"In the world of business and sustainability, John Elkington's work soars above all – it is honest, practical, compassionate and deeply informed. *Cannibals with Forks* is a brilliant synthesis of his genius for cutting through the thicket of tough issues and producing elegant solutions that can be applied today."

Paul Hawken, Author, *The Ecology of Commerce*

"John Elkington forthrightly and clearly conveys that sustainability, as a new value, will be the *"price of entry"* that society will demand for business success in the 21st century. I believe this is an essential message for all forward thinking businesses."

Deborah D. Anderson, Vice President,
Environmental Quality Worldwide, Procter and Gamble

"The Triple Bottom Line is becoming an imperative. Environmental and social responsibility should beat at the heart of every business leader."

Anita Roddick, CEO, Founder of the Body Shop

"Leading edge corporations must be moving up a gear, beyond eco-efficiency. The winners are driving up the sustainability curve and and enriching social capital. Those idling, satisfied with "Beyond Compliance", will end up in the scrap yard. This book is the corporate citizen's route map."

Patrick Thomas, CEO, ICI Polyurethanes

"I commend this book. John Elkington has consistently both challenged us all to think differently and offered us a way to do so. The issue of how to define sustainability in day to day terms is one which all companies should face up to. There are no ready answers, but *Cannibals with Forks* provides us with a good compass. And it is both constructive and stimulating to read."

Rodney Chase, Deputy Chief Executive, British Petroleum

"While not everyone would accept John Elkington's assertion that most company boards are both deaf and blind when it comes to monitoring the emerging agenda on sustainable development, I suspect that almost all would benefit from a greater understanding of the issues he describes so well."

Sir Anthony Cleaver, Chairman, AEA Technology plc

"The face of corporate environmentalism has changed dramatically in the past few years. *Cannibals with Forks* is a testament to that shift, and shows how sustainable development has become a priority for astute CEOs. Companies are increasingly using eco-efficiency to achieve what John Elkington calls the triple bottom line: profitable operations, sound ecology and social progress. By encouraging business to be more resource efficient, to do more with less, eco-efficiency will benefit society at large."

Björn Stigson, Executive Director,
World Business Council for Sustainable Development

"John Elkington has reached new horizons in bringing to light some key trends you may have missed so far. *Cannibals with Forks* tests best management practices against the sustainability imperative and, in so doing, challenges managers to discover and examine their companies' blind spots. The result is a thought-provoking and practical guide to rising above the waves in the rough business seas ahead."

Claude Fussler, Vice President, New Businesses, Dow Europe

"Since the Brundtaland report, many have tried to answer the question: "what does sustainable development look like and how can we get there?", *Cannibals with Forks* not only gives us a glance at how business could be practiced in a more sustainable society, it also identifies 7 key parameters that can guide everyone involved, not only business, in evaluating and improving their practices, behaviour and policy making for a more sustainable future. As John Elkington rightfully concludes, changes will be fast and those who can anticipate them will be surfacing as the shapers and creators of a sustainable society. The next challenge for John is, once the cannibals know how to eat with a fork, to try and identify the most wholesome and healthy diet to expand their life expectancy."

Joke H. Waller-Hunter, Director, Division for Sustainable Development, United Nations

"This is not exactly the easiest agenda to have your finger on the pulse of – it's fast moving, multi-layered and often invisible to all but the most tutored observer. John Elkington is second to none in that department, and whisks his readers briskly and confidently through an enormous range of issues, case studies and trends. In the process he immerses us in the detail whilst never once losing sight of the bigger picture – which all makes for indispensable reading."

Jonathon Porritt, Forum for the Future

"In this book John Elkington shows that he possesses sensitive antennae for the aspects of sustainable development that are becoming increasingly important in today's civil society. Indispensable reading for anyone concerned with the relationship between business and society."

Maria Buitenkamp, Coordinator,
Friends of the Earth 'Sustainable Europe' Campaign

"John Elkington has done it again in helping those who care about how their enterprises can survive in the next century navigate what should be obvious routes for good business. In pulling the strands and tools together in a lively and convincing piece of work, the question is asked whether our business leaders are prepared for the local and global societal responsibilities thrust upon them by the revolutionary final decade of the 20th century. Working with and listening to the best and most far-sighted should not distract us from the frightening challenge of convincing the many of the imperatives of sustainability."

Robert Davies, Chief Executive, The Prince of Wales Business Leaders Forum

"*Cannibals with Forks* is a truly useful book. John Elkington pragmatically and convincingly spells out the agenda that business must deal with to survive and prosper into the next century. The book helps us answer the questions we must respond to if we are to keep our customers, attract the employees we really want, and keep the friendship and respect of our children and their friends."

Mads Øvlisen, President, Novo Nordisk

"In a time when doomsday prophecies sell best, John Elkington remains a well-grounded optimist. He argues that we can all do better in meeting the triple bottom line. This will demand new values, attitudes, concepts and tools. His powerful new book will help motivate the business leaders and executives who must now invest in innovation and help to drive the necessary transition."

Professor Ulrich Steger, Institute for Ecology and Business Administration, European Business School

CANNIBALS WITH FORKS

The Triple Bottom Line
of 21st Century Business

John Elkington

CAPSTONE

That's a brilliant idea.
But how could it possibly work in my organization?

How often do you think as you read a business book that if only you could ask the author a simple question you could transform your organization?

Capstone is creating a unique partnership between authors and readers, delivering for the first time in business book publishing a genuine after-sales service for book buyers. Simply e-mail **capstone_publishing@msn.com** to leave your question (with details of date and place of purchase of a copy of *Cannibals With Forks*) and John Elkington will try to answer it.

Capstone authors travel and consult extensively so we do not promise 24-hour turnaround. But that one question answered might just jump start your company and your career.

Capstone is more than a publisher. It is an electronic clearing house for pioneering business thinking, putting the creators of new business ideas in touch with the people who use them.

Copyright © John Elkington 1997, 1999

First published 1997 by
Capstone Publishing Limited
Oxford Centre for Innovation
Mill Street
Oxford OX2 0JX
United Kingdom

This paperback edition first published in 1999 by Capstone Publishing Ltd

British Library Cataloguing in Publication Data
A CIP catalogue record for this book is available from the British Library.

ISBN 1-84112-084-7

Designed and typeset in 10/12pt Century Schoolbook and Futura by
Kate Williams, Abergavenny
Printed and bound in Great Britain by
T.J. International Ltd, Padstow, Cornwall

This book is printed on acid-free paper

Contents

Part III   Transition

Part IV   Toolbox

FOREWORD

"Is it progress," the Polish poet Stanislaw Lec asked, "if a cannibal uses a fork?" I believe it can be, particularly in the case of corporate capitalism and corporate cannibalism. If this last phrase seems far-fetched, read this description of Microsoft's founder, William Gates III, "Bill Gates eats competitors with the methodical determination of a corporate Pacman."[1] Gates, it is true, is scarcely renowned for his environmental or social sensitivities. But in our rapidly evolving capitalist economies, where it is in the natural order of things for corporations to devour competing corporations, for industries to carve up and digest other industries, one emerging form of "cannibalism with a fork" – sustainable capitalism – would certainly constitute real progress.

The fork, sustainability's triple bottom line, is explained in Chapter 4. Its three prongs are economic prosperity, environmental quality, and social justice. *Cannibals With Forks* identifies seven revolutions which are already beginning to transform the world of business and will help drive major corporations and leading economies towards these goals. The book, for reasons which will become apparent, is skewed more to the environmental dimension of sustainability than to the social or economic dimensions, but the integration of these different dimensions of the emerging political agenda will be a central challenge for 21st century business. And we will need to maintain our focus and drive to sustain this agenda through the inevitable cycles of economic growth and recession, company mergers and demergers, public enthusiasm and disillusion, government activism and passivity.

Inevitably, a key part of the task will be effective stakeholder consultation. Larry Ellison, founder of the US software giant Oracle, showed the way when he took the unusual step of setting up a cyberspace polling booth on the Internet to canvas opinion on whether he should bid for troubled Apple Computer. Apple may be a special case, but many of the companies discussed in the following pages have decided to consult a much wider range of stakeholders than would have been usual even a few years ago. Moreover, some are trying to work out ways of doing so on a continuing basis, not simply when in the throes of takeovers, mergers, or – as the recent history of companies like ICI, Hoechst, and Monsanto suggests will increasingly be the trend – demergers.

In the following pages, I draw on first-hand experience over more than two decades with some of the world's best-known corporations, national and international government agencies, and non-governmental organizations, as they have struggled to embrace key elements of the sustainability agenda and to internalize a growing range of economic, environmental, and social costs. Most of these companies have acted because they have had previous, painful experience of what can happen when they, or other companies, misread or fail to act upon a major new economic, social, or political agenda. But growing numbers have also responded because they scented commercial opportunity.

Many of the case studies are drawn from companies with which SustainAbility has worked over the years, because these are the organizations I know best. Throughout, I will name companies we have worked with, explaining some of the things that have gone right for them and some of the things that have gone wrong. Alert readers will note that the geopolitical focus of the book is largely on Western Europe and North America, where many of the relevant trends first surfaced. But our ability to deliver longer term sustainability will also depend heavily on our ability to help switch on the capitalists, financial markets, entrepreneurs, managerial classes, and consumers of the emerging economies, developing nations, and less developed countries of the world.

As I have mentioned, much of the work described in the following pages has been carried out through SustainAbility, the London-based think-tank and consultancy founded in 1987 with the triple mission of foresight, agenda setting, and change management. It is interesting, however, to recall the problems we had with the name. For several years, my colleagues and I spent much of our time, whether on the telephone or at conferences, spelling out and defining the S-word for people who had never heard it before. Indeed, a recent university computer search suggested that our use of the word in this particular sense may have been the first in print. True or not, it was certainly among the first; hence our problems.

Today, the problem is very different, given that many people think they know what "sustainability" means, yet define it in almost infinitely various ways. Perhaps surprisingly, business, initially in the form of a few leading companies, has been at the cutting edge in terms of working out what sustainability might mean at the level of a product, a process, a company, an industrial sector, or even an entire economy. We have worked with many of these pioneers in depth and often with extraordinary mutual candor. As a result, we know what it takes to switch a company on to this complex agenda, and we know many of the barriers which then need to be surmounted as the company struggles to make business sense of the sustainability agenda.

I first tried to work out what sustainable development might mean for business in the early 1980s following the publication of the 1980 *World Conservation Strategy.*[2] As a co-founder (in 1978) and later managing director of Environmental Data Services (ENDS), I was involved in efforts to bring together leading companies with public sector agencies and non-governmental organizations. But this was still a very different world. When, in the wake of the Bhopal disaster, I sat down to write *The Green Capitalists,*[3] the Berlin Wall was still standing and stood for several years more. The Soviet Union was more or less intact, Eastern Europe still under its thrall. Yet the broad shape of the future was already clear.

Capitalism, in its many forms, was the wave of the future. But then so, the book concluded, was sustainability. *The Green Capitalists,* which ended with a perspective by Tom Burke, who went on to advise three consecutive UK Secretaries of State for the Environment, was first published in 1987. That year also saw the publication of the World Commission on Environment and Development's report *Our Common Future,*[4] which brought "sustainable development" into the vocabulary of international politics.

"Perhaps, what we are seeing is the emergence of a new age capitalism," Tom concluded on page 252 of *The Green Capitalists*:

"appropriate to a new millennium, in which the boundary between corporate and human values is beginning to dissolve. It is now clear from the results who won the nineteenth-century argument about capital and labour. Socialism, as an economic theory, though not as a moral crusade, is dead. The argument now is about what kind of capitalism we want."

We were interested in the central role of governments, but the real focus was on the emergence of a new breed of "green capitalist" (an oxymoron for which I must accept responsibility), which we saw as an enormously hopeful trend. A key message was that unless, and until, the environmental community learned to work with business and through markets, many of the changes we wanted to see simply would not happen.

Rather than leave things to chance, I sat down with another colleague, Julia Hailes, and wrote *The Green Consumer Guide*.[5] The idea was that by changing the consumer choices we made every day, often without thinking, we could send powerful signals to retailers and, through them, to the rest of the business world. And so it proved. Published in 1988, this book, and its various editions, sold around a million copies and, alongside US cousins like *Shopping for a Better World*[6] and *50 Ways to Save the Planet*,[7] had an extraordinary impact. It helped catalyze a wave of international consumer pressure on business.

Back in 1987, however, we had pointed out that "the 'profitability' of a given business very much depends on where those who run the business choose to draw their 'bottom line', with costs above the line and profits below." A core concept introduced in *Cannibals With Forks* is that of the "triple bottom line," against which individual businesses and, increasingly, entire economies will be held to account, and have to perform, as we move into the 21st century. Since we often find that a degree of humor helps to lubricate the thinking process, I offer on page xi the first of 19 Spotlight panels as a light-hearted *aide memoire* for readers trying to get their brains around this triple agenda.

By turns critical and complimentary of the efforts of business to date, *Cannibals With Forks* shows how far leading corporations have come, and how far they still have to travel to perform successfully against the triple bottom line. Over the years, my colleagues and I at SustainAbility have seen corporate cannibalism, and its effects, at close quarters. For example, we have worked with a range of companies as they merged or de-merged: with Manweb as it was taken over by ScottishPower; with ScottishPower as it took over Southern Water; with Volvo as it dallied with Renault; with Tioxide as it was almost sold to DuPont by ICI, and then went to Huntsman Chemicals; and with Monsanto as it split up into life science and chemical companies. But, even so, *Cannibals With Forks* is an optimistic book, accepting that, while corporate cannibalism may not be pleasant to behold or comfortable to experience, it will remain an intrinsic part of any competitive economy.

The challenge is to work out how we can get these corporations to embrace and sustain a wider set of values. Is it possible, for example, to evolve new types of corporation which are less inclined to operate as economic, social, and ecological predators? How can we restructure markets in such a way that sustainability begins to make real business sense? Given that competition will always be one of the most powerful driving forces in biological, economic, and social systems, how can we

SPOTLIGHT

THE BARDOT FACTOR

Future market success will often depend on an individual company's (or entire value chain's) ability to simultaneously satisfy not just the traditional bottom line of profitability but also two emergent bottom lines; one focusing on environmental quality, the other on social justice. As a result, companies and their boards will need to think in terms of the *triple bottom line*.

But what does this triple bottom line look like in practice? To help memorize the logic, let's resort to caricature. Think in terms of the "Bardot Factor." Film actress Brigitte Bardot has been described as the second most famous French person in the world, after General de Gaulle. Her contributions over decades to the financial bottom lines of the film industry, St Tropez, and, indeed, the French economy itself are beyond dispute. She also wins in terms of the environmental agenda, having emerged as a forceful animal rights campaigner.

Two bottom lines down, one to go. But here's the problem. The erstwhile sex goddess, whose form inspired busts of Marianne, the female figure symbolizing the French Republic, has suffered the indignity of having some of the busts removed from town halls and replaced by others based on Catherine Deneuve. Despite her economic and environmental contributions, Bardot's views on immigration, and her support for the extreme right-wing National Front party, alienated many supporters. In short, the social justice dimension prevented her achieving a win–win–win outcome.

End of caricature. In today's world, companies like Coca-Cola, McDonald's, Shell, or Virgin depend for their success on their media profiles, on their reputations, and, ultimately, on public, consumer, and investor trust. As we will see, growing numbers of companies already find themselves confronted by the Bardot Factor, requiring novel "triple win" strategies and partnerships designed to satisfy the triple bottom line of sustainable development.

get competitive corporations to switch to sustainable development? And how can we ensure that corporations continue to build triple bottom line commitment and performance as they go through their inevitable cycles of growth and decline, expansion and downsizing, merger and demerger?

The focus throughout the book is on some emerging forms of 21st century capitalism. The aim is to lay bare the nature, scale, and implications of the biggest, most far-reaching experiment currently under way on Planet Earth. The dramatic interest is guaranteed by the fact that the futures of six billion of today's global citizens and of tens of billions of their descendants ride on the outcome.

Notes

1. Emily Bell, "Bill's Net blink turns into stare," *Observer*, 4 August 1996.
2. IUCN, UNEP, and WWF, *The World Conservation Strategy*, 1980.
3. John Elkington and Tom Burke, *The Green Capitalists*, Victor Gollancz, 1987.
4. World Commission on Environment and Development, *Our Common Future*, Oxford University Press, 1987.
5. John Elkington and Julia Hailes, *The Green Consumer Guide: From shampoo to champagne*, Victor Gollancz, 1988.
6. Council on Economic Priorities, *Shopping for a Better World: A quick and easy guide to socially responsible supermarket shopping*, Ballantine Books, 1989; updated 1992.
7. Earthworks Group, *50 Ways to Save the Planet*, The Earthworks Press, Berkeley, 1989.

Postscript 1999

Happily, the hardback edition of Cannibals sold out early in 1999; hence this first UK paperback edition. Inevitably, there have been major changes in the business world since the book was first published.

Some leading companies – such as Levi Strauss (pages 134–5) – have stumbled financially. We have also seen the emergence of such super-companies as BP-Amoco, DaimlerChrysler and the merged Ford and Volvo. Green leader Joschka Fischer (page 223) actually became Foreign Minister of Germany, taking a lead role in the Kosovo crisis. And Monsanto dug its hand still deeper into the 'monkey trap' (pages 221–2) represented by GM foods in Europe.

But the basic trends in the real world remain as predicted in these pages. Indeed, as I made the final corrections for the paperback edition, I was flying back and forth to countries like Australia and the USA to work on the triple bottom line agenda with the boards of major companies like Dow Chemical, Ford, North and Queensland Cement (QCL). These are exciting times, but no one has a lock on the truth. As before, your comments on the book would be welcome. My e-mail address is elkington@sustainability.co.uk

ACKNOWLEDGEMENTS

To begin with, my thanks go to Elaine (Elkington) and Celia Catchpole for finding Sara Menguc at David Higham Associates, and to Sara for finding Mark Allin at Capstone. These were key stepping-stones on the path to *Cannibals* in its current form. And, most of all, thank you Mark.

The roots of my quest for understanding about what sustainable corporations might look like and how they might behave go back a long way. Many people supported that quest during the 1970s and 1980s: among them John Roberts at TEST; Dr Bernard Dixon, as Editor of *New Scientist*; Max Nicholson, David Layton, Georgina McAughtry and Marek Mayer at Environmental Data Services (ENDS); and Liz Knights at Victor Gollancz.

At SustainAbility, I offer heartfelt thanks to all who have helped build the organization over the years, but particularly, and alphabetically, to Mo Cummings-John, Christèle Delbé, Franceska van Dijk, Anne Dimmock, Shelly Fennell, Professor Tom Gladwin (Stern School of Business, New York University), Julia Hailes, Dr Vernon Jennings, Sally Kadir, Niklas Kreander, Tore Linghede (Miljöeko), Geoff Lye (who made key inputs to Chapter 12), Tania Martin, Charles Medawar (Social Audit), Jane Nelson (Prince of Wales Business Leaders Forum), Catherine Priddey, Patrice van Riemsdijk, Hein Sas (Centre for Energy Efficiency and Clean Technology (CE), Delft), Professor Jim Salzman (American University), Andrea Spencer-Cooke (a vital Muse in the development of my triple bottom line thinking), Helen Stibbard, and Dr Alex Trisoglio (Environmental Strategies). Special thanks to Andrea, Jane, and Steve Viederman (Jessie Smith Noyes Foundation) for their comments on a late draft. All remaining faults are my own.

I am very grateful to Pieter Winsemius of McKinsey for permission to use the two figures reproduced in Chapter 14. Thanks, too, to Rupert Bassett for his designs, versions of which are used in Chapter 4.

Over the years, other friends and colleagues have helped spur the quest, among them: Roger Adams at the Chartered Association of Certified Accountants (ACCA); Jacqueline Aloisi de Larderel and Nancy Bennet at the Paris office of the United Nations Environment Programme (UNEP); Frances Cairncross at *The Economist*; Roger Cowe at *The Guardian*; Wouter van Dieren at IMSA; Claude Fussler at Dow Europe; Professor Rob Gray at CSEAR, University of Dundee; Kazue Harako and Masuo Ueda of the Valdez Society, Tokyo; Paul Hawken; Peter Hindle and David Hammond at Procter & Gamble; Helen Holdaway at The Environment Foundation; Dr Mike Jeffs, Dr Vanja Markovic, Richard Stillwell, Patrick Thomas and Lucia Timmermans at ICI Polyurethanes; Lise Kingo and Steen Riisgaard at Novo Nordisk; Kim Loughran and Martin Wright at *Tomorrow* magazine; Judy Pitts, Dave Porter and John Russell at Tioxide; Nick Robins, now at IIED; Dr Peter Scupholme at BP; Jonathan Shopley, now at ADL; Gus Speth and Janet Welsh Brown, when at the World Resources Institute (WRI); Tessa Tennant at the National Provident Institution (NPI); Teoh Cheng Hai at Golden Hope Plantations, Berhad; Professor Bob Worcester at MORI; and Dr Simon Zadek at the New Economics Foundation (NEF).

And, to end where I began, *Cannibals* once again represents a considerable investment of time that should have been theirs by my family, particularly Elaine, Gaia, Hania, and the denizens of Hill House, Little Rissington. I hope that they will conclude that this latest cuckoo in their nest has been worth the discomfort.

EXECUTIVE SUMMARY

Adapting to a 7-D World

Business will be in the driving seat.
Yet this will not make the transition any easier.
For many corporations, it will prove impossible.
For others, thinking and acting in 7-D
will become second nature.

We are all used to operating in a 3-D world. Even so, making sense of, let alone beating the competition in, a 3-D world can be pretty complicated: ask anyone who has played 3-D checkers. Now sustainable capitalism, with its emphasis on the triple bottom line performance of companies, industries, and economies, presents business people with an even more complex challenge: a 7-D world.

The sustainability agenda, long understood as an attempt to harmonize the traditional financial bottom line with emerging thinking about the environmental bottom line, is turning out to be much more complicated than some early business enthusiasts imagined. Increasingly, we think in terms of a "triple bottom line," focusing on economic prosperity, environmental quality and – the element which business has tended to overlook – social justice.

To refuse the challenge implied by the triple bottom line is to risk extinction. Nor are these simply issues for major transnational corporations: they will increasingly be forced to pass the pressure on down their supply chains, to smaller suppliers and contractors. These changes flow from a profound reshaping of society's expectations and, as a result, of the local and global markets business serves. Anyone who has worked in this area for any time knows that there are *waves* of change. Some of these waves, as we see in Chapter 2, are driven by triple bottom line factors – most particularly in recent decades by environmental pressures. To accept the challenge is to embark on a process which is likely to be both intensely taxing and, potentially, highly rewarding. With its dependence on seven closely linked revolutions, the sustainable capitalism transition will be one of the most complex our species has ever had to negotiate.

Cannibals With Forks comes in four parts:

♦ Part I reviews progress to date in the early "greening" of capitalism, markets, and industry, exploring some of the implications of the emerging triple bottom line for 21st century business;
♦ Part II, Chapters 5–11, outlines seven great revolutions which are already under way and on whose eventual success ride our hopes for a sustainable future;
♦ Part III focuses on the "sustainable corporation," and on some of the market changes needed to make it a reality;
♦ Part IV includes a blueprint of the sort of "sustainability audit" which shareholders, financial markets, managers, employees, customers, environmentalists, and other stakeholders will increasingly insist on applying as we move into the third millennium, and Appendix 1 provides some sketchy notes on some of the new words and phrases now surfacing in boardrooms around the world.

As we move into the third millennium, we are embarking on a global cultural revolution. Business, much more than governments or non-governmental organizations, will be in the driving seat. Paradoxically, this will not make the transition any easier for business people. For many, it will prove grueling, if not impossible. For others, thinking and acting in 7-D will come to seem like second nature. They will be pushing towards the sustainable corporation, some of whose key characteristics are outlined in Chapter 12.

The seven dimensions of a sustainable future outlined in Figure 1.1 and Chapters 5–11 may come as a surprise to many of those used to

Revolution	Focus	Old paradigm	❯	New paradigm
1	Markets (Ch. 5)	Compliance	❯	Competition
2	Values (Ch. 6)	Hard	❯	Soft
3	Transparency (Ch. 7)	Closed	❯	Open
4	Life-cycle technology (Ch. 8)	Product	❯	Function
5	Partnerships (Ch. 9)	Subversion	❯	Symbiosis
6	Time (Ch. 10)	Wider	❯	Longer
7	Corporate governance (Ch. 11)	Exclusive	❯	Inclusive

FIGURE 1.1   Old and new paradigms

dealing with the environmental revolution in terms of issues like population, global warming, biodiversity, the collapse of fisheries, or land contamination. But these revolutions are the deep currents underlying much of the surface turbulence we see in today's world. These are issues which will ultimately make or break our chances of achieving the sustainability transition. Companies wanting to get a sense of how they will measure up to the challenge should consult Chapter 14, which provides guidance on how to develop a sustainability auditing program.

Seven Revolutions for Sustainability

Let's look at each of these impending sustainability revolutions in outline. For each transition, we will also spotlight the most important blind-spot which currently impairs the vision of business leaders.

1 Markets

Revolution 1 (Chapter 5) will be driven by competition, largely through markets. For the foreseeable future, business will operate in markets which are more open to competition, both domestic and international, than at any other time in living memory. The resulting economic earthquakes will transform our world.

When an earthquake hits a city built on sandy or wet soils, the ground can become *thixotropic*: in effect, it becomes fluid. Entire buildings can disappear into the resulting quicksands. In the emerging world order, entire markets will also go thixotropic, swallowing entire companies, and even industries. Learning to spot the market conditions and factors which can trigger this process will be a key to future business survival, let alone success. As we will see, some analysts predict that global financial markets will begin to behave like "super conductors," with changes that would once have taken months or even years now happening in the space of days, minutes, or even seconds.

In this extraordinarily challenging environment, growing numbers of companies are already finding themselves challenged by customers and the financial markets about aspects of their triple bottom line commitments and performance. Although we will undoubtedly see continuing cycles based on wider economic, social, and political trends, this pressure can only grow over the long term. As a result, business will shift from using competition as an excuse not to address the triple bottom line agenda to a new approach, using the triple bottom line as part of the business case for action and investment.

Blind-spot 1 The worst blind-spot today's business leaders suffer from in this area is the deep-seated, if often unstated, belief that "sustainability" is a new form of religion, a late 20th century aberration of the human soul, rather than a new form of value which society will demand and which successful businesses will deliver through transformed markets.

2 Values

Revolution 2 (Chapter 6) is being driven by the worldwide shift in human and societal values. Most business people, indeed most people, take values as a given, if they think about them at all. Yet our values are the products of the most powerful programming that each of us has ever been exposed to. When they change, as they seem to with every succeeding generation, entire societies can go thixotropic. Companies that have felt themselves standing on solid ground for decades suddenly find that the world as they knew it is being turned upside-down, and inside out.

Remember Mrs Aquino's peaceful revolution in the Philippines? Or the extraordinary changes in Eastern Europe in 1989? Recall the experiences of Shell during the Brent Spar and Nigerian controversies, with the giant oil company later announcing that it would in future consult non-governmental organizations on such issues as environment and human rights before deciding on development options. Think, too, of Texaco. The US oil company paid $176 million in an out-of-court settlement, in the hope that it would bury the controversy about its poor record in integrating ethnic minorities. Just as financial markets can turn into quicksands or superconductors, so can entire business environments and, indeed, societies.

Such shifts in values are among the most powerful influences faced by politicians and business leaders alike. Swimming against the tide can be difficult, if not impossible, although swirling eddies may sometimes make it seem as though the process is going into reverse, back towards the comforting certainties of "business as usual." Companies misreading the direction of flow risk running aground or being swept aside into the commercial doldrums.

The transition from "hard" commercial values to "softer" triple bottom line values does not mean that life will become any easier for business; far from it. To reverse the analogy, while the values shift can turn the established order to jelly, individual companies or industries facing values-based opposition will increasingly be discomfited to find soft, spongy opposition turning almost overnight into the consistency of reinforced concrete.

Few technologies challenge our values and ethics as profoundly as genetic engineering. When *Nature* published the news that a Scottish lamb, number 6LL3 but better known by her alias, "Dolly," had been cloned, it triggered an ethical earthquake.[1] As the tempo of such announcements builds, ethical issues will continuously be in the public eye. But, in the process, which values will win out? Will a new morality – or moralities – evolve, or will most people simply regard such events as one more form of soap opera?

Cannibals With Forks suggests that we are already seeing the emergence of a new – or renewed – set of values, many of which will be central to the sustainability transition. No one imagines that we will ever reach the point where everyone on the planet shares a common set of values, but there is very likely to be convergence around at least a minimum set. This trend is likely to be critical as companies increasingly come to see their future as global. Although many triple bottom line campaigners see globalization as inimical to an economically, socially or environmentally sustainable future, this is the direction we will be driven in for decades to come. "Customer requirements dictate that we operate globally so that boundaries don't limit the best thinking, the best people or the best solutions," explained IBM senior vice-president Ned Lautenbach.[2]

Globalization has economic, social, and environmental dimensions. But the notion that sustainable development has a social dimension is still controversial. This is worrying. As Professor Tom Gladwin puts it, while sustainability is often thought of as "eco-efficiency for the rich," this definition is dangerously narrow. "Sustainable development is more than that," Gladwin stresses. "It's equity, justice, alleviation of poverty, and redistribution of opportunity."[3]

Nor are all business people fighting this analysis every step of the way. "Sustainable development requires collaborative thinking and partnerships with other non-business organizations," accepts Björn Stigson, executive director of the World Business Council for Sustainable Development (WBCSD). "These partnerships only make sense in the global scheme: to address poverty in the Third World, as much as to deal with pollution control." Stigson warns that "business can't tackle all the issues, nor can it do it alone," but observes that "the most enlightened corporations have integrated a social dimension into their corporate strategies."

Yet, even as we see some areas of convergence, it is clear that societal and business values differ widely around the world. This is the context within which sustainable development must be put into practice. The concept of sustainability is entering the business language at different speeds in different parts of the world, with current and emerging values acting as brakes, gearboxes or accelerators. As a result, our focus in future must not only be on changes in technology and in management systems, but also on values and mindsets. "My principal concern," says Whitman Bassow, long with the New York-based World Environment Center, "is that the emphasis is on changing the engineering of manufacturing, on things but not the attitudes of the people who produce the products, nor their behavior, nor the resistance to change inherent in human nature."[4]

Blind-spot 2 The worst blind-spot today's business leaders suffer from in this area is that the business of business is about the creation of economic value, and not about social or ethical values. This is not particularly surprising: a full generation of business leaders have been taught to stay out of politics and that they meddle in the affairs of governments (even oppressive regimes) at their peril. It is clear that attempts to drive corporations towards sustainability objectives and targets will trigger both action and reaction, support and resistance. Managing these trends and counter-trends will involve working with both individuals and groups to help them change their mindsets and, even more importantly, to transform the corporate culture. As a result, the sustainability transition will be as much a political transition as it will be an economic or social transition.

3 Transparency

Revolution 3 (Chapter 7) is already under way, is being fueled by growing international transparency and will accelerate. As a result, business will find its thinking, priorities, commitments, and activities under increasingly intense scrutiny worldwide. Some forms of disclosure will be voluntary, but others will evolve with little direct involvement from most companies. In many respects, the transparency revolution is now "out of control."

This process is itself being driven by the coming together of new value systems and radically different information technologies, from satellite television to the Internet. The collapse of many forms of traditional authority also means that a wide range of different stakeholders increasingly demand information on what business is doing and planning to do. Increasingly, too, they are using that information to compare, benchmark, and rank the performance of competing companies.

Companies that have previously sought to justify no disclosure or low-disclosure policies will find that they – and their entire value chains, linking suppliers and customers – are increasingly operating in a global goldfish bowl. They face growing pressures for right-to-know legislation and new corporate governance rules. As a result, the difficulty of keeping secrets will become immeasurably greater. Sooner or later, most things a company thinks or does will become public knowledge. Companies that fail to plan with this fact in mind must be prepared to pay the price.

But as more and more companies start to report elements of their triple bottom line commitments, targets, and performance, the field remains haunted by a paradox. As illustrated in Figure 7.1 (p. 171), corporate reporting has often outrun supporting activities in such areas as accounting, management systems, and auditing (see Chapter 3). This is perhaps not surprising, but the lack of synchromesh is emerging as a major barrier to progress.

The 21st century will see various reactions to these elevated levels of transparency. Some companies forced to operate in the global goldfish bowl will respond by trying to develop sophisticated "stealth" strategies designed to let them slip in under society's "radar." Others will develop aggressive competitive intelligence strategies to defend their interests, feeding on the new forms of information that are becoming available. Yet others will see the need to integrate triple bottom line considerations into their core business strategies. It is these companies that we will mainly focus on in later chapters.

Blind-spot 3 The worst blind-spot today's business leaders suffer from in this area is the belief that if they can just manage to keep their heads down, they can avoid the sorts of challenges that have buffeted companies like Shell and Texaco. Instead, the evidence increasingly suggests that even companies that normally operate well outside the spotlight – and therefore often have little or no experience of dealing with the new stakeholders and their complex, interlocking agendas – will find themselves inexorably drawn into the wrenching controversies triggered by the sustainability transition.

4 Life-cycle Technology

Revolution 4 (Chapter 8) is being driven by and – in turn – is driving the transparency revolution. Companies are being challenged about the triple bottom line implications of either industrial or agricultural activities far back down the supply chain, or of their products in transit, in use, and, increasingly, after their useful life has ended. Here we are seeing a shift from companies focusing on the acceptability of their products at the point of sale to their performance from cradle to grave and, increasingly, from cradle to cradle; i.e. from the extraction of raw materials right through to recycling or disposal. Managing the life-cycles of technologies and products as different as batteries, jumbo jets and offshore oil-rigs will become increasingly challenging, transforming key elements of R&D and product design processes.

New techniques are being developed to explore and, to a growing degree, measure the economic, social, and environmental impacts of new technologies, products, and processes. Most of these tools have been hugely expensive and have often produced confusing results, but they are beginning to escape from the laboratory environment to the market. In the process, they will mutate and evolve in unexpected ways. The surging power of computers and growing use of the Internet are parallel trends which are likely to further amplify developments in this area. As a result, companies operating in a wide range of different industries will suddenly find themselves exposed to a new form of "X-ray environment," in which their value chains and product life-cycles will be exposed (often in excruciating detail) to wider scrutiny.

Early environmentalists were often anti-technology, in addition to being anti-industry, anti-growth and anti-profit. But over a couple of decades our interest in such appropriate low technologies as biomass digesters and small-scale windmills has expanded to include everything from satellite remote sensing (great for monitoring environmental change) and supercomputers (handy if you are trying to model such complex systems as the atmosphere or a rainforest) through to new materials (which hold the key, for example, to lightweight, hyper-efficient vehicles) and molecular engineering (which could enormously boost the benefits of chemistry while cutting out most of the unwanted side-effects).

Chapter 8 introduces the "Need Test," which all technologists should assess their new ideas against. We also look at one of the fastest-emerging areas of technology; genetic engineering. Many environmentalists would assume that genetic engineering would fail the Need Test, without question. But my personal view – based on over fifteen years working with the biotechnology industry – is that we face a paradox. On the one hand, the inappropriate use of genetic engineering could easily derail our attempts to build a sustainable economy and, on the other, sustaining a human population of 10–12 billion will probably be impossible without genetic engineering. Ensuring that the gene revolution works with, rather than against, the grain of the sustainability revolution is one of the greatest challenges ahead of us.

Blind-spot 4   The worst blind-spot today's business leaders in companies suffer from in this area is the assumption that their responsibilities end at the factory fence, and that any triple bottom line impacts of their operations, products, or services will be sorted out in the "normal course of events." In today's business environment this a potentially fatal delusion. New forms of "X-ray environment" can switch on without warning, illuminating activities, processes, and companies way back down a value chain.

5 Partnerships

Revolution 5 (Chapter 9) will dramatically accelerate the rate at which new forms of partnership spring up between companies, and between companies and other organizations, including some leading campaigning groups. Organizations which once saw themselves as sworn enemies will increasingly flirt with, and propose new forms of relationship to, opponents seen to hold some of the keys to success in the new order. As even groups like Greenpeace gear up for this new approach, we will see a further acceleration of the trends driving the third and fourth sustainability revolutions.

Early on, some companies contented themselves with trying to mimic some aspects of their opponents' behavior, in the hope of developing a form of camouflage. The late 1980s and 1990s, for example, saw a number of companies trying to position themselves as "corporate environmentalists." Assumed by many campaigners to be little more than a case of corporate camouflage, "greenwashing," this trend reflected a new sense of mission in some parts of the business world. Indeed, some companies – among them BAA, RTZ (which recently changed its name back to Rio Tinto) and Shell – have recruited individuals who once ran anti-industry campaigns. Discussions of whether we are seeing "watchdogs turned lapdogs" can blind us to the fact that some of these people are having a real influence in their new organizations.

Increasingly, too, companies are seeking to develop longer term strategies congruent with the new alignment of triple bottom line forces. Some, as a result, are beginning to explore new forms of "strange alliance," linking up with former critics in new forms of company–NGO and public–private partnerships. None of this means that we will see an end to friction or even outright conflict. Instead, campaigning groups will need to work out ways of simultaneously challenging and working with the same industry, or even the same company. This trend has already triggered schizophrenic responses in some of the leading environmental organizations and in some of the companies that have formed innovative partnerships. Such tensions are likely to grow when the focus of the partnerships inevitably expands to embrace an integrated triple bottom line approach. But there is no reason why the various partners cannot learn to manage these complexities in the same way that they deal with complexity in other areas of their activities.

Blind-spot 5   The worst blind-spot today's business leaders suffer from in this area is the belief that, even in areas where there are admitted challenges to be dealt with, business can handle them on its own. If the sustainability transition were simply a matter of continuous improvement, this blind-spot would not be too serious. But we are talking about major dislocations in established markets and trading relationships. In short, of an emerging world in which the "2 + 2 = 50" power of "strange alliances" will transform the competitive advantage of industry sectors and of companies which manage to tap into it.

6 Time

Time is short, we are told. Time is money. But, driven by the sustainability agenda, Revolution 6 (Chapter 10) will promote a profound shift in the way we understand and manage time. As the latest news erupts through CNN and other channels within seconds of the relevant events happening on the other side of the world, and as more than a trillion dollars sluices around the world every working day, so business finds that current time is becoming ever "wider." This involves the opening out of the time dimension, with more and more happening every minute of every day. By contrast, the sustainability agenda is pushing us in the other direction, towards "long" time.

Given that most politicians and business leaders find it hard to think even two or three years ahead, the scale of the challenge is indicated by the fact that the emerging agenda requires thinking across decades, generations, and, in some instances, centuries. As time-based competition, building on the platform created by techniques like "Just-in-time," continues to accelerate the pace of competition, the need to build in a stronger "long time" dimension to business thinking and planning will become ever more pressing.

Walk into the lobbies of many international companies today and you see a series of clocks giving the time in the various world regions where they operate. In the future, companies will need to watch and respond to clocks providing windows onto very different dimensions of time. But it will be interesting to see whether any company has the nerve to install a version of the "Millennium Clock" (Spotlight, p. 254). The use of scenarios, or alternative visions of the future, is a more mainstream way in which we can expand our time horizons and spur on our creativity.

Blind-spot 6   The worst blind-spot today's business leaders suffer from in this area is the belief that the time-scales dictated by Wall Street and other financial centers are "reality." Instead, they are bubble environments which – as illustrated by the history of spectacular economic crashes around the world – can delude and destroy even the deepest-rooted businesses. Unless companies can balance the short-termism of most "wide time" markets with a real sense of "long time," they are extremely unlikely to survive the sustainability transition.

7 Corporate Governance

Ultimately, whatever the drivers, the triple bottom line agenda is the responsibility of the corporate board. Revolution 7 (Chapter 11) is being driven by each of the other revolutions and is also resulting in a totally new spin being put on the already energetic corporate governance debate. Now, instead of just focusing on issues like the pay packets of "fat cat" directors, new questions are being asked. For example, what is business for? Who should have a say in how companies are run? What is the appropriate balance between shareholders and other stakeholders? What balance should be struck at the level of the triple bottom line?

The better the system of corporate governance, the greater the chance that we can build towards genuinely sustainable capitalism. To date, however, most triple bottom line campaigners have not focused their activities on boards – nor, in most cases, do they have a detailed understanding of how boards and corporate governance systems work. This, none the less, constitutes the jousting ground of tomorrow.

To provide guidance on ways forward, Chapter 12 focuses on 39 steps towards the sustainable corporation. Chapter 13 highlights some of the things political leaders, opinion leaders, business leaders and the financial markets will need to do to help drive the process.

Blind-spot 7 The worst blind-spot today's business leaders suffer from in this area is an inability to see things in the round, to view the world and emerging challenges in "7-D." New forms of sustainability audit will help to clear the mists, but by illuminating the complexities in this area, they may well cause some companies to mimic the centipede which, when asked how it could possibly manage to walk on a hundred legs, tumbled into the ditch. Managing complex organizations through complex changes is a furiously demanding task. For companies and other organizations wanting to know how they are positioned for the transition, Chapter 14 outlines a sustainability audit framework.

Notes

1. Harry Griffin and Ian Wilmut, Seven days that shook the world, *New Scientist*, 22 March 1997.
2. Louise Kehoe, "IBM puts emphasis on global operations," *Financial Times*, 14 December 1996.
3. "Sustainable development: is it industry's business?," *Business and the Environment*, February 1997.
4. Whitman Bassow, "Get an attitude," *Tomorrow*, Issue 5, September/ October 1996.

PART I

Sustaining Capitalism

♦ 2 ♦

INTRODUCTION

Is Capitalism Sustainable?

What began as a scattered patchwork of protest groups grew into the most powerful social movement of the second half of the 20th century and will shape the markets and industries of the 21st century.

Can we rely on capitalism to ensure that the 21st century will be the Sustainability Century? Probably not, but current trends suggest that business is beginning to wake up to the necessity of change, and to the scale of the challenge. Ironically, however, many of those who are advising major corporations have yet to understand fully what is beginning to happen around them.

When I was still a boy in shorts, Nikita Kruschev, then President of the seemingly unstoppable Soviet Union, grabbed the world's headlines by saying that communism would bury capitalism. No doubt he believed it and much of the rest of the world feared he might well be right. Capitalism, whether in the Soviet Union or in other major industrial powers, had a decidedly mixed press for generations. In *Das Kapital* (1867) Karl Marx wrote that "capital is dead labor that, vampire-like, lives only by sucking living labor, and lives the more, the more labor it sucks." Really, who would want to live in a capitalist society? And, for much of the 20th century, many critics of the industrialized world order wondered aloud – sometimes very loudly – whether the future would be unsustainably capitalist or sustainably communist?

By the time I went to university in the late 1960s, many baby-boomers were in the thrall of sundry gurus, from Marx and Mao Tse-tung to Herbert Marcuse and Che Guevara. Their basic message was that capitalism's time was up. My taste, instead, was for people like Paul Ehrlich, Barry Commoner and Teddy Goldsmith: environmental thinkers who argued that the combined trajectories of population growth, industrial pollution, and ecosystem destruction threatened to undermine the future, whether capitalist or communist. Most, but not all, of these doomsayers were politically left-of-center. In fact, leading environmentalists and Greens came from a much wider political spectrum than most right-wing critics (with their *watermelon* jibe, "green on the outside, red on the inside") were prepared to admit.

Even so, and despite the success of the right-wing Reagan and Thatcher administrations in helping to reverse what seemed like the tide of history, many wondered whether this was simply an interlude on an inevitable path to something much closer to what Marx had in mind. Then came the fall of the Berlin Wall in 1989 and the subsequent collapse of much of the communist system, spotlighting the equal, and often greater, vampirism of most state-run economies. A few people had seen the collapse coming, recognizing that communism, too, had its internal contradictions, but for most people it came as one of the greatest surprises of the most surprising century on record.

The parallel "environmental revolution," also reaching its second great peak in 1989 (see Chapter 3), exposed the increasingly aggressive predation of the natural world by industry, whether capitalist or communist. Today we must ask what sorts of financing, enterprise, and industrial activity will a sustainable world require and foster? The following pages aim to provide at least some of the answers.

What's Going On Here?

Why read this book? Simple. The sustainability crisis is going to get a lot worse before we have any hope of turning the corner. As a result, the trends identified in the following pages look set to turn the world of business inside out over the next few decades. As Monsanto CEO Robert (Bob) Shapiro put it, "We are looking at one of those huge discontinuities in social and economic history that create incredible opportunity. At moments like this, everything is up for grabs."

For companies alert to the deep currents, the prospects are extraordinarily bright. "As this crisis becomes more and more evident," Shapiro explained, "the world is going to demand a set of changes that give us a chance of survival. The world is going to be prepared to pay people who can help it survive." At the same time, the world will be increasingly willing to hammer those whose business activities or plans threaten, or are seen to threaten, our future. Monsanto, for example, has been hammered in Europe on its plans to introduce such genetic engineering products as bovine somatotropin (BST) and herbicide-resistant soybeans.

Paradoxically, this period of history will be extraordinarily demanding for the movement that got the bandwagon started. What started out

THE TRIPLE BOTTOM LINE AGENDA

What is sustainability? Sustainability is the principle of ensuring that our actions today do not limit the range of economic, social, and environmental options open to future generations.

Why is it important? Simply stated, this is the emerging 21st century business paradigm. Sustainable development is proposed by governments and business leaders as a solution for a wide range of problems now racing up the international agenda. These range from global warming, ozone depletion, and the collapse of some ocean fisheries through to social problems such as the deaths of 37,000 children under the age of five every day (mostly from diseases for which there are inexpensive cures) and the death of some 585,000 pregnant women and mothers every year. The first UN *Global Environmental Outlook* report, published in 1996, argued that the world still lacks "the necessary sense of urgency" needed to pull back from the "environmental precipice."

What has this got to do with business? Many business people will argue that it is not their business to save the world. But the expectation is growing around the world that business will deliver. In part, this flows from the activities of organizations like the World Business Council for Sustainable Development (WBCSD), but it also flows from a recognition that business needs stable markets – and, uniquely, has the technology, finance, and management skills needed to achieve the sustainability transition. The triple bottom line agenda (see Chapter 4) is fast evolving – and on a broad front, with one of the most challenging tasks being that of coordinated delivery, to ensure both efficiency and effectiveness in resource use.

Isn't this a job for the law-makers and regulators? In part, of course, it is. But industry's often effective lobbying over the years for less regulation and, in some cases, active deregulation may now be coming back to haunt it.

Wall Street won't let us do this! Wrong. In the coming decades, the world's financial markets will insist that business delivers against the triple bottom line. Long blind to most environmental issues, the financial markets are beginning to worry and agitate for change. Leading banks and insurers are signing charters on sustainable development. Insurers, who often have to pick up the tab for other industry's losses, may never have actively campaigned for deregulation or for lax enforcement of pollution control laws, but are now in the front line as the costs come home to roost. They will increasingly insist that industry and governments take action.

as a scattered patchwork of protest groups, and then grew into the most powerful social movement of the second half of the 20th century, now looks set to shape key elements of the markets and industries of the 21st century. These trends will eventually impact all sectors of the global economy, without exception. But groups like Friends of the Earth, Greenpeace, and the World Wide Fund for Nature (WWF) now face changes in their own environments every bit as extraordinary as those that rocked IBM as the era of "Big Iron" gave way to the era of the PC – and those that then rocked Microsoft as the era of the PC, in turn, began to give way to the era of the Internet.

But, surely, things are getting better? In some key respects, they are. But ask most environmental or sustainability experts whether they think things are improving overall, and the most common answer is absolutely not. When Japan's Asahi Glass Foundation sent out its fourth annual questionnaire on "environmental problems and the survival of mankind" in 1995, it mailed a total of over 2,500 forms to experts and opinion-formers in 201 other countries. Asked to say how concerned they were in terms of a 12-hour clock, their average response was 8:49; close to the "extremely concerned" range of 9.01–12.00. Since the survey first started, the average response has shifted to one hour later, indicating growing concern.

When asked about conditions in 50 years time, over 50 per cent of respondents believed that conditions would be worse. They may well be right, but, given that pessimism can act as a self-fulfilling prophecy, the challenge now is to develop a more optimistic vision of the future and the social, economic, and environmental strategies needed to make it a reality. As we enter the third millennium, sustainability potentially provides us with a powerful framework for doing just that.

Upsides, Downsides

Trojan Horse?

Let's look at some of the downsides first. For several decades, business has mainly focused on the downside of the environmental revolution. This has also been true of the sustainability revolution, which really began to take hold from 1987. And, at least for some, the short-term downside was real enough, and intensely personal. One UK director of a US corporation we worked for in the early 1990s flew across the Atlantic to explain the sustainability imperative to the US board. Big mistake – disaster. When he convened a small group of us for a post-mortem on his return, he reported that, metaphorically at least, his blood had been left all over the boardroom carpet. By the end, his colleagues told us, he was all but dragged out of the room feet first.

The problem was that some corporate Americans saw sustainability as a plot, a late twentieth century version of the Trojan Horse. They argued that Gro Harlem Brundtland, the Norwegian Prime Minister who had chaired the World Commission of Environment and Development, was a quasi-communist and that the Commission's report, *Our Common Future*,[1] was little more than a ploy to transfer advanced US technology to the Third World for free. Ironically, the company was already an acknowledged leader in terms of pollution control. But its knee-jerk reactions to sustainability were repeated in boardrooms across the USA and in some European member states.

Things have changed in the intervening years, of course. But nowhere near as fast as they need to, despite the fact that any business that ignores the trends outlined in the following pages risks committing commercial suicide. As a result, the casualty list is growing longer all the time. We will look at the problems that have hit such companies as:

- ◆ **ABB**   How the Swiss–Swedish company, long fêted in sustainable development circles, ran into major problems when it won contracts to build two massive dams, Bakun in Malaysia and Three Gorges in China.
- ◆ **DreamWorks**   How an old Indian curse came back to haunt Steven Spielberg's new Hollywood studio.
- ◆ **Intel**   How the thirst of the world's leading chip maker left it with a virtual hangover.
- ◆ **Monsanto**   How the US company's attempts to introduce new genetically engineered products – among them the dairy hormone BST and herbicide-resistant soybeans – into the European market led to an acute attack of societal and corporate indigestion.
- ◆ **Shell**   How the world's largest oil company was surprised by a series of public relations disasters, despite its reputation for scenario planning and seeing far into the future.
- ◆ **Synthesia**   How a Czech explosives company's reputation blew a hole in the credibility of a major environmental award scheme.
- ◆ **Texaco**   How an ethnic diversity controversy led this oil major to examine its "very soul."

But for every casualty, every loser, there are dozens of potential winners. The upside is that those adapting to – and in some cases driving – this new business revolution are not only going to compete more effectively for some of the great market opportunities of the future, they will also connect more powerfully with their own values and those of their colleagues, customers, and other stakeholders. Some will also have a good deal of fun along the way. We will look at the experience of a number of companies that have begun the long march towards sustainability, although most of the cases will be skewed towards our client base and towards economic and environmental performance – rather than towards full triple bottom line performance. Hopefully, there will be more relevant experience to draw on if *Cannibals With Forks* is updated a decade from now. Among the companies discussed are:

♦ **Dow Chemical**   How one of the world's largest chemical companies came to challenge the need for some key industrial products, including chlorine.

♦ **Electrolux**   How this leading international "white goods" company is rethinking its corporate and product strategies with sustainability in mind.

♦ **Golden Hope Plantations**   How one of Malaysia's top plantations companies learned how to give up "smoking" and protect the environment.

♦ **ICI Polyurethanes**   How a leading European chemical company is planning to help us all sleep more easily by coming up with recyclable mattresses.

♦ **Interface**   How a carpet maker has learned to build its business around selling function, not product.

♦ **Monsanto**   How one of the leading US chemical companies is trying to redefine its role in life and focusing growing attention on sustainability as a guide to future market opportunities.

♦ **Novo Nordisk**   How one of Denmark's leading companies, operating in the healthcare and industrial enzymes markets, engaged its stakeholders in Europe and North America.

♦ **Procter & Gamble**   How the giant detergent and consumer goods company is using "value : impact" assessment to boost value delivered to consumers while shrinking the impacts caused in the process.

♦ **Tropical Marine Centre**   How this small company is working with people up and down its entire supply chain to ensure "zero loss" as exotic fish travel from tropical reef to the tanks of European fish fanciers.

♦ **Unilever**   How the Anglo–Dutch company turned the spotlight on the sustainability of its agricultural and food chains.

- ♦ **Volvo** How the auto-maker challenged its global supply chain to build in environmental quality.
- ♦ **Xerox** How the copier company learned to close the loop with "remanufacturing" and other techniques.

A New Interest in Capitalism

Problem or Solution?

Capitalism and sustainability, however much we may wish it otherwise, do not make easy bedfellows. As *Fortune* recently put it:

> "Corporations were put on this earth, after all, to make money, and to some minds, profit maximization will never seem all that different from greed. But profits, of course, pay for the latest equipment and technology that produce economic growth and more jobs. If corporations weren't greedy like that, they'd go out of business and then we'd all be in trouble."[2]

Well maybe. But the sustainability lobby points out that we are in trouble already, often because of the self-interested way in which most corporations have interpreted their missions. So, it asks, can the capitalist system change not only its spots but also its very nature? Can these corporate cannibals, in short, not only learn to use more civilized tools but also begin to shift their diet towards inputs that are less ecologically, socially, and economically damaging?

Meanwhile, although it is far from clear that capitalism is significantly more environmentally damaging than the alternatives, it has been in the spotlight recently both because of its rising global power and because of what some would have us believe is the "end of history." In 1989, Francis Fukuyama wrote an influential article arguing that the world was seeing the development of a quite remarkable consensus on the legitimacy of liberal democracy as a system of government. This system, he suggested, had conquered rival ideologies such as hereditary monarchy, fascism, and communism. In this narrow sense, he believed that we were seeing the end of history, the "end point of mankind's ideological evolution" and the "final form of human government."

The almost immediate crackdown by the Chinese communists after the Tiananmen Square protests in 1989, and the 1991 Iraqi invasion of Kuwait and ensuing Gulf War led many critics to argue that Fukuyama

– who followed up with a controversial book, *The End of History and The Last Man*[3] in 1992 – was wrong. Whatever the facts, some analysts fear that the world may potentially be even more unstable after the end of the "Cold War" than it was when the West and the Soviet Union were poised in nuclear deadlock. Certainly, the potential for "rogue" states to develop their own nuclear, chemical, or biological arsenals appears much greater now that many of the defence industry skills of the old USSR are available on the open market. In this context, any transition to more sustainable forms of economic development will have to cope with – and may even trigger – major political dislocations. If we fail to wake up to and manage these challenges in time, they may well derail key elements of the sustainability transition.

But, whatever the foreign policy outlook and implications of such trends, the "free" market is now the pre-eminent development model in most world regions. When, for example, the central bank chairmen from five of the largest post-communist countries – Russia, Ukraine, Poland, Hungary, and Romania – recently spelt out their monetary policies for the investment elite of the World Economic Forum, those present were delighted at how *boring* the speeches were. "There is no longer a debate about economic theory," commented Rodric Braithwaite, a former UK ambassador to Russia who had moved on to Deutsche Morgan Grenfell. "The fundamentals are not contested anymore."[4]

So capitalism it is, but we are seeing an interesting shift towards a debate about the limits and weaknesses of market mechanisms. One of the most forceful recent books on the theme is Robert Kuttner's *Everything for Sale*.[5] Markets work much better than command-and-control economies in most respects, but as Kuttner puts it, "A society that was grand auction block would not be a political democracy worth having." As a result, as we will see in Chapter 6, there is a now a resurgence of the debate about a broader range of human and societal values – and about ways in which they can be integrated into the operation of international markets and of the corporations that serve them.

Stripped to its essence, capitalism – of whatever brand – is an economic (and, necessarily, political) system in which individual owners of capital are (relatively) free to dispose of it as they please and, in particular, for their own profit. As we will see, there are many different ways of calculating, defining and valuing capital, but a key question for all capitalist societies in the 21st century will be whether their particular version can be sustained in the face of broader economic, political, social, and environmental challenges? This question is becoming more urgent as we see a shift in the balance of international power, with nations tending to lose power and transnational corporations tending to become increasingly powerful.

Can We Rely on Capitalism?

In the end, it all depends on what we want capitalism to do. Wealth creation is rarely a comfortable process and the world's capitalist societies have been undergoing a period of wrenching change. Nor are the most urgent problems facing politicians and business leaders related to environmental or sustainable development pressures, at least as conventionally defined.

The problem is deeper still in the eyes of many of those running the capitalist system. Even in the USA, capitalism now faces a fundamental challenge to the legitimacy of the largest corporations and to the way rewards are distributed in the free enterprise system. This is because of the perception that stock markets boost shares and reward executives (through stock options) when they lay off workers. Indeed, there are echoes of the time earlier this century when Teddy Roosevelt and others campaigned against what Roosevelt dubbed the "malefactors of great wealth."[6]

In Japan, too, waves of corporate restructuring have caused a spate of suicides among middle-aged corporate samurai. Until recently, the goals of corporations and employees coincided. "Workers look to the company rather than their families or other activities for self-fulfilment," explained Makoto Nakume, a psychiatrist who counsels stressed office workers.[7] But, increasingly, we live in what *Business Week* dubbed "The Age of Anxiety."[8] Everywhere, the threat of unemployment is felt to be imminent. Sometimes the casualties of change are small, but sometimes they are large enough to shake an entire nation. In the Netherlands, for example, enormous shock-waves followed the announcement by Germany's Daimler-Benz AG that it planned to pull the plug on NV Fokker, the loss-making, cash-strapped aircraft maker – a move it was thought could cost the country a total of 20,000 jobs.[9]

None of this is new, of course. More than 50 years ago, economist Joseph Schumpeter noted that the essential feature of the capitalist system is "creative destruction," which he defined as an organic process of "industrial mutation that incessantly revolutionises the economic structure from within, incessantly destroying the old one, incessantly creating a new one."[10] But one of the most worrying aspects of the latest wave of mutations has been that many of the layoffs have been permanent, not temporary as was the case during the recession of the mid-1970s.

Leading business people may still be fêted as heroes of the modern age, but growing numbers of people are wondering whether we can rely on capitalism to deliver anything approaching a sustainable future. As a result, it seems likely that the internal political challenges to the capitalist system will grow as the communist threat hopefully recedes and the pace of economic change accelerates in response to the process of globalization. Among the most urgent warnings of the dislocations that the globalizing market will trigger in the future is William Greider's *One World, Ready or Not*; "If I am compelled to guess the future, I would estimate that the global system will, indeed, probably experience a series of terrible events – wrenching calamities that are economic or social or environmental in nature – before common sense can prevail."[11]

What Are the Implications?

The economic and social dislocations now rocking all industrial nations make for an extremely unsettled political environment within which to attempt to pursue long-term goals such as sustainability. Partly as a result, business will find itself in a new, more central position. The relative weakening of government influence and control as globalization proceeds will ensure that business will increasingly be held to account for issues which would once have been seen as political – and therefore, necessarily, the preserve of government.

Some may even see this as a desirable outcome. Capitalism has proved itself perhaps uniquely capable of reinventing itself when presented with apparently insuperable threats and constraints. We have seen the raw capitalism of the Industrial Revolution progressively molded into new forms of "social," "green," or, increasingly, "stakeholder" capitalism. Hopefully, over the next few generations, we can also evolve more "sustainable" forms of capitalism.

One key shift that will drive us in this direction is the awakening of financial markets to key elements of the triple bottom line agenda over the next decade. The scale of the losses sustained to date by the insurance industry are mind-numbing. For example, as much as a fifth of the losses which rocked Lloyd's insurance market to its financial foundations were linked to policies covering risks related to asbestos, soil contamination, and toxic or radioactive wastes, but now something new is looming on the horizon. When Hurricane Andrew hit Palm Beach, Florida in 1992, Lloyd's of London was devastated once again. Underwriters and "Names" alike could only watch their TV monitors in horror as houses and cars went flying. The resulting claims soon totalled $16 billion and the losses were so catastrophic that the reinsurance market – insurers who insure insurers – shrank almost overnight. The real fear was that such hurricane damage might be linked to the global warming trend, implying that future losses would be on an even greater scale.[12]

The insurance industry is determined not to be taken by surprise again. As a result, it is investing considerable sums of money in global climate modelling. Some forward-looking insurers are now leading the charge in the financial markets to ensure that industry is alert to environmental risks and that it is investing sufficient time, effort, money, and other resources to keep the risks to an acceptable level. Some, too, are sitting down with groups like Greenpeace and exploring ways in which they can work together to drive the necessary changes.

The problem is that even the very largest, global corporations have little control over key elements of the sustainability agenda. Which is unfortunate for them. For, while the world is increasingly persuaded that sustainable development is a necessary direction, politicians rarely yet have the vision, let alone the courage, to steer their governments, parties, and electorates in this new direction. As a result, it is inevitable that a growing portion of the sustainability agenda will land, by default, in the lap of business and of what is increasingly called "civil society;" all the institutions and public activities which create the social context within which markets evolve and business is done.

The Politicians

What do Politicians Say?

With a few honourable exceptions, politicians say as little as they can get away with. But every so often, a major world leader breaks rank and tells it as they – or their trusted advisers – see it. Early cases were the "green" speeches of Prime Minister Thatcher and Presidents Gorbachev and Bush in the late 1980s. The 1992 Earth Summit in Rio de Janeiro also saw over a hundred world leaders lining up for their few minutes in the spotlight and, for the most part, reading the words scripted for them by others. Very few, insulated by their air-conditioned, body-guarded existences, seemed able to draw on much in the way of relevant personal experience.

Then came one of the more extraordinary developments of the first Clinton Administration in the USA: the eleventh-hour conversion of Secretary of State Warren Christopher to the environmental cause. Al Gore may have claimed the headlines with his book *Earth in Balance*,[13] but

Christopher's conversion was less expected. The very nature of his job meant that he had traveled the world constantly and, in the process, had been briefed on the issues most taxing the governments he was negotiating with.[14]

Cynics saw as significant the facts that Christopher would probably retire after the 1996 election (he did) and that there would be no comprehensive Middle East peace deal before he left office: politicians like to leave a legacy. Whatever his motives, he did just that. He ordered the State Department to produce an annual report on global environmental challenges, echoing an annual report on human rights. And he also called for a system whereby the main US embassies in each global region would establish environmental centers, to raise the profile of natural resources issues and the sustainability agenda.

It is interesting to recall how many experiences helped open his eyes. One was walking, just a month before, through the children's ward of a hospital treating patients from around the Chernobyl nuclear plant. Another was working his way around the Middle East, where he constantly came across problems of soaring populations and limited water resources. His brief on the prospects for the central Asian republics spotlighted "Soviet irrigation policies that turned much of the Aral Sea into an ocean of sand." The message was clear. "I kept running into political or security problems that had a very large environmental content," he recalled. "Haiti stuck in my mind, with the overpopulation and deforestation of that country. And, in eastern Europe, those new democracies are struggling with a legacy of environmental abuse – and may never recover."

Nor were these the only issues. "We must not forget the hard lessons of Rwanda, where depleted resources and swollen populations exacerbated the political and economic pressures that exploded into one of the decade's great tragedies," he continued. Christopher became more engaged the more he heard, said one aide:

> "He heard in one briefing that by the year 2025, there would be more people living in cities than are currently alive. He heard in another briefing, on the flood potential from global warming, that 40 per cent of all cities are on coasts or tidal estuaries. He put those two together, and began diving into the reading list."

He was streets ahead of most politicians in that respect.

And then there is China. Like the National Economic Council staff in the White House, President Clinton began to wake up to the fact that China's growing appetite for grain and oil imports would have major implications for sustainable economic growth, commodity prices and inflation in other world regions. As Christopher put it:

> "With 22 per cent of the world's population, China has only seven per cent of its fresh water and cropland, three per cent of its forests, and two per cent of its oil. The combination of China's rapid economic growth and surging population is compounding the enormous environmental pressures it already faces."

Tibet is unlikely to be the last country to feel the impact of China's *lebensraum* policy, as the country's giant population seeks new lands in which to live and from which to draw sustenance.

Many critics remain sceptical, however, knowing the unspoken rule of politics; "real men don't do environment." But Warren Christopher helped to open up the way for others, further legitimizing the sustainability agenda as a key item on the political agenda for the 21st century. This is an interesting contrast to the perspectives afforded to business leaders by most of the management consultants to whom they pay so much attention and money.

The Management Gurus

What do Consultants Say?

Consultants say too much, according to some, and surprising numbers change their minds a few years later. But there are many helpful gurus and, good or bad, these people are listened to by those corporate leaders. Their ideas, usually custom-designed to create bandwagons, also help to trigger convulsive waves of change in the world of business. In 1995 alone, according to the trade newsletter *Consultant News*, corporations spent $20.6 billion on management consultancy.

When, in the mid-1980s, I settled down to write *The Green Capitalists*, there was very little in the way of relevant management literature to draw on. Michael Royston had produced *Pollution Prevention Pays* in 1979, focusing on the early experience of companies like 3M.[15] An even more influential book in terms of the evolution of my thinking appeared the following year: Alvin Toffler's *The Third Wave*.[16] But the book which I adopted as my overall benchmark was *In Search of Excellence*, by two McKinsey consultants, Thomas (now universally known as Tom) J. Peters and Robert H. Waterman.[17] I read the book on a flight to France, where I was to help the United Nations Environment Programme (UNEP) with the first World Industry Conference on Environmental Management (WICEM). Like many others, I quarried elements of the book that took my fancy, coining the phrase "environmental excellence" in the subsequent WICEM report.

In Search of Excellence went on to sell over 6 million copies: good news for the publishers, but not for the environment. The book did nothing to advance the WICEM agenda, failing to make even a single passing reference to the environmental agenda. But, that sorry state of affairs is now changing. Some modern management gurus – including Michael Porter (see p. 108) – are beginning to pay serious attention to the environment, others to sustainable development, and others still are beginning to use ecological metaphors in outlining the winning business strategies of the future.

So in each chapter, we take a look at what business gurus are saying, and then consider, by way of contrast, what the much smaller number of environmental and sustainable development gurus have to offer. Most of the mainstream gurus, it turns out, have had very little to say to date about sustainability. Where the S-word is used, as by senior McKinsey consultants Lowell Bryan and Diana Farrell in *Market Unbound*,[18] it is typically used in a different sense.

But probably the biggest recent tome on the subject of capitalism is George Reisman's 1,046-page *Capitalism*.[19] This is strongly recommended reading for anyone interested in the subject, but listen to what Reisman has to say on the subject of environmentalism, which he concludes is the greatest current threat to capitalism. "The green movement," he argues, "is the red movement no longer in its boisterous, arrogant youth, but in its demented old age." Reisman, in short, seems to exhibit exactly the same mental disease that business people have long accused environmentalists of suffering from: a pathological inability to distinguish the good from the bad in a target population.

So why bother reading some of this stuff? The answer is that when we consider the prospects for the seven "sustainability revolutions" covered in Chapters 5–11, we need to take into account the advice which business leaders are currently receiving from this quarter. There is fierce competition not only between products and between services, but also between rival ideas and the linked ideologies. Mercifully, after a decade of books on "reengineering" and "downsizing," a new wave of strategy gurus are developing such concepts as "coopetition," "co-evolution," "business ecosystems," and "value migration," all of which, it turns out, are strongly related to the triple bottom line agenda.

THE GURUS:
MATTER MEETS ANTI-MATTER?

I imagined that pulling together the thoughts of a range of business and management gurus would be like making a salad out of matter and anti-matter. Put all the various ingredients in a bowl, stir vigorously – and watch your salad disappear as they cancel each other out! Far from it. What is remarkable about the sample of gurus brought together in the following pages is the convergence of their thinking in key areas.

With concepts like "stakeholder capitalism," "coopetition," and "business ecosystems," they are, wittingly or unwittingly, helping to sketch out some of the bridges to a world of sustainable capitalism. But how many of them are really switched on to sustainability and the triple bottom line agenda? Precious few, it turns out.

Fused/Switched Off

◆ George Reisman (capitalism is the solution to every economic problem) – see Chapter 2 of *Cannibals With Forks*
◆ Peters and Waterman during *In Search of Excellence* days – Chapter 2
◆ Most 1990s management writers

But the tide has changed. By 1991, Tom Peters had written *Lean, Green and Clean*.[20] Another interesting indicator of change is that the top two articles in the January–February 1997 *Harvard Business Review* were titled "Beyond Greening: Strategies for a Sustainable World" and "Growth through Global Sustainability."[21] Below we look at some who are further along the path.

Showering Sparks

◆ Lowell Bryan and Diana Farrell (superconductivity of financial markets) – Chapter 5
◆ Jean-Marie Dru (disruption) – Chapter 13
◆ Charles Hampden-Turner and Fons Trompenaars (cultures of capitalism) – Chapter 6
◆ Rosabeth Moss Kanter (concepts, competence, connections) – Chapter 12
◆ John Kotter (kill complacency) – Chapters 11–12

◆ Barry Nalebuff and Adam Brandenburger (coopetition, complementors) – Chapter 9
◆ Fred Reichheld (role of conditional loyalty) – Chapters 5–9
◆ Dava Sobel (search for longitude as metaphor for sustainability quest) – Chapter 10
◆ Edward Tenner (why accidents happens and things bite back) – Chapter 8
◆ James Womack and Daniel Jones (lean thinking) – Chapter 8

Switching on

◆ James Collins and Jerry Porras (guidelines for long-life companies) – Chapter 10
◆ Francis Fukuyama (central role of trust, social capital) – Chapter 9
◆ Bob Garratt (new forms of board accountability) – Chapter 11
◆ Gary Hamel and C.K. Prahalad (competing for the future) – Chapter 5
◆ Charles Handy (what is a company for?) – Chapters 10–11
◆ Hans Küng (need for shared values) – Chapter 6
◆ Robert Kuttner (virtues and limits of markets) – Chapters 13–14
◆ James Moore (business ecosystems) – Chapter 5
◆ Tom Peters (lean, green, clean companies) – Chapter 12
◆ Michael Porter (value chains, green competition) – Chapter 5
◆ Peter Sandman (moving beyond "outrage") – Chapter 7
◆ Peter Schwartz (art of the long view) – Chapter 10
◆ Peter Senge (the learning organization, proactivity) – Chapter 12
◆ George Soros (internal contradictions of capitalism) – Chapter 13
◆ Lester Thurow (the future of capitalism) – Chapter 2

Switched on

◆ Claude Fussler (eco-efficiency, eco-compass) – Chapter 8
◆ Tom Gladwin (the sustainable corporation) – Chapters 6–11
◆ Rob Gray (full-cost accounting) – Chapter 4
◆ Paul Hawken (the ecology of commerce) – Chapter 2
◆ Kevin Kelly (multiple goals, change changes itself, honor your errors) – Chapter 15
◆ Amory Lovins (natural capital, Factor 4–Factor 10 engineering) – Chapter 4
◆ Jane Nelson (mainstreaming) – Chapter 13
◆ David Packard (The H–P Way) – Chapter 11
◆ Ernst Ulrich von Weizsäcker (Factor 4–10) – Chapter 4

What's Driving the Agenda?

The economic and demographic forces now at work are spotlighted by Lester Thurow in *The Future of Capitalism*. Thurow, professor of management and economics at the Massachusetts Institute of Technology (MIT) and Dean of MIT's Sloan School of Management from 1987 to 1993, compares the shifts in today's global economy with ideas taken from the natural sciences.[22]

One of these is "plate tectonics" from geology, where spectacular earthquakes and volcanoes are seen as linked to the thrusting of underlying continental plates. Another is "punctuated equilibrium" from biology, which accepts that evolution occurs very slowly in the normal course of events, but suggests that every so often there is a dramatic change in the environment, with the result that species that were highly fit in the old world order die out and are replaced by something quite different.

Five fundamental economic forces are now responsible for changing the face of the world economy and pushing us towards a period of punctuated equilibrium. As a result, we live in highly uncertain times. "We are watching the 'dinosaurs' die," Thurow says, "but we don't know what will take their place." The five great changes driving this great economic convulsion are:

♦ The end of communism. A third of humanity used to live in the old communist world – and are now beginning to play a growing part in the global economy.

♦ The shift from an economy based on natural resources to one based on brain power.

♦ Demography, in the senses that there is likely to be a 50 per cent increase in world population by 2030, a huge increase in economic migration, and a "greying" of the populations of most industrialized nations.

♦ The development of a global economy. Increasingly, anything can be made – and sold – almost anywhere. But as the old rules, based on the GATT–Bretton Woods System, become redundant and the world breaks up into trading blocs where there will be freer trade within the blocs and more government management between them, there is no guarantee that effective new rules will replace them.

♦ There is no longer, Thurow asserts, a dominant economic, political, or military power. But what happens if, and when, China takes over as the world's largest economic and, very possibly, political superpower?

In China, as Thurow notes, one of the worst things you can say to your neighbors is, "May you live in interesting times." The Chinese know that fundamental uncertainty is among the worst things we can experience. Capitalism, in short, has a future but for most of us the next couple of decades will be extremely interesting times. And the early decades of the 21st century will be even more "interesting" for the corporate brain because of the failure of most corporate advisers to understand – and alert their clients to – the profound, inevitable implications for their clients of the impending sustainability revolution.

The Business World

What do Business Leaders Say?

In truth, most business leaders have still not even got as far as avowing that they are, really, environmentalists at heart. Take Steven Spielberg and his colleagues at DreamWorks (Case Study, p. 36). They tried this approach when they ran into heavy environmental flak, but found it hardly helped them. More directly engaged is Intel chief executive Andy Grove, whose book, *Only the Paranoid Survive*,[23] notes that the challenge in today's markets is to find rational ways to survive what he calls the "10×" – or tenfold – factors that can change everything almost overnight. Examples have included the arrival of sound in the movie industry, the transformation of the computer industry in the late 1980s, and the break-up of AT&T's telephone monopoly.

It is interesting to note that Intel was also one of the first companies in the world to be targeted by campaigners operating over the Internet (Case Study, p. 168), bringing an issue which once would have been purely local on to a much wider stage. But it is not yet clear from Andy Grove's writings or public pronouncements whether or not he suspects that the sustainability challenge might represent one of those "10×" shocks for Intel and for its customers and suppliers. This conclusion, as the companies involved in organizations like the World Business Council for Sustainable Development are beginning to recognize, is entirely reasonable – and supported by a growing body of evidence.

The Sustainability Century

Who Will Win, Who Lose?

It is not yet remotely clear whether capitalism can ever become sustainable, as that term is currently understood. But there is enough evidence to suggest that the free enterprise model offers the best hope of moving

CASE STUDY

DREAMWORKS, USA

Who would have imagined it? When movie mogul Steven Spielberg, record boss David Geffen, and former Disney executive Jeffrey Katzenberg joined forces to form DreamWorks, a new Hollywood studio designed to take the film industry into the digital age, the world of cinema and TV viewers looked forward to further blockbusters from the maker of box-office smashes like *Raiders of the Lost Ark* and *Jurassic Park*. Yet a few months later, Spielberg and his colleagues were cast as the villains in one of LA's most dramatic environmental controversies.[27]

The controversy was even more media-worthy because of the involvement of Microsoft chief Bill Gates and co-founder Paul Allen among Spielberg's co-villains. At stake was the future of an area called the Ballona Wetlands. Ballona is a corruption of the Spanish *ballena*, or whale, and the 1,087 acre site just north of LA international airport is home to a huge number of species. There are 128 birds species, five of them endangered; 35 mammal species; 13 types of reptiles and amphibians; and nursery grounds for ocean fish. The 329 recorded plants include medicinal herbs still used by the Shoshone people, who lived here long before the early Spanish colonists arrived and forced them into the San Gabriel mission. Problematically, too, the site is also said to contain a Shoshone Gabrielino cemetery.

The time-bomb that DreamWorks detonated when it announced plans to build Playa Vista, an "electronic garden city," on the site clearly had been primed centuries back. The developers' lawyers made things worse by refusing to believe that there had been burials there, demanding that the 400-strong tribe prove their claim. Chief Vera Rocha refused, saying that to do so would violate the sanctity of the dead. Significantly, perhaps, Californian law rules that six Caucasian graves makes a cemetery, but the rule does not apply to Indians.

Work was to have begun on the site, which also has a long history as a Hollywood studio backlot, in the summer of 1996. Then a coalition of 38 environmental groups and Shoshone Gabrielino native Americans blocked the project – handing in a petition signed by a million people and, perhaps more significantly, launching a series of lawsuits against Dream-Works and calling for a boycott of Spielberg's *Jurassic Park* sequel.

Matters were made worse by the fact that the billionaires behind DreamWorks had been offered a $44 million, tax-free subsidy by the city authorities, who at the same time closed a hospital for lack of funds.

Chief Rocha claimed that the Ballona site was "cursed" for the white man, a graveyard of their dreams. Drawing on late 20th century mythology, he also suggested that Spielberg see again the 1982 film *Poltergeist*, which focused on a family haunted after occupying an Indian burial site. It was at this backlot, in 1924, that newspaper tycoon Randolph Hearst is thought to have accidentally shot Tom Ince when Hearst caught Charlie Chaplin *in flagrante* with his mistress Marion Davies. Later, Howard Hughes housed his ill-fated giant "Spruce Goose" seaplane here. It took off just once, with Hughes struggling at the controls, and managed to get only a few feet above the water.

Whether or not DreamWorks finally gets off the ground at Ballona, the travails of Spielberg, Gates, and partners – most of whom claim to be environmentalists at heart – spotlighted the complex dynamics (economic, social and ecological) of late 20th century environmentalism.

in that direction – provided that it is suitably shaped by social and regulatory pressures. Its real strength is that, more than any other model subjected to large-scale testing, it promises to helps harness human creativity and innovation to the sustainability cause.

Despite the fact that very few modern business best-sellers even mention the environmental and sustainability challenges, among the most deep-seated trends that will make business life increasingly "interesting" are the seven impending "sustainability revolutions" spotlighted in Chapters 5–11. These seven revolutions are not sufficient conditions for global sustainability, even when taken together, but they will most certainly be necessary conditions.

Even companies like DreamWorks and Intel, at the very heart of the emerging economy and thought by many to be infinitely more environment-friendly than the steelworks and auto-makers of the past, have been among the recent casualties of environmental controversies. But the focus of today's debate is no longer simply on errant corporations, but on the sustainability of the emerging capitalist world order.

Marx, it turns out, was right in much of his analysis but his prognosis was deeply flawed; Kruschev's, too. Even so, the last thing 21st century corporations will be able to do is put their corporate feet up. On top of all the other changes under way, the sustainability transition will destroy some industries and force the radical restructuring of others. It will be the unmaking of tens of thousands of companies and businesses around the world. But it will also provide the seedbed conditions for hundreds of thousands, indeed millions, of new businesses.

Faced with the threat of the Internet, which he had persistently ignored, Bill Gates transformed Microsoft in amazingly short order into a key Net player. He was helped by the fact that his 20,000 over-achievers were convinced that they – indeed we – are moving into the "Microsoft Century." Maybe so, but it is even more likely to be the "Sustainability Century."

Companies able to engage their stakeholders with a clear vision of their shared future and, in the process, to outperform their competitors against the triple bottom line will be much better placed to win people's hearts and minds – along with their money. Readers wanting to get straight to the heart of the matter of the triple bottom line agenda should now turn to Chapter 4. Those wanting a personal perspective on the trends, events and turning points that lie behind the evolving triple bottom line agenda should turn to Chapter 3.

But recognize that we are still a long way from sustainability. Systems thinking tells us that sustainability cannot be defined for a single corporation. Instead, it must be defined for a complete economic–social–ecological system, and not for its component parts.[24] Think of an industry directly based on a renewable natural resource, such as the fishing industry. A captain of a fishing vessel might fish for his entire life without depleting fish stocks in an area, but if he were joined by a sufficiently large fleet of identical vessels, the fishery could be destroyed. The behavior of the captain and his vessel would not have changed, but in the first case it would be sustainable and in the second not.

Worse, as Paul Hawken has pointed out in *The Ecology of Commerce,*[25] is that:

> "we are faced with a sobering irony: If every company on the planet were to adopt the environmental and social practices of the best companies – of, say, the Body Shop, Patagonia, and Ben and Jerry's – the world would still be moving toward environmental degradation and collapse."

Ultimately, Paul Hawken argues, the problem we face is not so much a management problem as a *design* problem. "In order to approximate a sustainable society," he concludes, "we need to describe a system of commerce and production in which each and every act is inherently sustainable and restorative." This is the challenge implicit in the sustainability transition. Even the best companies, as Chapter 13 explains, will only be sustainable when the institutions and markets surrounding them have been redesigned to support and promote sustainability.[26] This recognition, in turn, will require triple bottom line campaigners to invest much greater efforts in such fields as the recalibration of international trade agreements and the operations of global financial markets. In many respects, the challenge has only just begun.

Notes

1. World Commission on Environment and Development, *Our Common Future*, Oxford University Press, 1987.
2. *Fortune*, 15 April 1996, page 26.
3. Francis Fukuyama, *The End of History and the Last Man*, Hamish Hamilton, 1992.
4. Steve Liesman, "Post-communist bankers sing a capitalist tune," *Wall Street Journal Europe*, 15 July 1996.
5. Robert Kuttner, *Everything for Sale: The virtues and limits of markets*, Alfred A. Knopf, 1997.
6. Irwin Stelzer, "Capitalism under fire," *Sunday Times,* 17 March 1996.
7. Emiko Terazono, "Death of a salaryman dream," *Financial Times*, 22 March 1996.
8. "The age of anxiety," *Business Week*, 11 March 1996, page 52.
9. Terence Roth, "Fokker's fall sends jarring shock waves across the Netherlands," *Wall Street Journal Europe*, 29 January 1996. See also Jay Brenagan, "Daimler's nose dive," *Time*, 5 February 1996.
10. Rob Norton, "Job destruction/job creation," *Fortune*, 1 April 1996.
11. William Greider, *One World, Ready or Not: The manic logic of global capitalism*, Simon & Schuster, 1997.
12. Marie Woolf, "Come hell, hurricane or high water," *Observer*, 3 November 1996.
13. Al Gore, *Earth in Balance: Forging a new common purpose*, Earthscan, 1992.
14. Martin Walker, "Diplomat with a cause," *Guardian*, 1 May 1996.
15. Michael Royston, *Pollution Prevention Pays*, Pergamon Press, 1979.
16. Alvin Toffler, *The Third Wave: The revolution that will change our lives*, William Collins & Co, 1980.
17. Thomas J. Peters and Robert H. Waterman, Jr., *In Search of Excellence: Lessons from America's best-run companies*, Harper & Row, 1982.
18. Lowell Bryan and Diana Farrell, *Market Unbound: Unleashing global capitalism*, John Wiley & Sons, 1996.
19. George Reisman, *Capitalism: A complete and integrated understanding of the nature and value of human economic life*, Jameson Books, 1997.
20. Tom Peters, *Lean, Green and Clean: The profitable company of the year 2000*, The Tom Peters Group, 1991.
21. Stuart L. Hart, "Beyond Greening: Strategies for a sustainable world," and Joan Magretta, "Growth Through Global Sustainability: An interview with

Monsanto's CEO, Robert B. Shapiro," *Harvard Business Review*, January–February 1997.

22. Lester Thurow, *The Future of Capitalism: How today's economic forces will shape tomorrow's world*, Nicholas Brealey Publishing, 1996.

23. Andy Grove, *Only the Paranoid Survive*, Currency Doubleday, 1996.

24. Module 3, *From SMAS to SMAS: The EPE workbook for implementing sustainability in Europe*, Version 1.1, edited by Andrea Spencer-Cooke, SustainAbility for European Partners for the Environment, May 1996.

25. Paul Hawken, *The Ecology of Commerce: How business can save the planet*, Phoenix, 1993.

26. Paul Hawken, "A Declaration of Sustainability," *Utne Reader*, September/October 1993.

27. Christopher Reed, "Raiders of the lost park," *Observer*, 29 September 1996.

♦ 3 ♦

THE THIRD WAVE
Storming the Boardroom

The sustainable development agenda is in the process of becoming a competitive and strategic issue for major tracts of industry and commerce.

It is no surprise today to see leading environmentalists and social activists wearing pin-stripes, rather than jeans and "Save-the-Rainforests" T-shirts. And they are just as likely to be carrying the *Financial Times* or the *Wall Street Journal* as the *Co-Evolution Quarterly*, *Ecologist* or *Utne Reader*. Have the powers of Mammon turned watchdogs into lapdogs – or have the revolutionaries taken the castle? The answer is a bit of both.

It was a chill, autumn morning. On the pavement outside the smart London hotel huddled a small group of protesters. As the business conference delegates filed in, the protesters asked them to take packs of information. But something was not quite right. What was going on here? Environmentalists picketing a mining company's annual general meeting? Animal rights campaigners? Human rights activists? None of the above, it turned out.

I came across this scene as I entered the hotel to help kick off the conference. The protesters were not from Greenpeace. Instead, they were "Chlorophiles;" chlorine industry employees campaigning to save their industry and their jobs. The conference, the first organized by Greenpeace for business people, played to a capacity audience and unwittingly turned the spotlight on the extraordinary shift of influence and power now under way.

Only a few years earlier, Greenpeace would have been outside on the pavement, or busily clamping plugs on to a polluting company's effluent outfall. For a couple of decades, the resulting images have been splashed over the front pages of newspapers and the TV news headlines. These days, however, the triple bottom line movement is not only inside the factory fence but, increasingly, in the boardroom. And Greenpeace is making no secret of the fact that the chlorine industry is one of the sectors it wants to drive into extinction.

The business brain keeps hoping that the environmental and other social challenges will go away, but they keep coming back deeper and stronger. Given that the environmental movement has been the real power behind the sustainability agenda for two decades, we will focus on its evolution, although a full analysis would necessarily cover many of the economic and social campaigns that co-evolved over the same period. Some of these, however, are touched on in Chapter 3. Inevitably, too, what follows is very much a personal perspective on the events and trends of the past three decades, but one which has been extensively tested over the years with others in the environmental and sustainable development communities.

These, in short, have been some of the key stepping stones which led me to the analysis and forecasts presented in *Cannibals With Forks*. For simplicity's sake, and for clarity, I have tried to distill the huge complexity of a worldwide movement into a few story-lines. Anyone wanting a more balanced account of the environmental revolution, and of the contributions of a wider range of revolutionaries, should read some of the growing number of books dedicated to this task.[1]

As an early baby-boomer I, literally, grew up with environmentalism. That has been my great good fortune. In 1949, the year I was born, the environment as such was simply not on the international agenda. However, as we see below, that same year some critical experiments were taking place in the Arctic. By the time I turned 21 in 1970, the first wave of environmentalism was in full flow. That year saw the first Earth Day, held in the USA. I started an environmental postgraduate degree in 1972, the year of the UN Stockholm environmental conference, and began work in an environmental consultancy in 1974, towards the end of the first wave's peak. By the time I turned 40, in 1989, we were in the midst of the second great environmental wave, or "green wave," as I dubbed it in a 1990 report of that name.[2] By 1999, half a century later and on the threshold of the third millennium, environmentalism will be recognized as one of the greatest contributions of the 20th century to posterity.

None of this has been easy for older generations of business people to understand, let alone empathize with. I have often said, impolitely if accurately, that death and retirement are the environment's greatest allies in the corporate boardroom. But, whatever age they may be, corporate executives now have no option but to try to understand what is going on. The urgency of the task is increased if, as I believe, we are in the early stages of the third great wave of environmental pressure. This time, however, the pressure will come across a much broader front – because the focus will be on the triple bottom line (see Chapter 4).

Bottom Lines

Corporate Citizens or Competitors?

Worldwide, business people are waking up to the fact that key markets are on the verge of rapid change driven by new environmental standards and related customer requirements. As a result, new bottom lines are being drawn alongside the old profit-and-loss statements. Once rated a low priority corporate citizenship issue, the sustainable development agenda is in the process of becoming a competitive and strategic issue for major tracts of industry and commerce.

The past three decades have seen environmentalism emerge as the most pervasive new social movement of the post-1945 period. During that time, representing little more than a single human generation, this rapidly growing movement has helped to transform the way people see both themselves and their future. Along the way, it has catalyzed major shifts in government policy and regulation, in the technologies we use and hope to develop, and – increasingly – in the very structure of our economies.

Today, the global environmental movement is experiencing a major paradigm shift. Increasingly, campaigners are expanding their remit from the analysis of problems to the identification, refinement, and implementation of solutions. Even organizations like Greenpeace are switching away from unadulterated confrontation to mixed strategies, including innovative partnership approaches with leading corporations – designed to shape and, increasingly, "make" markets.

To understand why such changes are revolutionary and to build a picture of where they might lead, it helps to understand where we have

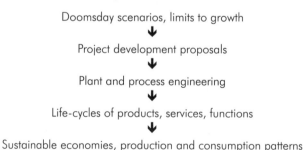

Corporate focus on:

Doomsday scenarios, limits to growth
↓
Project development proposals
↓
Plant and process engineering
↓
Life-cycles of products, services, functions
↓
Sustainable economies, production and consumption patterns

FIGURE 3.1   From Externalization To Internalization (*Source:* SustainAbility).

come from. The shift of emphasis over the past three decades is summarized in Figure 3.1. The early focus on nightmares and doomsday scenarios has given way over the years to a new interest in the question of how we can shape and harness the dreams and ambitions of ordinary citizens to the sustainability crusade. There has also been a significant shift from the externalization of environmental and other triple bottom line costs to their progressive internalization by business.

In the process, the baton has passed from project development professionals, through process engineers and new product development experts, to the very top levels of companies; those involved with strategy, investor relations, and, as explained in Chapter 11, the intimate workings of the board.

Are These Really Waves I See?

The environmental revolution hit the business world like a series of tidal waves, eventually carrying some environmentalists and other campaigners into the most unlikely places. To take just one example, Tom Burke, my co-author on *The Green Capitalists*,[3] subsequently served three successive British Secretaries of State for the Environment and ended up as an adviser to, of all people, RTZ (once Rio Tinto Zinc, then RTZ/CRA, now Rio Tinto again). In the 1970s, Tom ran Friends of the Earth – which had led the campaign to keep RTZ from mining in the unravaged wilderness of Snowdonia and more recently tried to stop the giant mining company despoiling Madagascar.

This same pattern has been repeating itself around the world as senior environmentalists have begun to be recruited not only by business but also by governments and the investment community. To anyone who remembers the daggers-drawn hostility in the early days of the collision between the worlds of business and environment, this all takes some getting used to.

What is going on? How can we make sense of the events and trends we have seen through the second half of the 20th century? Once, we would have been tempted to draw a straight line through all of these points and argue the case for inevitable progress towards doomsday or, alternatively, sustainability. But human history rarely, if ever, moves in a straight line. Today, by contrast, we see other, more complex, patterns in the data. Trying to make sense of these extraordinary changes, SustainAbility has so far plotted two great waves of environmental pressure across the OECD region, followed, to date, by two great downwaves. Before looking at what the future may hold, let's see what impact these past waves and downwaves have had on the ways in which business has defined its agenda.

Wave One: Environmentalism

Silent Springs?

If any one person can be credited with sparking the "environmental revolution," a term used by Max Nicholson in the title of a book published in 1970, it was Rachel Carson. But, as we shall see, *Silent Spring* was itself a direct result of one of the most momentous inventions of the 20th century.[4] First published in 1962, the book was largely responsible for turning the world chemicals industry from savior into demon.

"For the first time in the history of the world," Carson argued, "every human being is now subjected to contact with dangerous chemicals, from the moment of conception until death." At a time when there was mounting evidence of massive wildlife destruction caused by the new insecticides and other biocides, she pointed out that:

"we have allowed these chemicals to be used with little or no advanced investigation of their effect on soil, water, wildlife, and man himself. Future generations are unlikely to condone our lack of prudent concern for the integrity of the natural world that supports all life."

Worse, she warned, there was still:

"very limited awareness of the nature of the threat. This is an era of specialists, each of whom sees his own problem and is unaware or intolerant of the larger frame into which it fits. It is also an era dominated by industry, in which the right to make a dollar at whatever cost is seldom challenged."

TABLE 3.1   Wave 1 (peak 1969–73)

Environmentalism		Mainstream	
1970	Earth Day, USA	1970	Gaddhafi takes power in Libya
1972	UN Stockholm Conference	1972	US troops leave Vietnam
1972	*Limits to Growth, Blueprint for Survival*	1973	Watergate scandal
1973	OPEC 1 oil shock	1973	Yom Kippur war

But the public challenge was beginning to build. In *The Environmental Revolution*,[5] Max Nicholson noted that the public had become uncomfortably aware of the downside of scientific and technological progress. "The pride of having reached the moon," he suggested, "is cancelled out by the humiliation of having gone so far towards making a slum of our own native planet." It had taken a considerable number of years for this first great wave of concern to build, but Nicholson was writing just as the wave reached its peak. "Old values, habits of thought and established practices are being challenged all over the world," he reported.

In 1961, aged 10 or 11, I recall raising money for the newly founded World Wildlife Fund (now the Worldwide Fund for Nature). WWF was a wildlife conservation organization, whose founders – Peter Scott and Max Nicholson among them – were mavericks but also very much establishment figures and pro-business. But, as Nicholson himself concluded, "revolutions, unfortunately, have a way of overtaking the revolutionaries, defeating their attempts to understand or control what is going on, and baffling or alienating those at the receiving end." Indeed, a new breed of environmentalist would soon be bursting upon the scene, with the formation of such organizations as Friends of the Earth and Greenpeace. But, first, let's take a brief look behind the scenes.

Midwife to the Greens?

Few people, not even leading environmentalists, were aware that modern environmentalism had been sparked by the behind-the-scenes work of an unassuming British scientist, James Lovelock. Because Lovelock's work has helped drive each successive wave of environmentalism, his story is worth briefly summarizing here. I first came across Lovelock's work in 1976, when *New Scientist* published an article on his "Gaia Hypothesis." But, even then, Lovelock's contributions to the environmental world dated back almost three decades. In 1948, when looking for the causes of the common cold, he built a piece of equipment which would become the precursor of the environmental revolution.

Early in the 1990s, I nominated Lovelock for the Volvo Environment Prize. In 1996, he won the prize and, in his nomination lecture in Brussels, reviewed the history of that early invention, the electron capture detector (ECD) and its contribution to the evolution of the green movement.[6] In 1949, he recalled, the detector – originally designed to measure air movements – was taken on an Arctic expedition. Here it was soon found to have a worrying sensitivity: cigarette smoke upset its delicate workings. Lovelock tried out other gases, to see whether this was a part of a more general problem. It was. Among the different gases to which the instrument was acutely sensitive were CFCs – chlorofluoro-carbons.

"We did not at that time need a device to detect low levels of halocarbons," Lovelock recalled, "and so the electron capture detector was in a sense prematurely discovered." What he had, in fact, invented was "the most sensitive, easily portable and inexpensive analytical device in existence." Indeed, as he explained, the ECD is "exquisitely sensitive. If a few litres of a rare perfluorocarbon were evaporated somewhere in Japan we could with little effort detect it in a 100 cubic foot sample of the air here in Brussels a few weeks later."

Soon, serious scientists were applying the detector to the practical analysis of pesticide residues in foodstuffs. In the USA, scientists at the Food and Drug Administration (FDA), and in the UK scientists at Shell, did work which helped to spawn the environmental movement. It was discovered that chemicals like DDT and dieldrin could be found through-out the global environment; in the fat of Antarctic penguins and in the milk of nursing mothers in Finland. Enter Rachel Carson. Lovelock supported her work and recalls that:

"some parts of the chemical industry reacted in a shameful and fool-ish way by trying to discredit her as a person. It did not work. Quite the reverse. It made Rachel Carson the first saint and martyr for the infant and innocent Green movement."

Spaceship or Global Village?

Nor was it simply a matter of one new instrument being developed. Someone else who captured key aspects of what was going on in the infosphere was Marshall McLuhan, who immortalized the phrase "the medium is the message" in the early 1960s. McLuhan was so preoccu-pied with the social implications of the burgeoning web of electronic communications technology that he overlooked the environmental implications. Or perhaps it would be more accurate to say that the environmental impact of the mass media and communications revolution was a special case of the general trend which McLuhan had identified.[7]

The spread of communications technology, he argued, "establishes a global network that has much of the character of our central nervous system." McLuhan's conviction that this developing global network represented, in effect, "a single unified field of experience," enabling humanity to experience in depth the consequences of all of its actions, led him to the conclusion that the all-embracing reach of electronic communications technology was shrinking the world into what he dubbed the "global village." Events on the other side of the planet were projected into our homes and the messages of small campaigning groups were massively amplified, triggering – as we can now see – an accelerating values shift.

McLuhan argued that mechanization, as embodied in the Industrial Revolution, had extended the reach and power of the human body without a corresponding adjustment in the reach and sensitivity of the human nervous system. This necessary development has come much more recently, with the emergence of technologies like the electron capture detector, satellites, personal computers, and the Internet. But equally important, at least psychologically and emotionally, were the images of the planet seen from space which the various NASA missions brought back. These did more than anything else to boost the environmentalist version of the global village. The term environmentalists began using was *Spaceship Earth*, the title of two books, published independently in 1966 and written by Professor Kenneth Boulding and by Barbara Ward.

Images of the earth featured strongly in the campaigns of the new breed of environmentalist organization, including Friends of the Earth (which split from the more traditional Sierra Club in 1969) and Greenpeace (which started to emerge in 1971 and was soon using the new information technologies to dramatic effect). The center of gravity in the debate began to shift from wildlife and landscape conservationists to the new, more radical environmentalists. The latter came with a new set of values; baby-boomer values. Typically half the age of those who ran groups like WWF, these people were from the outset anti-business, anti-profit, and anti-growth. Their early campaigns did more than anything else to turn environmentalism into a worldwide movement and to propel the first wave of public pressure.

1970 saw the first Earth Day, in the United States, with activists taking to the streets across the country. In New York, they took sledgehammers to "gas-guzzlers" and dumped barrels of waste on to the carpet in the lobbies of major corporations. Most business people fought the environmental lobby at every opportunity, convinced that the wave would eventually turn and they would be allowed to get back to business as usual.

This first wave, peaking between 1970 and 1974, was largely driven by grassroots pressure and amplified by the power of television, forcing the hands of governments, policy-makers, and regulators alike. A pivotal year was 1972, which saw the publication of two key books – *Limits to Growth*[8] (Club of Rome) and *A Blueprint for Survival*[9] (*The Ecologist*) – and saw the doors open on the UN Conference on the Human Environment, held in Stockholm.

A range of new environmental management tools began to emerge. Some pioneering companies, including oil companies like BP and Sohio opening up the North Slope oil-fields of Alaska, began to develop environmental impact assessment methods. Some companies also experimented with environmental audits, sometimes to test out whether the impacts predicted by the assessments had been effectively tackled by the control measures – or whether new, unexpected areas of impact had emerged. But even great waves peter out. The first wave soon lost its energy and was followed by the first great downwave (Table 3.2).

TABLE 3.2   The first downwave (trough: 1974–87)

Environmentalism		Mainstream	
1974	Seveso disaster, Italy	1975	Fall of Saigon; first North Sea oil ashore
1978	San Carlos de la Rapita gas explosion kills 200, Spain	1976	Mao dies, China
1979	OPEC 2 oil shock	1977	Elvis Presley dies
1983	Greenham Common protests, UK	1979	Shah of Iran exiled; Khmer Rouge genocide exposed in Cambodia
1984	Bhopal disaster, India; Band Aid	1981	Pope, President Reagan shot
1985	BAS discovery of Antarctic ozone hole; Live Aid; French blow up Greenpeace's *Rainbow Warrior* in Auckland harbour, New Zealand	1982	Falklands War
		1984	China sets off down capitalist road
		1985	Gorbachev new Soviet leader
1986	Chernobyl disaster, USSR; Rhine disaster	1986	Mrs Aquino forces out Marcos, Philippines
1987	*Our Common Future*; Montreal Protocol signed; "storm of century" lashes UK	1987	"Black Monday" stock market crash

The First Downwave: Band Aids

Limits to Growth?

Just as the first OPEC oil-shock of 1973–74 seemed to confirm the Club of Rome's gloomy *Limits to Growth* forecasts, soaring energy prices triggered an international economic recession. The environment slipped down the political agenda, a trend eagerly exploited by industry lobbyists. Not that this meant that the environment slipped completely off the business agenda. In 1978, for example, the Brussels based Management Centre Europe carried out a survey of chief executives in eleven European countries.[10] At the time, Europe was "barely emerging from the most severe economic recession since the 1930s." Competition with major trading partners, most particularly the USA and Japan, was forcing massive restructuring of industries like textiles and shipbuilding. Yet environmental protection, it turned out, was seen as a more pressing management issue, for the period 1973 to 1978, than consumer protection, high levels of unemployment, the demands of organized labor, and even shareholder relations.

The 1970s had certainly been a busy time for environmental legislators. The period saw the formation of the first of hundreds of national environmental protection agencies, ministries, and departments. Ironically, even though the first wave had begun to fall back in 1974, its political impact continued for many years. When the Organisation for Economic Co-operation and Development (OECD) published its first state of the environment report in 1979, it included a listing of the new laws passed in OECD countries during the decade. The figures showed that the trend really took off in 1972, with the period between 1972 and 1976 representing the peak years.

Following the second OPEC oil shock of 1978–79, the downwave took hold in the USA during the early 1980s, under President Ronald Reagan and, in the UK, under Prime Minister Margaret Thatcher. "Environmentalists tremble" read one headline in *Science* shortly after the election of Ronald Reagan as President. If they did, they had good reason to do so: the ex-actor had been, to put it mildly, an uninspiring candidate as far as environmental issues went. At one stage, he went as far as to assert that trees were a major source of air pollution. He also claimed that air pollution was under control – on the same day that a pea-soup photochemical smog prevented his plane from landing at Los Angeles airport.[11]

The Republicans took their lead from a crop of think-tank reports which had argued that regulation was almost an un-American activity. Some observers feared a gutting of the Environmental Protection

Agency (EPA). Outgoing EPA administrator Doug Costle warned the incoming Republicans that:

> "there are fundamental demographic changes that we're going through in this country. As you look at the polls, the young people feel a lot more strongly about environmental issues than the age group that will be represented in the government leaders in the next four years. I don't think society is going to permit a turning back of the clock."

But that did not stop the Republicans. Indeed, an editorial in the *New York Times* described the ensuing chaos at the agency as follows:

> "Seldom since the Emperor Caligula appointed his horse a consul has there been so wide a gulf between authority and competence. Mr Reagan's EPA appointees brought almost no relevant experience to their jobs. His administrator, Anne Burford, was a telephone company attorney and two-term legislator who learned about environmental issues fighting Clean Air Act provisions in Colorado."

Not surprisingly, environmentalists saw these appointments as equivalent to putting foxes in charge of the chicken-houses. They were not far wrong: the resulting scandals rocked the EPA. Its staff halved at a time when its responsibilities more or less doubled. The American experience, as usual, simply took a trend to extremes.

No-one disputed that the USA had introduced an unprecedented succession of powerful and sweeping new regulations since the late 1960s. And there was a growing body of opinion that the time had come for the whole process of environmental regulation and enforcement to be streamlined or "fine-tuned." Indeed, the incoming administration had used such words to describe its intentions. But like the knights who assassinated Thomas à Becket in 1170, Burford and others took their instructions too literally. President Reagan, like Henry II, eventually found himself having to do penance for the resulting damage.

What is Zero?

The ability to measure vanishingly small quantities of toxins inevitably led to over-reactions. "Before the ECD was used," as Lovelock explained:

> "it would have been quite easy and reasonable to set zero as the lowest permissible limit of pesticide residues in foodstuff. Zero really

means the least that can be detected. After the electron capture detector appeared, zero as a limit became so low that to apply it in full would cause the rejection of nearly everything that was edible. Even natural vegetation contains measurable levels of pesticides, so sensitive is the device."

While the world struggled with this new problem, however, Lovelock was already accidentally stumbling on a new one. In 1968, the year we baby-boomers were taking to the streets in protest against the Vietnam War and other issues, Lovelock's family bought a holiday cottage in far western Ireland, on the shores of Bantry Bay. He noticed that the air was sometimes clear, and sometimes hazy so that objects less than a mile away became invisible. "The haze looked and smelt to me just like the photochemical smog of Los Angeles," Lovelock recalled, "but how could it have reached this remote rural region?" Next summer, he lugged a portable gas chromatograph on holiday. To cut a long story short, he found that the smog was coming from as far away as Southern France and Italy. More significantly still, his equipment picked up startlingly high levels of CFCs in what was meant to be clean Atlantic air.

So where were the CFCs coming from? Were they drifting across the Atlantic from America, or were CFCs – whose only source was industry – accumulating in the atmosphere? To find out, Lovelock put together an ECD instrument able to measure parts per trillion of gas and sailed to the Antarctic with it. What he found along the way lit a fuse which would eventually blow up, once again, under the embattled chemical industry.

The data were used by two American scientists, Sherwood Rowland and Mario Molina, to develop a theory on ozone depletion which – after much controversy – destroyed the future of the global CFC industry.[12] This issue helped catalyze the second great wave of environmentalism, just as the ECD data on pesticides had catalyzed the first wave.

Anyone for Clean Technology?

Throughout the first downwave, the continuing activities of environmentalists and regulators kept the pressure on environment-intensive industries. Among other things, they promoted energy efficiency and clean (or cleaner) technologies. One company which took the US EPA at its word when it began to talk in terms of "zero emissions" was 3M. During the 1970s, the company asked Dr Joseph Ling, then its vice-president for environmental engineering, to review the costs of meeting existing and likely new laws. The conclusions were grim.

Dr Ling concluded that traditional pollution control technologies were already consuming financial and other resources at an uneconomic rate. Worse, if environmental standards continued to rise, as seemed likely, the total costs would increase exponentially as companies tried to remove the last few percentage points of pollution. 3M came up with a radically different approach. As part of its new 3P (Pollution Prevention Pays) program, it adopted the following formula: "*Pollution (waste materials) + knowledge (technology) = potential resources.*" I first came across the 3P story thanks to Michael Royston, author of *Pollution Prevention Pays*,[13] who I had first met in Iceland in 1977.

The major thrust of the 3P program, which soon saved 3M many hundreds of millions of dollars worldwide, was directed into reformulating products, modifying processes, redesigning equipment, and recovering waste materials for re-use. As one example, 3M switched from a cotton herbicide which generated 12 pounds of pollutants per pound of product to one which generated two pounds per pound of product – and was also cheaper to make.

Paradoxically, the good news started to flow during the downwave. In fact, in 1978 Max Nicholson, David Layton and I were the founders of Environmental Data Services, a new company dedicated to researching and communicating best business practice. But the good news was accompanied by a steady stream of bad news. Among the issues on the environmentalist agenda were the following:

♦ The world's population had swelled from about 1.6 billion in 1900 to 5.2 billion by 1990 – and looked set to exceed 8 billion by the year 2025.

♦ Largely because of human pressures, it was estimated that the world was losing about a hundred species of all kinds every day. In 1987 alone, up to 50 million acres of species-rich tropical forest were estimated to have been destroyed.

♦ Oil was still being spilled into the oceans at ten times the rate of the already substantial natural seepage from oil fields.

♦ In Europe, the proportion of forests showing damage caused by acid deposition had grown from 8 per cent in 1982 to 52 per cent in 1988. More than a third of Europe's forests were thought to be blighted by acid pollutants – and the situation in Eastern Europe was turning out be even worse.

♦ In 1987 alone, human activity added the equivalent of 6.5 billion tonnes of carbon to the atmosphere – in the form of carbon dioxide and other greenhouse gases. This represented more than 1.25 tonnes for every person on the planet.

The odd thing about the first downwave was that it continued despite the growing availability of such statistics, and despite the fact that the period also saw some of the biggest environmental disasters in history, including the 1984 Bhopal poisoning deaths (5,325 people if you believe the official estimate, nearer 15,000 if you believe some unofficial estimates), and the 1986 Chernobyl nuclear accident.

Anyone for Sustainable Development?

None of these disasters was sufficient to trigger directly a second wave of protest. But there were reactions at other levels. 1987, for example, saw the publication of one of the most important books of the late twentieth century: *Our Common Future*.[14] This was produced by the World Commission on Environment and Development, chaired by Norwegian Prime Minister Gro Harlem Brundtland. The "Brundtland Report" put sustainable development – a concept which had been around at least since 1980 – firmly onto the international political agenda.

Sustainable development was defined as "development that meets the needs of the present world without compromising the ability of future generations to meet their own needs." Key objectives, the Brundtland Commission noted, include the following: reviving economic growth, but in a new form ("less material- and energy-intensive and more equitable in its impact"); meeting essential needs for jobs, food, energy, water, and sanitation; ensuring a sustainable level of population; conserving and enhancing our natural resource base; reorienting technology and managing risk; and merging ecological and economic considerations in decision making.

The Commission argued that feeding, clothing, housing, transporting, and fueling the expanded world population will imply a 5–7-fold increase in industrial production by the middle years of the 21st century. *Cannibals With Forks* is built around many of the same assumptions. It may not be the best option as far as the planetary ecosystem is concerned, but it is almost certainly the option we will have to plan for and manage in practice.

For those who find the Brundtland Commission's definition of sustainability too vague, here is a more precise definition, advanced by Herman Daly while an economist with the World Bank.[15] A sustainable society needs to meet three conditions: its rates of use of renewable resources should not exceed their rates of regeneration; its rates of use of non-renewable resources should not exceed the rate at which sustainable renewable substitutes are developed; and its rates of pollution

TABLE 3.3 Wave 2 (peak 1988–90)

Green		Mainstream	
1988	"Greening" of leading politicians (e.g. Thatcher, Gorbachev, Bush); Green consumer movement starts	1988	USSR withdraws from Afghanistan; George Bush elected US President; Harvard awarded patent on genetically engineered mouse
1989	*Exxon Valdez* disaster; 15% of UK voters back Greens in Euro-elections	1989	Massacre in Tiananmen Square, China; collapse of communism in Eastern Europe
1990	Earth Day, international; start of corporate environmental reporting trend	1990	Re-unification of Germany; Iraq invades Kuwait
		1991	Gulf War/Operation Desert Storm; disintegration of former Yugoslavia; coup against President Gorbachev; demise of USSR

emission should not exceed the assimilative capacity of the environment.

Going Green

Invisible Elbow?

Downwaves also end. The second great wave of environmentalism reached full force in the late 1980s, picking up through 1987 and peaking between 1988 and 1990. It was sparked by a wide range of issues and disasters, but a key contributory factor was the discovery of the Antarctic ozone hole in 1985. The glowing maps of the southern hemisphere published in the press and shown on TV gave ordinary people clear, visible evidence that something they were doing every day – using aerosols with CFC propellants – was helping to tear the global environmental fabric. Consumers suddenly felt that their fingers, quite literally, were on the button of environmental destruction. Here, at last, was conclusive proof of the global damage caused as the benefits brought about by Adam Smith's "invisible hand" began to be canceled out by the impact of the market's "invisible elbow."

Governments woke up to the fact that environmental problems were no longer simply local, national, or regional. Increasingly, we face global problems. In 1987, 35 nations signed an unprecedented international agreement, the Montreal Protocol, designed to control CFC emissions. In addition, industry began to recognize that it could no longer abdicate responsibility for such problems until the relevant environmental science was completed – in the expectation that the scientists would ultimately prove industry's innocence. As a result, we saw the emergence of early business champions of the "precautionary principle."

Regulators again had something of a field day, although the pace of development was slower in this second wave. By the early 1990s, the Commission of the European Communities alone had brought into effect some 250 environmental directives, with nearly another 50 in the pipeline. The success of the green parties in a number of member states during the 1980s had also given the political screw another fierce twist.

Can Consumers Save the World?

This time, as far as business was concerned, the pressures came via a wider range of channels. The publication of our own *Green Consumer Guide*[16] in October 1988 caught the spirit of the time – giving ordinary citizens the information they needed to make choices between named brand products. The idea caught on. By the time the book's US edition appeared the following year, it was joined by half a dozen others, including *50 Ways to Save the Planet*.[17]

Although this time the advantage was with organizations and companies working with environmentally aware consumers, green consumerism was an expression of a much wider tide of concern sweeping through society. Like "green capitalism" before it, "green consumerism" was an oxymoron. Again, I must accept the blame for spot-welding two apparently incompatible visions of the future. Anyone who genuinely thought that we could shop our way out of our troubles would certainly have been disappointed. But that was not our message. Our goal was empowerment – and the consumer pressures triggered by the book sent powerful new market signals to both retailers and manufacturers.

Paradoxically, business often found these pressures much harder to deal with than government-led initiatives. With governments, business could lobby, through trade and industry associations, stopping or at least slowing proposed regulations and other controls. When the market tripped in, however, things could move much faster – and often did so in a less predictable fashion.

As a result, business leaders began to accept that the future would not allow them to continue with business as usual. "One issue, more than any other, will affect Dow's prospects in the '90s and beyond," ran the message emblazoned across the front cover of the US chemical company's 1989 annual report. "That issue is the environment." The perception grew that a company's actual – and perceived – environmental performance increasingly determined the ease and degree of success with which it enters markets, makes and sells products, wins permission to develop new facilities, and attracts capital and skilled new recruits.

This time the environmental management toolbox expanded at an extraordinary rate. Among the phrases that business people learned to use were "environmental audit," "life-cycle assessment," "design for the environment," and "eco-labelling." These were ideas that had been in gestation since the first wave, but which had needed a new burst of energy to drive them on to the desks of ordinary executives.

By 1990, twenty years on from its inception, Earth Day had become an international event. When Earth Day co-founder Denis Hayes invited me to join the Earth Day International Board, I found the mood very different from what it had been in 1970. There was a greater focus on solutions, although the organizers still had great difficulty in working out how to involve major corporations without compromising themselves. Earth Day 1990 got campaigns, initiatives, and stunts off the ground in over 130 countries. At the time, like many others, I felt that we were on a roll that would continue at least until 1992, the year of the long-planned Earth Summit. I was wrong. The second downwave was about to hit.

The Second Downwave

Summit in a Downwave?

Unlike the UN Stockholm conference twenty years earlier, the 1992 Earth Summit was held against the background of the worst international recession of the post-1945 period. Two locomotives of economic growth in the 1980s – the German and Japanese economies – were almost derailed. Even on government estimates, nearly 20 million Europeans found themselves unemployed. Ordinary citizens became much more concerned about holding onto their jobs and with finding affordable products than about protecting the environment. The second downwave probably began by the end of 1990, and was certainly well under way by 1991 – when the world began to run into a number of

TABLE 3.4   Downwave 2 (trough 1991–)

Sustainability	Mainstream
1992 UN Earth Summit, Rio de Janeiro	1992 Bill Clinton elected US President; riots in Los Angeles
1995 Brent Spar controversy, Europe; Shell Nigeria; French nuclear tests in Mururoa	1993 Peace agreement between Israel and PLO; President Yeltsin clashes with Russian Parliament
1996 BSE/"mad cow" disease, Europe; road protests at Newbury, UK; publication of *Our Stolen Future*, Body Shop's *Values Report*	1994 Democracy breaks out in South Africa; Rwandan civil war, massacres; ceasefire in Northern Ireland
	1995 Financial crisis in Mexico; collapse of Barings; Oklahoma City bombing

other major issues, among them the Gulf War, Somalia, and the collapse of ex-Yugoslavia into bloody chaos.

But throughout this period, although there was a relative decline in environmental concern from the peak year of 1990, most opinion polls continued to show higher levels of awareness about a broader range of environmental issues than would have been the case during most of the 1980s. The environmental and sustainability agendas had not so much disappeared as been professionalized. A great deal was now happening behind the scenes. The paradoxical implication was that if growth resumed on the old pattern, environmentalism would likely enjoy a resurgence – and do so from a much higher base of public support, professionalism, and influence than in previous business cycles.

One of the more interesting moments of 1992 came with the publication of *Beyond the Limits*,[18] by some of the same team that had given us *Limits to Growth* twenty years earlier. Again, the conclusions reached were unsettling. "The human world is beyond its limits," we were told:

"The present way of doing things is unsustainable. The future, to be viable at all, must be one of drawing back, easing down, healing. Poverty cannot be ended by indefinite material growth; it will have to be addressed while the material human economy contracts."

"Like everyone else," the authors noted, "we didn't really want to come to these conclusions."

Corporate Environmentalists?

Most business people didn't like the conclusions, either. But the late 1980s had seen business investing a growing amount of energy and senior management time, via organizations like the International Chamber of Commerce (ICC) and the Business Council for Sustainable Development (BCSD), in preparing its position for the 1992 Earth Summit. Ironically, as we have seen, the second great green wave peaked in late 1990 or early 1991, well before the Earth Summit, leaving many business initiatives hanging in mid-air, without the political and market pressures to properly sustain them.

This time, however, there was a much more powerful ratchet effect at work. Perhaps a key reason for this was that the second wave had hit business much harder than it had hit governments. The president of the ICC noted that "the withering away of the Marxist challenge leaves the environmental challenge as the most fundamental one that business [people] all over the world are going to face in the foreseeable future."[19]

From the Bhopal disaster onwards, we had seen growing numbers of companies – most particularly US chemical companies like Dow Chemical, DuPont and Monsanto – committing themselves to environmental targets that began to take them well beyond what the regulators currently required. There was much talk of moving "beyond compliance" and of a new mood of "corporate environmentalism." Business leaders began to recognize the need for business people to act as environmentalists, rather than simply as professionals with environmental responsibilities. "No corporation can be truly innovative until everyone in the company has adopted an environmentalist attitude," said Edgar Woolard, as chairman and CEO of DuPont. In the spirit of the times, Woolard also said that, at least in his case, CEO stood for "chief environmental officer."

As we will see, this sort of claim was more than a little optimistic. But at least the conversion was now under way – and the second downwave simply slowed progress, rather than sending it into a tail-spin. Business leaders, increasingly, recognized the need to "change course," to use the phrase introduced in 1992 by the Business Council for Sustainable Development's 1992 book, *Changing Course*.[20]

Among the BCSD's key messages were:

♦ as the world moves inexorably towards deregulation, private initiatives, and global markets, economic growth and environmental protection will be inextricably linked;

♦ progress towards sustainable development makes good business sense, because it can create competitive advantages and new opportunities;

♦ sustainability requires new visions to energize society, together with new forms of co-operation between government, business, and society;

♦ open and competitive markets, both within and between nations, foster innovation and efficiency, and provide opportunities for improved living conditions;

♦ new regulations and economic instruments will need to be tailored to local circumstances, but must also be harmonized among trading partners; and

♦ some markets – for example those operating in the farming and forestry sectors – need to be reengineered so that price and other signals encourage progress towards sustainability.

But the area where *Changing Course* identified the greatest need for change was in the world's capital markets. Little was known, the BCSD noted, "about the constraints, the possibilities, and the interrelationships between capital markets, the environment, and the needs of future generations." This area was covered in greater detail in a subsequent WBCSD book, *Financing Change*.[21]

For many business people, the mid-1990s may not have felt like a downwave, but the period certainly saw reduced levels of public concern and activism in many countries. To some extent, however, the depth of the second downwave will only become clear when we can look back at it from the vantage point of riding – or being carried along by – the imminent third wave.

Wave 3: Sustainability

Will There be Another Wave?

I believe that the third wave has already begun. And the pressures on business this time around will be a complex mix of everything that went before, plus some new factors. Businesses developing a competitive edge in this area – a sustainability advantage – will be much better placed to identify and win a share of the new markets.

Through the 1990s we predicted that the third great environmental wave might start as soon as 1997 or 1998 (Table 3.5). This time, we concluded, the wave would be driven by such factors as strengthening

TABLE 3.5　Wave 3

Drivers	Characteristics
♦ Economic and social fall-out from globalization ♦ Economic recovery in some countries ♦ "Pre-Millennial Tension" ♦ Values shift(s) ♦ New generation of activists	♦ Acceleration and growing complexity ♦ Global goldfish bowl, spurred by Internet ♦ New focus on life-cycles, business ecosystems, time-scales, corporate governance ♦ Triple bottom line ♦ Value migration

science on global warming, growing concerns about the economic and social fall-out from globalization, and – in advance of the third millennium – more than a degree of "pre-millennial tension."

Through 1995, it seemed that our forecasts were beginning to prove a bit too conservative. A string of controversies once again sparked media interest in the environmental agenda. First, Shell UK ran into massive public resistance to its plans to dump its giant Brent Spar oil buoy at sea. Then the giant oil company became the target for an unprecedented international campaign as the Nigerian government executed environmental activist Ken Saro-Wiwa and his colleagues. That same year, too, President Chirac came under intense pressure from countries around the world to abandon his series of nuclear tests at the Mururoa atoll. As it happens, I was in New Zealand during the second test, sharing a platform with the country's Prime Minister, Jim Bolger. He was incandescent with anger at the French and very much on the side of Greenpeace in this latest dispute.

Time and again, we saw leading politicians beginning to be dragged into the debate. Britain's then Prime Minister, John Major, clashed with Germany's Chancellor Helmut Kohl over Brent Spar. President Chirac collided with Europe's President Jacques Santer on nuclear testing. And then, as the "mad cow" controversy broke across Europe, Major was again under fire from leading politicians across the Union.

Shell and others affected by these controversies noted that they had been hit out of the blue – and with unparalleled force. What, they wanted to know, was going on? Together with Paul Hawken and Geoff Lye, I spent a fascinating couple of days working through the evidence with top executives from Shell International. Some companies began to ask whether this was our third wave at last? No, we replied, the evidence suggested that this was exactly what we would have expected to see in the depth of a downwave.

Our logic worked like this. Ordinary people were now much more aware of the issues than they had been. They wanted to see the problems addressed, but desirably by someone else. The events of the 1990s had made them less confident that green consumerism and similar types of pressure would – at least in isolation – bring the necessary changes. This gap between their longer-term environmental concerns and their current unwillingness to act created a certain psychic friction, producing the equivalent of a static charge. When a potential scapegoat came along, the accumulated energy could discharge with surprising force. This was not the third tidal wave, we concluded, but a necessary series of precursor seismic events.

Will Gaia Surf the Next Wave?

The third wave, I suspect, will again owe a good deal to Jim Lovelock. This time, however, the catalyst he has contributed is an idea rather than a piece of equipment. Working for NASA, Lovelock began to wonder about life on earth. Working with Lynn Margulis, he developed the idea that the Earth might regulate its own climate and chemistry at a state favourable for the organisms that inhabit it. "I may be wrong but I do think that this idea, which the novelist William Golding suggested I call Gaia, has been my most useful contribution," he explained.

Lovelock first put forward the Gaia hypothesis as early as 1969, as the first wave built towards its peak. Together with Margulis, he defined Gaia as "a complex entity involving the Earth's biosphere, atmosphere, oceans and soil; the totality constituting a feedback or cybernetic system which seeks an optimal physical environment for life on this planet."

Gaia, Lovelock suggested in his 1979 book of the same title,[22] "is an alternative to that pessimistic view which sees nature as a primitive force to be subdued and conquered." Unlike most reductionist science, and this is the reason why I believe that Lovelock's thinking will be fundamentally important in the 21st century, Gaian science is not neutral. Vaclav Havel, then President of the Czech Republic, gave a speech when he received the Freedom Medal of the USA. Havel said that Gaia was part of a new science that offers moral guidance. It gives us something to which we are accountable. Or, to use Havel's words, "We are not here for ourselves alone."

In the context of our evolving triple bottom line accountabilities, the

CASE STUDY

ANGLIAN WATER, UK:
SURFERS OF THE THIRD WAVE?

Scene: A sewage works outside Cambridge, lit by a fitful sun, swept by a cold wind from the east.

Cast: Sundry members of Anglian Water's board environment committee, including yours truly, surveying the world from a metal gangway high above an experimental treatment plant.

Apparently random thought, staring down into the swirling brown liquid: Is this what we campaigned for all those years?

A few words of explanation. Twenty years ago, when I began to grill companies about their environmental problems, most loathed the idea of environmentalists getting anywhere inside the factory fence, let alone into the headquarters building. Anyone sporting an environmental label was assumed to be going for the throat. You counted yourself lucky if you got to speak to a public relations executive or environmental lawyer, even though you knew they were paid to keep you at arm's length.

Later, in energy companies like BP and British Gas, you met like-minded people whose working lives involved carrying out environmental impact assessments for major project proposals. They, at least, understood the issues. But their job was to shoe-horn new developments into the environment, not consider their sustainability or challenge the underlying need for such development.

Then came the late 1980s. Suddenly, the green world overflowed with exotic business breeds: new product development people, designers and – above all – marketers. Few were committed environmentalists: what they really wanted to know was how to give their products a sharp green spin into the marketplace. Many ended up in the ditch with their wheels spinning.

Now the not-so-random thought. Today the environmental agenda is attracting a different set: strategists, investor relations experts, and main board directors. The reason is that we are increasingly deliberating such questions as what companies are for, how they should meet stakeholder needs and expectations, and how they must be configured to succeed during the sustainability transition.

In the water industry, the regulators now insist that water efficiency is given a high priority. So among Anglian's projects designed to alert water-users to water conservation is the company's "Drought Garden." There is

)

also a WaterWise information pack, offering everything from the Triple Wax Dri-wash (clean your car without water) to "miracle watering cans," whose push-button devices ensure water goes where it is needed. Small beer, perhaps, but with almost a third of Anglian's customers admitting they waste "a lot" of water, such measures are timely.

Longer term, however, the route to sustainability will run through transformed water markets. Companies must learn how to earn more by selling less. Facing inexorably rising demand and an uncertain supply picture, Anglian is already pondering "demand side management." "Our normal response to the problem of a village with periodic water supply difficulties is to lay a larger pipeline," the company's water efficiency plan notes, "whereas a cheaper and more environmentally sensitive solution may be to reduce demand in that village by checking all the domestic supply pipes for leaks and fitting water-efficient appliances."

Fine, but how can we convert all consumers to water-efficiency? One way forward is obviously to install water meters. Anglian's current plan is to meter 95% of properties by 2015. And there's the rub: most consumers still see clean, almost free water as a right. This must – will – change. Watching the foam spiraling beneath our feet, I concluded that this was indeed what the first two waves of environmentalism were about: transforming leading companies into vigorous, effective campaigners for resource efficiency and sustainability. But will Anglian and its competitors get their act together in time to surf the third wave of environmentalism?

key question we must ask is this: are the models of growth that evolved in the post-1945 period the right, or sustainable, models for the 21st century? The answer, almost certainly, is that they are not. Indeed, it is interesting that the Commission of the European Communities, in its White Paper on *Growth, Competitiveness and Employment*,[23] spoke of the need to develop and adopt a "new model of development." Specifically, the Commission foresaw a growing imbalance in the main factors of production – land, labor, and capital.

For decades, the substitution of labor by capital, via technology, has been accompanied by growth in the use of energy and other raw materials, leading to the over-exploitation of increasingly scarce environmental resources. Because market prices do not adequately reflect the scarcity of many natural resources, nor the environmental opportunity costs involved in using such resources for short-term economic gain, the Commission notes that "their over-use has become systematic."

This time around, the challenge for business is likely to be of a very different order than in the previous waves and downwaves. There will be cycles, but the pressures are likely to increasingly converge on a number of principles which have been developed and applied by a number of environmentally and socially responsible companies. And the focus of political attention is likely to switch progressively to evermore sensitive parts of the environment and of the human population (for example, children's health), with the result that the challenge for business is characterized, over the long term, by a ratchet effect. The result, as illustrated by the Anglian Water case study (p. 64), is that growing numbers of companies are now considering elements of the sustainability agenda at board level.

Notes

1. See, for example: Tom Athanasiou, *Slow Reckoning: The ecology of a divided planet*, Secker & Warburg, 1997; Anna Bramwell, *Ecology in the 20th Century: A history*, Yale University Press, 1989; Mark Dowie, *Losing Ground: American environmentalism at the close of the twentieth century*, The MIT Press, 1995; Sara Parkin, *Green Parties: An international guide*, Heretic Books, 1989; David Pepper, *The Roots of Modern Environmentalism*, Croom Helm, 1986; Jonathon Porritt and David Winner, *The Coming of the Greens*, Fontana/Collins, 1988; Victor B. Scheffer, *The Shaping of Environmentalism in America*, University of Washington Press, Seattle, 1991.
2. John Elkington, *The Green Wave: Report of the first GreenWorld survey*, SustainAbility and British Gas, 1990.
3. John Elkington with Tom Burke, *The Green Capitalists*, Gollancz, 1987.
4. Rachel Carson, *Silent Spring*, Houghton Mifflin, 1962; Pelican Books, 1965.
5. Max Nicholson, *The Environmental Revolution: A guide for the new masters of the world*, Hodder & Stoughton, 1970; Pelican Books, 1972.
6. James E. Lovelock, *Midwife to the Greens: The electron capture detector*, Volvo Environment Prize lecture, Brussels, October 1996.
7. John Elkington, *The Ecology of Tomorrow's World*, Associated Business Press, 1980.
8. Dennis Meadows et al, *The Limits to Growth*, Earth Island, 1972.
9. *The Ecologist, A Blueprint for Survival*, first published as *The Ecologist* **2**(1) 1972, and then as a Penguin Special, 1972.
10. John Humble and Michael Johnson, *Corporate Social Responsibility: The attitudes of European business leaders*, Management Centre Europe, 1978.
11. John Elkington, *The Poisoned Womb: Human reproduction in a polluted world*, Viking 1985; Pelican Books, 1986.

12. M. J. Molina and F. S. Rowland, Stratospheric sink for chlorofluoromethanes – chlorine atom-catalyzed destruction of ozone, *Nature* **249**, 1974, p. 810. See also *Science*, 12 December 1975, p. 1036.
13. Michael Royston, *Pollution Prevention Pays*, Pergamon Press, 1979.
14. World Commission on Environment and Development, *Our Common Future*, Oxford University Press, 1987.
15. Herman Daly, "Institutions for a steady-state economy," *Steady State Economics*, Island Press, 1991.
16. John Elkington and Julia Hailes, *The Green Consumer Guide: From shampoo to champagne*, Gollancz, 1988.
17. Earthworks Group, *50 Ways to Save the Planet*, Earthworks Press, Berkeley, 1989.
18. Donnella H. Meadows, Dennis L. Meadow and Jørgen Randers, *Beyond the Limits: Global collapse or a sustainable future*, Earthscan, 1992.
19. John Elkington with Anne Dimmock, *The Corporate Environmentalists: Selling sustainable development – but can they deliver?,* SustainAbility and British Gas, 1991.
20. Stephan Schmidheiny with the Business Council for Sustainable Development, *Changing Course: A global business perspective on development and the environment*, MIT Press, 1992.
21. Stephan Schmidheiny and Federico Zorraquin, *Financing Change*, The MIT Press, 1996.
22. James E. Lovelock, *Gaia: A new look at life on Earth*, Oxford University Press, 1979.
23. *White Paper on Growth, Competitiveness and Employment*, Commission of the European Communities, 1993.

♦ 4 ♦

THE TRIPLE
BOTTOM LINE

Sustainability's Accountants

**Business executives wanting to grasp the
full scale of the emerging challenge
must audit current performance and future targets
against the triple bottom line.**

Driving companies towards sustainability will require dramatic changes in their performance against the triple bottom line. Some of the most interesting challenges, however, are found not within but *between* the areas covered by the economic, social, and environmental bottom lines. These "shear zones" are illustrated in Figures 4.1–4.7 and typical agenda items are covered in the three "shear zone" panels.

Like the ancient Trojans dragging the vast wooden horse through a great gap torn in the walls of their long-besieged city, some of the world's best business brains spent the 1990s struggling to take on board the emerging sustainability agenda. Many of their colleagues warned that success would end in disaster, just as it had done for the Trojans. Sustainable development, they argued, was a treacherous concept; basically, communism in camouflage. By the middle of the last decade of the 20th century, however, their fevered brows were being soothed by the concept of "eco-efficiency," promoted by the World Business Council for Sustainable Development (WBCSD). And then, as some had feared, the trap was sprung.

Communism had nothing to do with it. But the sustainability agenda, long understood as an attempt to harmonize the traditional financial bottom line with emerging thinking about the environmental bottom line, turned out to be more complicated than some early business enthusiasts had imagined. Today we think in terms of a "triple bottom line," focusing on economic prosperity, environmental quality, and – the element which business had preferred to overlook – social justice.

None of this was new, of course. *Our Common Future*, the 1987 report of the World Commission on Environment and Development, had made it perfectly clear that equity issues, and particularly the concept of inter-generational equity, were at the very heart of the sustainability agenda.[1] But most of the hundreds of companies that limbered up for the 1992 Earth Summit by signing the Business Charter for Sustainable Development, devised by the International Chamber of Commerce (ICC), had little idea of the deeper logic of sustainable development. As far as they, and the thousands of companies which have signed up since, were concerned, the basic challenge was simply one of "greening," of making business more efficient and trimming costs.

When the *Harvard Business Review* turned its spotlight on to the sustainability agenda in 1997, ten years after the publication of *Our Common Future*, it noted that, "Beyond greening lies an enormous challenge – and an enormous opportunity. The challenge is to develop a sustainable global economy: an economy that the planet is capable of supporting indefinitely."[2] This represents a profound challenge. Although some parts of the developed world may be beginning to turn the corner in terms of ecological recovery, the planet as a whole is still seen to be on an unsustainable course.

"Those who think that sustainability is only a matter of pollution control are missing the bigger picture," explained Stuart Hart, director of the Corporate Environmental Management Program at the University of Michigan:

"Even if all the companies in the developed world were to achieve zero emissions by the year 2000, the earth would still be stressed beyond what biologists refer to as its carrying capacity. Increasingly, the scourges of the late twentieth century – depleted farmland, fisheries, and forests; choking urban pollution; poverty; infectious disease; and migration – are spilling over geopolitical borders. The simple fact is this: in meeting our needs, we are destroying the ability of future generations to meet theirs."

And these problems are not simply economic and environmental, either in their origins or nature. Instead, they raise social, ethical, and, above all, political issues. The roots of the crisis, Hart concluded, are "political and social issues that exceed the mandate and capabilities of any corporation." But here is the paradox: "At the same time, corporations are the only organizations with the resources, the technology, the global reach, and, ultimately, the motivation to achieve sustainability."

There is no question that some of these issues can have – indeed, already have had – a profound impact on the financial bottom line. Think of the companies and industries making or using such products as asbestos, mercury, PCBs, PVC, and CFCs and it is clear that the long-term sustainability of major slices of any modern economy is already being called into question.

Worryingly, at least on current trends, things can only get worse. "It is easy to state the case in the negative," as Hart pointed out. "Faced with impoverished customers, degraded environments, failing political systems, and unraveling societies, it will be increasingly difficult for corporations to do business. But," he stressed:

"the positive case is even more powerful. The more we learn about the challenges of sustainability, the clearer it is that we are poised at the threshold of an historic moment in which many of the world's industries may be transformed."

The level of change implied by the sustainability transition is extraordinary. As the Worldwatch Institute put it in a recent *State of the World* report:

"We are only at the beginning of this restructuring. New industries are emerging to reestablish natural balances – based on technologies that can produce heat and light without putting carbon into the atmosphere; on metals made out of the scrap of past buildings and cars; on papers made out of what was once considered wastepaper. Some homes and offices are heated entirely by the sun or from electricity generated by the wind."[3]

But sustainable capitalism will need more than just environment-friendly technologies and, however important these may be, markets which actively promote dematerialization. We will also need to address radically new views of what is meant by social equity, environmental justice and business ethics. This will require a much better understanding not only of financial and physical forms of capital, but also of natural, human, and social capital.

Business leaders and executives wanting to grasp the full scale of the challenge confronting their corporations and markets will need to carry out a sustainability audit, outlined in Chapter 13, against the emerging requirements and expectations driven by sustainability's triple bottom line. In the spirit of the management dictum that what you can't measure you are likely to find hard to manage, we should ask whether it is even possible to measure progress against the triple bottom line?

The answer is yes, but the metrics are still evolving in most areas – and need to evolve much further if they are to be considered in an integrated way. In the following pages, we briefly focus on the relevant trends in relation to the economic, environmental and social bottom lines. In each case, we headline some of the current thinking on accountability, accounting, performance indicators, auditing, reporting and benchmarking. But we also look at the new concepts and requirements emerging at the interfaces between each of these great agendas, in the "shear zones" (see Figures 4.1–4.4).

FIGURE 4.1 SustainAbility is developing the concept of the "triple bottom line" of sustainable development. Society depends on the economy – and the economy depends on the global ecosystem, whose health represents the ultimate bottom line.

FIGURE 4.2 The three bottom lines are not stable; they are in constant flux, due to social, political, economic and environmental pressures, cycles and conflicts. So the sustainability challenge is tougher than any of the other challenges in isolation.

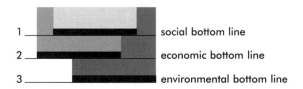

FIGURE 4.3 Think of each bottom line as a continental plate, often moving independently of the others. People often forget their dependence on wealth creation; and most of us are ignorant of our impacts on the ultimate bottom line.

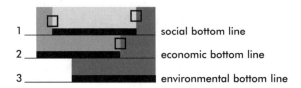

1 ___ social bottom line

2 ___ economic bottom line

3 ___ environmental bottom line

FIGURE 4.4   As the plates move under, over, or against each other, "shear zones" emerge where the social, economic, and ecological equivalents of tremors and earthquakes occur. The main shear zones are illustrated in Figures 4.5–4.7.

The Economic Bottom Line

Let's begin in the area where business should feel most at home. Given that we are using the "bottom line" metaphor, however, we need to understand exactly what it means in its traditional usage. A company's bottom line is the profit figure used as the earnings figure in the earnings-per-share statement, part of standard accounting practice. In trying to assess a company's conventional bottom line performance, accountants pull together, record and analyze a wide range of numerical data. This approach is often seen as a model for environmental and social accounting, but the challenge can be even tougher in these emerging areas of corporate accountability.[4]

Economic Capital

So how should a would-be sustainable corporation assess whether its business operations are economically sustainable? Obviously, a critical first step is to understand what is meant by economic capital. In the simplest terms, your capital is the total value of your assets minus your liabilities. In traditional economic theory, capital as a factor of production can come in two main forms: *physical capital* (including machinery and plant) and *financial capital*. But as we move into the knowledge economy, the concept is gradually being extended to include such concepts as *human capital* – a measure of the experience, skills, and other knowledge-based assets of the individuals who make up an organization. We will also consider the *intellectual capital* concepts adopted by companies like Skandia.

Among the questions business people need to ask in this area are the following. Are our costs competitive – and likely to remain so? Is the demand for our products and services sustainable? Is our rate of innovation likely to be competitive in the longer term? How can we ensure that human or intellectual capital does not migrate out of the organization? Are our profit margins sustainable?[5] Longer term, too, the concept of economic capital will need to absorb much wider concepts, such as *natural capital* and *social capital*, both of which are discussed below.

Accountability

In most countries, companies have an obligation to give an account of their financial performance. In the case of limited companies, directors are accountable to shareholders. This responsibility is partly discharged by the production and – in the case of public companies – publication of an annual report and accounts. An annual general meeting (AGM) theoretically provides shareholders with an opportunity to oversee the presentation of audited accounts, the appointment of directors and auditors, the fixing of their remuneration, and recommendations for the payment of dividends.

Typically, there has been little, if any, overlap between the areas covered by financial auditors in serving the interests of shareholders and the issues of interest to other stakeholders in terms of the environmental and social bottom lines. But one area where we see a growing degree of overlap between a company's economic and environmental performance is "eco-efficiency" (Spotlight, p. 78). At the same time, too, there are early signs that, as the sustainability agenda becomes a board-level issue, we will see growing overlaps with the whole corporate governance agenda (see Chapter 11).

Accounting

By the very nature of their work and training, most traditional accountants are short-sighted. Typically, the so-called accounting period is 12 months. Internal accounts are often prepared on a monthly or quarterly basis, with full results produced annually. Worldwide, however, the pressure to perform on a quarterly basis is intensifying as Anglo-Saxon approaches to stock management and investment banking spread.

In preparing their accounts, accountants are guided by a range of reasonably well-established concepts. These include the *ongoing concern concept* (with assets not stated at break-up value, unless there is evidence that the company is no longer viable), the *consistency concept* (which calls for accounts to be prepared on a consistent basis, allowing accurate comparisons between quarters or years), the *prudence concept* (accounts should be prepared on a conservative basis, recording income and profits only when they are achieved, and making provision for foreseeable losses) and *depreciation* (with the value of most assets progressively written off over time).

Despite 500 years – counting early clay tablets, some would say at least 5,000 years – of evolution in mainstream accounting, there remain huge controversies over how companies account for acquisitions and disposals, record extraordinary and exceptional items, value contingent liabilities, capitalize costs, and depreciate their assets. One of the most thought-provoking books of the 1990s was *Accounting for Growth*, in which Terry Smith stripped away the camouflage of creative accounting and helped shareholders, analysts, and others to assess how strong a particular company's finances really are.[6]

We have tended to see the bottom line as the hardest of realities, representing the unappealable verdict of impartial markets.[7] But it is increasingly clear that such accounting concepts are man-made conventions that change over space and time. Bottom lines are the product of the institutions and societies in which they have evolved. And, because accounting inevitably involves compromises, the bottom line turns out to be influenced by subjective interpretations, quite apart from "creative" accounting. So, for example, when Rover was taken over by BMW and subjected to Germany's stricter valuation criteria, a 1995 "profit" of £91 million became a £158 million "loss."

A key concept in relation to all three dimensions of sustainability – but particularly relevant in relation to environmental and societal costs – is that of "externalities." These economic, social, or environmental costs are not recorded in accounts. So, to take an economic example, the decision of a company to locate a high-technology plant in a relatively undeveloped region may have such effects as drawing technical talent away from local firms, or forcing up property prices locally beyond what local people can afford. We will look at examples of environmental and social externalities under the appropriate sections below.

Issues and Indicators

These are key tools of the trade. Among the items you would expect to see in a company's report and accounts would be a profit and loss account, balance sheet and statement of total recognized losses and gains. When it comes to wider economic sustainability, however, there is a surprising lack of generally acceptable indicators. Key considerations here might include the long-term sustainability of a company's costs, of the demand for its products or services, of its pricing and profit margins, of its innovation programs, and of its "business ecosystem" (see Chapter 5).

Auditing

Once we know what we should be measuring, the next question is how are we doing against the agreed benchmarks? Internal audits aim to ensure that management controls are working effectively. External audits involve an independent examination of – and an expression of an opinion on – the financial statements of an organization. The evidence collected draws on such sources as the company's accounting systems and the underlying documentation, its tangible assets, and interviews with managers, employees, customers, suppliers, and other third parties having some knowledge of the company. Only in exceptional circumstances are the key social and environmental issues fully on the radar screen.

Reporting, Risk-Rating and Benchmarking

Audits are designed to produce information for internal consumption, but there are growing demands for transparency. How far should a company be expected to go? Levels of reporting by companies vary widely, partly reflecting different accounting regimes, partly different opinions on what it is appropriate to report, and partly on the different needs of report users. The information generated by such reports, and available from other sources, is used by analysts in risk-rating. They are interested, for example, in working out the appropriate levels of share pricing, premiums for insurance policies, or security for loans. Even today, environmental and social risks are not high on the agenda for most companies, with the result that very few annual reports yet contain a robust section on social and/or environmental performance.

Another use for the reported data is benchmarking, which involves comparisons of processes and products, both within an industry and outside it, to identify and then meet or exceed best practice. Most benchmarking exercises in this area, however, now involve in-depth, in-company research, rather than simply relying on published reports. And it would be rare indeed in today's world for a company to spend

SPOTLIGHT

SHEAR ZONE 1: ECO-EFFICIENCY

The shear zone between the economic and environmental agendas shown in Figure 4.5 is probably the easiest for business people to grasp and manage. Yet it also represents a major set of emerging challenges even for the best-run companies. This shear zone is throwing up such agenda items as eco-efficiency, environmental cost accounting and ecological tax reform.

Let's focus on eco-efficiency. In the generally accepted definition, this involves the delivery of competitively-priced goods and services that satisfy human needs and bring quality of life, while progressively reducing ecological impacts and resource intensity throughout the life cycle, to a level at least in line with the Earth's estimated carrying capacity.[8]

To bring all of the world's growing population up to reasonable standards over the next few decades, we will need to achieve "Factor 4" change (involving 75% reductions) as a minimum – and maybe as much as "Factor 10" change, involving 90% reductions. Business leaders tend to be relatively relaxed about the concept, if still slow to push their companies towards the Factor 4 – let alone Factor 10 – goals now thought necessary to achieve a future which is both sustainable and equitable.

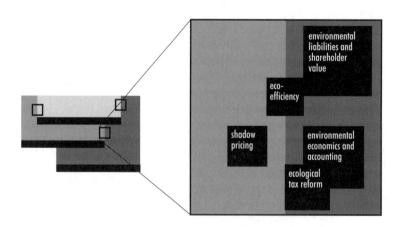

FIGURE 4.5 In the *economic/environmental shear zone*, some companies already promote eco-efficiency. But there are even greater challenges ahead, such as environmental economics and accounting, shadow pricing, and ecological tax reform.

much time on other aspects of the triple bottom line, unless it happened to be operating in a highly sensitive industry like waste disposal or nuclear power.

Environmental Bottom Line

The social agenda for business probably has a longer history than the environmental agenda. Think of the early controversies around slavery, child labor, and working conditions. But, following a flurry of interest in social accounting and auditing in the 1970s, the environmental agenda has tended to attract greater attention. The result, paradoxically, is that many business people these days feel happier being challenged on environmental issues than on social issues. This fact has had a marked impact on the way the sustainability agenda is defined by business.

Natural Capital

How can a would-be sustainable corporation work out whether it is environmentally sustainable? Again, a critical first step is to understand what is meant by natural capital. The concept of natural wealth is both complex and still evolving. If you try to account for the natural capital embodied in a forest, for example, it is not simply a question of counting the trees and trying to put a price-tag on the lumber they represent. You have to account for the underlying natural wealth which supports the forest ecosystem, producing – as just one stream of benefits – timber and other commercial products. Wider forest functions that need to be added into the equation include contributions to the regulation of water (in the atmosphere, water table, soils, and surface waters) and of greenhouse gases like carbon dioxide and methane.[9] And then there are all the flora and fauna, including commercial fisheries, whose health is linked to the health of the forest.

Natural capital can also be thought of as coming in two main forms: "critical natural capital" and renewable, replaceable, or substitutable natural capital. The first form embraces natural capital which is essential to the maintenance of life and ecosystem integrity; the second forms of natural capital which can be renewed (e.g. through breeding or relocation of sensitive ecosystems), repaired (e.g. environmental remediation or desert reclamation), or substituted or replaced (e.g. growing use of man-made substitutes, such as solar panels in place of limited fossil fuels).[10]

Among the questions business people will need to ask are the following. What forms of natural capital are affected by our current operations – and will they be affected by our planned activities? Are these forms of natural capital sustainable given these, and other, likely pressures? Is the overall level of stress properly understood and likely to be sustainable? Is the "balance of nature" or the "web of life" likely to be significantly affected?

The interesting thing about a company's ecological bottom line is that the carrying capacity of most ecosystems varies in relation to the number – and behavior – of the economic actors operating within them. As a result, these bottom lines will vary over time and space. The more efficient the actors, however, the more actors can be sustained. This is the basis of the Factor 4/10 approach discussed in the Spotlight (p. 78).

Accountability

In many countries, companies are held accountable by regulators for aspects of their environmental performance. In the USA, the Toxic Release Inventory (TRI) requires companies producing more than certain threshold limits of over 600 chemicals to report their emissions. Some countries, like the Netherlands, also back up their regulations with voluntary programs designed to push companies towards sectorally agreed targets.

Just as often, however, business is held to account by environmentalist and media campaigns, which may bear little relation to regulated or voluntarily agreed targets. And as companies begin to challenge their supply chains, a new dimension of pressure is being introduced. While planning this book, for example, I was invited by Volvo to help facilitate their first environmental conference for supplier companies. The company's top management told the 500-plus audience that Volvo had started off by focusing on safety, then added quality. Now, they said, environmental performance was increasingly in the spotlight – and suppliers would find environmental aspects being covered in Volvo's regular supplier audits (Case Study, p. 119).

Accounting

The field of environmental accounting is relatively embryonic, but is generating a growing literature.[11] Among other things, it aims to: re-balance the treatment of environmental costs and benefits in conventional accounting practice; separately identify environmental related costs and revenues within the conventional accounting systems; devise new forms of valuation which encourage better management decisions and increased investment in environmental protection and improvement; develop new performance indicators to track progress; and experiment with ways in which sustainability considerations can be assessed and incorporated into mainstream accounting.[12]

As far as environmental externalities go, many companies have been forced to take on to their books impacts and effects which were once externalized. Take the case of T&N, which as Turner & Newall was once one of the world's largest asbestos producers. For years, the company argued that the risks involved in the use of asbestos were acceptable. Eventually, however, the tide turned, not only against Turner & Newall but against the entire asbestos industry. At the time of writing, T&N had already paid out over £350 million over ten years to meet asbestos claims – and was busily selling off corporate assets to fund a further £323 million provision.[13] And, in an attempt to draw a line under its asbestos legacy, the company had announced a £515 million charge against annual profits to meet future personal injury claims and insurance costs. It was not alone in experiencing such problems.

Issues and Indicators

The sheer number of potential issues, and hence the expanding range of possible environmental risks, is reflected in the potential indicators. These include financial indicators such as: trends in legal compliance; provisions for fines, insurance, and other legally related costs; and landscaping, remediation, decommissioning, and abandonment costs. But there is also a growing need to measure environmental impacts in terms of new metrics, including: the number of public complaints; the life-cycle impacts of products; energy, materials, and water usage at production sites; potentially polluting emissions; environmental hazards, and risks; waste generation; consumption of critical natural capital; and performance against best-practice standards set by leading customers and by green and ethical investment funds.

At the company level, the task is being made somewhat easier by the development and publication of international environmental management standards. Globally, there is ISO 14001, developed by the International Standards Organisation (ISO) in the wake of the 1992 Earth Summit.[14] In Europe, there is the Eco-Management and Audit Scheme (EMAS), which takes a step beyond ISO 14001 by requiring companies to produce an environmental statement for each registered site. Both of these schemes are voluntary, but the expectation is that market forces will drive them down through value chains in the same way as the Total Quality Management (TQM) approach has spread.

But we will also need to consider environmental sustainability at the ecosystem level, where corporate environmental management systems are going to be of little help. This is an area where national and international government agencies and research organizations will continue to play a critically important role.

Auditing

The purpose of audits is to assess the state of a company's management systems and its progress against a range of indicators and targets. Environmental audits have a long history in the USA, but really took root in Europe in the 1990s. Indeed, SustainAbility helped spur the trend with *The Environmental Audit*, a report published jointly with WWF in 1990.[15] Such audits should focus on the environmental impact of the audited organization, but most still focus on management systems rather than real-world environmental effects. So, for example, they review such areas as: compliance against regulations and other standards; the performance of internal management systems; trends in energy usage, waste production, and recycling; and the use of eco-efficient technologies.

Reporting, Risk-rating, and Benchmarking

The environmental reporting and benchmarking trends are enormously significant and are discussed in Chapter 7. The first few corporate environmental reports (CERs), or environmental annual reports (EARs), were published in 1990 – and their number has subsequently mushroomed to many hundreds. Most of these reports have been prepared on a voluntary basis, with the result that the indicators used and the presentation of performance data are highly diverse, complicating comparisons. Nor are most much help yet for those trying to assess the risks associated with the operations of given companies.

These problems are, however, slowly being addressed as reporting companies begin to relate their performance against such indicators as the amount of emissions or waste produced per unit of either volume or value of production. So, for example, an oil company might link its

SPOTLIGHT

SHEAR ZONE 2: ENVIRONMENTAL JUSTICE

For the moment, the second shear zone – between the environmental and social bottom line agendas – is throwing up the most fundamental challenges for the business-as-usual paradigm. Among the early issues here have been the concept of "environmental justice" and, more specifically, of intra- and inter-generational equity.

The *intra*-generational agenda is largely concerned with equity issues affecting those now alive (e.g. haves *vs.* have-nots, North *vs.* South), and the *inter*-generational agenda mainly with the balance of advantage between different generations (as in pension rights or long-range health care entitlements) and between those currently alive and those yet to be born (e.g. loss of forests, biodiversity, or climatic stability).

Many companies have been unnerved by the environmental justice issue, focusing on the extent to which different people are relatively disadvantaged by environmental problems. But this is an area where environmentalists and human rights campaigners, traditionally two separate communities, have been finding common cause. To begin with, the focus was on the question of whether certain groups of deprived Americans were also selectively disadvantaged through exposure to environmental problems. Many companies fought the environmental justice lobby, but subsequent research found that economically and socially deprived groups *are* also more likely to be environmentally disadvantaged.

"On average, 230 times more toxic waste was emitted in neighbourhoods near the plants of the fifty largest industrial toxic polluters than in the communities of the CEOs responsible for the waste," noted Steven Viederman of the US Jessie Smith Noyes Foundation.[16] The agenda is now expanding to embrace such issues as the rights of the Ogoni people of Nigeria or the global warming-related threats to the livelihoods of people in countries like Bangladesh.[17]

And the evidence suggests that the tide can be reversed. In Louisiana, for example, a coalition of black people managed to trigger an historic ruling denying a consortium – which included British Nuclear Fuels – permission to build a uranium processing plant.[18] As one local white estate agent put it, "This isn't a case of NIMBY," or not in my back yard. "It's a textbook case of PIBBY – place in black back yards." Whatever the truth of the matter, the assertion made by CANT – or Citizens Against Nuclear Trash – resulted in an extraordinary reverse for the would-be developers. Said CANT lawyer Nathalie Walker, "it's the first time in the nation's history that judges have recognized that blacks have a valid claim in a case of environmental racism."

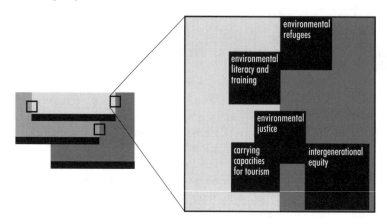

FIGURE 4.6 In the *social/environmental shear zone*, business is working on environmental literacy and training issues, but new challenges will be sparked by e.g. environmental justice, environmental refugees, and intergenerational equity.

environmental performance to a barrel of oil produced, while a water utility might compare its performance against sector averages.

But few, if any, companies have willingly reported on their performance against the sorts of indicators found at the interface between the environmental and social bottom lines. These include the challenging issue of "environmental justice," (Spotlight, p. 83) which in recent years has proved a painful thorn in the side of the US chemical industry.

Social Bottom Line

Some in the sustainable development community insist that sustainability has nothing to do with social, ethical or cultural issues. A sustainable world, they argue, could equally well be more equitable or less equitable than today's world. The real issues, they say, relate to resource efficiency. Like King Canute, they are trying to hold back the tide by sheer force of will, or prejudice. Their views may be a useful counterbalance to attempts to turn sustainability into a new form of communism, but in the end our progress against the social bottom line is going to be critically important in determining the success or failure of the sustainability transition. If we fail to address wider political, social and ethical issues, the backlash will inevitably undermine progress in the environmental area.

Social capital So, how should a would-be sustainable corporation think about social capital? In part, it comprises human capital, in the form of public health, skills and education. But it also must embrace wider measures of a society's health and wealth-creation potential.

One of the key recent books to address this area was *Making Democracy Work*, by Robert D. Putnam.[19] The book focuses on Italy and considers what makes some democratic governments succeed – and some fail. But the book which really switched me on to the notion of social capital was Francis Fukuyama's *Trust: The Social Virtues and the Creation of Prosperity*.[20] Fukuyama says that social capital is "a capability that arises from the prevalence of trust in a society or in certain parts of it." It is a measure of "the ability of people to work together for common purposes in groups and organizations." This ability is likely to be critical to the sustainability transition. It can be developed (or eroded) at every level in a society, from the basic family unit to the major institutions of international government. It depends on the acquisition and maintenance of such virtues as loyalty, honesty and dependability.

The central benefits flow from a lowering of social friction. So, for example, Fukuyama notes that:

> "if people who have to work together in an enterprise trust one another because they are all operating according to a common set of ethical norms, doing business costs less. Such a society will be better able to innovate organizationally, since the high degree of trust will permit a wide variety of social relationships to emerge."

In the same way, the degree of trust between a corporation or industry and their external stakeholders is likely to be a key factor determining their long-term sustainability. Conversely, "widespread distrust in a society imposes a kind of tax on all forms of economic activity, a tax that high-trust societies do not have to pay."

A key assumption in the work SustainAbility has done in recent years is that sustainable development is most likely – and will be achieved at the lowest overall cost to the economy – in those societies where there are the highest levels of trust and other forms of social capital. This, in turn, is likely to depend on the levels and equity of investment in human capital. According to Ismail Serageldin, the World Bank's vice president of environmentally sustainable development, human capital requires "investments in education, health and nutrition." Developing and spreading the necessary skills and training, particularly in the emerging economies and developing countries, will require new forms of public–private partnership.

Among the questions business people will need to ask are the following. What are the crucial forms of social capital in terms of our ability to become a sustainable corporation? What are the underlying trends in terms of the creation, maintenance, or erosion of these forms of capital? What is the role of business in sustaining human capital and social capital? To what extent are such concepts as environmental justice and intra- and inter-generational equity likely to change the ways in which we define and measure social capital?

Accountability

Whatever its critics may choose to believe, business is part of society. Governments try to regulate and otherwise control the social impacts associated with industry and commerce, but history is full of examples where the agenda was created outside the intertwined worlds of government and business. Whether it was the crusade to end slavery or the various campaigns to end child labor in European and North American factories, business people have long found their freedom of action being increasingly constrained by emerging social movements.

As globalization gathers steam, the interface between the economic and social bottom lines becomes increasingly problematic. Consider the abortive attempt by Germany's Krupp Hoesch to take over its rival Thyssen. This represented an attempt to make the German steel industry more competitive in the face of intensifying international competition. But, faced with massed rallies by tens of thousands of Ruhr steelworkers concerned about the implications for their jobs and protesting about "casino capitalism" and calling for "people before profit," Krupp – and its partner banks, Deutsche, Dresdner, and Goldman Sachs – backed down.[21] The decision was widely hailed by German politicians as evidence that the country's social consensus economy works; that "social responsibility" had prevailed. But there are short-term definitions of responsibility and longer-term definitions. The two companies may achieve the necessary efficiencies without redundancies, but if globalization continues Germany may simply have postponed the day of reckoning. In doing so, it may be ensuring that the inevitable economic and social quakes are worse than they need to have been.

It is against this background that we see a new stirring of interest in such concepts as social accounting and auditing. The evolution of social auditing, in particular, has more or less paralleled that of environmentalism, but with wilder swings between its "boom" and "bust" periods. In the USA, the pioneers in the late 1960s and early 1970s included Ralph

Nader and organizations like the Council on Economic Priorities. In the UK the charge was led by the late George Goyder with books like *The Responsible Company*[22] and, later, by the likes of the Consumers Association, Social Audit Ltd, and Counter Information Services.[23]

The idea was to expand the range of stakeholders involved in industry's deliberations. To begin with, the focus was on consumers and those directly affected by a company's products, but the new, more inclusive models of stakeholder capitalism have progressively drawn the boundaries so as to include an ever-widening range of stakeholders. The social statement produced by the Body Shop as part of its 1995 *Values Report* (Case Study, p. 139), and verified by the New Economics Foundation (NEF), provides a striking illustration of the trend.

One of the more interesting conferences on the whole area of social and ethical accounting, auditing and reporting happened in 1996 at, of all places, Windsor Castle.[24] The proceedings of the event, funded by the Environment Foundation, organized by NEF, and drawing together practitioners from as far apart as Canada, Denmark, India and the USA, were subsequently published by a new organization, the Institute of Social and Ethical AccountAbility (ISEA), which is dedicated to developing and promoting this dimension of the emerging corporate agenda.[25]

This is the wave of the future, but this area, inevitably, will also prove to have its own ethical dilemmas. In summing up the conference, Simon Zadek of NEF, a devoted proponent of social auditing, noted:

"At the turn of the century, the dominant management systems were the so-called Taylorian systems – ways of controlling our bodies to maximise efficiency, productivity, and profit. As we moved into the 60s and 70s, we began thinking about flexible management systems, which used the imagination and flexibility of people's minds to further increase productivity and business success. Today, we have social auditing."

"There is a real possibility," he warned, "that it might be used as a way of controlling people's hearts and souls."

Accounting

Social accounting aims to assess the impact of an organization or company on people both inside and outside. Issues often covered are community relations, product safety, training and education initiatives, sponsorship, charitable donations of money and time, and employment of disadvantaged groups. "Socio-economic sustainability," says Professor Tom Gladwin, "requires poverty alleviation, population stabilization, female empowerment, employment creation, human rights observance and opportunity on a massive scale."[26]

As far as social externalities are concerned, an example from Japan would be *karoshi*, the word for death caused by overwork. The case of Ichiro Oshima is not unusual. By the time he committed suicide, he had worked eighteen months with only half a day off. The advertising agency executive started work at 7am each day, often returning home at two in the morning. What was unusual was that his parents decided to sue his employer.[27] A flurry of litigation in the country has been forcing Japanese corporations to introduce "no overtime" days, in an attempt to give employees time off to spend with their families. How can such social costs be captured? Clearly, social accounting is another area where a great deal of further work is needed.

Issues and Indicators

Among the issues for which performance indicators have been developed are animal testing, armaments or other military sales, community relations, employment of minorities, human rights, impacts on indigenous peoples, involvement in nuclear power, irresponsible marketing, land rights, oppressive regimes, political contributions, trade union relations, wages and working conditions, and women's rights. Aspects of the indicators debate are covered in the Spotlight on page 93.

Auditing

Social auditing is usually considered as covering the non-financial impact of companies. In this sense, environmental audits are often seen as a form of social audit. The purpose of social auditing is for an organization to assess its performance in relation to society's requirements and expectations. Like it or not, sustainability auditing and reporting will be all about triple bottom line performance – and social and ethical accounting, auditing, and reporting in particular are likely to come up the curve like so many rockets.[28]

It is now over 20 years since pioneering organizations like Britain's Social Audit Ltd started to put companies such as Avon Rubber, Coalite and Tube Investments under the microscope. Then things went horribly quiet for about fifteen years. Now it's almost possible to watch the penny dropping in some CEOs' brains. Try reading through the forewords of recent corporate environmental reports (CERs), for example. Social issues are clearly back on the sustainability agenda.

"It's now clear that the doubling of world population over the next 40 years will place unprecedented pressure on social and biological systems," noted Monsanto chairman and CEO Bob Shapiro in the company's 1995 environmental annual review:

> "This means that we have to broaden our definition of environmental and ecological responsibility to include working towards 'sustainable development' – 'sustainable' because countless generations will need to live on this planet, 'development' because they shouldn't be condemned to live in poverty."

On the other side of the Atlantic, check out the 1995 NatWest Group environment report. "At NatWest," said Derek Wanless, as the giant bank's chief executive, "we are convinced that the triangle of society, economy and the environment are the determinants of the future and we will continue to take account of that fact in the way we run our businesses." NatWest ran into some major financial problems a couple of years later, suggesting that the economic side of the bank's triangle had been somewhat neglected. But growing numbers of banks will be focusing on this triangle in the future.

Reporting, Risk-rating, and Benchmarking

How do we get from words to action? The Danish health care and enzymes company Novo Nordisk, whose environmental reporting has consistently won plaudits internationally, is one of the companies that has been thinking through how to tackle the social reporting agenda. These areas are even more complex and political than the environmental agenda. But such companies are beginning to see social auditing as potentially offering a vitally important way of managing complexity.

The problem, says Dr Chris Tuppen, who led BT's charge in the area of environmental reporting, is that all of this is "rather like learning a new language." And when you are learning a new language, nothing slows things down as much as different teachers speaking different dialects and disagreeing publicly on how the new language is to be used – or what it means. Unfortunately, this is exactly what has been happening, although a degree of turmoil is to be expected in any area undergoing rapid evolution. More positively, Professor Peter Pruzan of the Copenhagen Business School is fairly optimistic, noting that there is currently "a strong convergence in terminology, methodology and practice."

The financial community remains largely unconvinced of the value of all of this, however. "Environmental issues are bottom line sensitive," comments Tessa Tennant of the National Provident Institution (NPI), a major pensions provider. But, she adds:

> "the bottom line implications of social issues are not clear. It would be difficult to justify why a company should produce a social report, although information on the level of absenteeism and employee turnover rates would be very relevant."

That said, she acknowledges that:

> "we are interested in seeing what companies are producing. Social reporting by most companies is quite incoherent. There may be sections on community relations, and perhaps charitable giving, but getting comprehensive data on social issues is still very difficult."

So, how to make things more coherent? One possible answer may be the new Institute of Social and Ethical AccountAbility – dedicated to the task of keeping an eye on the latest trends in social and ethical accounting and auditing, worldwide. Welcoming the Institute, BT chairman Sir Iain Vallance said that he believed that "in today's society, companies not only need to operate in an ethical manner, but also need publicly to demonstrate they are doing so."

The 134-page *Social Statement* which formed part of the Body Shop's 1995 *Values Report*, is the report to beat.[29] This document figured large in SustainAbility's decision to rank this company as the world leader in sustainability reporting in our UN report *Engaging Stakeholders*.[30] But if there is one report that might be viewed from a 21st century perspective as the seed of an impending accounting revolution, it could well be *Vizualizing Intellectual Capital in Skandia,* a supplement to the Swedish financial services company's 1994 annual report.[31]

Skandia argues that a company's value consists of more than what is traditionally shown in the income statement and balance sheet. Hidden assets, which they see as including employees' competence, computer systems, work processes, trademarks, customer lists, and so on are increasingly important in determining the value of a company. Concluding that "our intellectual capital is at least as important as our

SHEAR ZONE 3: BUSINESS ETHICS

The third shear zone, between the social and economic bottom lines, is throwing up a range of issues revolving around such areas as downsizing, unemployment, minority rights, and business ethics. At a time when the traditional relationships between companies and their employees are changing fundamentally, with even the largest companies moving sharply away from life-time employment, the whole issue of trust is also becoming increasingly charged. The result is that individual agenda items, like business ethics, contain greater potential energy – and, if mismanaged, destructive power – than in the past.

Ethical behavior, whether of an individual, organization, or corporation, is judged to be good, just, and honorable. Much business behavior causes offence because it is unethical, but in some cases – because ethics can vary from person to person, from company to company, and from culture to culture – the problem is that different ethical principles are being applied inside and outside the company. Some ethical violations are also legal violations, as when there is fraud or corruption. But many are not. For example, a company may sometimes legally stretch the truth when making claims about its products or provide customers with less than full value.

The emerging field of ethical – or socially responsible – investment focuses not only on a company's behavior but also on the industry it is in and the markets it serves. So, for example, products such as tobacco and armaments (particularly when indiscriminate in their action as is potentially the case with mines or germ warfare weapons) are often considered unethical and companies making them are usually screened out of investment portfolios.

The triple bottom line itself potentially raises a range of ethical issues. How, for example, should economic, social and environmental priorities be assessed and, more importantly, traded off? A company may successfully make pollution control technology, yet sell its products in countries which – like Burma – are considered out of bounds on ethical grounds.

financial capital in providing truly sustainable earnings," Skandia provides some "out-of-the-box" ideas on how a company's brainpower might be valued.

The company's 1996 report was entitled *Power of Innovation*,[32] and concluded, "Our responsibility is to turn the future into an asset." In

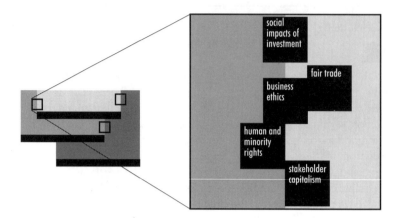

FIGURE 4.7   In the *economic/social shear zone,* some companies are looking at the social impacts of proposed investment, but bubbling under are issues like business ethics, fair trade, human and minority rights, and stakeholder capitalism.

trying to assess the contribution that various forms of human and social capital could make to value creation, Skandia concludes that "organizational capital is generated by packaging competence and increasing the use of information and communication technology." This, the company concludes, "contributes to long-term sustainability."[33] Longer term, could a mutated version of Skandia's approach be used to value the triple bottom line relationships and reputation a company has developed?

Accounting for the Triple Bottom Line

It is clear that progress – or the lack of it – can be measured against a wide range of indicators associated with each of the three bottom lines of sustainability. But the next step will be to tackle this agenda in an integrated way. Key tools will be sustainability accounting, auditing and reporting. In many respects these concepts are still "black boxes," more talked about in generalities than defined in precise terms, but there is now fascinating work under way in each of these areas.

Ultimately, as Professor Rob Gray and his colleagues put it, sustainability reporting "must consist of statements about the extent to which corporations are reducing (or increasing) the options available to future

SPOTLIGHT

NEW SUSTAINABILITY INDICATORS

A future growth industry will focus on the development of new sustainability indicators. As an example of ongoing work, the social indicator movement has been trying to work out ways of measuring wealth creation and individual well-being more accurately than when conventional measures like gross national product (GNP) are used.

Until very recently, economists and business people alike thought of "quality of life" and "standard of living" as identical. They are not. Indeed, the sustainability transition will require a shift from the post-1945 paradigm based on quantity objectives to a 21st century paradigm based increasingly on perceived quality of life.

National surveys in countries like Norway have shown a disturbing trend: perceived quality of life grew until some time in the late 1960s or early 1970s, but has been falling almost constantly since. In the UK, too, the perceived quality of life deteriorated substantially between 1975 and 1990 – according to the country's first index of "real" social wealth – even though money incomes had continued to rise. According to the New Economics Foundation (NEF), despite a 230% increase in GNP over the period and a near-doubling in consumer spending, the costs of commuting, pollution, policing, and cumulative environmental damage all rose significantly.

Emerging indicators include the Human Development Indicator (HDI) and the Index of Sustainable Economic Welfare (ISEW). The latter adjusts normal measures of welfare by subtracting, for example, the costs of unemployment, commuting, automobile accidents, and all forms of environmental pollution. Increasingly, companies will need to use such measures to assess their net contributions to society's real wealth.

generations."[34] This is an extremely complex task, but one which will probably look much easier once we have worked our way through a decade or two of experimentation in sustainability accounting, auditing and reporting. A key area of activity in this respect will be "full cost pricing" – underpinned by new forms of full cost accounting. The idea of full cost pricing is that all the costs associated with a product or service should be internalized, and, as a result, reflected in its price. Even where no markets exist for the values being considered, the "shadow pricing" approach can provide at least some guidance on relative values.

Very often, we will be unable to say whether or not a particular company or industry is "sustainable," but we will become increasingly sophisticated in terms of our ability to assess whether or not it is moving in the right direction. The triple bottom line approach clearly complicates matters. It is one thing to suggest, as some do, that a sustainable corporation is one which "leaves the biosphere no worse off at the end of the accounting period than it was at the beginning," but when we include the social and ethical dimensions of sustainability the range of sustainability-related issues and impacts grows dramatically. This does not mean that we should not try to move in this direction, but simply that we should be very careful about over-hyping the likely early benefits or pace of progress.

Most medium-term progress, in fact, is likely to be made against the first and second bottom lines (economic and environmental), although the rate of progress in social accounting, auditing, and reporting suggests that at least a core set of indicators could be available and in use within a matter of years. Meanwhile, the concept of the "sustainable corporation" is still evolving (see Chapter 12).

Our Common Future gave, at best, anecdotal suggestions on what a sustainable corporation might look like, although we can apply some of the principles applied to countries.[35] In the most general terms it would not only conserve and use nature and natural resources for the benefit of present and future generations, but also respect a range of human rights – including the right to a clean, safe environment – in the process. And it would contribute to progress against a range of new human welfare indicators which are currently still in development (Spotlight, p. 93).

Notes

1. World Commission for Environment and Development, *Our Common Future*, Oxford University Press, 1987.
2. Stuart L. Hart, "Beyond Greening: Strategies for a sustainable world," *Harvard Business Review*, January–February 1997.
3. Hal Kane, "Shifting to sustainable industries," *State of the World 1996*, Worldwatch Institute.
4. Many of the definitions under the "Economic bottom line" section are based on the *Oxford Dictionary of Business*, Oxford University Press, 1996.
5. Daniel Blake Rubenstein, *Environment Accounting for the Sustainable Corporation: Strategies and techniques*, Quorum Books, 1994.
6. Terry Smith, *Accounting for Growth: Stripping the camouflage from company accounts*, Century Business, 1992.

7. Simon Caulkin, "When black means red," *Observer*, 14 April 1996.
8. Business Council for Sustainable Development, Antwerp Eco-Efficiency Workshop, 1993.
9. Daniel Blake Rubenstein, *ibid*.
10. Jan Bebbington and Rob Gray, "Sustainable development and accounting: incentives and disincentives for the adoption of sustainability by transnational corporations," in *Environmental Accounting and Sustainable Development: The final report*, Limperg Institute, The Netherlands, 1996.
11. See, for example, Rob Gray, Jan Bebbington and Diane Walters, *Accounting for the Environment*, Paul Chapman Publishing Ltd, 1993; Daniel Blake Rubenstein, *Environmental Accounting for the Sustainable Corporation: Strategies and techniques*, Quorum Books, 1994; and Wouter van Dieren (editor), *Taking Nature Into Account: Towards a sustainable national income*, a report to the Club of Rome, Copernicus, 1995.
12. Rob Gray, Jan Bebbington and Diane Walters, *Accounting for the Environment*, Paul Chapman Publishing Ltd, 1993.
13. Tim Burt, "T&N raises £42m for asbestos costs," *Financial Times*, 15 April 1997.
14. Christopher Sheldon (editor), ISO *14001 and Beyond: Environmental management systems in the real world*, Greenleaf Publishing, 1997.
15. John Elkington, *The Environmental Audit*, SustainAbility and WWF, 1990.
16. *From Prudent Man to Prudent Person: Sustainability and institutional investment for the 21st century*, Steven Viederman, Harvard Seminar on Environmental Values, Cambridge, Massachusetts, USA, 12 December 1996.
17. Environmental Justice, *Developing Ideas*, International Institute for Sustainable Development, Issue 3, May 1996.
18. Tony Allen-Mills, "Louisiana blacks win nuclear war," *Sunday Times*, 11 May 1997.
19. Robert D. Putnam, *Making Democracy Work: Civic traditions in modern Italy,* Princeton University Press, 1993.
20. Francis Fukuyama, *Trust: The social virtues and the creation of prosperity*, Hamish Hamilton, 1995.
21. Michael Woodhead, "A Pyrrhic victory for Germany," *Sunday Times*, 30 March 1997.
22. George Goyder, *The Responsible Company*, Basil Blackwell, Oxford, 1961.
23. Rob Gray *et al.*, *op. cit.*
24. Claudia Gonella and Richard Evans (editors), *6th Environment Foundation Consultation on Corporate Social and Ethical Accounting, Auditing and Reporting*, Institute of Social and Ethical AccountAbility, April 1997.
25. Claudia Gonella and Richard Evans *op. cit.* See also: Simon Zadek, Peter Pruzan and Richard Evans, *Building Corporate Accountability: Emerging practices in social and ethical accounting, auditing and reporting*, Earthscan, London, 1997.
26. Thomas N. Gladwin, Tara-Shelomith Krause and James J. Kennelly,

"Beyond Eco-efficiency: Towards socially sustainable business," *Sustainable Development* **3**, 35–43, April 1995.

27. Peter Hadfield, "Overwork death case jolts Japan," *Sunday Times*, 4 May 1997.
28. John Elkington and Helen Stibbard, "Socially challenged," *Tomorrow*, March/April, 1997.
29. The Body Shop International, Social Statement as part of *The Values Report*, 1995.
30. SustainAbility, *Engaging Stakeholders*, Volume 1: The Benchmark Survey, 1996.
31. Skandia, *Visualizing Intellectual Capital in Skandia*, supplement to 1994 annual report.
32. Skandia, *Power of Innovation*, supplement to Skandia's 1996 interim report.
33. Skandia, Intellectual Capital Development, 1996 (booklet and CD).
34. *Ibid.*
35. Daniel Blake Rubenstein, *Environmental Accounting for the Sustainable Corporation: Strategies and techniques*, Quorum Books, 1994.

Part II

Seven Revolutions

7-D QUESTIONS

For each of the seven sustainability revolutions covered in Chapters 5–11, we ask a series of questions. These are:

- **Why worry?** Why is this trend important for our future? And why, more particularly, should business and others invest time, money and other scarce resources in understanding the trend and in responding?
- **What's new, gurus?** Given the growing competition for a share of the increasingly stretched business brain, we look at some new ideas from the world of business and management gurus. Do they see the same triple bottom line trends? Do their ideas conflict with or reinforce those discussed in *Cannibals With Forks*? And are there ideas we can borrow to help drive forward the sustainability transition?
- **Boardroom views** What is the view from the boardroom? Is the director class aware of what is going on? Which sectors and companies are most awake to threats and opportunities? And how should any self-respecting board prioritize triple bottom line agenda items against other board imperatives?
- **Bubbling under** What are the triple bottom line trends and issues that only a few pioneers are so far working on – but which are likely to surface in the 21st century?
- **Winners, losers** As the revolution takes hold, which products, companies, industries, nations and world regions will prosper – and which suffer? Who will be members of the leading business ecosystems, who left out in the cold?
- **Keys to the 21st century** For each revolution, we identify three keys to business success during the sustainability transition.

MARKETS

Going for the Triple Win

Business and markets are increasingly seen as the way forward. But the results will be less predictable than when the agenda was mainly driven by governments.

Revolution 1 has been building for many years. It focuses on the use of market mechanisms, rather than traditional command-and-control measures, to deliver improved performance against environmental and broader sustainability targets. In the process, it is shifting the center of gravity from the world of government to the world of business. The key question: are business leaders and major corporations ready for the impending challenge?

Revolution	Focus	Old paradigm	❯	New paradigm
1	Markets	Compliance	❯	Competition

The goal is simply stated. Over the coming years and decades, as the role of government changes and billions more people come to live in market economies, the world must learn how to work with business and through markets to achieve sustainable development. With the decline of the nation state, business will become even more important as an agent of change. What is far from clear, however, is whether business can really be turned into a restorative force as envisaged by sustainability gurus like Paul Hawken.

We have made extraordinary progress during the first three decades of the environmental revolution, but if sustainable development is to become a reality the first thirty years of the third millennium will need to see levels of change that make our progress to date look pedestrian.

As we have seen, even core bastions of business thinking like the *Harvard Business Review* are beginning to acknowledge the scale of the necessary transition. "The more we learn about the challenges of sustainability," concluded a recent keynote paper in the journal, "the clearer it is that we are poised at the threshold of a historic moment in which many of the world's industries will be transformed."[1]

The shift in business thinking has taken off from a relatively small base, is accelerating at an extraordinary rate, and is increasingly embracing the triple bottom line. In moving towards a sustainable global economy, it is now recognized, we will depend on the motivation, ambitions, and performance of corporations – and on the restructuring of the markets which they serve. "The achievement of sustainability will mean billions of dollars in products, services, and technologies that barely exist today," explains Stuart Hart, director of the Corporate Environmental Management Program at the University of Michigan:

"Whereas yesterday's businesses were often oblivious to their negative impact on the environment and today's responsible businesses strive for zero impact, tomorrow's businesses must learn to make a positive impact. Increasingly, companies will be selling solutions to the world's environmental problems."

But the challenge of developing, sustaining and implementing sustainability visions should not be underestimated. Those who are currently building tomorrow's markets know just how volatile the business can be. Markets and technology co-evolve, and the current pace of technological evolution threatens to keep many industry sectors almost perpetually off balance for the foreseeable future. Worse, the inevitable push towards "life-cycle technology," explained in Chapter 8, can only aggravate the problem.

Let us focus for a moment on the world of information technology. Just as the car turned horse buggies into museum pieces, so new technology like the Internet will send thousands of companies to the scrapyard. *Who says?* A man whose business has teetered on the verge of extinction a number of times as the information technology revolution swept around the world. *His name:* Andy Grove. *His job:* at the time chief executive (later chairman) of Intel. *His problem*: cataclysmic, unpredicted changes in Intel's markets. And his problems are critically relevant here because it is now clear that the sustainability transition must be delivered through dynamic markets with the capacity to move at warp speed.

Only the Paranoid

Few companies fared as well in the closing years of the 20th century as Intel. The microprocessor giant rode the crest of the IT revolution. The extraordinarily tight linkage between ever more processing-power-hungry Microsoft software and increasingly powerful Intel chips became known as the "Wintel" combination. It seemed unbeatable. Nothing, it seemed, could go wrong. But it is no accident that when Grove came to write a book on his company's evolution he finally chose as the title a phrase he often uses, *Only the Paranoid Survive*.[2]

Here is a man who knows exactly what it is like to stand on the edge of the sort of precipice which today's competitive pressures are beginning to open up underneath even the highest of high-tech industries. And he recognized an earthquake in the making when faced by the rapid evolution of the Internet. Nor was this the first time that Intel had teetered on the brink of a precipice. Intel faced a terrible choice in the mid-1980s. Having invented dynamic random access memory, better known as DRAM, Intel was forced to watch as lower-cost Japanese producers took over the DRAM market. What should Intel do? Intel did the unthinkable, walking away from the memory business. Instead, the company focused on microprocessors and, in the space of a few short years, became much more prosperous as the world's largest microchip producer.

As a result of such experiences, Grove now keeps an eye out of for what he calls "strategic inflection points," which he described as "times in the life of a business when its fundamentals are about to change," and for "10×" changes – moments when the forces affecting a given company suddenly multiply ten-fold. But how can a company recognize one of these 10× market transformations in advance? It's difficult. Even Grove cannot provide infallible clues on how to spot strategic inflection points in advance. But his description of how such shifts can transform markets is worth repeating.

"Strategic inflection points can be caused by technological change, but they are more than technological change," he notes:

> "They can be caused by competitors but they are more than just competition. They are full-scale changes in the way business is conducted, so that simply adopting a new technology or fighting the competition as you used to may be insufficient. They build up force so insidiously that you may have a hard time even putting a finger on what has changed, yet you know something *has*."

Having faced at least three strategic inflection points himself, including Intel's failure to respond adequately to customer concerns when the company shipped defective Pentium chips in 1994, he stresses that "a strategic inflection point can be deadly when unattended to."

As it happens, Intel also came unstuck in the environmental area (Case Study, p.168). This may seem paradoxical, given the success of the IT industry's amazing pursuit of the Moore's Law curve, which means that it continuously creates greater value out of ever-shrinking inputs (at least per unit of product) of energy, materials, and other environmentally significant resources. But as we will see, Intel – like all other industries, many of which are its customers – now faces another 10× change in the form of the Factor 4–Factor 10 objectives of eco-efficiency. Potentially, this will be another huge opportunity for Intel, where Factor 4 change probably seems tame, but not for all of the company's current customers. Grove himself notes, "You can be the subject of a strategic inflection point but you can also be the cause of one." So will Intel commit to becoming a catalyst for future sustainability inflection points?

Why Worry?

Goodbye to Predictability

For those who are uncomfortable with change, there are plenty of reasons to worry. The number of 10× changes can only grow. Whatever the feelings of individual governments, companies, or campaigners, the direction of change is clear. Trade liberalization is the name of the global game. "The liberalisation of trade and foreign investment has stimulated innovation, encouraged efficiency and promoted growth," stresses Donald Johnson, secretary-general of the Organisation for Economic Cooperation and Development (OECD).[3] "Open trade has been a driving force for stability and prosperity. It has been a precondition for the fourteen-fold expansion in world trade in goods since 1950 and a six-fold increase in world production. As closed trade ushered in depression and war in the 1930s, open trade has paved the way for continued postwar growth and prosperity." As a result, the OECD is committed to helping the World Trade Organization (WTO) push forward with trade liberalization.

Some environmentalists recognize that this trend could bring benefits in terms of global development, efficiency, and innovation, but most remain profoundly skeptical. Nor is this simply a matter of old-style environmentalists having favoured command-and-control measures to solve the environmental crisis. New-style environmentalists, among them the CEOs of a growing number of leading companies, may see business and markets as the way forward – but many are uncomfortably aware that the results will be less predictable than when the agenda was mainly driven by governments.

As liberalization proceeds, organizations like the WTO and OECD are hard-selling the values and principles of markets and competition around the world. They are also working to remove or reduce anti-competitive practices, public or private, that threaten to impede the openness of markets to international competition.[4] Unfortunately, some of these practices are rules, standards, and regulations put in place with the explicit aim of protecting both people (in such areas as labor standards and human rights) and the natural environment.

Many business people, it has to be said, welcome this process. During the first wave of environmentalism, a company's need to compete in the marketplace was often advanced as an excuse for inaction, or – at best – slow progress. But even those who have called loudest for deregulation are beginning to recognize that lawlessness, or even the process of re-regulation, can be highly disruptive to their business activities. Indeed, by the time the second wave hit, many business people, particularly marketing professionals, woke up to the fact that the environmental performance (both real and perceived) of their products was becoming a competitive issue, whatever might be happening on the legal front.

Now, as the third – sustainability – wave builds, companies are beginning to recognize that they need to think and invest strategically in order to stay in the existing game or break into new ones. The globalization process is one key factor driving change. Companies that have already traveled up the learning curves for total quality management, *kaizen* (continuous improvement), reengineering, and now virtuality, are finding that the pace of events is accelerating further. "It's an avalanche kind of thing, a snowball effect," explained Egon Zehnder, an international headhunter based in Zurich and charged with finding the sort of global executives able to survive and thrive in these new conditions.[5] "In the last five years, it's been really dramatic."

Short-sight is Infectious

Among the factors driving this acceleration and complexification is the growing need for companies to raise funds on the international money markets. This, in turn, brings companies – for example German outfits like Hoechst – into the arms (some would say clutches) of the investment banks. Investment bankers play an increasingly important role in shaping both the world economy and the fate of particular companies. "They have gotten very, very adept at spotting underperformers anywhere in the world and finding potential bidders from anywhere in the world," notes Louis Turner of the UK–Japan High Technology Industry Forum.

This trend, as we see in Chapters 10 and 11, probably does not bode well for sustainable development, since the result is to force companies to adopt the Anglo-Saxon focus on short-term financial results. The result is a form of collective myopia. This convergence is increasingly seen in capital markets, with even Japan saying that it will have its own "Big Bang" to keep pace with New York and London, which went through massive deregulation in the 1970s and 1980s. The obvious question is are the Japanese about to contract the short-sight virus?

The convergence is fueled by new techniques which have major implications for the ways in which companies are run. Benchmarking, for example, involves measuring some aspect of the performance of a process, business unit, or company and then comparing it with the performance of competitors and, often, the "best-in-class" performers in other sectors. The growing business appetite for benchmarking is itself both a symptom and a cause of the underlying convergence of economic systems and practices.

What's New, Gurus?

Recipes for Industrial Extinction

If sustainability requires long-sighted corporations, there are good reasons for believing that the reengineering and downsizing trends of recent years will prove to have had a massive negative impact. Indeed, there is a growing recognition that the downsizing trend is not of itself the path to future competitiveness – let alone sustainability. Even Stanley Roach, the chief economist at Morgan Stanley, one of the leading US investment banks, has expressed concern. "For years I have extolled the virtues of America's productivity-led recovery," he wrote to his clients. "I must confess I am now having second thoughts." More specifically, he had come to the conclusion that, "Tactics of open-ended downsizing and real wage compression are ultimately recipes for industrial extinction."[6]

Nor was Roach alone in spotting the growing downside of downsizing. Listen to Frederick Reichheld, a Bain & Co consultant, thinking aloud in his book *The Loyalty Effect*.[7] "Downsizing cuts away at the very foundation of trust," he concludes:

> "If you take the energy and motivation out of a company it suffers. Even more important is the fact that you are losing experienced employees. They know your business and your customers. When you burn them you incinerate your business."

No one disputes the need for companies to be leaner and meaner when the market requires it, nor – in competitive markets – to make "assets sweat." But the chances are that we will begin to see more business leaders putting down their axes and reflecting on what their companies are for – and where they are headed. Not that further slimming is out of the question. Indeed, we will see more and more companies adopting "lean thinking," a more complex, sophisticated approach and the title of a book by James P. Womack and Daniel T. Jones.[8] The key to this strategy is the elimination of all forms of waste. The idea is that each business needs to map its "value streams" and build new types of relationship with customers such that products are pulled through the value chain by customer demand, not pushed by producers.

The result, a seditious thought, is that, as the *Financial Times* put it, "only what is needed will actually be made." Indirectly, this is clearly an approach that could help companies drive towards their eco-efficiency goals. In setting out the case for companies to look well beyond their operations, with a view to transforming the value stream, Womack and Jones also blaze the trail for those committed to persuading more companies to adopt a life-cycle approach to their products and activities. Unfortunately, as they are quick to admit, not even Toyota, a long-time pioneer in lean production, has yet gone as far as they would like. But one thing is certain. Companies that are better at managing the flow of value through their businesses will generally be more eco-efficient.

Approaching "Absolute Zero"

More worrying is *Market Unbound*, by senior McKinsey consultants Lowell Bryan and Diana Farrell.[9] They describe the accelerating shift of power from national economic and political elites to global elites – and to the global capital market. "Like an awkward adolescent," they report:

"the global capital market is just now discovering its own strength and potential. Increasingly, millions of global investors, operating out of their own economic self-interest, are determining interest rates, exchange rates, and the allocation of capital, irrespective of the wishes or political objectives of national political leaders."

This global capital revolution will result in astounding changes:

"As the market becomes unbound from the constraints of national governments, it is creating the potential for a tidal wave of global capitalism that could drive rapid growth and highly beneficial integration of the world's real economy well into the next century."

"There is also," they admit:

"a somewhat less probable, but nonetheless significant, chance that the power of this market could turn destructive and unleash financial instability and social turmoil such as the world has not seen since the 1920s and 1930s."

These trends will no longer be evolutionary, they suggest, in the sense that they will be smooth and predictable. Instead, they will often be discontinuous. All participants, whether they are involved willingly or unwillingly, will face new opportunities, threats, and risks. The implication is that, "Like it or not, we are becoming citizens of the world. To take advantage of the global capital revolution, we must adopt a global mind-set, embrace the market changes, and adapt to them."

As the process takes hold, Bryan and Farrell predict the global financial market will reach a state very much like some materials achieve when their temperature approaches absolute zero: *superconductivity*. Superconductors are dramatically more efficient at carrying electrical current. Similarly, as the market grows in size and power, and as capital mobility increases, the resistance to the flow of capital and new production techniques is very likely to fall around the globe.

No doubt this is the direction in which most of us are headed, but we should be very wary of assuming globalization will take us in one pass to anything approaching total financial or, ultimately, economic superconductivity. For any action, there are reactions. As for the triple bottom line, the words "sustainability," "sustainable," and "unsustainable" are used frequently through *Market Unbound*, but not in anything like the sense meant here. The trends Bryan and Farrell herald are seen to be neutral with respect to the environment. This is unduly optimistic.

The idea of a "perfect" market omnisciently allocating resources and ensuring the protection of the environment is far-fetched, and even dangerous.

Standing on a Precipice

But we could perhaps imagine real triple bottom line progress if these financial market trends were to be coupled with those identified by Gary Hamel and C. K. Prahalad in *Competing for the Future*.[10] "We are standing on the verge, and for some it will be the precipice, of a revolution as profound as that which gave birth to modern industry," they argue. "It will be the environmental revolution, the genetic revolution, the materials revolution, the digital revolution, and, most of all, the information revolution." Technologies waiting in the wings, they conclude, include microrobots, virtual meeting rooms, and custom-designed environmental bioremediation techniques.

Fine, but many of these revolutions will take us in unexpected directions, short-circuiting some of the well-laid plans of would-be revolutionaries. They will help to create new rules of the game. The explosive controversy in Europe when Monsanto tried to import genetically modified soybeans provides a dramatic example. Although the US company is convinced that genetic engineering will make agriculture more sustainable, environmental concerns, the power of the media, and the ability of campaigners to operate over such media as the Internet meant that the opposition built quickly and hit harder than once would have been the case.

Ecology *vs.* Economy?

Despite such upsets, perhaps the most reassuring signal of the emerging new paradigm came when Michael Porter, Harvard Business School professor and leading international competitiveness guru, contributed a joint-authored paper to the *Harvard Business Review* forging strong links between environmental protection, resource productivity, innovation, and competitiveness.[11]

The current assumption, he and co-author Claas van der Linde note, is that in today's world "there is an inherent and fixed trade-off: ecology versus the economy." The result is a form of arm-wrestling match, with one side trying to force through new rules and standards, and the other trying to roll them back. Tomorrow, Porter and van der Linde argue, resource productivity will be directly linked both to environmental protection and competitiveness. Environmental constraints drive innovation and, as a result, eco-efficiency.

They point to the success of the Dutch flower industry, responsible for around 65% of world exports of cut flowers. The Netherlands is short of land for growing flowers and has an unsuitable climate, just some of the factors that have forced the country's growers to innovate all along the value chain. Their very resource poverty forced the Dutch to develop high-tech systems for year-round greenhouse cultivation. More could still be done to reduce the inputs of fertilizers and pesticides, it is true, but such examples underscore the point that a resource-constrained economy, whether the constraints are "real" or created by environmental policies, can be highly competitive, so long as other key factors are in place.

The conclusion, Porter and van der Linde suggest, is that top executives should spend less time resisting new environmental legislation, and more rethinking the nature and future of their businesses to ensure they are well adapted for the sustainability transition.

Boardroom Views

Tyranny of the Bottom Line

So much for the theory: what is the view from the boardroom? Do mainstream board directors spend much time thinking about the environment, let alone the triple bottom line? Which sectors and which companies are awake to the threats and opportunities – and which are likely to suffer from the Rip van Winkle syndrome a few years hence?

You can always find CEOs and other business leaders who see the shape of things to come and even some who are beginning to talk of the triple bottom line. Companies like the National Westminster Bank and General Motors refer to the economic, social, and environmental dimensions of sustainability in their corporate environmental reports. But few CEOs are as vociferous on the subject – and on the emerging perils of globalization – as the Body Shop's Anita Roddick. "Free trade holds much of the blame for continued international conflict," she argues:

"Markets are said to possess wisdom that is somehow superior to man. Those of us in business who travel in the developing world see the results of such Western wisdom, and have a rumbling disquiet about much of what our economic institutions have bought into."[12]

And what about the bottom line, as traditionally defined? "Our current economic indicators are inadequate for measuring global trade's human effects," Roddick insists, "we are tethered by the tyranny of the bottom line. What about putting emotion, compassion and caring into the economic equation?" For her, the attempted ethical neutrality of major corporations was best summed up by Shell Nigeria's general manager, when he said, "For a commercial company trying to make investments, you need a stable environment. Dictatorships can give you that."

Nor is Roddick alone in making such statements. Early pioneers are also emerging in other sectors, even banking. "Business ecology must be seen as an opportunity, not a threat," according to Terry Thomas, managing director of the UK's Co-operative Bank:

> "It represents the sea-change in business values since the 1980s and the way ahead for the next century. Generally, however, we still lag behind our competitors in the US and Scandinavia in fostering environmental reporting and encouraging sustainability."

Turning up the Heat

Some companies have seen customer pressures building for years in this area. In 1992, for example, Michael Adams of US computer-maker Digital Equipment was already reporting that major industry customers were turning up the heat.[13] "Please confirm that your products do not contain any of the hazardous chemicals on this 3-page list," demanded one international aerospace customer. "We are returning this computer because it was packaged with materials containing CFCs," wrote another conglomerate. And for those wondering whether environmental performance would ever provide competitive advantage, a German metals fabricator told Digital, "Your solutions are similar [to your competitors']. We will purchase from the one which we feel is the most environmentally friendly."

Even so, most major international companies still view the triple bottom line as something for the future. For example, when fund managers attended a Boston conference to listen to what Niall FitzGerald, the new UK chairman of Anglo–Dutch consumer products giant Unilever had to say, they heard him mention an S-word, as in "sustainable, profitable growth."[14] But the triple bottom line was clearly not at the forefront of his mind. Looking for global market leadership in the 21st century, FitzGerald said that Unilever had failed in two important respects: it had not made enough money in the relatively mature markets of Europe and North America, and it had not grown as rapidly as it should have in the fast-developing markets of Asia and Latin America. The growth of such markets, he said, "is the most dramatic shift in industrial power that has taken place in the last 100 years."

Paradoxically, the sweeping top management changes that Fitz-Gerald was announcing to take the company into the 21st century had been largely sparked by one of the great marketing fiascos of recent years. When Unilever introduced its new Persil Power washing powder product in 1994, based on a new ingredient (or accelerator), the aim had been to outflank arch-rival Procter & Gamble's Ariel. But P&G found that the accelerator damaged some clothes over multiple washes and attacked Unilever so forcefully that the product had to be withdrawn. As Unilever's detergents co-ordinator, FitzGerald's head could well have been on the block, but he turned the disaster into a hugely powerful accelerator for corporate change.

What the media didn't say – and probably didn't know – was that the vigour of P&G's attack on Unilever flowed from P&G's highly developed life-cycle assessment approach to product development. The company had previously tested the Unilever accelerator compound for possible use, rejecting it because of the problems that were later to bubble to the surface with Persil Power. P&G's approach is described in more detail in Chapter 8.

But at the same time as FitzGerald was talking in Boston, using what looked like – and was – a very narrow definition of sustainability, relevant work was already under way behind the scenes. Unilever had already linked up with WWF to develop a sustainable fisheries program, and my colleagues at SustainAbility were also busy alongside Dutch consultants TME with a major international piece of work on the implications of sustainability for Unilever's agricultural, fisheries, and food value chains.

Unilever, in fact, was beginning to wake up to the fact that in pursuing "long-term value creation for our shareholders and employees," to use FitzGerald's words, superior value would most likely come to those competitors with a superior understanding of the triple bottom line of sustainability. But the real competitive advantages, it was recognized, would flow not from marginal "greening" improvements to products but from deep – albeit carefully phased – structural changes to value chains and markets.

Bubbling Under

Six major trends which are "bubbling under" as far as the current boardroom agenda is concerned are covered in the next six chapters. For the moment, however, let's look at three issues linked to a number of these trends and likely to challenge company boards in future. The first of these is the assessment of "sustainable competitive advantage." The second is the emerging concept of "business ecosystems," with competition taking place not just at the level of the individual company but also at the level of constellations of linked companies. And the third is the dematerialization agenda advanced by the Factor 10 Club (see Spotlight, p. 78).

Waking up the Chairman

In most companies, the environmental agenda has been handled by environmental professionals, rather than by the board. Now, as argued in Chapter 10, the corporate governance dimensions of the sustainability agenda need urgent attention. So how can we get boards to wake up in time? One answer is to publish surveys ranking companies in terms of their understanding of, and, increasingly, performance against, the triple bottom line. Let's look at two recent survey reports, one by Morgan Stanley, the US investment bank, the other by the UK green business organization, Business in the Environment.

The Morgan Stanley analysts were asked to identify companies worldwide enjoying what was called a "sustainable competitive advantage."[15] Again, their definition of "sustainable" was much narrower than would be required for a full triple bottom line analysis. Their aim was to produce a map of global competitiveness. Some of the results came as no great surprise. The US advantage is overwhelming, for example, with 125 American companies among the 238 world leaders identified. More surprisingly, the UK came second, with 21, ahead of Japan with 19, and Germany with 10. Among the UK-based companies flagged up as highly competitive are GlaxoWellcome, British Airways, Unilever, Reuters and RTZ. A perhaps less obvious leader was Spirax Sarco, an engineering company which controls 30% of the global steam controls market. According to Morgan Stanley, Spirax Sarco's competitive advantage is likely to be "sustainable," a key aspect of the study, for 10–20 years, since it would take that long for a competitor to overtake it.

Of course, all sorts of things can go wrong along the way. And there is also the question of the survey's methodology. Because the survey was aimed at Morgan Stanley's investment clients, it only looked at publicly quoted companies, in which the USA and UK are unusually strong. But the underlying point was clear: Japan, which had dominated the 1980s with new techniques such as *kaizen* and just-in-time management, was now seeing a range of international competitors gaining a new head of steam having made major technological and structural changes.

As a means of describing the competitive performance of whole economies, the *Financial Times* argued, the Morgan Stanley approach is "rough and ready." Its main advantage, on the other hand, is that it approaches the issue of competitiveness from "an unfamiliar angle." And the same can be said for the Business in the Environment (BiE) Index of Corporate Environmental Engagement,[16] described in Chapter 11.

The BiE survey focused on the Financial Times Stock Exchange (FT-SE) 100 companies. The goal was to wake up company boards to the emerging challenge. The stratagem worked. The phones rang off the hook in the three organizations that produced the survey. Many calls were from environmental specialists in companies where the chairman, CEO, or other board members had woken up to find themselves publicly listed as less than perfect in some aspect of their environmental engagement. Even more galling, they saw competitors coming higher up the rankings. As Chapter 7 explains, such novel forms of accountability are likely to be a key feature of 21st century capitalism.

Goodbye to Competition?

Hardly. The name of James Moore's book is actually *The Death of Competition*, but that isn't what he forecasts.[17] "Competition as we know it is dead," he says.[18] "Not that competition is vanishing. In fact it is intensifying. But we need to think about it differently." Interestingly, Moore's book draws heavily – powerfully – on ecological metaphors. Whereas traditional competition has focused on products and markets, with one company's products competing head-on with another's, the new approach sees business ecosystems developing very much like biological ecosystems. As they do so, they move through similar stages: pioneering, expansion, authority, and renewal.

The focus now is not just on a given company, but on its entire environment. "Companies need to coevolve with others in the environment," Moore explains, "a process that involves cooperation as well as conflict. It takes generating shared visions, forming alliances, negotiating deals, and managing complex relationships." Business networks like BiE and the World Business Council for Sustainable Development (WBCSD) represent early steps in this direction in relation to some key aspects of triple bottom line performance. But the implications are far broader. In a global survey of green business networks we forecast the emergence of green *keiretsu*; consortia of companies dedicated not simply to talking about sustainable development but also to financing and delivering it.[19]

This process will be accelerated by another trend identified by Moore; the erosion of traditional industry barriers. As a result, we are seeing companies finding themselves competing with unlikely rivals. "The most creative and aggressive companies exploit these wider territories," Moore observes, "transforming the landscape with new ecosystems. The dominant new ecosystems will likely cross several different industries, and they will joust with similar networks spread across still other industries." For the moment, it is sufficient to say that the real test for 21st century businesses will be to outperform their rivals at creating the new business ecosystems needed to build and sustain their triple bottom line performance.

The Ultimate 10× Challenge

When the history of the late 20th century is written, the first meeting in October 1994 of the Factor 10 Club could rank alongside the early meetings of the Bolsheviks or the early garage days of Apple Computer as one of the century's formative moments. Held in Carnoules, France, on the initiative of the Wuppertal Institute, the German think-tank, this was a group quite explicitly modeled on the Club of Rome and dedicated to accelerating the shift towards a dematerialized economy.[20]

The basic idea, and one which has been further developed by Amory Lovins of the US Rocky Mountain Institute, is that our economies – to be sustainable during a period when the global human population will likely double and living standards in some parts of the world approach current western standards – need to increase their resource conversion efficiency by a minimum of Factor 4 (i.e. 75% reductions in resource use for any unit of consumption). Given that western societies typically consume 20 to 30 times more than their counterparts in the less developed world, the Carnoules Declaration calls for Factor 10 improvements (i.e. 90% reductions).

Inevitably, this trend will proceed at different speeds in different world regions. But over a time-scale of decades it is as likely to be driven by price increases and tax reforms as by changing values – the subject of Chapter 6. True Factor 10 dematerialization would convert not only companies but also, very likely, entire existing business ecosystems into dinosaurs.

Winners, Losers

Point of Differentiation

Those taking an active interest in all of this – and trying to pick out potential winners and losers – will now include a growing range of investors and analysts. "We believe in a sustainable world, that its resources are finite and that we should preserve them," said Derek Maughan, chairman and CEO of US investment bankers Salomon Brothers. "And," he added, "that's good business."[21] Yes, but it is taking a long time to get even such pioneering firms to recognize the need to apply triple bottom line principles to their core businesses.

Even so, there are signs that the message is getting through. Salomon Inc CEO Robert Denham noted:

"Environmental issues are very important to a lot of the industries we're involved with, and if we can have a better understanding of those issues and deliver better advisory services in transactions or acquisitions, then that's another factor to distinguish us from our competitors."

With brains like these trying to spot winners and losers, the chances are that the natural selection pressures on industry are about to go up several notches. And when it comes to *where* future growth, sustainable or unsustainable, will most likely happen, Jim Rogers is a man worth listening to. In the 1970s, he was the other half of the team that helped George Soros start up as a fund manager: Soros traded, Rogers did the research. Between 1969, when they set up, and 1980 they managed a gain of 3,365 per cent, while the US market – as measured by the Standard & Poors composite index – rose just 47 points. In the end, having made his fortune, Rogers bailed out and traveled around the world by motorbike.

In his book, *Investment Biker*,[22] Rogers thought he could discern the outlines of one major future economic growth area. "When you stand back and look at Asia," he explained:

"a few facts leap out. China has abundant labour but lacks capital and has undeveloped natural resources. Japan has lots of money, but no natural resources and little labour. And north of China sits Siberia, brimming over with natural resources but without labour or capital. A natural partnership stares you in the face: Japanese capital, Siberian natural resources and Chinese labour."

A pipe dream? No, he argued. "On my motorcycle ride through Siberia, I saw Chinese workers operating Russian enterprises in Khabarovsk and Blagoveshchensk with the benefit of Japanese capital and management. This golden triangle will be the most productive and prosperous arrangement on the planet throughout the 21st century." It will also, consequently, be a place to watch for major ecological disasters.

Such development will help skew the business agenda towards new issues. Some key triple bottom line objectives will clearly not be achieved as fast as most campaigners would like; indeed, we may sometimes see progress going into reverse. Take child labor. Despite the fact that the International Labour Organization (ILO) is dedicated to abolishing child labor worldwide, it reports that a quarter of children under the age of 15 are employed in parts of Ghana, India, Indonesia, and Senegal. Their work is often considered essential to maintaining the financial health of the family. Given these facts, it seems likely that companies trading with such countries will continue to find themselves – as Nike and Reebok have been – attacked by values-led campaigners.

Some relatively advanced countries will also try to attract inward investment by explicitly holding down social standards, as Britain did in refusing to implement the European Union's "Social Chapter." Sometimes this will work: certainly Britain has attracted a high proportion of incoming investment. But some companies will opt for the higher standards anyway, as have companies like brewers Scottish & Newcastle, engineers GEC-Alsthom, chemicals group BOC, banknote printer De La Rue, and Securicor.[23] Longer term, as the Shell executive quoted by Anita Roddick explained, investors and businesses alike want a degree of security. As a result, real or perceived social sustainability is likely to be a key factor in many 21st century investment decisions.

No Gain Without Pain

Business needs government help to make the sustainability transition. Growing numbers of countries, like Singapore, will be doing their best to position themselves for the sustainability transition. Take Sweden, one of the world's most environmentally conscious countries. When environment minister Anna Lindh announced that the government planned to double a carbon emissions tax first introduced in 1990, there was understandable concern on the part of business – even though energy-hungry sectors like cement, glass, and chemicals were to some degree exempted.

This meant that Sweden would soon have the highest carbon tax in the world, complained Sven Olof Lodin, deputy director of the Confederation of Swedish Industries.[24] Doubling the tax, he argued, will:

> "mean Swedish companies will lose market share to companies using methods that generate more emissions. It is completely counterproductive from the point of view of the environment, employment growth and future investment."

Well maybe, but if the principles developed by Michael Porter are correct, Sweden may also be positioning itself as one of the key industrial economies of the 21st century. Nor is it simply a matter of companies and national economies fighting for a share of the global environmental technology market. Instead, we will see a growing focus on technologies, products, and services that are themselves clean or resource-efficient, rather than needing strap-on environmental technologies for pollution control or environmental clean-up.

That said, the environmental technology market alone – worth $200 billion by the late 1980s – is expected to grow to somewhere between $300 billion and $600 billion by the end of the century; clearly, not a market to be sniffed at and some countries are doing particularly well here. US exports of eco-technology, for example, rose 50% between 1993 and 1996 to $14.5 billion. In Germany, it is estimated that nearly one million people now make a living from environmental protection, almost as many as from vehicle manufacturing. And the needs are still growing. In Poland alone, it was estimated that the country would need $10 billion between 1996 and 2000 to fund environmental clean-up.

The clean-up industry will include many winners, clearly, but anyone whose employment or income depends on curing environmental problems should keep an eye out for new technologies or approaches which make clean-up unnecessary and end-of-pipe solutions obsolete.

Stealing Markets

Finally, one of the most interesting sectors to watch for winners and losers will be the global chlorine industry. In part this is because its problems are intrinsically interesting, but also in part because where chlorine goes tomorrow other sectors will follow not long after. After years of conventional campaigning, Greenpeace is now turning to markets as a mechanism for driving change. The group's approach, illustrated by the stunningly successful "Greenfreeze" campaign to disrupt the refrigeration market and drive the industry out of CFC refrigerants, was well summed up by Greenpeace solutions campaigner Corin Millais, "Our approach is to enforce the solutions by stealing the market. We're going to get into their territory and take their customers."

So, extinction for the chlorine industry and all its applications? Too early to say, but just as Greenpeace can evolve to meet new market conditions, so can industry. Don't bet on chlorine's early demise, but the challenge all sectors of industry face is on the verge of expanding dramatically. One thing of which we can be certain, meanwhile, is that the 21st century chlorine industry – along with its customers – will spend less time using competition as an excuse for inaction and a great deal more using it as a reason for changes which a previous generation of chemical engineers and CEOs would have thought inconceivable.

Three Keys to the 21st Century

The first sustainability revolution focuses on markets, requiring that we understand and use the following keys to sustainable enterprise:

- ◆ First, sustainable development will increasingly be delivered by business through markets. Those markets, however, will need to be powerfully shaped or reshaped by governments, with a switch in focus from the externalization to the internalization of triple bottom line costs (see Chapter 13).
- ◆ Second, even the best-run corporations will face a number of "strategic inflection points." Some of the resulting "10×" changes will have little to do with the sustainability agenda, except in the sense that they distract management attention. But, as the transition takes hold, few companies or sectors will escape strategic inflections driven by regulators, market-makers (i.e. those who shape market expectations and priorities), and competitors in pursuit of radically improved performance against the triple bottom line.
- ◆ Third, business leaders determined to ride out the waves of change need to be focusing today on "lean thinking," Factor 4/10 dematerialization and the opportunities that will be created by the

CASE STUDY

VOLVO, SWEDEN:
RATTLING VALUE CHAINS

What was it John Lennon said at that Royal Variety Show a generation ago? Something like, "Those in the cheaper seats clap: the rest of you, rattle your jewelry!" Today, more and more companies are tiring of the cheap applause for shallow greening and turning, instead, to more challenging life-cycle-based strategies. One such company is the Swedish auto-maker Volvo, now part of Ford. And the late Beatle came to mind as I flew to Gothenburg to help with the launch event for Volvo's new environmental supplier challenge – because the company was beginning to rattle its supply chain with rare enthusiasm.

Volvo's then CEO, Sören Gyll, told the assembled suppliers that this was just the beginning of a multi-year, global campaign. Hundreds of suppliers had been invited to hear about the new campaign, designed to ensure that environmental care is given equal priority alongside two long-established core values; safety and quality. Now Volvo planned to add a third performance dimension; environment. The company announced that it would begin to include environmental factors in its audits of suppliers. "The race has started," said Han-Olov Olsson, Vice President responsible for marketing at Volvo Car Corporation.

Some years ago, the company even invited its customers to think whether they needed to take their cars when traveling into city centers. Better, its CEO noted, to take public transport. Volvo, as it happens, also makes buses! But we still seem light years away from the day when auto companies happily invite customers to complete some form of Need Test (see Chapter 8) before suggesting that they buy – or lease – a car. That will depend on a radical restructuring of the pricing structure in transport markets – and of the way in which we see and prioritize the need for access, mobility and different forms of transport.

sustainability transition. The focus, as Chapter 13 argues, needs to be on adding value, not adding volume.

Notes

1. Stuart L. Hart, "Beyond Greening: Strategies for a sustainable world," *Harvard Business Review*, January–February 1996.

2. Andrew S. Grove, *Only the Paranoid Survive: How to exploit the crisis points that challenge every company and career*, Currency Doubleday, 1996.

3. Donald J. Johnson, "The imperative of free trade," *The* OECD *Observer*, no 201, August/September 1996.

4. Crawford Falconer and Pierre Sauvé, "Globalisation, trade and competition," *The* OECD *Observer*, no 201, August/September 1996.

5. Michael Hirsh, "Meet GloboBoss!," *Newsweek*, 25 November 1996, pages 34–7.

6. David Smith, "The jobs axe that fell but failed," *Sunday Times*, 19 May 1996.

7. Frederick Reichheld, *The Loyalty Effect: The hidden forces behind growth, profits and lasting value*, Harvard Business Press, 1996.

8. James P. Womack and Daniel T. Jones, *Lean Thinking: Banish waste and create wealth in your organisation*, Simon & Schuster, 1996.

9. Lowell Bryan and Diana Farrell, *Market Unbound: Unleashing global capitalism*, John Wiley & Sons, 1996.

10. Gary Hamel and C.K. Prahalad, *Competing for the Future: Breakthrough strategies for seizing control of your industry and creating the markets of tomorrow*, Harvard Business School Press, 1994.

11. Michael E. Porter and Claas van der Linde, "Green and Competitive: Ending the stalemate," *Harvard Business Review*, September–October 1995, pages 120–34.

12. Anita Roddick, "Myth behind the idea of an unfettered global economy," *The Times*, 21 November 1996.

13. Michael Q. Adams, *Environment: Our customers are helping us to lead*, presentation to IMD Workshop, Lausanne, Switzerland, 23–4 November 1992.

14. Andrew Lorenz, "New Unilever aims to transform value," *Sunday Times*, 1 September 1996.

15. Tony Jackson, "Global competitiveness observed from an unfamiliar angle," *Financial Times*, 21 November 1996.

16. Business in the Environment, with AEA Technology and SustainAbility, *The Index of Corporate Environmental Engagement*, Business in the Environment, 1996.

17. James F. Moore, *The Death of Competition: Leadership and strategy in the age of business ecosystems*, John Wiley & Sons, 1996.

18. James F. Moore, The Death of Competition, *Fortune*, 15 April 1996.

19. John Elkington and Anne Dimmock, "The Green *Keiretsu*: An international survey of business alliances and networks for sustainable development," *Tomorrow* supplement, 1994.

20. Factor 10 Club, *Carnoules Declaration*, Wuppertal Institute, Germany, 1995.

21. Ann Goodman, "King Salomon minds," *Tomorrow*, No. 5, September/October, 1996.

22. Richard Thompson, "Get on your bike and let the money roll in," *The Times*, 6 April 1996.
23. Anthony Barnett, "British firms defying the Social Chapter opt-out," *Observer*, 4 August 1996.
24. Hugh Carnegy and Leyla Boulton, "Sweden moves at the double," *Financial Times*, 20 March 1996.

VALUES

Ghost in the System

Are values really crucial to the longer term future
of capitalism? Or are they, instead, little more
than flies in the economic ointment?
Can business afford to leave this area to public
affairs professionals and industry chaplains?
The answer to these questions are
yes, no, and absolutely not.

The emerging triple bottom line of sustainability implies that the resulting controversies are as likely to be fueled by economic and social issues as by environmental controversies. The underlying shift from "hard" to "soft" values does not mean that life will become easier for business: indeed, until we learn the rules of the new game, exactly the opposite.

Revolution	Focus	Old paradigm 〉	New paradigm
2	Values	Hard	〉 Soft

Will someone please tell me what is going on? This plaintive cry has echoed around a growing number of corporate boardrooms in recent years. Indeed, in the wake of Shell's mishaps with the Brent Spar and Nigerian controversies, Royal Dutch Petroleum president Cor Herkströter worried about Shell's inability – "with the best will in the world" – to assess some of the new problems correctly. "There appears to be something of a ghost in the global system," he noted, "some sort of blurring that causes us to make subtle, but in the end far-reaching, mistakes in assessing development."[1]

The nature of the problem, I believe, is that we are seeing a profound values shift in countries around the world. For the most part, this is not something that is being regulated: instead, it is happening as a natural outgrowth of people's evolving awareness and concern. And a key dimension of this shift is the way in which what would once have been seen as "soft" values (such as concern for future generations) are now coming in alongside – and sometimes even overriding – traditional "hard" values (such as the paramount importance of the financial bottom line).

Below, we look at the experiences of companies that have offended the values of their day, among them I.G. Farben, Green Cross, Nike, Wal-Mart, Volkswagen, Texaco, Astra USA and Mitsubishi Motor Manufacturing of America. To list companies like I.G. Farben and Nike in the same sentence is monstrous, given that the former was a criminal organization and the second is often considered an ethical company, but the point is that both managed to trigger public outrage by offending moral values. We will then review thinking on the subject of values, before looking at some of the ways in which such companies as Shell, the Body Shop International and Levi Strauss are trying to come to grips with the values agenda.

However, before we look in more detail at the values shift, it is worth stressing that the post-1945 period has been something of an aberration in human history. New technologies have driven unprecedented rates of social change around the world. As Hardin Tibbs of the Global Business Network has put it:

"Much of the technology introduced during the 20th century, and particularly since World War II, has had the effect of expanding personal freedom. The birth control pill, for instance, was midwife to sweeping changes in the sexual mores of the Western world, and through the power of the mass media and travel this has extended to much of the developing world also. People have been eager to explore the limits of these new freedoms – in personal mobility, affluence, and styles of living."[2]

These explorations and experiments have been critically important in driving the ongoing values shift. Unfortunately, however, some of these experiments have:

"bumped up against frustrating reversals and contradictions. Cancer and AIDS reversed the sense that life-threatening disease was in retreat. Material accomplishments were tarnished by family disharmony, stress, and lack of time. A belief in the inevitable progress of scientific materialism was taunted by growing polarization in democratic industrial countries, and the existence of starvation in a world where science was in principle capable of eliminating material need."

As a result, the coming years are likely to see a dramatic new focus on values. Business, somewhat surprisingly, is also being driven to focus on values by the downsizing trend. As companies opt for flatter hierarchies, bosses will be unable to look over their employees' shoulders to the same degree. As a result, more employees will be taking decisions which would once have been passed up the hierarchy. In the process, they will do as they think best. "If you want them to do as the company thinks best too," Tom Stewart warned senior executives in *Fortune*, "then you must hope that they have an inner gyroscope aligned with the corporate compass."[3]

These inner gyroscopes and corporate compasses are rooted in values. Stewart distinguished "hard" corporate values (e.g. profitability) from "soft" values (e.g. integrity, respect for employees, and sustainability). Where employee surveys have been carried out by companies aspiring to embrace both types of value, most people think their organization takes the hard values seriously – but the proportion believing that it respects the softer values turns out to be very much lower.

Shifts in our values often take place over extended time-scales, but attitudinal research suggests that this process is well under way in relation to the values necessary to drive and support the sustainability transition. The sorts of areas where campaigners have been focusing their efforts were well illustrated by a 1991 book, *Changing Corporate Values*,[4] produced by New Consumer. New Consumer, like the longer-established Council on Environmental Priorities (CEP) in the USA, assessed a range of companies in terms of their commitment to and performance against targets in such areas as disclosure of information, clean and safe working conditions, industrial democracy, equal opportunities, employee training, community involvement, environmental protection, animal welfare, political donations, relationships with oppressive regimes, and military sales.

None of this was happening in a vacuum, of course. The World Values Survey, which tracks the replacement of "materialist" values by "postmaterialist" values has involved research in some 40 countries, representing around 70% of the world's population. The conclusion is clear. The underlying values shift may often be invisible to the naked eye, but:

"its impact is pervasive. It is changing social, political and economic life. And because it is transforming entire lifestyles, including consumer patterns, fertility rates and the priority that people give to environmental protection, it constitutes a major component of global change."[5]

In the process, even values which once seemed to have the consistency of sponge have periodically – often suddenly – become as hard as concrete.

Ultimately, it will not be enough to green the products people buy or even the industries that make those products. The necessary switch to more sustainable lifestyles can only come with an appropriate shift in our values. And it matters which values we adopt, as Lester Thurow has pointed out:

> "If the world's population had the productivity of the Swiss, the consumption habits of the Chinese, the egalitarian instincts of the Swedes and the social discipline of the Japanese, then the planet could support many times its current population without privation for anyone. On the other hand, if the world's population had the productivity of Chad, the consumption habits of the United States, the inegalitarian instincts of India, and the social discipline of Argentina, then the planet could not support anywhere near its current numbers."

Why Worry?

Barbarians at the Gate

Despite the recent reverses suffered by a string of companies as their values got out of phase with those of wider society, the years following the collapse of the USSR and other communist states were glory days for the values of capitalism and of those sitting around most boardroom tables. Or that was the way things looked on the surface. Whether it was Chrysler's Lee Iacocca, ICI's John Harvey-Jones, Microsoft's Bill Gates, or Virgin's Richard Branson, business leaders enjoyed an era in which they were seen as the new super-heroes in the vanguard of Western culture alongside Hollywood actors and rock musicians.[6]

To be sure, there were films, among them *Wall Street* (perhaps best remembered for Gordon Gekko's motto, "Greed is good!") and *Barbarians at the Gate* (based on the hostile takeover of R J R Nabisco), which warned of the perils of unbridled capitalism. But such was the cultural fascination with the world of business that by the late 1990s the criticism often seemed strangely muted. That period is now coming to an end, with profound implications for boardrooms around the world.

Whatever business leaders may say about the power and wonders of the market, one of the key lessons of the 20th century must be that industrialism, be it of the capitalist, communist, or some other variety, needs to be moderated very much as a nuclear reactor must be shielded or a potentially harmful organism absorbed into a new complex of ecosystem checks and balances.

The best places to look for evidence of what raw capitalism or other forms of enterprise can be like include Amazonia and the ex-communist world. In the absence of the sorts of controls that have developed in the west, enterprise – and its fraudulent cousins – develop rapidly. "Few industries can rival the short-termism of the timber trade," concluded a recent report from the Environmental Investigation Agency.[7] Arguing that the $100 billion world timber industry was "running out of control," the EIA noted that the unbridled plunder of the planet's remaining rainforests is increasing at an alarming rate. Among a list of timber companies branded as "forest rapists," with Japan's Mitsubishi heading the list, a number are accused of corruption and other illegal practices, in addition to "cut-and-run" policies which leave large areas of regions like Amazonia and the Russian Far East devastated.

Greed, not surprisingly, is also rampant in many of the erstwhile communist states. In Albania, the poorest country in Europe, hundreds of thousands of people were left penniless by a pyramid savings scam run by a gypsy and former shoe factory worker who promised to make huge interest payments to savers. Albanians succumbed in droves to her offer of 50% interest on their life savings, failing to recognize that new deposits were being used to pay off the interest of the first wave of deposits. The innocence, indeed the greed, of some of the victims was shown by the fact that when the media interviewed one of a group of investors who received part-repayment following a near-riot in Tirana, she said she planned to immediately re-invest the money in one of the other crooked pyramid savings schemes operating in the country.[8] Shortly afterwards, riots sparked off by public outrage over these schemes helped trigger virtual civil war in the country.

In the more advanced economies, we may pride ourselves – to quote an editorial in *Barron's*, the Dow Jones business and financial weekly – that "It Can't Happen Here."[9] But the publication was making the point that stock markets like Wall Street are themselves still subject to wild fluctuations. This is a subject to which we will return briefly in Chapter 13. Eventually, we must hope that even an Amazonia, Albania, or Zaire may develop the necessary social and political infrastructure needed to temper human greed and sustain a successful capitalist economy.

Meanwhile, whatever may be going on in the world of stock markets, the evidence from elsewhere in the world suggests that the range of issues over which well-known companies can stumble even in the long-industrialized economies is growing almost by the day. Let's work our way quickly through a wide spectrum of recent controversies, starting with the most heinous, war crimes, where most people would accept that the wrongdoing was absolute and unforgivable. Next we will turn to a number of more recent issues where some would argue that the failure of the companies involved to spot significant changes in society's values was more understandable.

Any company believing that its operations are sustainable if they meet economic efficiency and environmental quality standards, but fail to meet emerging social and ethical standards, needs to understand what lies behind the historic failings of companies like I.G. Farben and Green Cross, and – on a very different scale – the recent troubles of companies like Nike, Wal-Mart, Astra USA, Shell, and even the Body Shop. In each case, the offended values are highlighted.

I. G. Farben

Don't Employ Slave Labor

Some of the worst crimes ever committed by a company were carried out by Germany's giant chemical combine, I. G. Farben. Among other things, the company invented and manufactured the Zyklon B gas used by the Nazis in their gas chambers. It also worked some 30,000 slave laborers to death at Auschwitz alone. With a record like that, you would assume that the company would have been shut down decades ago: not so.

Although I. G. Farben today is only a shadow of its former self – having been stripped in 1953, as a punishment, of its production facilities, most of which ended up in such companies as BASF, Bayer, and Hoechst – it is still very much alive and in business. Indeed, it caused a storm when it recently filed suit to reclaim extensive holdings in eastern Germany, where it had been the biggest landowner in 1945.[10] Outraged Holocaust survivors argued that the company should not be allowed to exist, let alone reclaim the land seized by the communists in the wake of the war. Their demand was that I. G. Farben should be immediately liquidated and its assets distributed among the survivors. "We created the wealth I. G. Farben owns today," explained Hans Frankenthal, founder of "Never Again," a lobbying group which represents some 10,000 forced labor survivors.

These arguments sent shudders through corporate boardrooms in Germany, because the outcome could set costly precedents. Many of the country's best-known companies used forced labor during the war, although few were as closely linked to the Nazis as I. G. Farben. Even though the company pleaded that it had paid its debt to survivors in

1957, when it handed $8 million to the Jewish Claims Conference, it won little public sympathy.

Other companies raced to pre-empt similar campaigns, hiring respected historians to tell their untold wartime stories before someone else did it for them. In a 558-page tome, Daimler–Benz documented how it had used 30,000 forced laborers in 1945 alone. A new chapter of Deutsche Bank's corporate history discussed its "Aryanization" program, and included an admission by chairman Hilmar Kopper that the bank "fell to low depths." A spokesman for Siemens noted that corporations had been "a part of, and used by, a totalitarian regime." Who would be brave enough to say it will never happen again?

Japan's Green Cross

Don't Put Profits Ahead of Lives

"I was raped," Hiroshi Shimizu protested. "I never thought that doctors would give me bad medicine." A Japanese man in his thirties, and using an assumed name, Shimizu was one of more than 2,000 Japanese hemophiliacs and their loved ones infected by the deadly HIV virus before heat-treated blood products became available in Japan. This is the tragedy; the scandal was that a number of companies and the Japanese government turned out to have colluded to keep safe blood products off the market to give local companies a chance to develop their own.[11]

As long ago as 1983, a health ministry investigation had recommended that all imports of untreated blood products should be banned immediately. Patients like hemophiliacs need regular blood transfusions, but risk AIDS if the blood has been drawn from already infected donors. The inquiry team, led by Dr Takeshi Abe, the country's leading hemophilia expert, also urged that emergency imports of treated blood should be allowed from US drug giant Baxter International. But just a week later, the recommendation was reversed. According to memos recovered from government records, it was reversed because it threatened to "deal a blow" to Japan's own blood products industry. Instead, the health ministry insisted that Baxter conduct two years of clinical testing in Japan before its heat treatment could be introduced there. In the meantime, local companies like Osaka-based Green Cross raced to come up with their own alternatives. Baxter and other foreign importers were forced to continue selling untreated products if they wanted to stay on the market.

There were many factors at work in causing this tragedy. For one thing, there was a long-standing aversion in Japan to talking frankly and in public about the AIDS problem. Even a decade after the problem was first recognized, some Japanese doctors were still not informing patients when they tested positive for the HIV virus, while some hospitals simply turned HIV patients away. But there were also deep-rooted weaknesses in the country's regulatory system. Many blood products companies employ retired health ministry bureaucrats, as part of a process called *amakudari*, or "descent from heaven." In short, those still working in government were too close to those they were supposed to be regulating.

Green Cross, which expected its liabilities to run into hundreds of millions of dollars, was subsequently accused by the health ministry of having dumped infected stock on the market to clear its inventory. It was also accused of having falsified documents to show that it had stopped selling contaminated products before it actually did so. Although the company denied the charges, the controversy was moving too quickly. Victims sued Green Cross, the country's leading blood products supplier, along with two other Japanese companies and the local units of Germany's Bayer and of Baxter. Before long, Japanese TV viewers saw an unusual spectacle. Top executives of Green Cross knelt before a group of victims and family members, pressing their heads to the floor and mumbling apologies for ten minutes.

Although the company's admission of guilt may help it in Japan, where criminal sentences are often lighter for those who have expressed remorse, there was a downside: all five companies would be even more exposed to possible criminal charges in Japan, and the foreign companies could face civil suits in the USA and Europe.

But the whole saga can be seen in a different light if you know that Green Cross founder Ryoichi Naito was himself a war criminal. He had been a doctor at the infamous Unit 731, an Imperial Army germ-warfare group that conducted terrible experiments on prisoners of war during World War II. Under Naito, who died in 1982, just before the AIDS issue really hit, Green Cross pursued an aggressive business strategy, which he once summed up in the terrifying words: "Money is more important than blood."

The Green Cross example raises questions about whether corrupt companies are born corrupt or have corruption thrust upon them. Clearly, the older a company is, the greater the likelihood that it will have experienced corruption problems, and that it will have adopted society's values – pure or impure. But there is probably a Nobel prize awaiting the social scientist who works out what it is about some corporate cultures that resists corruption, and millions of dollars if it can be bottled and sold.

Nike, Wal-mart

Don't Employ Child Labor

Ugly stories about a different form of forced labor and about the social conditions of production have dented the reputations of a series of western companies – and led to major new pressures on suppliers based in such countries as Indonesia, Pakistan, Bangladesh, and Thailand. At a time when rich world countries are embracing the sustainability agenda and beginning to worry about their children's children, consumers around the world have been made uncomfortably aware of the way that hundreds of millions of today's young people are abused in sweatshops and other forms of child labor.

The issue had been around for years, but 1996 brought into American living rooms stark images of Pakistani children stitching footballs, Haitian workers sewing Walt Disney T-shirts and tearful celebrity confessions.[12] If any single moment defined the new agenda, it was the confession by American talk-show host Kathie Lee Gifford that her Wal-Mart outfits were made by Honduran girls paid 31¢ an hour – but, she said, she hadn't known. Her admission was picked up by a tiny human rights organization, National Labor Committee, whose director went on to a congressional hearing on labor abuses and increased the pressure on Gifford and other celebrities who, like basketball star Michael Jordan, endorse products made in this way.

Jordan, who at the time earned $20 million a year endorsing Nike sneakers, was presumably embarrassed to find that this sum was a great deal more than the annual payroll for the thousands of Indonesians who actually made the shoes. The fundamental issue was further highlighted by a report from the International Labour Organization concluding that about 250 million children are working in developing countries – nearly twice earlier estimates. The report also documented many examples of children doing dangerous work putting them at risk of death, crippling accidents, disease, poisoning, and sexual abuse.[13]

Rather than lying low in the hope that the storm would blow over, Gifford went on *Larry King Live* and launched a crusade to end child labor. "The flaying of celebrities like Gifford and Jordan made it easy for Americans to miss the point," reported *Time*:

"For years, children have been sold as slaves, blinded or maimed for crying or rebelling or trying to return home, ill-fed, bone-weary, short-lived. They file the scissor blades, mix the gun-powder for the firecrackers, knot the carpets, stitch the soccer balls with needles longer then their fingers."

As the issues hit the front-pages and TV headline news, consumers were faced with an urgent question: "How much are Americans willing to sacrifice the children of other countries to give their [own] children what they want?"

Activists were quick to exploit the historic opportunity to get their priorities on the agenda. "American companies cannot escape the moral responsibility," said Kailash Satyarthi, a leading Indian campaigner for children's rights. "They are the people placing the orders. So they are the principal employers of the children."

Companies like Gap, Levi Strauss, and Sears pledged themselves to fight exploitative practices. Reebok called on its arch-rival Nike, the market leader in trainers, to join it in a bid to end child labor and improve working conditions in their Asian factories. Reebok, which had long taken a public stance on social issues, was edging into the lead in this new form of values-based competition. Nike, however, had already stressed that its contractors had been subject to a "memorandum of understanding" binding them to rules on child labor, worker, and environmental standards. Even so, the company became a lightning rod for protests, not least because of the extraordinary contrast between Michael Jordan's earnings and the $2.23 basic daily wage paid by Nike's Indonesian sub-contractors.

Shortly afterwards, the World Federation of the Sporting Goods Industry pledged to try to eliminate child labor in their operations worldwide by 2000. Nike, which had commissioned labor practice audits of its factories, was beginning to release selected data, while Reebok was calling upon activists to alert it to abuses. And one US importer noted that: "Virtually every retailer is asking for certification from vendors that they are complying with codes of conduct."

If the pressures are sustained, the long-term implications for countries like Bangladesh, Indonesia, and Pakistan could be profound. A ban on the use of cheap child labor in Bangladesh's booming garment industry was soon announced – with government officials pleading with international customers to continue buying. The ban followed intense pressure from the International Labour Organization and – more importantly – from the US, which imports 60% of Bangladeshi textile exports.

CASE STUDY   **LEVI STRAUSS, USA:**
GLOBAL SUCCESS SHARING PLAN

Most major international companies these days can produce some sort of mission or values statement, but precious few yet devote much attention to putting their principles into practice. One notable exception is Levi Strauss, best known for its 501 jeans. With 1995 profits of $700 million on a turnover of $6.7 billion, the company was way ahead of its competitors. The interesting question is: did the company's ability to focus on values flow from its profitability, or vice versa?

The company has long roots – starting back in the 1850s, when the original Mr Strauss began selling early versions of Levis to San Francisco's gold-rush miners – but only began to work on the ethical side of its business in recent decades.[14] The real progress dates from 1974, when Bob Haas, a company employee since 1973 and a member of the founding family, took over as chief executive. Within twelve months, he had carried out a highly leveraged management buy-out of the 63% of the firm's equity in public hands, ending Levi's 14 years as a listed company. Haas was motivated by a concern that any company with a public listing suffers because the demands of shareholders, analysts, and other financial outsiders can seriously impair corporate vision.

Unusually, Haas also looked for ways in which he and the Haas family could share the company's profitability more broadly with employees. In Haas's own words, the resulting Global Success Sharing Plan (GSSP) came about for both philosophical and commercial reasons:

> "Throughout our history, we have sought to conduct our business in ways that are consistent with our values, which include recognition – both psychic and financial – for those who contribute to our success. This plan is particularly faithful to our values because everyone will work towards a shared objective in order to receive individual rewards."

The company's ethics code defines commercial achievements as "broader than merely financial success." Like many other companies, as *Management Today* put it, "Levi's also publishes a paper mountain of aspiration statements, ethical guidelines, codes of conduct – you name it, they most certainly have it." But they try to live up to the pledges. So, for example, Levi's is phasing out all its operations in China, including marketing and distribution, because of that country's human rights record.

❭

The upside, it hopes, is that motivated employees will help drive innovation and continuously renew competitive advantage. If the GSSP targets are met, the 2001 payout to employees will be equivalent to about a year's profits at current levels. Given that some 94% of the company's stock is owned by descendants of the original founder, with the lion's share in the hands of Bob Haas and his uncle, Peter Haas Snr., the company has had a much easier ride of it than would have been the case if it had to contend with dividend-hungry institutional investors.

Levi's is also strongly committed to diversity, with the idea that the workforce in every country where the company operates should reflect the local ethnic and social mix. Recruitment policies are tailored to this end and job ads are placed in magazines that are known to reach minorities like black and disabled people.

Among many other initiatives, the company's Global Sourcing Guidelines are designed to ensure that it does not buy products from sweatshops using – and often abusing – child labor. But Levi's has been sensitive in the way it has implemented the policy. According to one consultant who has worked with the company, examples include Bangladesh and Turkey, "where children were working for contractors, providing their family's only source of income. Levi's paid the contractors to keep them in school until they were 14; it costs them more, but it's a long-term view."

So, does Levi's ethical stance help motivate employees and sell more jeans? The answer appears to be that it does. But the company also appears to be the corporate equivalent of a Rorschach Test: what you see in Levi's very much depends on your own priorities and ethics. Some see a privately-held company with an attitude which would not be ethical if applied to a listed company – where the main goal is to maximize owner value. Others see the company as an early experiment in business ethics which will soon spread to many other companies, sectors, and countries.

The message is that the globalizing economy can be as vulnerable to well-targeted activism as were some national economies. The difference is that much more of the pressure on human rights and other ethical issues is now likely to be directed at major international companies rather than governments. And the problem here is clear. As Nike chief executive Philip Knight put it, "We're dealing with governments that are less than ideal." An interesting example of how a company can deal effectively with this new agenda is provided by Levi Strauss (see Case Study, p.134).

Volkswagen

Don't Steal Trade Secrets

It was a punishing blow. The loss of José Ignacio López, VW's head of purchasing and production optimization, came after VW chairman Ferdinand Piëch had fought a long, drawn-out battle with arch-competitor GM to save López's skin – and VW's own critically important cost-cutting drive. After four years at the VW wheel, Piëch had steered Europe's leading car-maker out of the ditch and onto the road to recovery.[15] But he had been enormously aided in the task by ace cost-cutter López, whom he had lured from GM and who, unfortunately, was subsequently charged by German prosecutors with stealing GM trade secrets.

The dispute between VW and GM had become highly personalized for the top managers of the two giant companies. "There is a sort of pathological hatred of López at GM," explained one motor industry analyst. "They will now want to get their pound of flesh and keep VW squirming." But there was much more to it than that. When López quit GM to become a top executive at VW, it was alleged that he had also taken with him top secrets covering such areas as supplier price lists, future GM products, and plans for a new experimental factory. GM not only wanted an apology from top VW management; it was also seeking damages running into hundreds of millions of dollars, perhaps even billions.

The case spotlighted the growing importance of information about the economic aspects of the entire life-cycle of the auto industry – and of other sectors (see Chapter 8). But it also came at an appalling time for VW. With materials accounting for up to 60% of the value of a vehicle, the company still had a long way to go with the process of cost-cutting that López had led. And, just as worryingly for Piëch and his supervisory board, VW was also one of the German companies that had recently decided to come clean about its wartime use of slave labor and other issues. A 1,056-page book by historian Hans Mommsen, *The Volkswagen Factory and Its Workers in the Third Reich*, details how VW used forced labor to build personnel carriers, mines, and other war materials. Piëch's father, Anton, had been plant manager at the time.

With a record like that, you would have thought that VW in general, and Ferdinand Piëch in particular, would have been trying to be squeaky clean in all of their business dealings. Did they simply not know what was going on? Did Piëch, like many of his countrymen before him, choose not to know? Or perhaps competition, as the modern version of war, forces so many compromises that in the end the ethical boundaries blur in business brains?

Astra USA

Don't Tolerate Sexual Harassment

Companies faced with ethical challenges often seek to lay the blame on individuals. But, it is fair to ask, would the unethical behavior have surfaced and flourished if the corporate culture had been better attuned to the values and expectations of wider society? This question was raised repeatedly when the US subsidiary of the giant Swedish drugmaker Astra was accused of tolerating widespread sexual harassment and other abuses.

Following an exposé published by *Business Week*, the parent company suspended Lars Bildman, for 15 years head of Astra USA. Astra group chief executive Hakan Mogren said that Bildman had "abused his position" and developed an "unacceptable leadership style." More specifically, former female employees with Astra USA alleged that they had been fondled or required to accompany male executives to bars, nightclubs, and hotel suites. A female sales representative with the company agreed, describing Astra USA as "a sick company."

Astra, now part of AstraZeneca claimed that the problems were the result of "a single man who abused his power." The company also alleged that Bildman had spent $2 million of its money on renovating three houses he owned. If it could be shown that the parent company knew – or perhaps even suspected – that these problems were part of the company's culture, any employee successfully suing would win very much higher damages. But, as *Business Week* put it:

> "To some degree, demonizing Bildman may serve to deflect blame from Astra itself. Many outsiders believe that Bildman could not have run amok for most of his 15 years at the helm of the US unit if he had been properly supervised by the parent company."

The same is true of Nick Leeson at Baring's, clearly, or of José Ignacio López at VW.

The Body Shop International

Don't Let Hype Outrun Performance

Paradoxically, as mainstream business begins to wake up to the ethical challenge long advanced by companies like ice-cream makers Ben &

Jerry's and cosmetics group the Body Shop, so some of these pioneering, "alternative" companies are themselves coming under ethical fire.[16] These companies may be almost at the other end of the ethical spectrum from an I. G. Farben, yet they are also being attacked for sins of commission or omission. The Body Shop, for example, has been attacked in relation to the way it was set up, its trading practices, and most particularly for its "Trade Not Aid" development projects – now renamed "Community Trade."

When Jon Entine wrote his article "Shattered Image" for the magazine *Business Ethics*, he challenged Body Shop founder Anita Roddick's claims for the company's social, ethical, and environmental goals, comparing them unfavourably to the company's actual performance. The Body Shop fought back with a barrage of dossiers and letters denouncing both Entine and the magazine. The result was that the article was never published in the company's home country and the controversy faded. But the Body Shop, shaken, pushed ahead with an extensive survey of the company's stakeholders – initiated before the controversy broke. The results appeared in the form of the ethical auditing, and social statements in its 1995 *Values Report* (Case Study, p.139).

Like Ben & Jerry's, the ethical ice-cream maker, the Body Shop had found that it is dangerous to allow a gap to open up between the myth a company weaves about its commitment and ambitions and the day-to-day realities of operations. As US academic Kirk Hanson wrote in his evaluation of the company:

> "Any company which makes socially responsible claims a key element in its marketing will be scrutinized to a much greater extent than a company which does not. The company must demonstrate extraordinary transparency and a willingness to hear and act on criticism of any dimension of its behavior."

Behind the Parables

Each of these half-dozen case studies underscores a basic fact of human life. First, even the best-run companies can come unstuck when their values are seen to be out of alignment with society's values. Second, every business community has its actual and potential criminals, generally individuals but sometimes entire company boards. Third, and most worryingly, when societies mutate under extreme conditions

---

CASE STUDY   **THE BODY SHOP INTERNATIONAL, UK:
DAMNED IF WE DO, DAMNED IF WE DON'T**

"We went into the social audit with a sense of 'damned if we do, damned
if we don't,'" said Body Shop founders Anita and Gordon Roddick in the
foreword to the social statement – which formed part of the company's
innovative 1995 *Values Report*.[16] They also noted their long-standing
belief that "business is primarily about human relationships. We take the
view that the more we listen to our stakeholders and the more we involve
them in decision-making, the better our business will run." The question,
then, is how to measure the quality of these relationships.

The company had been attacked by a US journalist for alleged failures
to live up to its declared ethical and business principles. Although Anita
Roddick had declared her support for social auditing before the Body
Shop was attacked, this challenge was undoubtedly a key spur for the
134-page social statement. This reviewed the results of surveys of, and interviews with, some ten different stakeholders groups, including employees, shareholders, customers, franchisees, suppliers, and NGOs.

Some parts of the document may have made painful reading for senior
managers, but the surveys also showed strong support for the company's
values and values-based training. With its environmental, ethical, and
animal welfare statements, in addition to the social statement, the *Values
Report* is the closest we have yet seen any company get to triple bottom
line reporting. The report is a must-read, or at least a must-skim, for anyone trying to work out where stakeholder capitalism might take us.

---

companies can be effectively programmed to carry out what most reasonable people would consider to be the "work of the devil." Given these
facts, it is clear that we ignore the issue of corporate values at our peril.

What's New, Gurus?

Wealth Creation Needs Values

So values are important, but are they really crucial to the long-term
future of capitalism? Or are they, instead, little more than flies in the
economic ointment? Can business afford to leave this area to company
public affairs professionals and industry chaplains? The answers to

these questions, to paraphrase Charles Hampden-Turner and Fons Trompenaars in *The Seven Cultures of Capitalism*,[18] are yes, no and absolutely not.

Based on a questionnaire survey of 15,000 senior managers in the USA, the UK, France, Germany, Sweden, the Netherlands, and Japan, the book explains how different business cultures and value systems influence behavior and chances of success. All seven countries call themselves capitalist and subscribe to a free enterprise philosophy. But there, it turns out, the similarities end. When Hampden-Turner and Trompenaars focused on day-to-day details, such as the meaning found in work, styles of managing employees, attitudes towards stakeholders, negotiating tactics, and so on, they found that the differences were unexpectedly wide. Now that we see "world competition between rival cultures of capitalism," it is more important than ever to understand these differences if we are to catalyze and direct the sustainability transition.

The first surprise is that wealth creation, it turns out, "is in essence a moral act," driven by values. These values, in turn, flow from national and corporate cultures. "In any culture," we learn:

> "a deep structure of beliefs is the invisible hand that regulates economic activity. These cultural preferences, or values, are the bedrock of national identity and the source of economic strengths – and weaknesses."

The failure of so many economists to properly understand wealth creation, Hampden-Turner and Trompenaars argue, flows from the fact that they have studied how people use money, not why they do this or what their motives may be. "Economics," they conclude:

> "is so concerned with counting and itemizing that it has lost sight of the one component, almost unmeasurable, that makes all economic activity possible: human relationships. Behind every economic transaction are people making choices, acting on their values, giving one thing high priority, another one low."

Each of the seven nations evaluated turns out to have its own unique combination of values. "This value set is an economic fingerprint," Hampden-Turner and Trompenaars argue, which "correlates with specific types of economic achievement and failure." In a world aspiring to achieve sustainable development, an in-depth understanding of these differences – and of the best ways of managing them – is clearly going to be essential.

Indeed, as Hampden-Turner and Trompenaars point out, the environmental revolution described in Chapter 3 itself resulted from a values meltdown in the main capitalist nations. Business people schooled in analytic skills rather than holistic perceptions knew the "price of everything" but "the value of nothing." As a result, the world of business and industry was seen to be "prosaic, ugly, and uninspiring." Through the 1960s and early 1970s, millions of young Europeans, Scandinavians, and North Americans who might otherwise have played a key role in transforming their economies "turned their backs on business as a worthwhile commitment." Sadly, however powerful a draw the sustainability agenda may ultimately prove, "a decade of disenchantment is not easily recoverable."

The Challenge of Social Sustainability

The third guru whose ideas we will briefly review here is Professor Tom Gladwin. He comes at the issue from a different angle. "After devoting my entire career toward bringing industry into harmony with nature," he recently told a gathering of senior business people, "I have become increasingly convinced that the more difficult challenge lies in bringing industry into harmony with people."[19]

Whereas most business organizations are comfortable with the economic and (increasingly) environmental bottom lines, Gladwin notes that the same cannot be said for the third – social – bottom line of sustainability. Eco-efficiency, he accepts, is a necessary condition for fully sustainable development, but far from a sufficient one. "Genuine sustainability," he argues, "also demands poverty alleviation, population stabilization, female empowerment, employment creation, human rights observance and opportunity redistribution on a massive scale." On the environmental front, he suggests, there is good news. "The incentives pushing and pulling for the greening of industry are increasingly strong and positive." But the same cannot be said on the social front. Here, "the signals being sent to industry by global economic forces for enhanced human and community development are variously weak or negative." So, the eco-resource challenge may prove to be the relatively easy part of the sustainability transformation, while the socio-economic challenge looks likely to be more intractable.

Gladwin is not simply talking about ways of understanding cultural diversity or of handling outrage. He calls for "a much deeper, soul searching, revolutionary and indeed painful process of transforming the moral order." In short, a radical redefinition of the social contract between business and society.

Sustainability, in this definition, represents a fundamental paradigm shift. It will transform human values, political visions and the societal "rules of the game" from:

> "economic efficiency towards social equity, from individual rights to collective obligations, from selfishness to community, from quantity to quality, from separation to interdependence, from exclusion to equality of opportunity, from men to women, from luxury to necessity, from repression to freedom, from today to tomorrow, and from growth that benefits a few to genuine human development that benefits us all."

Challenge to the World

But the problem that international companies can trip over is that even if different cultures decide to pursue sustainability, they are very likely to define and pursue it in different ways. So what chance is there of developing a global consensus on business ethics? The answer is that although globalization and information technology seem to be driving us in this direction, the transition is likely to prove a very tough challenge. Even if we eventually achieve elements of a global consensus, it will take decades, even generations, and the risks for companies straddling different cultures look set to grow rather than shrink.

One thinker who has been trying to sketch out elements of a global ethic is the Swiss theologian Hans Küng, director of the Global Ethic Foundation, based in Tübingen, Germany. He argues that the need for consensus has become critical in the wake of the rapid changes in technology, science, and global trade.[20] "Business must have its place, must be efficient, must make a profit," he argues. "But an interest *only* in business, as an interest *only* in oneself, is dangerous. The economy is not an end in itself: it is there to serve human needs."[21]

On globalization, Küng notes that it is an "ambiguous process." He accepts that it is inevitable, but argues that:

> "it has limits and it can be controlled. Since we have globalisation of capital, we must seek to globalise the ethical principles which are above it. A struggle for profit is ethically legitimate *only* if higher values prevail."

Ethics, Küng explains, "is not a description of the world. Ethics is a challenge to the world." In the past, religions have attempted to codify ethics, but have all-too-often ended up inspiring intolerance, hatred, cruelty, and war. Now, as we move into the 21st century, "pure capitalism endangers the basic social contract and will inevitably provoke a backlash."

As a result, Küng believes, there is a growing need for a basic minimum ethic, to guide international politics and trade. And what would it involve? According to Küng, "A global ethic means a fundamental consensus on binding values, irrevocable standards and personal attitudes which can be shared by people of all religions and also by nonbelievers." Unfortunately, the major religions have found it impossible to reach consensus on specific ethical issues, including contraception, abortion, and euthanasia. But, Küng insists, "the great religious traditions agree on most basic principles, as they have been formulated for the first time with the Declaration Toward a Global Ethic." Adopted by the Parliament of the World's Religions in Chicago in 1993, the Declaration enshrines two fundamental demands: "Every human being must be treated humanely. And what you do not wish done to yourself, do not do to others, which is known as the golden rule in most religions."

Whether, like Tom Gladwin, we call these "rules of the game" or, like Hans Küng, "golden rules," it is increasingly clear that sustainable capitalism will depend on a shared understanding not only of the importance of values but also of the adoption of specific principles. A tall order indeed, even if all politicians and business leaders were aware of the problems and committed to tackling them. So how much of this challenge is visible to those on the bridge of these great corporate supertankers as they surge forward into the third millennium?

Boardroom Views

Shell-shocked

1995 shocked Shell rigid: first the Brent Spar controversy, then Nigeria. Top managers were forced into a rapid rethink. "The fact that parts of Shell have been in business for 100 years is no guarantee that the future will be OK too," warned Cor Herkströter, chairman of the company's committee of managing directors. At first, Shell thought in terms of persuading society that the company's values and operating principles were sound. But the scale of the reaction ultimately convinced top management that this was not going to be enough.

During the following months, I heard a number of Shell executives comment on what seemed to be the quite disproportionate scale of the public reaction to the two controversies. My own view was that there was no mystery about these reactions. Working with Dow Europe, SustainAbility had already identified deep-seated trends which seemed to indicate a fundamental shift in society's values. The first trend was a decline in the legitimacy of governments and other political institutions; the second was a growing tendency for product life-cycles to become more transparent to outside scrutiny, an issue to which we will return in Chapter 8; and the third we summed up in the phrase "*values shift*".

When the events of 1995 began to unfold, it appeared increasingly obvious that Shell was going to be the first major casualty of all three trends. The giant oil company had itself begun to detect warning signs in 1994 – but failed to react in time. Market research carried out on the Shell brand during the development of the company's new retail visual identity revealed that among significant sections of the West European population, and particularly among the young, Shell was seen as being (to use the company's own words) "somewhat old-fashioned and out of touch."

After the shocks of 1995, Shell launched a series of roundtable meetings, taking in 14 locations in Europe, the USA, the Middle East, the Asia-Pacific region, Australasia, Africa, and Latin America. The meetings, in places as different as Oslo and Seoul, each brought together around a dozen Shell staff face-to-face with senior figures from business, NGOs, the media, academe, and government for a "full and frank exchange of views."

What really marked out this "Society's Changing Expectations" initiative was that Shell was being dramatically more open than in the past. "This initiative could probably have been carried out in confidence," allowed Herkströter:

"but to have done so would have struck at the heart of what it is about. We work in 'society' around the world. Can we hope to successfully touch base with that society if we do something like this, and then try to keep it quiet?"

To succeed, stakeholder engagement initiatives must be genuinely interactive. "I firmly believe that you do not only extract value, because then the process does not really work," Herkströter explained. "You have to make absolutely certain that if you involve others, particularly third parties, you give value as well."

Not a New Challenge

In the wake of the Brent Spar controversy, I had found myself drawn into the debate. As the signatory of a letter to *The Times*,[22] I had positioned SustainAbility alongside those who argued that Shell's decision on the Brent Spar had been wrong, but for new reasons. Before long, I had a number of opportunities to observe Shell's reactions to the new values-based agenda at close quarters.

With a group of colleagues from organizations like the New Economics Foundation and Traidcraft, I helped Shell UK think through the issues around social accounting, auditing, and reporting. Separately, I took part in a session during which Shell UK's managing director, Chris Fay, exposed his senior management team to external challenge. One of my own questions to Chris Fay focused on the extent to which Shell could see the values shift taking place among the company's own younger employees And, on a third occasion, Paul Hawken, Geoff Lye, and I spent two days with senior Shell International people working through what the company should be doing in response to the new challenges.

But, to my mind, by far the most interesting Shell perspective came from Cor Herkströter, musing on the lessons learned from 1995.[23] The problems Shell was facing, he stressed, were not as new as some critics might assume. In earlier centuries, Dutch multinational companies – among them the Compagnie van Verre, the Vereenigde Oost-Indische Compagnie and the Nederlandsche Handel Maatschappij – also faced the challenge of operating in different cultures. "Managers back then struggled with clashing value systems, conflicting moral standards and rapid technical change," Herkströter recalled, "along with their primary responsibility of producing a good product and a decent profit!"

The 20th century, he noted, had been "particularly bloody." Catastrophes, disruptions, and wars had repeatedly tested Shell's management. "In the process," he said, "we have always had to face up to many dilemmas – to the questions of where to invest, how to balance differing demands and how to meet contradictory expectations." But the late 1990s saw a new set of challenges. "The vast majority of us are living in relative peace and prosperity," he continued:

> "yet, for reasons that we find difficult to identify, the institutions with which we grew up no longer appear to be as strong and healthy as they once were. Why are they not operating in the ways we have come to expect? Why are we coming up against problems that, with the best will in the world, we cannot seem to assess correctly?"

His answer, as we have seen, was that there appeared to be a ghost in the global system. Take the Brent Spar controversy. Shell had gone through a three year process to identify the "best practical environmental option" for disposing of the structure. Deep sea disposal emerged as the best option, satisfying all the appropriate regulations and being approved by the UK Government. "But," as Herkströter put it:

> "we found that what appeared to be the best option in the UK was not acceptable elsewhere. We were caught between two different approaches to the environment. The public reacted in a way that we did not expect and the pressure groups used the Spar as a symbol in a way we did not anticipate."

At least for the top brass at Shell, the two key factors behind this emerging "ghost" were the communications revolution and the gradual loss of trust in established institutions. The two, it turns out, are closely interrelated. Earlier generations learnt about the world directly from figures of authority – their parents, teachers, coaches, and local political leaders. The media were important, but they also tended to be more deferential to authority, less given to attacking established institutions. How things have changed.

New technologies enable us all to compare what these authority figures say to the thoughts and perspectives of different, competing authority figures. As a result of the transparency trend examined in Chapter 7, the public has suffered a "loss of innocence." As Herkströter concluded:

> "once it is gone, it can never be regained. Today the world visible to any one person, anywhere on the planet, is becoming increasingly fragmented. The speed and immediacy of modern communications ensures that this process will continue. National governments, political parties, institutionalised religions, academic institutions, will never regain the authority they used to have – that ability to exclusively define the world view of large segments of the population."

Imperialist or Relativist?

Internally, Shell's own management culture was also clearly responsible for a fair proportion of the company's problems. The company, according to Herkströter, suffered from "a type of technical arrogance which is rather common in companies with a strong technical base.

Most of us in Royal Dutch/Shell come from a scientific, technological background. That type of education, along with our corporate culture, teach us that we must identify a problem, isolate it, and then fix it. That sort of approach works well with a physical problem – but is not so useful when we are faced with, say, a human rights issue. For most engineering problems there is a correct answer. For most social and political dilemmas there is a range of possible answers – almost all compromises. So, starting off with a strong, scientifically grounded mind-set, we tended to misjudge some of the softer issues and consequently make mistakes."

Which was odd, given that Shell had a long head start. Its ethical standards were published in the 1970s, in the form of a Statement of General Business Principles. These have underpinned the company's efforts to build a reputation for honesty and integrity, but were subsequently revisited in the wake of the 1995 controversies to see whether they were likely to be well-tuned to the needs and expectations of the 21st century.

Shell – along with many other companies – will have to wrestle with some fundamental ethical dilemmas. "The question of so-called double standards is a classic example," notes Herkströter:

> "There are groups who call for one set of standards – whether it be for wages, environment or any other issue – to be applied world wide. It seems that some people believe that their values are universal and that they can be applied no matter what the cost or the social implications for those concerned."

The danger for international companies is that they will inevitably and increasingly find themselves uncomfortably squeezed between those Shell dubs the "moral relativists," who argue that they should apply local standards, and those it sees as "moral imperialists" – who would impose a single standard on the whole globe. Both are wrong, Shell would argue. Certainly recent controversies have shown that what is acceptable in one country can be totally unacceptable in other countries. And developing countries and transition economies will often insist that they must strike a different balance between triple bottom line priorities – to build or protect their competitive edge. All of which can leave the multinational corporation as the "piggy in the middle."

These issues are not simply philosophical: they are fundamental to the future of capitalism and to the societies that have chosen to develop capitalist economies. Part of the answer, as we will see, lies in new forms of social accountability, part in some of the new types of partnership now emerging between such companies and their critics (see Chapter 9), and part in new approaches to corporate governance (Chapter 11). But in a world of continuing economic, social, and political diversity there will be no total solutions.

Bubbling Under

Drawing the Line

The evidence suggests that the global collision of value systems will intensify in the future. A good place to look for signals on how this debate is going to evolve is the World Trade Organization (WTO), which is charged with wiping out barriers to global trade. The late 1990s saw a widening philosophical gulf between the developed and developing countries on the role of the WTO. For example, the US Clinton Administration, pressured by unions and corporations, has been pushing to remove "invisible" barriers such as corruption, which drives up the costs of entering some markets, and poor labor conditions, which US unions argue give Asian producers an unfair advantage.[24]

Asian trade negotiators, however, see western pressure on such issues as an unwarranted intrusion into their societies and cultures. "Where do you draw the line?" demanded Aznam Yusof, deputy director general at the Malaysian Institute of Strategic and International Studies. "Do we discuss the climate or traffic jams? You could go on and on."

These are fair questions. And, at least in the world of business, international research shows that there are major differences between the values of executives based in different world regions. When Wirthlin Worldwide surveyed executives in Asia and the USA, for example, it asked respondents which of 17 "universal values" they considered to be most important on a six-point scale.[25] Of the values, only two appeared high on both lists: hard work and self-reliance. North Americans tended to prefer freedom of expression, personal freedom, and individual rights, while Asians were more likely to prioritize respect for learning, openness to new ideas, and accountability. There were differences, too, within world regions. In Asia, the Japanese were much more inclined to favour harmony, Singaporeans an orderly society, the Taiwanese self-reliance, and Thais the achievement of financial success.

Future corporate strategies must clearly recognize this diversity. But Shell's experience suggests both that companies with international operations need to heed the call for the observation of basic triple bottom line principles wherever they may operate and that the early years of the 21st century will see information technology and other trends driving a continuing convergence between the values of different – but probably not all – world regions.

Daddy, Can I Have the Keys to the Industry?

The question appeared as the title of a *Business Week* profile of the Suharto family's stranglehold on Indonesian politics and industry. Corruption may be a way of life in some parts of the world, but it will increasingly be in the headlines as globalization proceeds. "In the Indonesian version of Camelot," reported *Business Week*, "it is well-nigh impossible to get a deal done without a Suharto clan-member as ally, agent, or partner."[26] US, Japanese or European companies that refuse to play the game lose out on huge new opportunities in such areas as telecommunications, power plants, finance, automobiles, and heavy industry. "Without them, you wouldn't have a project," said one foreign executive with a major investment in the country. "It's as simple as that."

So called *quanxi* capitalism, or "crony capitalism," is endemic in many parts of Asia.[27] In such countries as Thailand and Indonesia, military and political groups control access to markets and demand cash payments, "royalties," and other inducements for permission to invest. As the Green Cross AIDS scandal illustrated, in Japan and Korea crony capitalism takes the form of giant *keiretsu*, formed of interconnected corporations allied with government ministries. In China, once-public property is now often controlled by People's Liberation Army officers – and local payments are seen as an inevitable part of doing business.

What can be done? The simplest position for ethically challenged companies would be to steer clear of countries like China and Indonesia altogether. But few companies are prepared to go this far. In terms of social and political sustainability, foreign investors have been calculating that whoever followed President Suharto would almost certainly come from the clan or its supporters – and would be wary of seriously disrupting the Indonesian economy. Very few Indonesian politicians, military leaders, or businessmen have escaped the net of patronage and that means, as one western diplomat put it, that "No matter who ascends the presidency, he will be part of the elite and caught up in all this."

History has an uncomfortable knack of taking most of us by surprise. But assume that the diplomat was right. Would it be better to be outside and free of blame, or inside working for change? In a globalizing economy, made increasingly transparent by the Internet and other emerging technologies, these issues will tax growing numbers of companies and business leaders. And the sheer speed with which such controversies can erupt will ensure that growing numbers of corporate boards will be discomfited.

Winners, Losers

Winners

The new agenda for business will increasingly revolve around values and ethics. Successful companies will be better at identifying, understanding, and responding to the values of those they work with and serve. Their number will include a growing proportion of businesses that have carried out social audits, to find out how they are viewed by stakeholders – and what those stakeholders' expectations are likely to be in future.

Figure 5.1 illustrates the fact that previous values shifts, driven initially by "Innovators" and "Early Adopters," have moved through the "Early" and "Late" Majority stages to the point where they are ignored

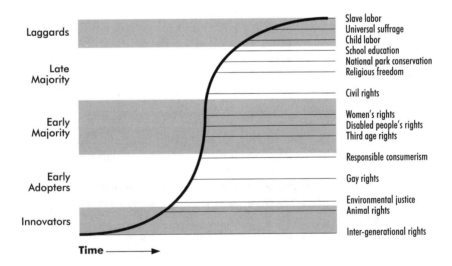

FIGURE 5.1   The Impending Values Shift

FROM "GLOBAL CONSUMER" TO "WORLD CITIZEN"

Global Consumer		World Citizen
Me	➜	We
More	➜	Enough
Materialism	➜	Holism
Quantity	➜	Quality
Greed	➜	Need
Short-term	➜	Long-term
Rights	➜	Responsibilities

FIGURE 5.2   Values for the Future

only by small numbers of individual, organizational or national "Laggards." Among the values likely to move rapidly up the "S" curve over the next few decades are responsible consumerism, business ethics, environmental justice, and inter-generational rights. Figure 5.2 spotlights some of the likely underlying transitions.

There have been self-declared ethical companies since the Industrial Revolution, but their number has been growing fairly rapidly in recent years as the baby boom generation move into the top echelons of business. Among their models are Bill Hewlett and Dave Packard of Hewlett-Packard. Indeed, one of the most accessible books describing the evolution of a company's ethics is *The HP Way*, by David Packard.[28] As explained in Chapters 10 and 11, Packard – who died in 1995 – was also among those who recognized the problems of developing a long-term vision and moving to address triple bottom line responsibilities at the same time as keeping Wall Street analysts happy.

But how, in the midst of all of this, can we judge the direction and pace of change? One area to watch will be the emerging ethical investment sector. Once led by organizations well outside the business mainstream, we are now seeing the sector attracting well-known financial names. Inspired by the "Tomorrow's Company" inquiry, for example, Kleinwort Benson Investment Management announced that it planned to raise £100 million for a fund dedicated to identifying 80 UK companies taking a stringent stakeholder approach to their businesses.[29] According to Kleinwort's Paul Sheehan:

"It makes sense. The companies that have clear values, invest more in training employees and put money back into the communities actually buying their products will have more success over the long term than those still caught up in a bottom-line-only culture."

For most companies, however, values and ethics will only be one component of the winning formula. Brave experiments will be needed to work out just how far particular companies or industries can push the envelope at any moment in time. In France, Mouvement E Leclerc – the hypermarket chain – experimented with advertisements showing a range of social problems, including youth unemployment, blighted housing estates, and crime, and explaining what its customers could do about them.[30] The message was, "You may think everything has gone to pot. Let us show you what we can do." As an example, the company became the first of the main hypermarket chains to stop selling hunting rifles and ammunition, a move it said would mean sacrificing Fr100 million (£13 million) a year.

It remains to be seen how such experiments work out in reality, but from such small initial steps a 21st century values revolution may be in the process of forming. Whether or not it ultimately succeeds, one group of professionals seems bound to win out. Ethical auditors may be thin on the ground in today's world, but the business of helping companies clean up their ethical acts can only grow.

Some analysts even calculate that this is already a $1 billion-a-year industry. Certainly, ethical overhauls can cost a good deal of money.[31] After running foul of regulators, one small US utility – Orange & Rockland Utilities – hired Price Waterhouse and a law firm to do an independent investigation. A team of nearly 50 produced a 1,200-page report costing some $7 million. Consultants charged over $200,000 to design an internal ethical watchdog system. And they recommended opening a two-person ethics office, at an annual cost of $175,000. This is, perhaps, an expensive way to develop a corporate conscience, and there are definitely much cheaper ways of addressing the same problem. But the company's president, Larry S. Broedsky argued that the investment had paid off: "There's no question that we have regained the confidence of the regulators."

Even the World Bank has now appointed an executive with a brief to explore the links between values, even spirituality, and the bottom lines of companies and the health of entire national economies. Richard Barrett landed the new job of World Bank values co-ordinator and is convinced that companies can help themselves if they successfully help employees to find more meaning and vision in their jobs. It is perhaps no accident that such appointments are being made in the wake of massive downsizing around the world. "Corporate fitness is great,"

Barrett says, "but what worries me is it's not being done with values in mind."[32] For any chief executive pondering whether to embark on this path, he notes, "Personal transformation is a prerequisite to corporate transformation. It must begin at the top."

Losers

There *will* be losers. Some of them will be those who ignored the social and ethical dimensions of the new business agenda, some those who tried to adapt but failed. In the new world order, even companies that – like Shell – regularly delight the financial analysts will risk coming unstuck where they fail to fully recognize the other bottom lines of sustainable development. Any company which, like Texaco (Case Study, p.154) or Mitsubishi Motor Manufacturing of America (MMMA), violates emerging expectations risks being forced to examine their "very soul."

In fact, MMMA's disastrous mishandling of a US sexual harassment suit by the Equal Employment Opportunity Commission unintentionally illustrated the dangers that companies face as they expand into foreign cultures. For years, Japanese firms have been warned that they should do a better job of absorbing top American and European executives and giving them real authority. Unfortunately, most Japanese companies continue to suffer from a deeply ingrained "us *vs.* them" mentality.[33] Ask some Japanese companies how many people they employ and they often count only Japanese nationals. Most also insist that key decisions are taken in Tokyo. And these problems, in turn, generally mean that Japanese companies have great difficulty in attracting top foreign talent.

Different parts of Mitsubishi in the US report separately to Tokyo, which meant that experienced Mitsubishi people in other parts of the company were kept out of the loop until too late. In the time-delay created by this structure, local managers tried to frighten MMMA employees into staying silent by threatening their jobs – and organized an ill-judged employee demonstration which simply succeeded in turning the issue into front-page news.

By contrast, some companies, including some profiled in these pages, will decide to push the ethics envelope faster and further. Levi Strauss can do so partly because it is privately held, but there is every likelihood that other companies will choose to adopt at least some of the ideas that such pioneers have helped place on the agenda. But they should recognize the risks involved. The experience of the Body Shop International shows that the very act of promoting a company's social conscience can

CASE STUDY   **TEXACO, USA:**
                              EXAMINING THE CORPORATE SOUL

Texaco provided a warning to the world. Shareholders saw $1 billion wiped from their shares on the day the scandal broke. *The New York Times* ran the story on its front page, reporting that senior managers at the giant US oil company had shredded documents relevant to a race discrimination lawsuit. Following stonewalling over a number of years by the company, tapes finally showed Texaco executives allegedly calling black employees "niggers" and "black jelly beans" as they discussed plans for destroying evidence. On 15 November 1996, the company settled the suit, filed on behalf of 1,400 employees, for $115 million in cash plus salary adjustments for the plaintiffs and other expenses.[34]

Some commentators saw the outcome as a victory for equal rights, others as one more example of trial by media ordeal. Texaco CEO Peter I. Bijur attracted a good deal of media attention with his promises to "wipe out" discrimination in the company and to examine its "very soul." One reason for the controversy was that drilling for and refining oil does not require much in the way of consumer research, with the result that oil companies are often less in touch with people issues than are consumer products companies like Procter & Gamble or Unilever.

Worse, Texaco had been forced to declare bankruptcy following a failed court battle against Pennzoil and then spent years fighting off corporate raider Carl Icahn, paying down debt, and shedding operations and employees. People issues had been sidelined. Ironically, the whistleblower on the racial abuse front was himself a downsized employee, suffering either from remorse or post-downsizing anger.

"Corporate directors typically have paid scant attention to workplace diversity," noted the *Wall Street Journal Europe*, "largely because they rarely viewed it as a bottom-line concern. But now, as civil-rights activists revive the push for affirmative action, boards are starting to scrutinize management's diversity efforts." One possible outcome could be more female and minority directors on company boards. "You are going to take this [diversity] issue much more seriously if you have someone at the table who has a personal and social interest in making sure those issues are addressed," was the way one recruitment expert put it.

One of the few institutional investors to have voted for increased diversity before the storm broke was New York State comptroller H. Carl McCall, who managed a portfolio including 1.2 million Texaco shares.

)

"As shareholders, we have a responsibility to demand an accounting from companies on how they plan to deal with these kinds of issues, because it's clear that if a company has an image of diversity, it's more acceptable to consumers and therefore more profitable,"

he explained. "The market reacts negatively to companies where there's a perception that the culture supports discrimination."

The acid test, however, will be whether in the future other mainstream investors bring more pressure to bear on Texaco and other companies on the diversity issue than they did in the past.

attract attacks either from out-and-out trouble-makers, or from those who have deeper – or simply different – definitions of the ethical principles at stake.

There is no way that business alone can reverse the erosion of trust, or rebuild society's sense of shared values. But business success is going to depend increasingly both on a strong sense of internal purpose and values within companies, and on the congruence of these values with those of a growing range of external stakeholders. Such stakeholders will want to hold the companies they invest in, work for, or buy from to account for their performance against the triple bottom line. The problem for multinational companies, as Shell knows to its cost, is that the balance between the different elements of the triple bottom line will be struck in very different ways in the various world regions – and in the same region at different points in time.

Three Keys to the 21st Century

The second sustainability revolution focuses on values, requiring that we understand and use the following keys to sustainable enterprise:

- ◆ First, values are essential to wealth creation – and will also be central to the sustainability transition. Human and social relationships are often ignored in all of this, but now need to be brought to center stage. And, while many values are shared in cultures around the world, the sustainable development community must learn to recognize – and work with – diversity in values.
- ◆ Second, integrating the triple bottom line into corporate strategies can bring new values to the fore. Companies should conduct regu-

lar social and/or ethical audits of their operations and plans, reporting publicly on progress. Economic values (e.g. "Don't steal industrial secrets") may be recognized by some companies, but are not observed by all. Social and ethical values (e.g. "Don't use slave or child labor," "Don't tolerate sexual harassment") are also evolving in some countries. Meanwhile, the environmental and sustainability values pioneered by a few companies are further from universal acceptance, but are likely to gain wider support.

♦ Third, sustainable development will require that we move rapidly to address such issues as population stabilization, poverty alleviation, employment creation, female empowerment, and human rights observance. Because these goals are ethical, social, and political, they will need to be addressed by society as a whole – but focused, sustained business support will be a necessary condition of success. Companies should consider whether they need to become "social activists," driving new thinking and values down through their value chains.

Notes

1. C. A. J. Herkströter, *Dealing with contradictory expectations – the dilemmas facing multinationals*, 11 October 1996, Amsterdam, published as a paper by Group External Affairs, Shell International, 1996.
2. Hardin Tibbs, correspondence with the author, 1994.
3. Thomas A. Stewart, "Why value statements don't work," *Fortune*, 10 June 1996.
4. Richard Adams, Jane Carruthers and Sean Hamil, *Changing Corporate Values: A guide to social and environmental policy and practice in Britain's top companies*, Kogan Page, 1991.
5. R. Angleheart, *World Values Survey: Modernization and post-modernization*, Princeton University Press, 1997.
6. Stephen Amidon, "A triumph for boardroom values," *Sunday Times*, 26 May 1996.
7. Environmental Investigation Agency, *Corporate Power, Corruption and the Destruction of the World's Forests*, 1996. See also: David Harrison, "Loggers in chainsaw massacre," *Observer*, 8 September 1996.
8. Joanna Robertson, "Penny drops in Albania as savings scam collapses," *Guardian*, 21 December 1996.
9. Alan Abelson, "It can't happen here," *Barron's*, 17 March 1997.
10. Theresa Waldrop, "Corporate confessions," *Newsweek*, 21 August 1995.
11. Edith Hill Updike, "Anatomy of a tragedy," *Business Week*, 11 March 1996; Anthony Spaeth, "Ceremony of blood," *Time*, 25 March 1996.

12. Glenn Burkins, "US Labor Department cites firms for buying sweatshop products," *Wall Street Journal Europe*, 22 May 1996; Nancy Gibbs, "Cause celeb," *Time*, 17 June 1996; Mark C. Clifford, Michael Shari and Linda Himelstein, "Pangs of conscience," *Business Week*, 29 July 1996; Roger Cowe, "Reebok leads child labour purge," *Guardian*, 28 September 1996; Kasra Naji, "Dhaka bows to pressure on child labour," *Financial Times*, 2 November 1996; Frances Williams, "Rise in child labour to 250m," *Financial Times*, 12 November 1996; Mark C. Clifford, "Keep the heat on sweatshops," *Business Week*, 23 December 1996.

13. *Child Labour: Targeting the intolerable*, International Labour Organization, 1996.

14. Rhymer Rigby, "Jeans genius," *Management Today*, November 1996.

15. David Woodruff and Kathleen Kerwin, "Can VW ride out the storm?," *Business Week*, 25 November 1996; Haig Simonian, "A big blow for Europe's biggest car manufacturer," *Financial Times*, 30 November 1996; Haig Simonian and Andrew Fisher, "López quits VW over dispute with GM," *Financial Times*, 30 November 1996; Brandon Mitchener and Gabriella Stern, "VW and GM still face major disagreements in three-year dispute," *Wall Street Journal Europe*, 2 December 1996.

16. Roger Cowe and Jon Entine, "Fair enough?," *Guardian*, 14 December 1996.

17. The Body Shop International, *The Values Report*, 1996.

18. Charles Hampden-Turner and Fons Trompenaars, *The Seven Cultures of Capitalism*, Doubleday, 1993; Piatkus, 1994.

19. Thomas N. Gladwin, *Socio-economic Challenges of Social Sustainability*, Third Senior Executives' Seminar, "Sustainability and Profitability: Conflict or Convergence?," HRH The Prince of Wales' Business & the Environment Programme, Cambridge University, UK, 15–19 September 1996.

20. "New rules to live by," *Newsweek*, 12 August 1996.

21. John Lloyd, "Global enfant provocateur," *Financial Times*, 29 March 1997.

22. John Elkington (and Geoff Lye), "Pollution concerns over Brent Spar," Letters to the Editor,*The Times*, 20 June 1995.

23. C.A.J. Herkströter, *Dealing with Contradictory Expectations – the Dilemmas Facing Multinationals*, 11 October 1996, Amsterdam, published as a paper by Group External Affairs, Shell International, 1996.

24. Bruce Einhorn, Amy Borrus and William Echikson, "Why the WTO is stuck in the muck," *Business Week*, 16 December 1996.

25. Paul M. Sherer, "Executives are oceans apart on values," *Wall Street Journal Europe*, 5 March 1996.

26. "The Suharto Empire," *Business Week*, 19 August 1996.

27. "Crony capitalism takes its toll," *Business Week*, 22 July 1996.

28. David Packard, *The HP Way: How Bill Hewlett and I built our company*, HarperBusiness, 1995.

29. Ardyn Bernoth, "Companies show they care," *Sunday Times*, 8 December 1996.

30. Alex Duval Smith, "Hypermarket campaign puts conscience first," *Guardian*, 10 February 1996.

31. Mike France, Peter Elstrom and Mark Maremont, "Ethics for hire," *Business Week*, 15 July 1996.

32. Suzanne Miller, "World Bank turns to spirituality to increase profile and profits," *The European*, 31 October 1996.

33. Edith Hill Updike and William J. Holstein, "Mitsubishi and the 'cement ceiling,'" *Business Week*, 13 May 1996.

34. Mike France and Tim Smart, "The ugly talk on the Texaco tape," *Business Week*, 18 November 1996; Joann S. Lublin, "Texaco case causes a stir in boardrooms," *Wall Street Journal Europe*, 25 November 1996; Jolie Solomon, "Crisis management," *Newsweek*, 25 November 1996; Holman W. Jenkins Jnr, "Texaco ransoms its image for $176 million," *Wall Street Journal Europe*, 29 November 1996; and "Texaco: Lessons from a crisis-in-progress," *Business Week*, 2 December 1996.

TRANSPARENCY

No Hiding Place

Be warned: the same bowl that makes the corporate goldfish visible to the outside world can also distort – and the more extreme the viewer's angle of vision, the greater the distortion.

To work efficiently and effectively, markets need information. For decades, business resisted demands for greater corporate transparency in such areas as environmental protection and other triple bottom line priorities. Today, however, leading companies are competing with one another in a modern version of the Dance of the Seven Veils. The predominant paradigm is flipping from "closed" to "open."

Revolution	Focus	Old paradigm	❭	New paradigm
3	Transparency	Closed	❭	Open

"None of your business!" was the typical reply a few decades back when environmentalists and others asked leading companies for information on their operations and plans. And as the first sustainability revolution pushes business toward the globalized, accelerated, and hyper-competitive markets of the future, it would be natural to assume that commercial secrecy will become ever more important. This is true, up to a point.

Theft and leakage of corporate and industrial secrets in the US more than trebled between 1992 and 1995 – and may now be costing US companies alone $2 billion a month.[1] The VW *vs.* GM dispute discussed in Chapter 6 was an example of this deep running trend. The inevitable result is a growing focus on ways of keeping business secrets under wraps.

But the second – values – revolution is now pushing business in a completely different direction: towards openness and disclosure. As Shell put it in the wake of the Brent Spar and Nigeria controversies, we now increasingly live in "a CNN world." New information technologies, coupled with employee allegiance to much broader social agendas, mean that companies can no longer count on their ability to maintain secrecy over time. Nor are new values the only drivers: their effect is both fueled and amplified by parallel trends in such areas as information technology, disclosure rules, life-cycle assessments, and supplier challenges.

The days when Aristotle Onassis could tuck his whalers out of sight behind convenient icebergs are almost gone. New technologies and open borders render most forms of economic, environmental, and social abuse increasingly visible. Indeed, far from being drowned in a flood-tide of useless information, many of the world's citizens – thanks in large part to the public interest groups a growing number of them support – are becoming increasingly adept at keeping track of the activities of corporations and governments. The emergence of "green," "responsible," "political," or "vigilante" consumers is just one facet of this emerging megatrend.

This is a profound change from the early days of the environmental revolution. A surprising number of the books on my shelves from the 1970s and early 1980s have titles like *The Politics of Secrecy* or *Cover Up: The facts they didn't want you to know*.[2] *Cover Up*, published in 1981, was dedicated by its author, *New Ecologist* editor Nicholas Hildyard, to his niece – "in the hope she will grow up in a world which has learnt to live without cover-ups." Sorry, Nick, but as you know, cover-ups are still the stuff of political life and probably always will be. But these days the chances of sustaining them over time have shrunk dramatically.

Glasnost vs. Chernobyl

Secrecy almost always backfires in the environmental area. History has shown that too much secrecy damages the health not only of individuals but of nations. Indeed, the perils of living in countries wedded to secrecy have been powerfully illustrated by the fate of millions living in the lands once controlled by the Soviet Union. It is extraordinary to recall that even president Mikhail Gorbachev, fêted in the West as the architect of the *glasnost* policy of increased openness, was himself kept in the dark about the sheer enormity of the 1986 Chernobyl nuclear accident and of the radiation problems the USSR faced as a result.[3]

Despite the fact that the disaster had already been detected by Swedish scientists and American space satellites, the Soviet cover-up was determined and, unlike many of the fall-out victims, long-lived. Early assessments by the International Atomic Energy Agency (IAEA), based mainly on Soviet information, suggested that the immediate and long-term effects within the Soviet Union would be considerably less serious than had been feared. Outside the Soviet Union, the IAEA concluded, the impact would be negligible. Nothing, unfortunately, could have been further from the truth. By the tenth anniversary of the meltdown, the disaster was still growing and the real truth was only just beginning to emerge.

A report presented in 1995 by the secretary-general to the 50th UN general assembly revealed the extraordinary scale of the humanitarian, health, and economic impacts caused by the Chernobyl nuclear accident. "The lives and livelihoods of around 10 million people have already been affected by the disaster," Anthony Tucker reported:

"Half a million people have been displaced. Predictably, the abandoned villages and forests of the 30-kilometre exclusion zone around Chernobyl have become the wild, sinister, no-go haunt of criminal and bandit communities. But in Belarus, in the Russian Federation and in the Ukraine, where weather-determined fallout was greatest, agriculture is corrupted by contamination, there is massive social and industrial dislocation, and humanitarian, health and economic problems are of such immensity and complexity that they are beyond available resources. These are conditions that are perhaps comparable only to the aftermath of civil war."

As the radioactive plume worked its way around the world, it triggered public anxiety everywhere it went – or was suspected of having gone. The Swedish public stepped up its demands that the country's nuclear power stations be phased out, but elsewhere governments kept their heads down in the hope that the political storm would blow over. For most it did, but for those in the contaminated regions the nightmare had, literally, just begun. It was soon clear that contaminated land the size of England and Wales would be unworkable well into the 21st century. And, contrary to early claims that thyroid cancer would affect "just" one in a million infants (aged 0–3 years) in the highest fall-out areas, the latest data suggested that the actual figures would be closer to one in every four or five exposed infants.

Red Lake

Nor were the problems bequeathed by the old USSR simply nuclear in origin. A few months after the tenth anniversary of the Chernobyl nuclear accident, Greenpeace declared Lake Kaskovo, near the Russian industrial town of Dzerzhinsk, as the most chemically polluted lake in the world. Average life expectancy for people living near the lake was estimated at 42. According to the *Sunday Times*:

> "Green slime oozes from charred toxic waste barrels onto the thin layer of orange ice covering Lake Kaskovo; passing birds that mistake the lake for water die as soon as they hit the surface; rivers feeding the lake are red and bubbling with poison; countless babies in the area are born with deformities."[4]

So was this mere media hyperbole? No. This was the legacy of living in a "closed city," which did not even appear on the maps for many years. "For so long, we knew so little and said so little," said Serafim Krivin, who could recall the lake when it had contained trout – before Dzerzhinsk became the capital of the Soviet chemical industry.

But now, as the problems become common knowledge, many ordinary Russians are beginning to behave in very much the same way that their western counterparts have done for decades. In the central agricultural region of Kostroma, for example, local people voted against the completion of a nuclear power plant, left unfinished after the Chernobyl disaster. Although the project would have created 20,000 jobs in an area desperate for employment, local activists – many of them pensioners – persuaded more than 80% of the voters in a legally binding referendum to reject the plans of the once omnipotent Ministry of Atomic Energy.

The problems faced by the citizens of Dzerzhinsk and Kostroma may seem outlandish to those living in countries where the environmental revolution has been running for a generation or so, but the fall-out from cover-ups and other forms of secrecy is simply a matter of degree. As a result, the impacts of the transparency revolution – which is essential for the sustainability transition – will increasingly be felt around the world. Furthermore, as we shall see, new technologies and communication channels will enormously complicate the task for anyone trying to keep triple bottom line misdemeanors secret.

Why Worry?

Corporate Goldfish

Worldwide, business increasingly operates in a "goldfish bowl." Any acquisition, any merger, and any investment may potentially come under close scrutiny from environmentalists and other stakeholders.[5] In some countries, regulations require corporate disclosures, in others the process still proceeds, if at all, on a voluntary basis. But it is hardly coincidental that most of the companies responding effectively to the transparency revolution operate internationally. Although environmental concerns may wax and wane in individual countries, these companies are exposed to diverse pressures and also often feel the need to think long-term. The resulting time-horizons help them spot the underlying social and political trends, building decade on decade.

The growing demand for transparency and stakeholder consultation is one of these deep-seated trends. Companies that have faced public outrage, and have been in fear of losing some part of their licence to operate, have found that early, honest disclosure can help immeasurably in building or rebuilding public support. But be warned: the same bowl that makes the corporate goldfish visible to the outside world can also distort – and the more extreme the viewer's angle of vision, the greater the potential distortion. Corporate transparency on its own, in short, is no guarantee of a quiet life. That said, just as the first two sustainability revolutions have their own momentum, so does the transparency revolution.

Stakeholder pressures will be critically important in driving this trend. Although a handful of companies have adopted ethical values which provide an internal driver for sustainability, most companies will only move forward in response to strong, sustained pressures from the growing array of external stakeholders. Not surprisingly, many of these external stakeholders tend to talk in terms of "corporate disclosure," whereas business people prefer to talk in terms of "corporate communication and reporting." Both phrases are legitimate, but it is important to recognize the sheer number of involuntary, mandatory and voluntary channels through which disclosures now occur (Table 7.1).

Some types of disclosure and reporting are mandated by law; some are becoming key ingredients in industry's "licence to operate," required by local communities and, increasingly, by leading business customers; some, so far at least, are in the voluntary domain; and others, including some of the most disconcerting and painful, are involuntary.

Warts and All

Throughout three decades of environmentalism, industry had tried to minimize the amount of information communicated to shareholders and the public – relying on the "safety of the herd." But the decision of

TABLE 7.1   Forms of triple bottom line disclosure

Involuntary	Mandatory	Voluntary
◆ Accidents ◆ Campaigns ◆ Press and media exposés ◆ Whistleblowing ◆ Court investigations ◆ "Dirty tricks" campaigns by competitors or others	◆ Annual reports and accounts ◆ Stock exchange requirements (e.g. Securities & Exchange Commission reports, USA) ◆ Toxic Release Inventory (USA) ◆ Pollution registers (France, UK)	*Confidential* Disclosure required by: ◆ banks ◆ insurers ◆ customers ◆ joint venture partners *Non-confidential* ◆ Social reporting aspects of annual reports ◆ One-off or free-standing corporate performance reports ◆ Eco-audits, social audits ◆ Product labeling (e.g. eco-, fair trade labels) ◆ Answering benchmarking questionnaires ◆ Industry federation initiatives (e.g. the chemical industry's Responsible Care program) ◆ Briefings of, e.g. analysts, employees, media, campaigners ◆ Press releases and media briefings ◆ Staff newsletters ◆ Open-house days, on-site visitor facilities ◆ Toll-free numbers for stakeholders

Sources: SustainAbility/Deloitte & Touche/IISD

companies such as Monsanto (in the US), Norsk Hydro (in Norway) and BSO/Origin (in the Netherlands) to publish revealing environmental reports marked the beginning of a dramatic shift in business attitudes to disclosure. Such reports represent only one of a number of involuntary, voluntary, and mandatory channels of disclosure, but they are now perhaps the most widely accepted.

To their considerable surprise and relief, most early corporate reporters found a warm welcome for their efforts. Honesty was enormously appreciated in most cases, although many North American companies remain acutely sensitive about the prospect of disclosure leading to litigation – and Japanese companies, some of which have been known to use reports produced by foreign competitors for intelligence purposes, remain concerned about the competitive implications.

Certainly, it is worth thinking hard before deciding to report. As we warned in our 1993 report *Coming Clean*, "any company that forgets that the [sustainability] debate can be a minefield is in danger of losing its corporate legs. Don't expect bouquets just because you have decided to open your books." In some countries, plant managers can be jailed for failing to comply with emission controls. And any reporting company would be well advised to read its final draft report with the eye of a committed enemy of capitalism. If not, it risks being ambushed.

That said, some of the most effective, and best received, reports have been those where the reporting company has been prepared to adopt a "warts-and-all" approach. Those who have taken this path have found that stakeholders are much more likely to believe the good news where there is also a frank, detailed discussion of the remaining problems.

Am I a Stakeholder?

It is difficult to overstate the importance of stakeholders in driving – or stalling – the sustainability transition. And any stakeholder analysis needs to distinguish between "traditional" and "emerging" stakeholders.[6] Traditional stakeholders include shareholders, lenders, regulators, and government policymakers. Emerging stakeholders include employees, customers and consumers, trade associations and coalitions, professional and academic organizations, and community and environmental groups. Emerging stakeholders can also include "surrogate stakeholders" for interests not traditionally represented – including the planet's biosphere, the world population, and future generations. If business is to satisfy the growing demand from both stakeholder groups for improved triple bottom line standards and performance, it must learn to manage the dialogue in radically new ways.

Yesterday's stakeholders, almost exclusively, were concerned with maximizing return for shareholders and investors (asking such questions as, "Is my money safe?" and "Will this be a profitable company longer term?"). Companies were only accountable to their owners, and, in any event, were not typically in business to pursue broader social and environmental objectives.

Today, by contrast, business operates in a much more complex and heavily regulated world ("Is the company in compliance with current standards and emerging expectations?" "What are the potential liabilities?"). Now the concept of sustainable development, with its triple bottom line, is helping to ensure that tomorrow's stakeholders will include increasingly powerful representation of natural resource, biospheric, North/South, and inter-generational equity interests ("Is this company – indeed, this industry – sustainable?").

Remember, as argued in Chapter 4, sustainable development will be most likely, and will be achieved at the lowest overall cost to the economy, in those societies where there are the highest levels of trust and other forms of "social capital." Difficult decisions will be easier to take and the time-scales for change will be shorter. Conversely, low trust societies typically experience higher friction, resulting in added costs.

The levels, and credibility, of information disclosure both by companies and by government agencies will play a key role in influencing the extent to which social capital is created, conserved, effectively invested, or eroded in any given society. Indeed, as we see in Chapter 9, the reporting activities of recent years have done a great deal to prepare the way for some of the new strategic partnerships now beginning to form between far-sighted companies and pragmatic campaigning groups.

What's New, Gurus?

Emotion is OK

Transparency, of course, can be achieved before or after the event. However much disclosure there may have been, however much information may already be in the public domain, the outcome of a controversy often depends on how the major players approach the debate. If they become emotional about the issues, the chances of a major dispute obviously increase. But does that mean emotion is bad? Not at all, says our first guru, Peter Sandman, the leading US expert on public outrage and environmental risk communication.

Regardless of whether the company involved is DreamWorks trying to develop a sensitive site (Case Study, pp. 36–7) or Intel applying to take "too much" water in a dry region (Case Study, p. 168), corpora-

CASE STUDY

INTEL, USA: VIRTUAL CAMPAIGNS

"Part of the price of being in the limelight," as one semiconductor analyst put it, "is that you're expected to meet much higher standards, you're more accountable, and you have to act very, very differently." Indeed, the experience of Intel, the world's biggest and most profitable microprocessor manufacturer, suggests that even the best companies may find themselves suffering from blind-spots and mishandle the resulting controversies. More interestingly, Intel's experience suggests that "progressive companies attract even more progressive stakeholders."[7]

Intel is probably best known for its "Intel Inside" message on PCs. With 1995 earnings of nearly $3.6 billion on revenues of $16.2 billion, the company had every reason to expect a positive response when it announced plans early in 1993 to invest $2 billion in an expansion of its Rio Rancho manufacturing site in New Mexico. The expansion was expected to double production at the site, already Intel's largest, and create over 2,000 new jobs. But such plants need a lot of water. Unfortunately, a few months later the US Geological Survey concluded that the aquifer supplying the region's water was far smaller than had been thought.

The New Mexico state engineer ruled that Intel could only pump just over 70% of the water it had said it would need. More seriously, however, the issue triggered an investigation by a local grass-roots environmental justice group, the South West Organizing Project (SWOP). The resulting study, "Intel Inside New Mexico," came to a vote at the company's annual meeting in New York City. In the event, however, the vote went against SWOP. Intel could point to its previously excellent environmental track-record. It was spending hundreds of millions of dollars each year on environmental protection. More specifically, it more than halved hazardous waste production in the previous decade, despite the fact that it also produced a nine-fold increase in revenues over the same period.

Initially, Intel responded defensively to the SWOP campaign, just as it did in 1994 when its Pentium chips were found to be faulty. But the company said it had learned some important lessons. "As our stock has come to be more broadly held," Intel investor relations director Gordon Casey told *Tomorrow* magazine, "the portion of our investors who are socially responsible is growing, and going forward we'll give these issues more weight."

The SWOP campaign, enormously aided by the power of the Internet, suggests that companies breaching triple bottom line expectations will increasingly find themselves targeted by "virtual campaigns," with geographically separated individuals and organizations forming joint platforms courtesy of the Net.

tions and other business institutions undertaking major projects should expect to encounter public outrage. And the further globalization proceeds, the greater the risk that outrage will be caused by events in places which would once have been, in every sense, beyond the horizon.

Once confronted with outraged campaigners or communities, the natural tendency on the part of business people is to reject opposing views as "pure emotion," with the implications that they are thereby ruled out of court. But the likelihood is that business will face even greater eruptions of outrage as the values shift proceeds and the world moves into the globalized, highly competitive future now being sketched out and planned for by mainstream business gurus and their corporate clients. Major controversies stir emotions on all sides, not just among protesters. "Too often, my clients get locked into issues of control, ego and vindication," says Sandman.[8]

Based on his work with such corporate clients as ARCO, DuPont, Intel, and Union Carbide, Sandman explains that public outrage is a factor that almost every business risks having to deal with at some point. Perceived risk, he notes, is usually a complex, volatile mix of hazard and outrage. One of the first things he does is try to get business people to accept that emotions are legitimate – the public's and their own. "I tell them, look, just as the community's outrage gets in the way of their rational assessment of the hazard, your outrage gets in the way of your rational assessment of the community's outrage."

The best approach, Sandman believes, is to "come clean" with the public and other stakeholders. More radical still, he suggests that stakeholders be given a say in how the project – and even the company – is managed. As an example of best practice, he points to BP's handling of an oil spill at Huntingdon Beach, California. Although a contract carrier was to blame, when asked if BP was responsible BP's chief executive replied: "Our lawyers tell us it is not our fault. But we feel like it is our fault and we are going to act like it is our fault." Six months later, Sandman recalls, a survey showed that BP "had gained stature because of how they handled the spill."

Outrage is expressed in different ways in different countries. An issue that might be framed as a control issue in the USA may be seen as a trust issue in Germany. Sandman explains that,"Where people in the United States are basically saying, 'How dare you control my life,' in Germany they're saying 'I want a more reliable parent, a more trustworthy boss.' " These differences are becoming more important as companies increasingly trade across national boundaries and in different world regions. For those facing outrage, Sandman offers the following advice:

♦ Bring the concerns to the surface
♦ Stake out the middle ground, not the extremes
♦ Acknowledge prior misbehavior – repeatedly
♦ Acknowledge current problems – dramatically
♦ Discuss achievements with humility, and
♦ Share control and be accountable.

Usually, Sandman says he finds clients end up doing only around ten per cent of what he wants them to do. But, even then, he has learned to expect a certain amount of backsliding. "Rhetoric changes first," he notes, "behaviour changes next, and attitudes change last." Throughout, the core message he offers is clear. "More and more companies are realizing that having a good corporate ear is as important as having a good corporate mouth."

Engaging Stakeholders

Handling outrage is only the tip of the communications challenge represented by the triple bottom line. The second "guru" is not an individual, but my own organization, SustainAbility. Through the 1990s, the company emerged as one of the world's leading centers of excellence in relation to the accounting, auditing, and reporting requirements of the sustainability transition. Two early reports were *Coming Clean* and *Company Environmental Reporting*. But the following section draws on SustainAbility's two-volume report *Engaging Stakeholders*,[9] produced alongside the United Nations Environment Programme (UNEP) and 16 sponsoring companies from countries as diverse as the USA, Sweden, France, Belgium, Germany, the UK, and Australia, and representing sectors as different as mining, metals, energy, chemicals, water, transport, and health care.

As more and more companies join the ranks of report-makers, environmental reporting remains haunted by a paradox. Logically, before companies began to report externally on their environmental performance, initial efforts would have been focused upon developing appropriate environmental accounting methodologies and indicators for measuring performance and then installing systems for auditing against these. Only then would a company report be produced and verified. Instead, as Figure 7.1 suggests, the process has often seemed to run backwards. Many companies have tended to start off with auditing, followed by reporting – before realizing that their management systems were not really up to the task of producing the necessary information.

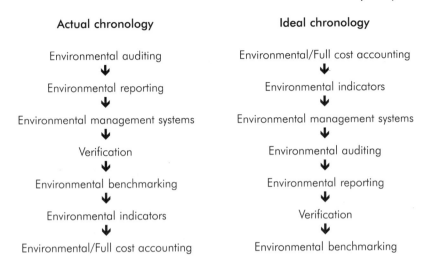

Actual chronology

Environmental auditing
↓
Environmental reporting
↓
Environmental management systems
↓
Verification
↓
Environmental benchmarking
↓
Environmental indicators
↓
Environmental/Full cost accounting

Ideal chronology

Environmental/Full cost accounting
↓
Environmental indicators
↓
Environmental management systems
↓
Environmental auditing
↓
Environmental reporting
↓
Verification
↓
Environmental benchmarking

FIGURE 7.1   The Inverted Chronology of Reporting
(*Sources:* SustainAbility/UNEP)

And the real interest in environmental and full cost accounting has begun to emerge relatively late in the day.

Even in the late 1990s, it was clear that most reporting companies still viewed their reports as public relations vehicles, designed to offer reassurance and to help with "feel-good" image building. Report users and other stakeholders had different ideas. As far as they were concerned, reports were increasingly seen as tools for monitoring, measuring, screening, comparing, and benchmarking. This trend towards benchmarking and benchmarkability raises the tricky issue of comparability. Early on, at least some reporting companies quite deliberately tried to ensure that their reported performance could not be directly compared with that of their competitors and best practice in other sectors. Others simply tried out whatever reporting method first occurred, rather than opting for formats which would have enabled direct year-on-year or pan-industry comparisons. But we are now beginning to see the first crop of reports specifically designed to show the reporting company's performance in the context of industry averages or linked to unit of production.

During SustainAbility's 1996 international benchmarking survey of environmental reporting, ten emerging trends were identified – as shown in Figure 7.2. Each represents a major challenge for companies aiming to achieve "triple wins" in highly competitive markets.

To get an idea of why these trends are important and, to a degree, inevitable, we will look briefly at each in turn.

	Established focus on:	➜	Emerging focus on:
1	One-way, passive communication	➜	Multi-way, active dialogue
2	Verification as an option	➜	Verification as standard
3	Single company reporting	➜	Benchmarkability
4	Management systems	➜	Life cycles, business design, strategy
5	Inputs and outputs	➜	Impacts and outcomes
6	Ad-hoc operating standards	➜	Global operating standards
7	Public relations	➜	Corporate governance
8	Voluntary reporting	➜	Mandatory reporting
9	Company sets reporting boundaries	➜	Boundaries set by stakeholder dialogue
10	Environmental performance	➜	Triple bottom line performance

FIGURE 7.2   Ten Transitions Towards Sustainability Reporting
(*Sources:* SustainAbility/UNEP)

1 Multi-way, Active Dialogue

This involves more than simply including feedback forms in a company's report. Even the pioneering reports from Monsanto and Norsk Hydro were essentially one-way vehicles. In subsequent years, a small number of companies have organized stakeholder forums to discuss the needs and expectations of report users. Examples include BP Chemicals and Novo Nordisk, the Danish pharmaceuticals and industrial enzyme producer.

In the case of Novo Nordisk, the process has probably gone further than with any other company. Each year since 1991, the company has invited stakeholders from across Europe, including some of its harshest critics, to spend several days challenging the company's senior management and other employees at close quarters. Although some of the information released as part of the process was used against the company in a consumer campaign in Germany, Austria, and Switzerland, the approach is seen as valuable by all those who have taken part – and has also been extended to Novo Nordisk's North Carolina site.

2 Verification as Standard

How do you work out whether a company report is credible? One answer is to check whether it is verified by an independent firm of auditors. When Norsk Hydro opted to have its first report verified in 1990, the move was universally welcomed. The company, however, subsequently published reports that were not verified. The other pioneer, Monsanto, did not opt for verification, nor, at the time of writing, is its latest report verified. But a growing number of reporting frameworks call for verification, including the European Union's EMAS scheme and the Danish and Dutch reporting requirements.

There are a number of emerging issues surrounding verification, however. First, there is a striking contrast between the styles of verification adopted by accountancy firms and the more challenging approaches developed by some environmental management consultancies. Furthermore, some companies are focusing on having their reports verified, while others (among them Bristol-Myers Squibb, Dow Europe and Sun Company) have simply had their environmental management systems or auditing programmes verified. It is often not easy to tell which approach to verification has been adopted without reading the text very closely.

Even so, research by the US Investor Responsibility Research Center (IRRC) suggests that environmental reports "have risen quickly to become a trusted source of information for advocacy groups, institutional investors, investment managers, news media, environmental regulators, and other stakeholders."[10] It is true that most stakeholders currently see basic forms of verification adding very little to the credibility of current reports, but many also see verification emerging as a standard requirement in future – as it has in financial reporting.

3 Benchmarkability

Anyone who has tried to compare or benchmark reports, even those produced by companies operating in the same industry sector, will recognize that the task is usually impossible. With companies choosing their own environmental performance indicators and other metrics, benchmarking is still often more a hope than a reality. This is a key problem, given the role comparability plays in making reports credible.

One reason for the current failure to ensure benchmarkability may be simple fear about the possible outcome. But another reason appears to be that report-makers are failing to recognize and respond to the emerging needs of report users, most particularly financial analysts and institutions. Whereas most reporting companies still see their reports as a form of reassurance for the outside world, growing numbers of report users want to use the data reported to compare, benchmark, rank, and rate companies.

4 Life Cycles, Business Design, Strategy

Inevitably, the initial focus of reporting was on the most visible aspects of a particular company's activities: its projects, its plants, and its products. Longer term, however, we will see companies recognizing a need to get a better grip on a wider range of triple bottom line issues and on performance up and down the value chain; from "cradle to grave" (see Chapter 8). In the process, some reporting companies are finding that what started out as a public affairs activity is beginning to have a strong influence on corporate strategy and business design.

Further pressure in this direction will be generated by interest in new concepts such as "eco-efficiency," "environmental space," and the "Factor 4" through "Factor 10" approaches to dematerialization. That said, there remains a real danger that the growing focus of many report-makers on continuous improvement, an approach drawn across from Total Quality Management (TQM), coupled with the spreading use of TQM-derived benchmarking tools, will blind them to the much more fundamental steps that may need to be taken on the road to sustainability. This sort of blind-spot is best dealt with through stakeholder dialogue processes which challenge current mindsets and promote lateral or "out-of-the-box" thinking.

5 Impacts and Outcomes

Data on industry's inputs and outputs are obviously welcome, but they are only really useful if they can be linked to real-world environmental impacts – and to programmes for reducing and making good those impacts. The necessary shifts here are from data to information and knowledge, from understanding to action. In short, what do all the emissions and waste data published in these reports actually mean in terms of environmental decline or progress, let alone of longer term sustainability?

One of the first steps in the right direction came in a recent Dow Europe report. "The figures we present often raise the question: 'How do these emissions impact the environment?,' " the company explained.[11] Interestingly, the report also included a review of the methodology by CE, the Delft-based environmental think-tank. To achieve genuine progress, such data and targets need to be linked firstly to government sustainability frameworks and targets, and secondly to market (and particularly financial market) requirements and incentives.

6 Global Operating Standards

In a globalizing economy, whatever Shell may feel about the dangers of pushing developing countries and transition economies too far, too fast, companies using different standards in different parts of the world will, at the very least, raise stakeholder eyebrows. The question of whether to adopt ad-hoc or global operating standards can tax even the best reporters.

The titanium dioxide producer Tioxide has produced both group-level and site-level reports covering countries as diverse as the UK, Spain, South Africa, and Malaysia. But such reporting remains the exception. More typical was the reaction from Ciba-Geigy, now part of Novartis. The company noted: "We do not report [Toxic Release Inventory] data because TRI data [are] collected in the US only. Sites outside the US collect data according to local legal requirements and according to Ciba-Geigy requirements."

The impending transition from local standards to global standards – particularly in respect of emerging triple bottom line requirements and expectations – looks set to be one of the toughest for business as we move into the 21st century. The challenge will be made more difficult because most companies have grown used to operating very different standards in different parts of the world.

7 Corporate Governance

The shift to a more governance-focused approach to accountability and reporting is signalled by the emerging views of the risk-rating agencies and financial institutions. This trend is likely to hit the financial markets in waves, switching on the insurers first, then the banks and other lenders, and last, but far from least, the equity markets.

The emerging corporate governance agenda is covered in more detail in Chapter 11. This transition will need to involve a wider set of stakeholders than is implied by the conventional relationship between managers, directors, and owners. It will also require a fuller and more integrated vision of corporate accountability. Meanwhile, at least for the equity and other fast-paced financial markets, environmental issues are often overshadowed by the sheer scale of the problems that have rocked institutions like Barings, Daiwa, and Sumitomo. But sustainable development is going to depend on the capacity of financial analysts to think longer term than they currently find possible.

8 Mandatory Reporting

We have consistently encouraged voluntary approaches – in the belief that they encourage greater experimentation by report-makers. This is still the case, but there are clear signs both among report-users and report-makers that there will be growing calls for mandatory reporting – to force non-reporters to report. The USA, with its Toxic Release Inventory (TRI) requirements, provides perhaps the best-known case of mandatory environmental reporting, but other countries – among them Denmark, the Netherlands, Norway, and Sweden – now also impose mandatory requirements on certain industry sectors and categories of company.

For some companies that are already reporting, their support for mandatory requirements flows from a desire to ensure that the pain is spread and to minimize the problem of "free-riders." But it also reflects the fact that market approaches to environmental management depend on the availability of life-cycle and value chain information which – for the overwhelming majority of companies – is still not available.

9 Boundaries Set by Stakeholder Dialogue

One of the main reasons why corporate environmental reporting has not yet transformed the credibility of the reporting companies is that the process of deciding when, how, and to whom to report is often controlled by the companies themselves. For such reports to be credible, and for external stakeholders to be genuinely engaged, they must be involved from the outset in discussing and negotiating the boundaries of the reporting process. As already noted, few companies have taken the logical next step of opening themselves up to "no-holds-barred" stakeholder dialogue, but those that have say they have found the process invaluable.

10 Triple Bottom Line Performance

Growing numbers of reporting companies are signalling their recognition of the need to address the triple bottom line. "Shell UK recognizes that others have a legitimate interest in how it conducts its businesses," the company said in its first report, published in 1996:

> "It has tried to be open about its operations, and the principles and standards which inform them. However, it recognizes that in a

changing world, in which people are increasingly concerned about the balance between environmental, social, and economic considerations, it has to do much more to engage the public in difficult environmental choices."

Boardroom Views

McLibel lessons

Personal experience suggests that most board directors are now aware that transparency is becoming an issue. Even so, most triple bottom line issues still rank low on a board's list of priorities. In part, as argued in Chapter 10, this is a generational problem. In general, there is an inverse relationship between the age of a company director and (almost always) his ability to engage with the sustainability agenda. Many directors – and, as a result, many boards – still have little understanding of what this third sustainability revolution will involve, let alone of where it will take us. Most of these people grew up when transparency technologies like television were relatively new; many still find it hard to use a personal computer for anything more advanced than word-processing; and for the overwhelming majority the Net and Web remain foreign, indeed hostile, territories.

The very real risks multinational companies now face in the global goldfish bowl created by such technologies are perhaps best illustrated by what happened when McDonald's served libel writs on five self-styled anarchists. Two chose to fight the battle through the courts and the resulting trial became the longest in English legal history.

I took a particular interest in the "McLibel" trial, having come to legal blows with McDonald's following the 1988 publication of our best-seller, *The Green Consumer Guide*.[12] Indeed, in 1989 we had encountered many of the senior McDonald's people who turned up in the McLibel trial.[13] Through the 1980s, McDonald's had been trying to deflect or kill a series of challenges, ranging from criticisms of "junk food" to allegations that the company's meat was sourced from land cleared of rainforest. McDonald's stretched every sinew, not always successfully, to persuade us that our beliefs about the company were wrong. During the same period, according to John Vidal, who monitored the McLibel trial from the outset:

"McDonald's was stamping out brushfires everywhere – in just a few years it forced apologies or retractions from the BBC, the *Guardian* and the Scottish [Trade Union Congress], effectively closed down the

CASE STUDY

GREENPEACE INTERNATIONAL, THE NETHERLANDS: MIND-BOMBS

What is it that has made Greenpeace so successful? To begin with, it was the camera. When the first ragged-trousered army of draft dodgers, hippies, yippies, journalists and assorted others got together on the Canadian coast at the end of the 1960s to form the "Don't Make a Wave" Committee, the aim was to "bear witness" to earth-shaking events like nuclear testing.[14] "We saw it as a media war," recalled Robert Hunter in *The Greenpeace Chronicle*.[15] "We had studied Marshall McLuhan." He described the film packages that resulted as "mind bombs, sailing across the electronic seas into the minds of the masses."

The Greenpeace icon became one of the most powerful symbols of the late 20th century. And the group proved to be consummate masters of the art of transforming everything from whaling ships to the Brent Spar oil buoy into symbols of environmental destruction. One veteran campaigner described the classic icon: "A whaling ship, an explosive harpoon, a fleeing whale and between them a tiny, manned inflatable with the word 'Greenpeace' emblazoned on the side – it says it all."

Or, as Fred Pearce notes:

"It did. But now things are changing in the media. No one disputes Greenpeace's command of state-of-the-art communication technology. When French commandos stormed aboard the *Rainbow Warrior* in the South Pacific in 1995, a piece of technology called a 'squisher' digitised and compressed the imagery captured by video cameras, compressed it and bounced it off an orbiting satellite before the metal doors of the *Warrior*'s communications room could be broken down."

But, as Pearce argues, access to the world media is getting more fragmented and more widespread. In the heyday of mass television one man could, in Hunter's words, "demand the attention of the world." In the future, it may be impossible for anyone to make such demands. At the same time, technology will spread the tools of testimony – video cameras and Net access – to every part of the world threatened by the greenhouse effect, the ozone crisis, the great extinction, the soil gap, and all the other eco-calamities. Hunter's planet-wide "collective mind" will know more than ever about the planet's state. But will Greenpeace – or anyone – be able to focus that knowledge, to set the agenda with an image?

Worse, the growing use of digital editing will dent people's willingness to believe even what they see with their own eyes. Chris Rose, campaigns director at Greenpeace UK, argues that the group has helped create a "new politics" based not on the production and distribution of wealth "but on the production and distribution of public attention." No doubt Greenpeace will continue to exploit new technology to considerable effect, but the question now must be whether this very technology, like the Net, will force the group into a massive restructuring of the way it operates.

Transnational Information Centre, stopped the transmission of at least one Channel 4 film, and silenced a play."[16]

The company had expected a quick, clean conclusion to its legal action against the London Greenpeace activists who had distributed a pamphlet, *What's Wrong with McDonald's?* Instead, it found itself in the public eye for two-and-a-half years, or a total of 314 days in court. Almost worse, there was a site on the Web devoted entirely to the company's alleged misdeeds. "It's McHell," was the way John Vidal put it. "There, for anyone who cares to log on, is 'McSpotlight,'" he explained:

"25 megabytes, 1,300 files, millions upon millions of critical words, clips of films that McDonald's thought it had suppressed, extracts of the banned play, every malicious cartoon and article that has ever appeared, all the information supposedly taken out of circulation by previous trials. Every testimony against the company, every revelation, every blunder and admission has turned up on international 'mirror' sites so they cannot be wiped out. It's the ultimate anti-McDonald's experience. In 14 languages. And top of the list is the *What's Wrong With McDonald's?* pamphlet."

And such is the speed of publishing these days, that John Vidal's book on the subject, *McLibel*, was out before the judge's decision.[17]
Whichever side of the McLibel fence you come down on, this trial marked a series of quantum jumps in the magnifying power of the global goldfish bowl. The rapidly evolving Net and Web are transforming the conditions in which business will be done in the future. And, ironically, another of the companies whose recent experiences illustrate this fact is the chip-maker Intel (Case Study, p.168). The take-home message from the Intel saga is that progressive companies attract even

more progressive stakeholders, and new communication technologies will accelerate and amplify their activities in ways which most of the architects of the Net and Web presumably never envisaged.

Many companies already offer financial and, indeed, environmental data on the Web. But anyone who tours the web-sites of the FTSE 100, Fortune 500 or *Business Week* 50 will find huge variations in quality and accessibility. When *Business Week*'s Stephen Wildstrom went surfing for annual reports, he found "some dramatic differences in approach. Offerings range from bare-bones financials, some with barely readable text, to colorful and sometimes animated annual reports with multimedia glitz."[18] When we went surfing for environmental reporting on the Web, we found pretty much the same. Many companies were simply reading their printed reports directly across onto their web-sites, arguing that if they didn't the verifications would no longer apply. But a few – among them Nortel and Xerox – were already beginning to play with the new medium to offer users a much more enticing and inter-linked package of information.

Meanwhile, the logic of the triple bottom line suggests that we will also see an accelerating convergence between financial, environmental and social reporting. Allan Kupcis, as president of Canada's Ontario Hydro, put it this way:

> "Ultimately, we will witness the disappearance of the corporate environmental report. We will know we are really changing course when one corporate annual report presents past performance and future goals integrating financial stewardship with environmental integrity and social responsibility."

Bubbling Under

Social Reporting

Reporting by companies will inevitably go through cycles, but the underlying trend is towards greater transparency and more attention to the triple bottom line. Indeed, when we recently assessed a range of corporate environmental reports, many published in 1996, the top-scoring report – by a wide margin – was the Body Shop's *Values Report* (Case Study, p.139). This four-volume report represented one of the earliest attempts to evolve the standard environmental report into a more holistic form of reporting, also covering a wide range of social and ethical issues.

"We're seeing a lot of interest in the social angle from major corporations with a good track record on environmental reporting," explained Dr David Wheeler, then head of the Body Shop's ethical auditing program. "The question is how you can measure your company's impact on stakeholders, and track progress towards more sustainable operations."[19]

As the sustainable development agenda increasingly embraces such social issues as human rights, we will see more companies focusing attention on the relatively new field of social accounting, auditing, and reporting. Early social audits may have been carried out several decades ago, as explained in Chapter 4, but today there is an important difference – in that companies are themselves now commissioning such audits, rather than being subjected to external processes commissioned and published by others. Some critics may see this as a recipe for the co-option of the auditors, but it is just as likely that processes "owned" by companies will be more effective in catalyzing real change.

Human Rights

One company which has recently found the human rights agenda bubbling up around one of its prize projects is British Petroleum (BP), soon to be BP Amoco. In the race to secure oil reserves for the 21st century, BP has had high hopes of its venture in Colombia, which it predicts will be the biggest oil prospect in the Americas since the opening up of the Alaskan fields in the 1970s.[20] Although BP chief executive John Browne immediately dismissed the allegations as "groundless and without substance," the *Observer* and others accused the company of complicity in human rights and environmental abuses in Colombia.

Among the accusations, BP was alleged to have colluded in the videotaping of meetings so that "death squads" could target activists. "Rubbish," the company retorted. The only videotapes taken at public meetings – at which the army would normally be present, in a region which has many of the characteristics of the old Wild West – were made in case the Ministry of the Environment ever asked for proof that public consultation had taken place. The Ministry had never asked to see the tapes, BP said, and they had never been made available to the military. But the company, which felt that it had been the subject of a campaign of disinformation and exaggeration, was left in the impossible position of trying to prove a negative.

Whatever the facts, the implication of Shell's Nigerian and BP's Colombian furores is that the human rights dimension of the sustainable development debate could well make discussion of the sustainability transition much more volatile and politically charged. The potential for outrage on a scale greater even than that which faced Shell is clear.

Will the Analysts Wake Up?

Another trend bubbling under is for the world's financial markets to pay more attention to a company's eco-efficiency, although so far it's hard to spot. When we held roundtables for financial analysts in London, New York, and Tokyo as part of the *Coming Clean* project, most financial analysts said they simply binned the environmental reports they received as useless. A few years on, most have yet to change their minds. Most analysts, according to Bill Birchard, still:

> "wrinkle up their noses at the thought of seriously studying green reports. So do the debt analysts. When Moody's Investor Service or Standard & Poor's come to figure out whether a company can pay quarterly coupons and return of principal on a debt issue, they find that environmental capital and operating costs simply consume too small a share of cash flow to make a difference."[21]

But insurance analysts and some banks are beginning to give some of these reports a closer look. "The forthrightness is a good indicator of the quality of management," noted Bill McElroy, an assistant vice president in Zurich-America's commercial real estate group in New York. Meanwhile, across at Swiss Bank Corporation (SBC), Franz Knecht, then vice president and head of environmental management services, foresaw the day when SBC bankers will summarily refuse loans to marginal clients because of their failure to provide environmental reports. Conversely, he suggests, companies that provide sound data could find their loan applications being processed faster, a considerable advantage when time is money.

Holy Grail?

As the interest of financial markets inevitably grows, so will the interest in ways of internalizing triple bottom line costs without wrecking companies. To this end, we will see increasing investment in new forms of accounting. A leading authority in this area is Professor Rob Gray, who heads the Centre for Social & Environmental Accounting Research

(CSEAR) at Scotland's University of Dundee. If we want to internalize such costs, he asks, "can accountants deliver the new holy grail of sustainability – 'full cost accounting?' "[22]

Ultimately, however, he argues that the voluntary approach is not going to deliver either full cost accounting or sustainability. "Internalisation of environmental costs has occurred – and continues to occur – to some degree," he says:

> "Changes in customer taste, increased (if patchy) regulation, new taxation initiatives, and increased costs of control have all added new costs (and perhaps opened new opportunities) for both organisations and individuals. They do so, however, in an uneven way. Some companies in some industries have been hit hard, others – perhaps even in the same industry – have, so far, escaped unscathed."

Most companies continue to enjoy a "free ride" at the expense both of those pioneering companies that have made a start on internalizing costs and of the wider environment. However transparent the operating environment in which it does business, a company ultimately must face financial reality. If internalizing a range of triple bottom line costs starts to threaten stock market valuations, salaries or jobs, then only regulations will swing the argument. So the challenge is not simply one of making the costs imposed more visible, a task which accountants can certainly help with, but also of forcing all economic players to internalize their fair share of costs.

Winners, Losers

The winners in this third sustainability revolution will be those who learn to work with the grain of – rather than against – the new media. The new technologies and the new spaces they open out in our brains threaten new forms of outrage: even faster and harder to counter than the problems that Peter Sandman has helped so many companies recognize and handle.

Many companies will also develop internal versions of the Internet, or "intranets." A typical intranet uses a web browser to access corporate web pages accessible only to staff members.[23] Web features like hypertext documents enable users to extract useful information from the blizzard of data. By linking isolated islands of information technology, intranets potentially can help companies respond to external challenges in an appropriate time-frame – and in a coordinated, coherent way.

The next question for companies that have invested in such intranets will be how fast and how far they open them up to outsiders; suppliers, customers, and, ultimately, the full range of triple bottom line stakeholders. If the experience of companies that have produced the first waves of environmental and social reports is anything to go by, those with the courage to open up in this way will, on balance, win.

The losers will include those companies which move too late, too early, or in the wrong direction. Increasing computerization also brings new risks in terms of internal or external sabotage and hacking, which may trigger some of the major disasters of the future. So companies that fail to think through sufficiently the implications of their cyberspatial activities, or which fail to adequately police the new cyber-realms, risk being among the early casualties. None of this argues against making the plunge, however: this is the wave of the future.

Countries which follow the lead of the military regime in Myanmar (Burma), outlawing the possession of computers with networking capability without authorization, risk being sidelined to an even greater extent in the new world order. And the casualties will also include those who need the oxygen of media coverage, but fail to win it. Academics such as the Cambridge sociologist John Thompson have talked of the "struggle for visibility" as being at the very heart of modern politics.[24] The same can be said of modern business, an insight that entrepreneurs like Steve Jobs, Bill Gates, Anita Roddick, and Richard Branson long ago recognized.

The opening out of cyberspace will bring new threats and opportunities for most businesses. The evolution of the triple bottom line agenda will itself be hugely influenced by the evolution of cyberspace – and of the culture that goes along with it. The leading anthropologist of this new realm is Shelly Turkle, author of books like *Life on the Screen*. Her conclusion is that, "We're at the beginning of a profound shake-up of that sense of what a self is and what you take responsibility for and what you don't."[25] The implication is that our understanding of what is meant by responsibility, accountability, and, indeed, sustainability, will be transformed by what happens along the cyberfrontier and in the new economic, social, and political realms opening up therein.

Three Keys to the 21st Century

The third sustainability revolution focuses on transparency, requiring that we understand and use the following keys to sustainable enterprise:

♦ First, no matter how successful some companies may be in devising "stealth" strategies to mask what they are doing, or intend to do, most businesses will increasingly operate in a high-visibility environment. International business will find that the Internet will enormously increase the geographical reach and magnifying (and distorting) power of the goldfish bowl.

♦ Second, voluntary reporting by a relatively small number of companies will help fuel demands for much higher levels of corporate disclosure. The focus will expand from environmental performance to progress against a range of triple bottom line indicators. Some countries will decide that the only way to achieve this is via mandatory reporting requirements.

♦ Third, for such disclosures to be helpful and boost a company's or industry's credibility, stakeholders will need to be actively involved in deciding on the indicators, targets and reporting methods. At the same time, however, business will need to engage emotions and perceptions, not just pump out science and "facts" (see Chapter 13).

Notes

1. Christopher Parkes, "Surge in US corporate espionage," *Financial Times*, 22 March 1996.
2. Nicholas Hildyard, *Cover Up: The facts they didn't want you to know*, New English Library, 1981.
3. Anthony Tucker, "The fallout from the fallout," *Guardian*, 17 February 1996.
4. Carey Scott, "Russia's green warriors march on Poison City," *Sunday Times*, 15 December 1996.
5. SustainAbility, Deloitte Touche Tohmatsu International and the International Institute for Sustainable Development, *Coming Clean: Opening up for sustainable development*, 1993.
6. International Institute for Sustainable Development and Deloitte & Touche, *Business Strategy for Sustainable Development: Leadership and accountability for the '90s*, 1992.
7. Ann Goodman, "Telling Intel," *Tomorrow*, No. 2, March/April, 1996.
8. Peter Sandman, "It's the outrage, stupid," *Tomorrow*, No. 2, March/April, 1996.
9. SustainAbility, in association with UNEP, the New Economics Foundation and 16 participating companies, *Engaging Stakeholders, Volume 1: The Benchmark Survey – The second international progress report on company environmental reporting* and *Volume 2: The Case Studies – Twelve users respond to company environmental reporting*, 1996.

10. Report reveals what makes environmental reports credible, *The Green Business Letter*, April 1996. *Environmental Reporting and Third Party Statements*, prepared by the Investor Responsibility Research Center (IRRC) for the Global Environmental Management Initiative (GEMI), 1996.
11. Dow Europe, *Environmental Progress Report 1994*, published 1995.
12. John Elkington and Julia Hailes, *The Green Consumer Guide: From shampoo to champagne*, Victor Gollancz, 1988.
13. John Elkington, *A Year in the Greenhouse: An environmentalist's diary*, Victor Gollancz, 1990.
14. John Vidal, "You and I against McWorld," *Guardian*, 9 March 1996.
15. Fred Pearce, "Greenpeace: Mindbombing the media," *Wired* UK, May 1996.
16. Robert Hunter, *The Greenpeace Chronicle*, Holt, Rinehart and Winston 1979; Picador, 1980.
17. John Vidal, *McLibel*, Macmillan, 1997.
18. Stephen H. Wildstrom, "Surfing for annual reports," *Business Week*, 14 April 1997.
19. Kate Victory, "Body Shop's 'Values Report' ups the ante on corporate reporting," *Business and the Environment*, March 1996.
20. Stephen Fidler, Sarita Kendall and Robert Corzine, "Oil giant in troubled waters," *Financial Times*, 8 November 1996; also David Harrison and Melissa Jones, "Europe presses Colombia to investigate BP," *Observer*, 27 October 1996.
21. Bill Birchard, "Does anyone read this stuff?," *Tomorrow*, No. 6, November/December, 1996.
22. Professor R.H. Gray, "Accounting for the environment?," *European Strategy Europe 1997*, Campden Publishing, London, 1996.
23. Ian Campbell, *The Intranet: Slashing the cost of business*, preliminary report by International Data Corporation, Framingham, Massachusetts, 1996.
24. Martin Woolacott, "When invisibility means death," *Guardian*, 27 April 1996.
25. Pamela McCorduck, "Sex, lies, and avatars," *Wired*, April 1996.

◆ 8 ◆

LIFE-CYCLE TECHNOLOGY

Conception to Resurrection

Combine intensifying market competition, evolving values and global transparency.

Result: an *X-ray environment* in which the entire life cycle of a product can be powerfully illuminated.

Leading companies have become increasingly comfortable using the language of Revolution 4, which involves a growing focus on product life cycles and value chains. But dangerously few yet understand the competitive implications. These seem set to turn key markets inside out – and existing competitive and customer-supplier relationships upside down. Technology will still be key, but the focus is switching from product to function.

Revolution	Focus	Old paradigm **)**	New paradigm
4	Life cycles	Product	**)** Function

The days when technology was a dirty word in environmental circles are long since gone, but we still have to deal with the fact that technology has had a bad press, at least since *Silent Spring*. Much of the criticism was justified, of course, but few campaigners would now dispute that technology – very different technology – will be a necessary condition for the more sustainable economies of the 21st century and beyond. Unfortunately, all technologies, even those introduced in the interests of sustainability, have unintended side-effects. But new life-cycle assessment and design techniques are now emerging, which at least give us the option of screening new technologies before they are widely marketed.

That said, the screening task gets progressively tougher. In the early years of the Industrial Revolution, most industrial products were made in small numbers, then sold and used close to the point of manufacture. Those who bought them mainly knew where these products came from and, at least in outline, how they were made. Because they were relatively scarce and expensive, products were cared for and repaired a number of times before the materials were discarded or re-used. Some even passed down through the generations. And if they had an environmental impact, it was generally close to the points of manufacture, use, and disposal.

Today, in contrast, we are offered products which – at least in historical terms – are amazingly complex and yet remarkably cheap. This is partly because they are made in huge numbers, in ways few of us have any hope of understanding. They are shipped around the globe, and bought and discarded in time-scales which would have struck our great-grandparents as literally incredible, and even sinful. Many seem near-magical to those who use them, yet are overtaken by new developments in the space of a few years, or even months. At times it seems that the computers we buy are obsolete before we get them home.

Unfortunately, however, the impacts many of these products now cause through their life cycles are beginning to cause damage at the planetary level. Think of the CFCs released by aerosols, refrigerators, and air-conditioning systems or the "gender-bending" chemicals found in industrial effluents and products alike. There is also a growing concern about the impacts of the sheer volume of materials and energy now used to sustain modern lifestyles. As a result, companies are finding that their responsibilities for a product cannot be shrugged off at the factory fence or even at the point of sale. They are being encouraged – and will, increasingly, be forced – to take "cradle-to-grave" responsibility.

Combine the first three sustainability revolutions – intensifying competition, evolving values, and global transparency – and you have the ingredients of a potentially explosive cocktail. The result, as we will see, can be an *X-ray environment* in which the entire life cycle of a product can, almost at the flick of a switch, be powerfully illuminated for all to see. One industry after another has suddenly found itself in versions of this X-ray environment, in which its operations and failings are exposed in excruciating detail.

More worrying still, recent controversies suggest that we will see an accelerating shift towards *vertical* rather than simply *horizontal* X-ray environments. What does this mean? Well, a few years ago an oil spill tended to switch the spotlight of public scrutiny on to a few oil companies and, if relevant, their shipping contractors. A chemical industry accident would raise questions about chemical handling or site emergency procedures across an industry. That was a horizontal X-ray and the industry's PR people got used to dealing with such problems and handling the outrage they caused.

Now, however, the penetrating power of the global media means that a controversy can suddenly illuminate not simply one site or product, one company or one industry, but instead an entire value chain. A recent case, to which we will return, was the "mad cow" scare in Europe. It is as if a company's, or industry's, opponents have been issued with complementary versions of Superman's X-ray specs. In the space of a few short hours, the world suddenly seems to know more about a company's value chain than most of its own executives do.

At the same time, those companies that have really begun to understand the sustainability agenda, know that the only way for a company to achieve the necessary progress against the triple bottom line is to focus on improving the performance of the whole value chain. The value chain model developed and popularized by Michael Porter has emerged as a key means of analyzing a company's operations and relationships as a source of competitive advantage.[1] This approach is based on an understanding that every single activity at every level in the product life cycle can have an impact on the product's, and company's, economic performance. By extension, it can also be used to understand the life-cycle dimensions of triple bottom line performance.

As some companies move in this direction, they are using the knowledge gained in the process to undermine their competitors. Let's get specific: think of arch-rivals Procter & Gamble and Unilever.

Life-cycle Power

"Taken to the cleaners" was one of the kinder headlines that greeted the news that Procter & Gamble's product tests showed that Persil Power, made by arch-rival Lever, rotted clothes. After a period of corporate fisticuffs, Lever withdrew the product. Like Intel with its defective chips, Lever had unintentionally demonstrated the perils of doing business in an increasingly sensitized world without fully understanding the life-cycle risks associated with their technology and products.

Procter & Gamble was able to go for its competitor's jugular because of the life-cycle research it had done some years earlier on the same accelerator compound that caused the problems. On the basis of that research, P&G had decided not to use the compound – and was astounded when Unilever subsequently did so.

Increasingly, companies must understand the full range of effects caused by their existing or planned products, throughout the product life cycle: from "cradle to grave," "sperm to worm," or "womb to tomb," as they say. Alternatively, given the growing market value placed on recyclability and ultimate recycling, perhaps we should talk in terms of "cradle to cradle" or "conception to resurrection." There will be few exceptions to this requirement. Even technologies which may seem totally benign and sustainable when only a few are in use may become problematic when millions are in use, and, as a consequence, the pace of product development accelerates. Products as simple as aerosol cans suddenly turn out to have the capacity to blow holes in the stratospheric ozone layer.

The Persil Power controversy illustrates an inescapable fact of business life: product life cycles are moving to center stage. Indeed, after years of media scare stories, many consumers – and, indeed, citizens – seem in danger of turning into neurotics. As leading PR expert Quentin Bell put it: "We can't have sex for fear of AIDS, we can't eat beef for fear of CJD, and we can't use mobile phones for fear of getting our brains scrambled." And this growing nervousness is beginning to have major implications for leading brands. Instead of the "Winner Takes All" society, with the economic rewards flowing disproportionately to a few key players, perhaps we should be beginning to think in terms of the "Loser Takes All" economy – with a few unlucky companies unwittingly serving as lightning conductors, earthing static charges built up by the activities and misdemeanours of the many?

Why Worry?

Brand Rage

"So what?" some people may say. If we get into difficulties, all we have to do is follow the commonsense rules of public relations. If there is a problem, own up. Be honest. Move quickly. Explain what really happened – and move the spotlight on to our plans for making sure such problems don't happen again. In desperate cases, remember Heineken and Perrier, and do something dramatic. Recall 17 million bottles in 152 markets, as Heineken did, or, even better, follow Perrier's lead and drive a bulldozer over thousands of "contaminated" bottles of mineral water.[2]

Well, yes, but the life-cycle revolution will bring some interesting new twists to the already tricky world of "brand rage." Market research in many countries suggests that consumers are increasingly prepared to take action against companies and brands that they see as having betrayed their trust. Perception often outweighs reality. And the risk is that the potential for unpleasant surprises may grow exponentially as the reach of the media extends and the range of triple bottom line issues brought to our attention explodes.

To get a sense of the range of issues that can switch on the X-ray environment, and of the different levels of penetration achieved once X-ray specs are issued, let's look at a small number of recent cases. First, all of us have used products made of aluminum, so let's focus on the plight of Canada's beluga whales. Then we will move on to alligator penises, mad cows, sustainable paper, T-shirts made by sweatshop labor, the growing pressure on those who make the 15 billion cigarettes smoked every day, and the airbags designed to save adults which turned out to kill children.

Life-cycle Detectives

As a modern parable, illustrating the complex, apparently chaotic way in which today's problems can evolve, consider the beluga whales of Canada's great St Lawrence river. "Because belugas make an extraordinary range of noises – from whistles and creaks to clicks and warbles," explains Pierre Béland, one of the scientists involved, "the seafarers who first heard them named them sea canaries."[3] Sadly, they have also turned out to play the same role that canaries once played in mines: signalling rising pollution levels by dying.

Hunted and trapped for thousands of years by those who lived alongside the river, these small white whales came under massive hunting pressure between the mid-1800s and 1900s. There were once an estimated 100,000 belugas; today there are fewer than 500. Yet, despite the fact that the belugas were totally protected in 1979, their population failed to recover. Among the possible reasons suggested were low natural reproductive rates and the destruction of beluga habitat by hydroelectric projects. But recent research has spotlighted a more worrying factor.

As industry began to develop in the region, dead belugas started to turn up. Laboratory tests showed that their bodies were so contaminated by industrial pollutants that they were soon being classified as toxic waste. A possible source of the pollutants was one of the world's largest aluminum-producing complexes, which for decades released large quantities of a highly potent carcinogen, benzo(a)pyrene, into one of the St Lawrence's tributaries, the Sanguenay.

To begin with, scientists found it hard to work out how the whales had become so contaminated. Admittedly, they fed on invertebrates in the river's headwaters, but – although the invertebrates were themselves contaminated – this source was insufficient to explain the belugas' problems. Then a new clue surfaced. Another species that can build up very high levels of persistent pollutants is the eel. The scientists suddenly realised that the migrating eels swim smack through the middle of the belugas' habitat. And it turned out that they might be contributing as much as half of the contaminants found in the whales. "I felt like a naive detective who had been trying to figure out how packages move between cities by searching highway vehicles at random," recalled Pierre Béland. "I got nowhere until I chanced on a mail truck."

Nor did the story stop there. It was found that female whales were consistently less contaminated than the males. Why? The answer turned out to be a key part of the explanation for the whales' low reproductive rate: the females were passing astounding amounts of pollutants on to their calves in their milk. The conclusion was that, far from recovering from pollution, successive generations of whales were becoming increasingly contaminated.

No one actively set out to poison the belugas. For years the damage continued without anyone understanding why it was happening. The St Lawrence, in effect, was being used as a giant environmental laboratory. This was simply one more case of the life-cycle effects of technology being swept under the ecological carpet. Nowadays, however, we can no longer plead ignorance.

Shrinking Penises

And just in case the fate of Canadian belugas seems a bit remote from the day-to-day cares of running any business but an aluminum smelter, it is worth noting that such problems can hit almost any business these days. Recall the enormous controversy when scientists showed that phthalates, which are suspected of causing human fertility problems, could be found in most brands of baby milk. Phthalates, widely used as "plasticizers" to make materials like PVC softer and more flexible, share with many other industrial chemicals the ability to mimic the effect on the body of estrogen, the female sex hormone. Environmental campaigners have linked phthalates to recent evidence of declining sperm counts and increasing testicular cancer in men.[4]

"What do the breakdown of the family, dead whales, shrunken alligator penises, hyperactive children, disappearing frogs, and breast cancer have in common?" the normally calm *Business Week* asked its readers. The answer was that, "they all may be linked to the modern era's witches' brew of pesticides, plastics, and other man-made substances."[5]

The book that really ramped up the debate on these issues in the late 1990s was *Our Stolen Future*,[6] which claimed that, "We have become unwitting guinea pigs in our own vast experiment."

Having myself published a book called *The Poisoned Womb* in 1985,[7] it was fascinating to see just how far the scientific research had come. As US vice president Al Gore put it in his foreword to *Our Stolen Future*:

"The scientific case is still emerging, and our understanding of the nature and magnitude of this threat is bound to evolve as research advances. Moreover, because industrial chemicals have become a major sector of the global economy, any evidence linking them to serious ecological and human health problems is bound to generate controversy."

An example of the way in which this area of scientific uncertainty can erupt into the news and dramatically upset major companies is the multimillion-dollar lawsuit launched against US chemical giant DuPont over allegations that one of its fungicides, Benlate, and particularly an ingredient called benomyl, can cause children to be born without eyes (a condition known as anopthalmia) or smaller-than-normal eyes (micropthalmia). Whatever the outcome, few issues are as likely to exercise the public and political mind in the 21st century as one which links chemicals that are everywhere about us and both our own reproductive health and the fate of the unborn.

Led to Slaughter

In normal circumstances, most people who buy meat in supermarkets give little, if any, thought to the myriad processes that bring these packages of beef, mutton, or pork to the supermarket shelf. Keen to discourage rampant vegetarianism, most supermarkets probably prefer it when their customers cannot peer right back down the food chain. But the "mad cow" controversy shows just how dramatically things can change in an X-ray environment.

It also shows how some such issues can damage the fortunes of a very wide range of industries. Stripped to its essentials, the issue was whether cows fed with products including waste products from sheep suffering from a disease called scrapie could, first, develop bovine spongiform encephalopathy (BSE) and, second, pass the disease on both to their offspring and – in the form of Creutzfeldt Jakob disease (CJD) – to those eating the contaminated meat. As the *Financial Times* put it early on in the controversy:

"Already the crisis is clearly damaging some sectors of a highly complex and interdependent industry. The immediate pain is being felt not by farmers, but by the industry that serves them further down the food chain – the auctioneers, abattoirs and processors, and meat hauliers. At the sharpest end are the slaughterhouses, which have seen their throughput grind to a standstill since the crisis broke."[8]

The impacts were extraordinary. In the immediate aftermath, some 4,000 people – or around half the workforce – were laid off by the 90 largest UK abattoirs. Companies that were sitting on stocks of meat estimated to have a potential market value of £79 million suddenly found their asset value more or less halved overnight. The Road Haulage Association said that about 8,500 drivers and support staff had been laid off and 5,000 trucks involved in transporting animals, animal feed, and meat had been forced off the road. In Germany, meanwhile, beef consumption plummeted by 70% in the first week after the scare broke – and only slowly recovered to the 50% level. Across the European Union, beef consumption was estimated to have dropped by 30%.

And what was perhaps most interesting about the disaster was that experts had been warning of the dangers for years. One had even called for the slaughter of six million cows six years earlier, warning that anyone under the age of 50 should avoid beef. He was derided in articles based on government briefings, excluded from expert panels and denied research funding.[9] The attempted cover-up was among the most blatant of recent times, but – as will increasingly be the case – failed to protect the government, the industries hiding behind its skirts, or the victims of the disease.

Once the lid came off the UK meat industry, it seemed incredible only that the disaster had taken so long to erupt. Not that the UK was alone in finding out extraordinary things when the X-ray environment switched on. In Switzerland, for example, it was discovered that thousands of human placentas from hospitals had been used since the 1960s to make animal feed. How could the practice, which breached hospital waste disposal guidelines, have gone undetected for so long? But, that said, the UK was the country with the real problems.

The root causes of these problems turned out to include the economics of the beef industry, the government's deregulation of the animal feed industry, and the unbelievably cavalier attitudes of the boards of some of the major companies involved.

When BSE first surfaced as an issue, in 1986, the UK Government decided to exclude from the food chain tissues most likely to include the suspected infective agents, proteins known as prions. If the bans on such tissue in animal feed and in products meant for human consumption had been properly enforced, the problem might have disappeared. But the beef industry is notoriously suspicious of outsiders, ruled by informal agreements, and often poorly managed.[10] Indeed, the *Observer* noted, "as BSE became more common, farmers got better at spotting it before it became obvious." In this way, it was feared, "thousands of diseased cows may have gone to market." Magistrates' courts handled a string of cases in which farmers were accused of passing off diseased animals as healthy.

One step further along the food chain were the abattoirs. They serve a market plagued by over-capacity, resulting in intense competition and very low profit margins. As a result, many middle range abattoirs constantly operate on the verge of financial collapse. Attempts to set up quality meat schemes were usually undermined by cut-throat competition. Internal quality controls were generally poor, with abattoir workers being semi-skilled and poorly paid, so quality issues are seen to be management's responsibility not the worker's. External controls were also deeply flawed, with former meat inspectors saying they had an average of only two minutes to check a carcass. To begin with, at least, serious shortcomings identified by spot-checks were insufficiently pursued by the health authorities, at a time when the authorities were, in any event, leaning over backwards to persuade the public that British beef was safe.

Another link in the chain turned out to be what is known as rendering, where abattoir wastes are cooked and crushed to make such products as tallow and bone meal. Inspections found that fully 75% of the renderers were failing to meet the relevant regulations. The rendering industry is dominated by a single firm, Prosper de Mulder. The firm accounted for around two-thirds of red meat waste acquired for rendering in England and Wales, enjoyed a return on capital of more than 30% and yet operated in what was politely described as a "highly informal way." According to the *Observer*, "there were no minutes of board meetings." Nor was it simply a case of inadequate management systems. "The company appeared to have little respect for the regulatory authorities," the paper reported.[11]

The conclusion was that "For a decade, at least, much of the industry has been governed by a culture of organized irresponsibility." But, inevitably, a massive price would be paid by the industry. For the short term, it was being kept alive by consuming itself:

"Renderers used to recycle unwanted animal parts to make products for industry; now theirs is largely a waste disposal business. As the cull comes to an end, over-capacity will be exposed and plant closures and job losses will come thick and fast. Then what is being slaughtered will be the industry itself.'"

This is a moral (or perhaps immoral) tale for our times. With public attention hooked, the media went into convulsions, squeezing every last bit of potential horror from the controversy. BSE, the public was told, might have got into milk or, through animal wastes in fertilizers, into rivers and drinking water. Such is the nature of discourse in the global village. But, in the end, as one farmer put it: "If the first priority of consumers is cheap food, it may not be entirely coincidental that the same objective is adopted all the way up the food chain."[12] The same can be said of our demands for cheap anything – cars, energy, homes, or holidays – and the extraordinarily complex value chains whose purpose in life it is to meet our ever-expanding needs.

From T-shirts to Cigarettes

Nor are Canadian belugas and British beef isolated examples. The list of technologies and products receiving the X-ray treatment is growing by the day. Let's quickly look at the way that a small selection have been affected by triple bottom line concerns.

Paper One of the most intensive life-cycle studies of any industry, anywhere, was published by IIED as *Towards a Sustainable Paper Cycle*.[13] The third most energy-intensive manufacturing sector in the world, the paper industry has often been in the spotlight in recent years, following controversies over such issues as chlorine bleaching, recycling, and sustainable forestry. Largely financed by the World Business Council for Sustainable Development (WBCSD), the IIED report concluded that bringing all paper mills up to uniformly acceptable environmental standards would cost at least $20 billion.

A few years ago, it would have been very difficult to find out how Asian mills compared with North American mills, for example, or European with Scandinavian. Increasingly, however, such data will be available, and the ability of pulp and paper companies to maneuver the spotlight onto single issues where their particular products happen to perform well will be increasingly constrained.

T-shirts and other clothes Retailers, whatever they sell, often complain that they lack the resources to track down malpractice in their supply chains. But the US labor secretary Robert Reich worked out an effective way to turn up the heat on issues such as sweatshop labor. "We have uncovered slavery here in the United States," he stormed, pointing to his department's discovery of a garment factory in California where Thai immigrants worked 18 hours a day in "sub-human conditions."[14]

Faced by the inevitable industry protests that it was impossible to discover what suppliers and their sub-contractors, and even sub-sub-contractors, were doing, Reich decided to pile on the pressure. "If they wished to know, they could know," as he succinctly put it, noting that what was needed was a "cultural shift" in the retail sector. To speed the process, his department published a "white list" of manufacturers which had submitted detailed proof that they avoid sweatshop suppliers. Publication was timed to have maximum impact over the Christmas period, with the hope that the media would come up with their own "black lists" by a process of deduction.

In the end, however, everyone knows that it all comes down to one thing. Will ordinary people be prepared to pay the price? "Ultimately, it's up to the consumer," said Jeff Hermanson of the Union of Needle Trades, Industrial and Textile Employees (UNITE!). "They are the ones with the power to spur retailers into action." Campaigners often find it hard to build sustained consumer pressure over long periods, unless it is on "black and white" issues like South African apartheid. But business has found that the "caring," "concerned," "ethical," "green," "militant," "political," or "vigilante" consumer can be mobilized if the issue is clear and immediate, and if there is a well-defined target industry, company, or product to go for.

Tobacco   This product category shows just how far public pressure can push an industry. It also demonstrates that if the issue affects people in their everyday lives, and particularly if it affects their health, pressure can develop and be sustained over a period of years.

Some health effects of smoking can take decades – in some cases, more than half a century – to appear. Even so, smoking remains one of the world's favourite addictions, or "habits" as the tobacco industry would prefer one to say.[15] An estimated 15 billion cigarettes are smoked every day, including more than a billion in the USA. And it is the USA, the home of the international tobacco industry, which has gone furthest in turning up the heat under the tobacco giants. Some states have passed laws restricting smoking in public, while the Food and Drug Administration (FDA) has been lobbying to have cigarette vending machines banned and to further restrict advertising. Smoking, at least under the Clinton Administration, has even been banned at the White House.

But much more serious for an industry whose main product is now widely acknowledged to cause cancer, and many other health problems, is the growing likelihood of a successful legal challenge by cancer victims. One retired air traffic controller, Grady Carter, sent shock-waves through the industry when his lawyer succeeded in persuading a jury to award his client and his wife $750,000 in damages for the loss of part of a lung following cancer surgery. The industry, which had faced hundreds of similar claims over the previous 30 years, had not previously lost a case.

The award, made against Brown and Williamson, an American tobacco company owned by BAT, was scarcely a show-stopper. The company would have no trouble in paying up even if its appeals failed. Indeed, BAT made a 1995 profit of £2.4 billion, including £1.6 billion contributed by its tobacco division, and spends £50 million a year fighting cases such as these. But what if the public mood continues to swing against the industry and more cases succeed? There are those who are dedicated to ensuring that this happens and, as in so many other areas, the advice given by science can so easily swing in unexpected directions as new evidence comes in.

The image that may come back to haunt the industry is the photograph of the "Tobacco Seven," all tobacco company heads, swearing before Congress that they believed that cigarettes are not addictive. Since then a raft of damning documents has appeared and hundreds of new lawsuits have been filed.[16] Tobacco industry analysts comforted themselves that the world market was predicted to grow 20% by the end of the century, with the potential markets in the developing countries barely scratched by western companies to date, but there are those who believe that – at least in some parts of the world – Marlboro Man could well join Stalin and other fallen 20th century idols on the junkheap of history. Meanwhile, there is a deep irony in the news that tobacco companies hope to fund the payments they now expect to make, and which will likely run into hundreds of billions of dollars, by selling more cigarettes in emerging markets like China.

Murderous Airbags

Faced with evidence of unacceptable risks, most people would prefer to change the technology than to change their behavior or lifestyles. One of the most extraordinary illustrations of this fact is the recent evolution of the humble auto airbag. Sixties America saw airbags as the sure-fire route to automotive safety; a way to drive fast, share the roads with maniacs, and still come out alive. Unfortunately, as the airbag story demonstrates, there is what some scientists call the "law of unintended consequences." Every time we act to address one set of problems, the chances are that we unintentionally set in train a new rash of problems. Often, the benefits of the action hugely outweigh the new problems, but not always. In the case of airbags, they have turned out to have a particularly nasty habit of killing young passengers. "Airbags have been blamed for the deaths of 22 babies and small children so far – eight last year," *Fortune* reported in 1996.[17]

One reason why Americans are so fond of airbags, it turns out, is that many of them refuse to wear seat belts. Only around two-thirds of Americans routinely wear belts when driving. The pressure for airbags developed as an alternative way of ensuring driver and, increasingly, passenger safety. This was despite the evidence of tests carried out by Volvo in 1974, with 24 small live pigs exposed to airbags in action to show the likely effect on 3- to 6-year-old children. The result was eight dead pigs, with a further 13 seriously injured.

Today's statistics suggest that, in any event, airbags work far better when a belt is also worn – and that one baby or small child dies for every 70 or so lives saved. As I wrote this chapter, the US government announced that less powerful air-bags would save the lives of dozens of children each year, yet could cost the lives of between 133 and 1,203 adults![18]

Complicated. Now imagine the same sort of problem, but with lives saved or enhanced today and the injuries suffered by future generations. What chance is there that we will not only learn to identify such impacts with any degree of confidence, but also move to tackle them effectively and in time? The answer almost certainly depends on how far we get with developing both our understanding of the law of unintended consequences and our use of new techniques like life-cycle assessment (LCA) and design for the environment (DfE) tools.

What's New, Gurus?

Why Things Bite Back

However clever our technology, unintended side-effects will continue to haunt us. Edward Tenner, in his book *Why Things Bite Back*, speaks of technology's "revenge effect."[19] Since we were on the subject of airbags, let's stick with cars. Tenner notes that power door locks, now standard on many new cars, increase the sense of safety, yet have helped triple or quadruple the number of drivers locked out of their own cars – costing $400 million a year in the USA and exposing drivers to the very criminals the locks were meant to defeat.

Or take the car and home alarms that in many cities seem to have displaced the dawn chorus. Maddened by the electronic squawking, some neighbors have trashed offending vehicles in an attempt to silence them. And the false alarms from cheap security systems required by insurance companies mean that two-thirds of recent alarm calls in Philadelphia were false – with the result that the equivalent of 58 full-time police officers were diverted from real crime to following up useless calls.

Time and again, our early expectations about a new technology turn out to be over-optimistic or otherwise flawed. The same electronic gear that allows us to work at home, for example, doesn't necessarily make us any freer. Urgent network messages, e-mail and faxes now arrive at our homes at all hours, tying us ever more closely into the business cycle. Nor is there simply one sort of revenge effect. Tenner identifies at least five distinct types:

♦ The first of these is the *rearranging effect*, as where the installation of air-conditioning equipment on trains raises platform temperatures for those waiting to board by as much as 10°Fahrenheit.

♦ Second, there is the *repeating effect*, where "labor-saving" equipment results in the same thing – such as the household laundry – having to be done more often, rather than the householder gaining more time to do other things.

♦ Third, there are *recomplicating effects*, as when the potential benefits of switching from rotary to digital telephone dialling are overwhelmed by single calls sometimes needing (when you add in carrier access codes and credit card numbers) thirty digits.

♦ Fourth, there are *regenerating effects*, illustrated by the greater damage caused, during the Gulf War, when Patriot missiles hit incoming Scud missiles aimed at Tel Aviv and converted a single object into lethal debris extending over as much as 5 kilometres.

♦ And, fifth, there are *recongesting effects*, as when innovation opens up a new space, only to result in it being rapidly filled with traffic (e.g. the electromagnetic spectrum) or potentially deadly waste (e.g. the 30,000–70,000 pieces of space debris clogging up earth's orbit).

All of these effects, it turns out, are characteristics of *systems*, rather than of single products or materials. Today, however clever the testing, so-called "bugs" can have an ever-greater impact as the scale of the systems they inhabit, and the number of people who depend upon them, becomes ever larger. Ironically, too, the very products and systems we have put in place to protect our lives and property are proving, like those airbags, to have unintended revenge effects. The X-rays used to diagnose cancer may themselves cause cancer. The asbestos used to control fire hazards turned out to cause asbestosis. The solvent tanks undergrounded in Silicon Valley, for fire protection purposes, began to leak invisibly into the local water supply. And the CFCs which made refrigeration "safe" will continue to corrode the planet's protective ozone layer through the 21st century.

Worse, we see a change in the very nature of disasters. Yesterday's involved clearly visible cause-and-effect chains (when the boiler blew up, you were either dead or not). By contrast, many of today's disasters are expressed as a statistical deviation from "normal" background rates (as with lung cancer caused by smoking). The old disasters were mainly sudden and local: the new ones are often gradual and global, from radioactive isotopes in the 1950s milk to climate change in the 1990s.

The technological dream of a self-correcting, risk-free world is as much an illusion as John von Neumann's 1955 prediction of energy too cheap to meter by 1980. In fields as diverse as medicine, the environment, the computerized office and sport, new technologies often fail to deliver the benefits that were promised – and bring problems that weren't. So the computer software on which so much of modern life now depends will almost certainly be a key source of future catastrophic risk.

But, there are also grounds for optimism. As Tenner concludes:

"One reason for optimism is that disaster is paradoxically creative. It legitimizes and promotes changes in rules – changes that may be resisted as long as the levels of casualties remain 'acceptable' prior to a disaster that leads to change."

The way forward, he suggests, is for technology to mimic nature: to become more diverse, to dematerialize, and to pursue *finesse* – abandoning frontal attacks on problems "for solutions that rely on the same kind of latent properties that led to revenge effects in the first place."

Lean Thinkers

For years, intensifying international competition has switched one industry after another on to the need for life-cycle thinking. In their extraordinary book, *The Machine That Changed the World*, James Womack and Daniel Jones explained how auto companies – inspired by Toyota – had been dramatically improving their performance through "lean production" techniques.[20] In their follow-up book, *Lean Thinking*, Womack and Jones came up with what they saw as "a formula for sustainable growth and success."[21]

The approach was stimulated by the Japanese concept of *muda*, which means "waste." More specifically, the word covers any human activity which absorbs resources but creates no value. Included would be mistakes which need making good, production of goods that no one turns out to want, processing steps which are not actually needed, useless movement of people and materials from one place to another, and goods which fail to meet customer needs and expectations. The lean thinking mind-set is based on five principles:

♦ First, companies need to understand the *value* created by each specific product.
♦ Second, they must identify the *value stream* for the product.
♦ Third, value should *flow* without interruptions.
♦ Fourth, the customer should be encouraged to *pull* value through the entire system.
♦ And, fifth, all those involved should pursue *perfection*. The focus of attention is directed at "the entire firm, indeed at the whole value stream for specific products, running from raw material to finished good, order to delivery, and concept to launch."

Womack and Jones believe that lean thinking is "counterintuitive and a bit difficult to grasp on first encounter (but then blindingly obvious once 'the light comes on')." Environmental issues only get a couple of quick look-ins as they spool out their thinking over 350 pages. In one case, lean thinking helped remove the need for producing radioactive acids. Once the light does switch on in the right way, this approach potentially provides an extraordinarily powerful boost for progress against the triple bottom line.

The Eco-compass

So how can we ensure that environmental considerations are fully taken into account in the development of new technology? One of the best people to ask is Claude Fussler, who as vice-president for environment, health, and safety at Dow Europe became one of Europe's best-known industrial proponents of the sustainability agenda. His book, *Driving Eco-Innovation*,[22] co-written with Peter James, explores some of the ways in which the fields of innovation and sustainability are now beginning to overlap.

The real problem we face, Fussler argues, is "innovation lethargy." Many of the technologies we have developed may seem hugely sophisticated to us, but in reality they are crawling along at the bottom of the evolutionary scale. When Professor Robert Ayres looked at the energy efficiency of a number of major end uses in the US, for example, he found that the efficiency of air cooling systems ranged between 0.7% and 5%; cooking and water heating between 0.3% and 3%; and lighting between 0.7% and 7%. Appalling.

Our innovation lethargy is simultaneously a problem for the environment and for our economies, Fussler points out. The problem, in a nutshell, is that we are too often happier focusing on smaller, incremental improvements to existing technologies rather than on the process of "super-innovation" which produces technologies "which reshape economic and social possibilities by creating a new performance curve and new forms of demand."

One real problem here is that the gap between the initial invention and widespread use can be a matter of decades, as in the case of the jet engine and the transistor. The jet engine was invented in 1928, took its first flight in 1941 and, even so, was only adopted in military aircraft during the 1950s and civil aircraft in the 1960s. Computer chips, which are currently subject to Moore's Law (which holds that they will double their power and halve their size every 18 months), are currently on the vertically climbing part of the standard "S-curve" of product innovation. Made in 1965 by Intel co-founder Gordon Moore, the forecast has been remarkably prescient and has held true for the past 35 years, helping to propel semiconductor production into a $150-billion-a-year industry.[23] But Fussler notes that it took the industry 25 years to move from the transistor's discovery to the first real integrated circuit, the Intel 8008 microprocessor.

The key to long-term success, then, is to keep an eye on emerging technologies and emerging inflexion points in the S-curves, when periods of super-rapid innovation and technical progress are about to begin. Not that "surfers of the S-curves" will always find it easy to spot the developing wave. How many businesses predicted the rapid phase-out of CFCs? "Surfers will follow the maxim: move before you have to," says Fussler. "Replace current products, ahead of competitors, with new ones which address fundamental long-term needs."

But how can you identify emerging vulnerabilities and opportunities ahead of someone putting up a sign saying "S-curve this way?" The answer, Fussler suggests, is to use the "eco-compass" developed by Dow Europe. The eco-compass has six poles or dimensions (see Figure 8.1), designed to capture all significant environmental issues. A key advantage is that, instead of thinking about each dimension separately, the compass allows new product development teams to explore all the dimensions simultaneously, including any significant inter-relationships between them. The six eco-compass dimensions are:

♦ health and environmental potential risk
♦ resource conservation
♦ energy intensity
♦ materials intensity
♦ revalorization (remanufacturing, reuse, and recycling)
♦ and service extension (a measure of improved service from a given quantity of inputs, for example by improving product durability)

The eco-compass is mainly designed to drive and record improvements towards the minimum "Factor 4" targets set by sustainability experts based at organizations like Germany's Wuppertal Institute and the US Rocky Mountain Institute. The data are always expressed for a given unit of activity or value; what life-cycle specialists call a "functional unit." For paint, this would be an area of surface covered, so the measure might be square metres of surface covered per kilogram of paint applied.

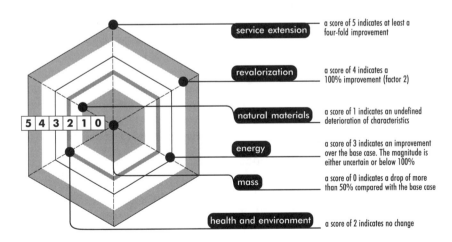

FIGURE 8.1   Dow Europe's Eco-compass (*Source*: Dow Europe)

Of course, in the end, such tools only constitute real progress if they are used by enough people, they work, and they do not trigger too many revenge effects. As Fussler concluded:

> "innovation is more than creating new ideas. It is a structured business process that plays out at the analytical, strategic and creative levels. It only adds value when it combines three operational disciplines: response to future market needs and openings; the creation of genuinely new ideas for meeting these needs; and the achievement of outstanding implementation of the ideas."

Throughout, Fussler contends, the aim must be to:

♦ reduce the mass intensity
♦ minimize the human health and environmental risk
♦ decrease the energy intensity
♦ increase the levels of reuse and revalorization of wastes
♦ boost the conservation of resources and the use of renewable materials
♦ extend the service and function.

A key element in success is likely to be a diverse, creative team. This needs to include expertise from different parts of the organization and different stages of the life cycle. It should draw on people with different styles of thinking; analytical, conceptual, emotional. The best participants tend to bring energy, creativity, and, indeed, a sense of humor to the proceedings. And it should involve at least some of those who will be responsible for putting the ideas into practice.

Boardroom Views

No Accident

So how does all of this look from the boardroom of the typical company? Frankly, it is rarely on the agenda. How many ordinary companies have the capacity to understand their value chains on an ongoing basis in the way that supermarkets came to understand the realities of their meat supply chains during the BSE crisis? How many companies running Total Quality Management-driven supplier challenges cover the full range of triple bottom issues? How many apply lean thinking directly to environmental and social issues? The answer, in all cases, is

CASE STUDY

SAINSBURY'S, UK:
VETTING THE FOOD CHAIN

If you are looking for evidence that supplier challenges are the wave of the future, turn to Sainsbury's 1996 environment report. Alongside all the data on Sainsbury's own direct impacts, there are five pages on the indirect impacts associated with the operations of the company's suppliers. The company's UK retail business relies on over 6,500 suppliers worldwide – and the report spotlights some areas in which suppliers are now coming under scrutiny. The benefits for Sainsbury's include cost savings and new market opportunities, together with improved environmental performance and security of supply.

Older issues are now covered by established sourcing policies. So, for example, Sainsbury's tuna products are all based on fish caught using "dolphin friendly" pole and line fishing methods. Now pressures are being exerted on suppliers in such areas as energy efficiency, integrated crop management, organic produce, animal testing, animal husbandry, timber and forest products, and peat. Let's look at two of these: the company's integrated crop management system (ICMS) and peat.

On the ICMS front, the requirement is that growers use biological and natural pest control methods, and half of all crops were covered by ICMS protocols by the end of 1995/96. The target was three-quarters by the end of 1996/97. This area requires a long-term, strategic approach because of the scale of the transition involved. But already three-quarters of UK crops sourced by Sainsbury's are grown according to these protocols and a third of overseas crops. The targets for the end of 1996/97 were 88% and 57%, respectively.

On the peat front, Sainsbury's Homebase stores have managed to meet 20% of demand through peat substitutes. The 1996/97 target was to build a database on peat substitutes, which seemed weak. But the company's reporting team told me that they needed to get the peat buyers on side before they tried to "distort" the market towards sustainability.

precariously few. But the pressures now building up are such that the limited best practice available today could spread rapidly.

Even those companies that use life-cycle assessment (LCA) as a key in-house tool have been slow to build life-cycle thinking into their corporate strategies. But, as we have seen, it was no accident that Procter & Gamble picked up Lever's Persil Power problem. Certainly, the competition between these two giants is unusually intense. Sustain-Ability has worked with both and it sometimes seems that they regard one another with a mutual loathing unrivalled since the Cold War. But P&G has emerged as one of the world's leaders when it comes to the use of LCA and of a related approach, value:impact assessment.

As Peter Hindle, responsible for environmental affairs in Europe, explains:

> "Society expects that the products and services that it buys and uses will be safe for people and for the environment. It also expects that those involved in making the products or providing the services will work in safe conditions and that the production processes will not injure the environment."

But, he notes, these "bold statements beg the question: 'How safe is safe?'" Each of us accepts certain levels of risk every day, whether we are crossing the road, driving a car, or traveling in an aircraft. That said, the ways in which we experience and respond to risks depend enormously on the degree to which we have control over, or at least a say in, the risk-generating activities:

> "For everyday consumer goods such as laundry detergents, dishwashing liquids, baby diapers, shampoos, toothpaste, skin cream and colour cosmetics, people expect the products to be safe under conditions of use and reasonably foreseeable misuse. This includes worker safety, user safety and environmental safety."

So far, so ordinary, you may say. But P&G has also been trying to internalize at least some of the new requirements of sustainable development. For much of the 1990s, the company distilled the complexity of the challenge down into a single phrase: "More from Less." "The on-going societal debate on the concept of sustainable development centers on the appropriate balance between economic growth (how much 'more') and environmental quality effects (how much 'less')," Hindle explains.

Achieving more from less requires a systematic approach that measures two comparatives: "more" and "less." In P&G's "value:impact assessment" approach, "more" relates to consumer value, "less" to environmental impact. Noting that many early "green" products turned out to offer "less from less," the company set out to ensure that products that offered an improved environmental performance also delivered the benefits that consumers want, ensuring that people want to buy and use them. Only if these improved products displace existing products, it argues, will the environmental benefits be significant.

The value assessment part of the process uses different criteria to evaluate a product's "fitness for use." How well a product works often depends on how the consumer uses it, which means that research needs to be carried out on actual, rather than just recommended, usage. Once these data are in, the company can proceed to the impact and risk assessment stages of the process.

Used in conjunction with the development of P&G's new "compact" detergents, designed to deliver more laundry benefits with a reduced volume of chemicals, the approach led in the space of a few years to European consumers using 386,000 tonnes less chemicals than would otherwise have been the case. A side-benefit was that the impacts that would have been associated with the manufacture, distribution, and use of these chemicals were also avoided.

An illustration, in short, of how lean thinking can help in the sustainability transition. But if we are to move towards the Factor 4 – let alone Factor 10 – improvements, corporate boards are going to need a sharp nudge from markets, particularly from the financial markets. Such pressures are beginning to build.

Sharpest Tool

Perhaps not surprisingly, the real board-level pressure is coming from sectors that have a vested interest in adopting a life-cycle perspective, most notably the insurers, rather than in optimizing short-term return on equity, like most financial analysts. Corporate boards have not seen insurers as sustainability campaigners, but many soon will. Insurers are no keener on losing money than the rest of us, and the potential losses they face because of environmental risks are getting ever larger.

"Insurance companies are both affected by environmental problems and can make an important contribution to sustainable development," says Frank Annighöfer, chairman of the board at Germany's Gerling Consulting, part of a major insurance group.[24] There are many ways in which insurance companies can cut the environmental impact of their activities, not least through green housekeeping measures – involving minimizing the impact of such areas as office cleaning, computing and furnishing.

But, as Annighöfer continues, "the sharpest tool that an insurance company has is not housekeeping but its insurance products – the risks covered or not covered in an insurance contract and the premium for the insurance cover. If no insurance cover is available for certain technologies considered unsafe or likely to cause environmental damage, the chances of this technology surviving decrease." And, he notes, "if the insurance premium for a business with bad [environment, health and safety (EHS)] management is higher than for one with an advanced EHS program, there will be a cost advantage for the latter."

Unfortunately, that is not the way that things have always worked in the past. But 25 years ago, Gerling decided to offer its EHS expertise to industry and government via Gerling Consulting, and now operates the service from 12 offices across Europe. Among the areas covered are site audits, risk control strategies, and hazardous waste remediation. Longer term, an even more important lever that Gerling and other insurers can pull is the investment one. Insurance companies have to invest billions of dollars earned from premiums and Gerling has also now entered the field of environmentally sound investment, working alongside Norway's Storebrand in building up the Environmental Value Fund described in Chapter 13.

If such initiatives take off, they will provide a further stimulus to corporate boards wondering whether they should pay greater attention to the risks lurking up and down their value chains. Few companies will be able to sustain a life-cycle worldview on an ongoing basis, let alone full 7-D vision. But every time a major new issue surfaces, we will see corporate auditing teams racing around the world to see whether the same thing could happen again, in a different place, to a different industry or company. As a logical end-point of the value:impact assessment approach, some companies may even find themselves beginning to think the unthinkable – and wondering whether the high-to-medium risk processes they operate or products they offer are really necessary.

Bubbling Under

Designing for Sustainability

Life-cycle assessment (LCA) has now escaped from the laboratory into the market. As a result, we are seeing growing numbers of companies trying to integrate life-cycle thinking into their new product development processes. One company SustainAbility has worked with throughout the 1990s as it addressed the task of environmental product design is ICI Polyurethanes (ICI PU). The company makes polyurethane foams, widely used in furniture and mattresses, as well as in building insulation, car steering wheels, and refrigerator insulation.[25]

The challenge, as Vanja Markovic (later with ICI Group) recalled, was to use LCA as a means "to develop a product with reduced environmental impact during the whole life cycle." This is a complex business, with two main types of polyurethane, TDI and MDI. Originally ICI PU (later sold to Huntsman Chemicals) was keen to find an additional way to use MDI, with the environmental story surfacing later. In developing its "Waterlily" foam product, LCA was used to carry out a broad brush analysis of the main environmental impacts throughout the life cycle of foams used in furniture. The exercise focused on five main stages of the process: raw material manufacture, product fabrication, packaging and transport, use, and waste management. The main benefit of the exercise, says Dr Markovic, was "to draw attention to the importance of the raw material manufacturing stage," which proved to account for 80% of life-cycle energy consumption.

Given that companies cannot do everything at once, one of the key advantages of LCA is to help identify priorities. In this case, ICI PU decided that its priority had to be design-for-recycling. The Waterlily foam, which is now being sold to companies like IKEA, can be chemically recycled and future Waterlily foams could contain as much as 70% recycled foam. Everything hangs, however, on how fast the pressures to recycle develop. Recyclability is one thing, recycling – coupled with the successful sale of products with a high level of recycled content – quite another. ICI PU will be worth watching to see whether it can scale up its recycling activities to ensure that future sleepers can rest assured that their mattresses will not end up further clogging the world's landfill sites.

It is worth noting, however, that a product's environmental performance is rarely the highest priority when it comes to determining competitive advantage. Other attributes, among them price, performance, reliability, and quality, are usually more important to commercial success. As we have seen in the P&G case, such attributes may themselves sometimes constitute environmental progress, but may not be advertised as such by the producer, let alone be seen as such by the end consumer. A recent study found that of a sample of 16 "green" products, environmental performance advantages alone were insignificant in conferring a competitive edge in 11 cases.[26] What that tells us is simply that environmental performance is not a sufficient condition for market success in most cases, but it will increasingly be a necessary condition.

Who Needs It?

If the life-cycle data continue to accumulate, the triple bottom line perspective will begin to raise real question marks over some products, processes and even industries. And, as the sustainable production and consumption imperative builds, we will also hear increasing discussion of Factor 4–10 strategies. In parallel, the growing use of LCA tools reflects both the pressures for higher levels of environmental quality and for continuous improvement of product quality.

Life-cycle thinking and techniques can be applied to products, processes, or systems. It can focus on economic, environmental, or social costs and benefits. In the economic area, for example, a company may investigate the life-cycle benefits, costs, and impacts of its products, either hoping to cut them or to prove to customers that high initial purchase costs will be offset by lower overall life-cycle costs.

Modern management approaches such as value engineering and value marketing depend on such life-cycle insights for their effectiveness. Now such techniques are being applied to products to identify their life-cycle economic, environmental, and, in some cases, social costs. What is interesting about the lean thinking approach is that it challenges the need for products and services. The sustainability agenda does the same – and to an even greater extent. As a result, companies determined to remain at the cutting edge should be thinking of applying some form of "need test" to their product or service offerings.

SustainAbility's "beta version" of a need test, developed alongside Dow Europe, is shown in Figure 8.2.[27] An outline application, focusing

---

The Diagnosis

1 What is the primary function of the product or service?
2 What other benefits does the product or service offer?
3 Is there likely to be a long-term need and/or demand for the product or service?
4 How does the value:impact assessment for the product or service look today?
5 Would the product or service be sustainable in an equitable world of 8–10 billion people?
6 Are there more sustainable ways of providing the function – or meeting the need?

The Prognosis

7 Given 1–6, what threats and opportunities will there be for the product or service during the sustainability transition?

FIGURE 8.2   The Need Test (*Source:* SustainAbility)

on the dairy hormone BST, can be found in the Spotlight on pages 214–15. Used in parallel with the eco-compass and by a diverse, committed working group focused not only on potential threats but also on the very real business opportunities likely to open up the Need Test can be a useful eye-opener and horizon-widener for product teams, business units and even entire companies.

Winners, Losers

Like any revolution, the life-cycle revolution will often disrupt, or even destroy, existing commercial relationships. With many companies already trying to slim down their supply chains to a smaller number of strategic suppliers, poor life-cycle performance (actual or perceived) will become a further reason for dropping particular companies. Many companies will not even know why they have been delisted.

The winners in this new world will be those companies that have already X-rayed much of their supply chain and operations for potential problems and moved to address any issues identified. The losers will include a high proportion of those that have not. For those determined to avoid this fate, the sustainability audit framework outlined in Chapter 14 suggests some of the questions they should be asking.

Even the most seductive business strategies will need to be reviewed against this trend. So, for example, one emerging business strategy has been for manufacturers of ingredients or components of final consumer products as different as soft drinks and personal computers to try to develop brand identities which come right through the supply chain. Examples include NutraSweet in soft drinks, Goretex and Lycra in clothing, Teflon in cooking utensils and Intel in computers. Other companies aiming to move in the same direction include ICI Acrylics, with products (Lucite in the US, Perspex in Europe) destined for use in baths, spas, and other "sanitaryware." The potential downside of this strategy is that, while it can massively boost the profitability of particular components or ingredients, it also helps build the X-ray environment. Companies which in the past simply had to worry about what industrial customers thought of them will increasingly have to worry – as Intel now does – about what end-consumers (and those who influence them) think.

And the fact that a technology offers major benefits in relation to one dimension of the triple bottom line does not mean it will prove to be sustainable. Genetic engineering has already produced a number of classic examples. Take the genetically engineered version of the dairy hormone bovine somatotropin (BST). Producers like Eli Lilly and

WHO NEEDS RECOMBINANT BST?

Let's apply the Need Test to a real-world product. Given that genetic engineering has the power to transform our world, for better or worse, let's take a bio-product: bovine somatotropin (BST).

The Diagnosis

1 What is the primary function of BST?

Recombinant (genetically engineered) BST is a hormone designed to supplement the natural hormone in dairy cows, where it controls lactation – or milk production. Injections of BST can boost a cow's milk production by some 10–15%.

2 What other benefits does BST offer?

BST manufacturers – among them Eli Lilly and Monsanto – claim more milk with fewer cows and less feed: a boon for milk-starved regions and, potentially, a way of tackling the dairy industry's contribution to global warming.

3 Is there likely to be a long-term demand for the primary function?

It depends on your vision of the future. If you are a deep green, almost certainly not. BST is very much part of the high-tech, intensive approach to husbandry, which, as a system, is unlikely to be sustainable. But if you are a pale green, let alone a "brown," the assessment could be very different. Population pressures, you might conclude, will drive growing demand for food and, in turn, growing intensification of all food production systems.

4 How does the value:impact assessment for BST look today?

At the level of the individual, large-scale farm, the assessment is probably weighted in favour of BST. In developing countries and the ex-communist bloc, recombinant BST has been welcomed as a means to accelerate the transition to western diets. But the wider implications, in terms of the likely negative impacts on the structure of the farming industry, on small farming units and on the communities and landscapes they sustain, remain a major concern. There are also important animal welfare issues.

❯

5 Would this approach be sustainable in an equitable world of 8–10 billion people?

If 8 billion people insisted on the sort of diets found today in America or Germany, for example, large-scale use of recombinant BST would be essential. But given that today's cattle-based industries are already raising major ecological issues, their future expansion along conventional paths is far from guaranteed.

6 Are there more sustainable ways of providing the same function?

Not in terms of boosting milk yields with injectable hormones, although the direct genetic engineering of cows might provide a more humane – if even less ethically acceptable – route to the same goal.

The Prognosis

7 On the basis of 1–6 above, what are BST's prospects?

In a world where cows and other farm animals are increasingly turned into machines, BST would be a sure-fire winner. In a sustainable world, hopefully based on the humane treatment of animals, the prospects seem less certain. That said, things might be somewhat different if the biotech industry came up with a version which could be ingested rather than injected.

Monsanto have argued that it can enormously boost milk production, enhancing dairy productivity and – incidentally – helping to cut down on greenhouse gas emissions from cow's intestines! The product, however, also has the power to radically transform the agricultural economy, together with many of the economic, social and environmental systems which depend upon it (Spotlight, above).

Predicting which technologies will meet the new requirements, and which will fail, is problematic since market resistance can itself spur new rounds of innovation. But one thing seems certain: companies wishing to develop and market new technologies and products in the future will need to apply some form of need test early on and then manage subsequent research, development and deployment activities in the light of the sort of thinking and priorities encapsulated in Dow's eco-compass.

Three Keys to the 21st Century

The fourth sustainability revolution focuses on life-cycle technologies, requiring that we understand and use the following keys to sustainable enterprise.

♦ First, the initial three sustainability revolutions – intensifying competition, evolving values, and global transparency – will increase the power and penetration of the X-ray environment. Successful companies will develop the capacity not only to look but also to manage both upstream and downstream in their value stream or chain. They will apply lean thinking to minimize the life-cycle economic, social, and environmental costs associated with their products.

♦ Second, life-cycle data on materials and products will become a necessary condition of sales in a growing number of sensitized markets. As a result of growing investment in life-cycle assessment and design tools, such as Dow's eco-compass, their power will grow, their complexity decrease and their cost tumble. The spread of value:impact assessment techniques will also encourage growing numbers of customers to think more about functions than about products (see Chapter 13).

♦ Third, the "Law of Unintended Consequences" will continue to apply – even in the work we do in pursuit of sustainability. Our ability to pick up and respond to emerging economic, social, and environmental side-effects early on will be a key factor in our success in managing the transition. Remember, however, that not all unintended side-effects are problematic.

Notes

1. Michael Porter, *Competitive Advantage: Creating and sustaining superior performance*, The Free Press, 1986.
2. *Management Today*, August 1996.
3. Pierre Béland, "The beluga whales of the St. Lawrence river," *Scientific American*, May 1996.
4. James Blitz and Mark Suzman, "Government 'fuelled scare on baby milk,'" *Financial Times*, 29 May 1996; also, Clive Cookson, "Implicated chemicals widely produced," *Financial Times*, 29 May 1996.
5. John Carey, "A scary warning – or a scare story?," *Business Week*, 8 April 1996.
6. Theo Colborn, John Peterson Myers and Dianne Dumanoski, *Our Stolen*

Future: How man-made chemicals are threatening our fertility, intelligence and survival, Little, Brown and Co, 1996.

7. John Elkington, *The Poisoned Womb: Human reproduction in a polluted world*, Viking 1985; Pelican Books, 1986.

8. Alison Maitland, "Links in the food chain wither and die," *Financial Times*, 4 April 1996.

9. Sarah Boseley, "How the truth was butchered," *Guardian*, 24 March 1996.

10. Charles Leadbeater, "Why the beef industry has led itself to slaughter," *Observer*, 22 December 1996.

11. See also Jean Shaol, *BSE: For services rendered?*, a paper available from the Department of Accounting and Finance, University of Manchester, Manchester M13 9PL, UK, 1996.

12. Oliver Walston, "Swept away on a tide of hysteria," *The Times*, 23 March 1996.

13. *Towards a Sustainable Paper Cycle*, International Institute for Environment and Development (IIED), 1996.

14. Afshin Molavi, "Power of publicity turned on America's sweatshops," *Financial Times*, 2 December 1995.

15. Alasdair Murray, "Now the tobacco giants begin to feel the heat," *The Times*, 23 August 1996.

16. Patricia Sellers, "Team Tobacco goes up in smoke," *Fortune*, 9 September 1996.

17. Rob Norton, "Why airbags are killing kids," *Fortune*, 19 August 1996.

18. Jayne O'Donnell, "Weaker air bags save kids, put more adults at risk," *USA Today*, 14 January 1997.

19. Edward Tenner, *Why Things Bite Back: New technology and the revenge effect*, Fourth Estate, 1996.

20. James P. Womack, Daniel T. Jones and Daniel Roos, *The Machine That Changed the World*, Macmillan, 1990.

21. James P. Womack and Daniel T. Jones, *Lean Thinking: Banish waste and create wealth in your corporation*, Simon & Schuster, 1996.

22. Claude Fussler with Peter James, *Driving Eco-Innovation: A breakthrough discipline for innovation and sustainability*, Pitman Publishing, 1996.

23. Robert E. Service, "Can chip devices keep shrinking?," *Science* **274**, 13 December 1996.

24. Frank Annighöfer, "Insurers and sustainable development," *Environment Strategy Europe 1997*, Campden Publishing, 1996.

25. "Polyurethanes business leads ICI on environmental product design," *ENDS Report 258*, Environmental Data Services, July 1996.

26. "Building the 'green' factor into product development," *ENDS Report 260*, September 1996.

27. SustainAbility with Dow Europe, *Who Needs It? Market implications of sustainable lifestyles*, 1995.

PARTNERSHIPS

After the Honeymoon

Stakeholders want to be treated as partners.

The greater the mutual, earned respect and loyalty,
the greater the chance that the organization
will be sustainable.

Sustainability can be a 2 + 2 = 5 (or even 50) game. To achieve outstanding triple bottom line performance, new types of economic, social, and environmental partnership are needed. Long-standing enemies must shift from mutual subversion to new forms of symbiosis. The resulting partnerships can help each partner perform traditional tasks more efficiently, while providing a platform from which to reach towards goals that none of the partners could hope to achieve on their own.

Revolution	Focus	Old paradigm ❭	New paradigm
5	Partnerships	Subversion ❭	Symbiosis

Effective, long-term partnerships will be crucial during the sustainability transition. Some will be between the public and private sectors, some between companies, and some between companies and groups campaigning for a broad range of triple bottom line objectives. The focus in this chapter will largely be on environmental partnerships, but we are also seeing the evolution of similar partnership approaches in such areas as Third World development and human rights.

The idea of trying to develop partnerships, both inside and outside the company, may seem common sense, but old perceptions and prejudices die hard. Potential partners continue to feel profoundly misunderstood by those they should be seeking to influence and engage. "I just wish I could give people a pill so that they could see the world the way we see it," the chief environmental officer of a major corporation once confided. "Forget it!" I replied. But the comment was an interesting window into at least one corporate soul.

Many business people – and many campaigners – still see the clash between companies and campaigners in terms of an unending battle between the forces of good and evil, of light and darkness. Right and wrong, however, depend on where you are standing and which way you are facing. Consider the views of Jim-Bob Moffett, the larger-than-life American chairman of Freeport McMoRan – the company which runs one of the world's largest copper and gold mines in the mountains of Irian Jaya.[1]

Freeport McMoRan and Rio Tinto, which owns a stake in the mine, found themselves plunged into the X-ray environment when a group of hostages were seized by members of the Free Papua Movement (OPM), as part of its independence struggle. The OPM see the mine, operated virtually as an extra-territorial part of America with the protection of the Indonesian military, as a symbol of the problems they face. Worse, the local tribespeople – in addition to having been driven off their lands – complain that run-off from the mine is polluting rivers and that the removal of forest cover is affecting the local climate. Paradoxically, the hostages included students from Cambridge University who had been working with local tribes to learn how they exploited nature without destroying it.

The Freeport McMoRan response to environmental challenges can only be described as robust. The scale of the pollution, Jim-Bob Moffett retorted, "is equivalent to me pissing in the Arafura Sea." He told *The Times* that he was involved in "a new Cold War" with local and international campaigners. "This," he said, "is not a job for us, it's a religion." All of which tends to make negotiation with the enemy, let alone the development of longer term partnerships, inconceivable.

Monkey Traps

Such reactions bring to mind the old "Monkey Trap" tale (Spotlight, p. 222). Companies like Freeport McMoRan would do well to learn and understand it. The history of the environmental revolution is full of examples of companies locking themselves into various forms of monkey trap. In the case of Freeport McMoRan and Rio Tinto, their corporate fists are locked in the earth by the thought of the billion tonnes of copper and gold ore to be won as giant mechanical shovels chew away at the mountain tops. And the nature of human beings and of corporations being what it is, the 21st century will also produce abundant examples of the corporate monkey trap in action. Some companies will escape empty-handed, some will work out ways of breaking the jar out of the earth, but more than a few will also be hammered senseless by their opponents.

THE MONKEY TRAP

A monkey comes into a village at night. He finds a hole in the ground and circles it warily, smelling food. His paw just barely fits into the opening, because the hole is actually a narrow-mouthed jug buried flush with the ground. He manages to scoop up a handful of rice, but can't run off with the food – since his closed fist can't be drawn back through the jar's opening. Not wanting to lose the food, he screeches, but keeps his fist closed. Shortly, a villager comes by with a rock or pole and kills the monkey, either as a pest or for food.[2]

Why Worry?

Tomorrow's CEOs are Green

Another reason for business to worry is that the environmental agenda is way up the list of priorities of the emerging generations of university graduates. "Europe's graduates put care for the environment top of their agendas," according to the European Graduate Survey, which covered 16,000 final-year students in 56 universities, business, and engineering schools across 14 countries.[3] But, while 68% said they were prepared to pay the price of a better environment, only 38% thought that the global picture would improve. These young people are also switching on to the Internet in a big way: 61% used it in this latest survey, compared with just 37% a year earlier.

For these, and many other, reasons, it is clear that we now stand on the threshold of a new era in the relationships between business and its many stakeholders, including potential new recruits. We also see, in the words of a recent book on green activism in America, environmentalism at the crossroads.[4] Faced by growing media skepticism and a degree of political backlash, environmentalists have been rethinking what they do and how they do it.

For business, the value of the multiple perspectives introduced by stakeholder dialogue processes has been demonstrated time and again for companies. The priorities and strategies emerging from such processes turn out to be better-rooted in emerging realities, more credible with all stakeholders, and, as a result, more robust. Not that this approach has been trouble-free: some of the information released by Novo Nordisk to visiting stakeholders turned up as part of a consumer campaign against the company's enzymes in Germany, Austria, and Switzerland. But that, the company believes, is part of the price you pay to build the relationships which are likely to be indispensable during the sustainability transition.

There is no question that these changes potentially represent a "10×" challenge for environmentalists and the traditional style of relationship they have developed with business. But it is still far from clear how many of today's campaigning organizations will successfully make the transition to the new ways of operating. Equally, the changing conditions will create opportunities for totally new forms of campaigning, pressure politics, and partnerships between campaigners and like-minded corporations. Indeed, these initiatives may well be developed from scratch by some of the students covered in the *European*'s survey.

Meanwhile, earlier generations of green activist are moving into the mainstream. Take German politician Joschka Fischer, who at the time of writing was leader of the Bundestag Greens (later Germany's foreign minister). Because Fischer is determined that the Greens will influence national, not just ecological, policy, he gave himself a crash course in economics and began to speak out positively on foreign policy issues like sending troops to Bosnia and European Monetary Union. His aim was to lead the Greens into a left–centre coalition "with an independent personality and high economic competence." He may or may not succeed, but jokes that, "I stand on my head day and night figuring out how I can become Chancellor."[5] Given enough time and the right breaks more of these people will play key roles in the sustainability transition. Expect to see growing numbers of them popping up on company boards before long.

As we shift towards the sustainable business paradigm, we will see companies like Freeport McMoRan and Rio Tinto trying to develop strategic partnerships with individual campaigners and with major campaigning groups. Some will succeed in attracting powerful partners, some not. But the terms and conditions of these partnerships will have changed profoundly. In the old order, very few campaigning groups, or non-governmental organizations (NGOs) as they are better known, were prepared to work directly with industry. Some never will, but longer term they will probably turn out to be in the minority. What is different today, however, is that the NGOs are increasingly in a position of power – and some are preparing to use it in novel ways, working with business and through markets.

Trapping NGO Fists

In the old order, the NGOs that decided to work with business generally wanted money, and were considered to be sell-outs by radical activists. Whether the funding was for core costs, campaigns, or other initiatives, the relationship was simple. Crudely stated, it was "Give us money and we will splash your name over some appropriate surface." A few leading NGOs, particularly those dedicated to wildlife conservation, developed huge corporate sponsorship departments dedicated solely to hunting down deep-pocketed corporate donors. And, like the monkey with its fist in the trap, they too then tended to find that they were in no position to run effective campaigns against their new-found funding partners. Some companies even offered funding with the explicit aim of locking up potential enemies, or even of using them as Trojan horses.

In any event, the conditions in which such partnerships were pursued changed dramatically when two things happened in parallel. First, companies, inevitably, became more discriminating. They began to insist on a bigger PR bang for their sponsorship buck. And they wanted their benefits in the form of an enhanced reputation with selected audiences. As "cause-related marketing" evolved, some of those NGO corporate sponsorship departments became almost indistinguishable from mainstream advertising or PR agencies.

The second shift was driven by NGO needs. They found themselves managing increasingly large projects and budgets. Their staffs mushroomed and demanded better employment conditions. They found they needed people, and project and financial management skills which, they noted, business was also rich in. So we saw downsizing companies seconding managers to NGOs, often as a way of easing them into retirement. And we also saw NGOs appointing people from business to their boards and top management posts.

In a parallel trend, we saw leading campaigners being recruited by major companies. Not all of these transfers worked. More than a few secondees, and some of those actively headhunted, proved to be fish out of water. But enough of these grafts "took" to ensure that NGOs remain interested in finding new ways to access the human resources and skills available within their business partners – and companies in finding ways to extract new forms of value from campaigning organizations or from ex-campaigners.

Greenfreeze and After

Now we are entering a new phase in the evolution of business–NGO relations, involving early strategic alliances between companies and selected NGOs. In the process, some NGOs are learning to punch with the weight of multinational corporations, in part by learning to work alongside and through corporations. An early example was the string of "strange alliances" that Greenpeace pioneered in its "Greenfreeze" campaign with companies like DKK Scharfenstein and Calor.

The aim was to use Greenpeace's marketing and communication muscle to help launch ozone-friendly technology, which the prevailing refrigeration industry consensus said was unworkable. The result was that the plans of the multibillion-dollar refrigeration and chemical industries were thrown into complete disarray.[6] What happens if and when Greenpeace starts to work with the real heavyweights?

In the world of business, environmental performance is increasingly seen as a competitive and strategic issue for companies. As a result, growing numbers are experimenting with novel forms of NGO relationship. In the world of NGOs, meanwhile, the mid-1990s marked a critical crossroads, with the environmental agenda opening out into a much broader, and more demanding, sustainable development agenda. As a result, more environmental NGOs are experimenting with partnership approaches to environmental and sustainability problems.

One pioneer has been the US Environmental Defense Fund (EDF), which has worked with companies as diverse as McDonald's and General Motors. Recently, it formed the Alliance for Environmental Innovation with the Pew Foundation – and set up a joint task force with S.C. Johnson & Son, Inc., to work on the cleaning products company's product formulation and packaging processes. "People have always expected products to be effective, while also being safe to use and dispose [of]," explained Joseph Mallof, an SCJ executive vice-president:[7]

> "We believe that our products can offer higher quality and value to people if we integrate eco-efficiency as a fundamental part of the initial product concept. This will enable us to use more environmentally friendly materials, and fewer of them, which in turn will reduce waste, risk and costs."

In the case of the EDF–S.C. Johnson partnership, each partner has borne its own costs, as did EDF in earlier projects with other companies. But other NGOs will be much less worried about accepting the corporate dollar. Indeed, they will increasingly need to do so to fund the growing scale of their operations. The ethical debate on such issues is already fairly heated and, on present evidence, the temperature is likely to rise further.

Strange Attractor

So just how important are these trends? Not just at the level of a company's public affairs department, but at the level of the board? The board of BP, now BP Amoco, wanted to have answers and SustainAbility was asked to investigate the growth of business–NGO alliances worldwide, with a view to helping the company develop an agenda for action.[8] Recently in the news because of alleged misdemeanors in Colombia, BP has a long track record of working productively with NGOs. But the company's board wanted to know whether it should be thinking in terms of developing a strategic alliance with one or more NGOs. And, if so, with whom, how and to do what?

To this end, we surveyed more than 60 environment and development NGOs and 20 companies worldwide, asking them to assess the sincerity of corporate environmentalism, the most important influences on environmental performance, and the elements which make for successful partnerships. We then analyzed the two groups separately. Although we knew a convergence process was already running, we all found the results surprising.

Rather than illustrating the gulf to be bridged, the survey showed a surprisingly high degree of convergence. Despite what some companies may believe, NGOs are watching environmentally proactive companies with great interest, and most are heartened by the upsurge in corporate environmentalism. Interestingly, though, NGOs are also acutely aware of the gap between leaders and laggards in a given industry. This knowledge is informing their selection of potential partners. We then went on to interview some 20 companies that had already developed strategic alliances with NGOs. Among their number, companies as diverse as the Body Shop, General Motors, McDonald's and Monsanto. Indeed, the project unfolded against a background of increasing collaboration between companies and NGOs, among them WWF's developing link with Unilever on "sustainable fisheries" (Case Study, p.227).

The inescapable conclusion is that as the environmental agenda broadens to incorporate sustainability's triple bottom line, some NGOs are recognizing the key role that business can, indeed must, play in forging workable solutions. Increasingly, stakeholder capitalism (see Spotlight, p. 298) will be the name of the game. Growing numbers of

CASE STUDY   **UNILEVER, UK/THE NETHERLANDS: SUSTAINABLE FISH FINGERS**

As the world's largest fish buyer, the Anglo–Dutch giant Unilever is backing a plan developed by WWF to set up an international labeling scheme for sustainable fish production. Unilever is the company behind such brands as Bird's Eye and John West. When the scheme was announced in 1996, the plan was that the first labeled products would be in the stores by 1998, with all of the company's fish products labelled by 2005.

The new standards, which will be policed by a new Marine Stewardship Council (MSC), will focus on two main issues: where the fish are caught and the methods used to catch them. Participating fisheries will be certified against the MSC criteria and their packs will bear the MSC logo. The project has been modeled on the Forest Stewardship Council (FSC), a similar program WWF set up in 1993 for the timber trade.[9]

But what is perhaps most interesting about the scheme is that it reflects disillusion on the part of both WWF and Unilever with government efforts to set and enforce catch quotas to control over-fishing. This is the first real attempt to offer a market-based approach. It remains to be seen, however, both whether the supermarkets and specialist fish stores will back the scheme, and whether the consumer will switch in significant numbers to sustainable kippers and fish fingers.

businesses are seeking to move beyond confrontation to forge more productive relationships with NGOs. The convergence of these trends creates an opportunity for new forms of partnership, but raises an interesting new issue. Many business people had argued that there were too many NGOs for comfort. If current trends continue, however, we may well see a shortage of credible NGOs willing and able to work alongside, and invest their credibility in, particular companies or industry sectors. Thus, we concluded, companies that lead their competitors in forging strategic alliances with key NGOs could enjoy a strong "first mover" benefit.

Nor is this just a European and North American phenomenon. Respondents from around the world recognized the trend. From Southern Africa, Jon Hobbs (at the time, executive director of the Industrial Environmental Forum of Southern Africa) observed:

"It is interesting that these questions should be raised at this time. A recent series of interviews with our members (mostly corporate executives) revealed that their priority requirement from the [Industrial Environmental Forum] is 'guidelines' on how to 'better engage' NGOs."

Schizophrenia Guaranteed

More than 85% of our NGO respondents believed that partnerships will increase over the next five years, and that NGOs should get involved in *more* company partnerships. Even so, confrontation is expected to continue in parallel – and several factors could reverse the trend toward collaboration. In the USA, for example, Speaker Newt Gingrich and his Republicans managed to trigger a major re-think among NGOs already working with companies with their attempts to undermine existing environmental regulations. In the event, NGOs and their allies fought off the challenge, but both they and the companies they work with will need to grapple with the internal "schizophrenia" partnerships can create within their own organizations. Partnerships, even when well managed, can fuel schizophrenia both in companies and NGOs.

Of course, it is difficult to generalize about NGOs, given that they are so diverse. They concentrate on a wide array of environmental (and often social and economic) issues; span local, regional, national, and international "jurisdictions;" represent numerous forms of decision-making structure and management; and are driven by widely different political philosophies. Some NGOs are staffed by a handful of people, relying largely on volunteer efforts, while others are large, international, highly professionalized organizations. These inherent differences in form, agenda, and style also extend to their views on developing relationships with business, whether in true partnerships or in dialogs. So before entering into an alliance with an NGO, a company would want to know where the organization fits into the overall sustainability movement.

To make the diversity easier to grasp, we distinguish between four main types of NGO, based on two separate sets of characteristics. First, consider the extent to which the NGO seeks to integrate the role of businesses and "public interest" groups in achieving environmental goals. At one end of the spectrum, as Max Nichsolson put it a couple of decades ago, are the *integrators,* placing a high priority on developing productive relationships with business, and striving to identify non-confrontational, "win–win" strategies. At the other end of this spectrum are the *polarizers*. They have typically made a strategic decision not to develop close working relationships with business, preferring to concentrate instead on a watchdog role.

Second, consider whether the NGO discriminates between companies within an industry with respect to their real or perceived environmental commitment and performance. At one end of this spectrum, we have the *discriminators*. For them, the challenge is to understand the issues facing a particular industry and to track the progress made by individual companies compared to industry benchmarks. At the other end of the spectrum, there are the *non-discriminators*. For them, a company's relative environmental performance is not of particular interest. Rather, the focus of attention is typically the environmental burden of the industry in general.

With these two dimensions in mind, we use a 4-celled matrix of NGO types (Figure 9.1) showing "Sharks," "Orcas," "Sealions," and "Dolphins." Most sane people and organizations tend to avoid sharks, although there are plenty of them about in most industries. The info-

	Polarizer	Integrator
Discriminator	**Orca (killer whale)** ♦ highly intelligent, strategic ♦ can adapt behavior, strategy to context ♦ fearsome, uses fear to coerce ♦ uncertain in behavior ♦ likes deep water, can cover great distances ♦ associates with own kind ♦ eats sealions (and, sometimes, dolphins)	**Dolphin** ♦ intelligent, creative, integrators ♦ adapts behavior and strategies to context ♦ can fend off sharks ♦ equally comfortable in deep or shallow waters, can cover great distances ♦ can be a loner – or intensely social ♦ empathy for other species
Non-discriminator	**Shark** ♦ relatively low intelligence ♦ tactical ♦ acutely responsive to distress ♦ poor eyesight, peripheral vision of prey ♦ undiscriminating in terms of targets ♦ swims, often attacks in packs	**Sealion** ♦ moderate intelligence ♦ tactical ♦ popular spectacle ♦ friendly ♦ menu item for sharks and orca ♦ tends to stay in "safe waters" ♦ believes in safety in numbers ♦ uneasy if too far from group

FIGURE 9.1   Four types of NGO (*Source:* SustainAbility)

TABLE 9.1   Drivers of "Strange Alliances"

Company perspective	NGO perspective
◆ markets are pushing us this way	◆ markets are interesting
◆ NGOs are credible with public on, for example, issues, priorities	◆ disenchanted with government as provider of solutions
◆ need for external challenge	◆ need for more resources, such as funding and technical and management expertise
◆ cross-fertilization of thinking	
◆ greater efficiency in resource allocation	◆ business is credible with, for example, government
◆ desire to head off negative public confrontations, protect image and reputation	◆ cross-fertilization of thinking
	◆ access to, for example, supply chains
◆ desire to engage stakeholders	◆ greater leverage

Source: SustainAbility

sphere, in particular, is full of them: the media thrive on bad news, so the natural selection pressures working in favour of shark-like behavior are often intense. On the other hand, the NGO type likely to be most in demand, both with business and public sector organizations, is also among the rarest to date: those pursuing what Brain Technologies Corp has dubbed the "Strategy of the Dolphin".[10] Our survey showed growing numbers of NGOs moving – or aspiring to move – towards this top, right-hand cell. This is the "Strange Attractor" of our BP report's title.

The drivers pushing us in this direction are summarized in Table 9.1. The resulting "strange alliances" between corporations and NGOs will demand extraordinary vision and new political and management skills from people who in the past have found it much easier to simply lob bricks at one another. They are now being asked to build together. If the approach works, they will need to accept shared responsibility for both the ends and the means. If they fail, as many experiments do, we need to recognize that even some failures should be celebrated if, in the process, we learn from our mistakes.

What's New, Gurus?

A Question of Commitment

Interestingly, some far-sighted management gurus have been flagging up similar trends in other areas. Among the ideas they are advancing are *business ecosystems*, *co-opetition*, and *stakeholder capitalism*. As we saw in Chapter 5, James Moore's book *The Death of Competition* introduced the notion of business ecosystems. The challenge for companies today is to work out how to integrate a growing range of partners and stakeholders into these ecosystems.

The advantages of this approach have also been explored by Fred Reichheld in two recent books: *The Loyalty Effect*[11] and *The Quest for Loyalty*.[12] But as Reichheld himself argues: "Loyalty seems to be dying in our society. Look at the way we treat friendships, community organizations, even marriage. You would think we were renting cars or motel rooms instead of making commitments." And, he points out, "it's not just our social lives that seem to be less permanent. As the *Financial Times* pointed out recently, business too seems to have entered the age of the one-night stand." The average US company, he notes:

> "now loses half its customers in five years, half its employees in four, and half its investors in less than one. Layoffs, stock-market churn, fickle customers, executive job surfing – all signs seem to point towards opportunism and disloyalty as the governing principles in commerce as well as in society."

Business leaders do not typically see loyalty, whether with suppliers, customers, or other stakeholders, as fashionable, lucrative, or even particularly relevant. Their view is that "they have more urgent problems to worry about – for example, growth, productivity, and profits." No one disputes that these priorities are indeed urgent, but the interesting thing about Reichheld's work is that he argues that many of the indicators of growth, productivity, and profitability seem to signal that the wrong approach is being used. As Reichheld explains, "ignoring loyalty in order to focus on these 'more pressing' problems may be exactly the wrong fix."

In short, he argues, what is dead is the old form of *unconditional* loyalty. Fifty years ago, he suggests:

> "loyalty played a much larger part in everyday life than it does today. People were deeply loyal to their families, of course. But people also displayed unquestioning loyalty to a long list of civic, religious, and professional authorities and even to the companies they bought from and worked for."

As a result, in today's world "very few of us feel unconditional loyalty to anyone or anything." But don't despair. Reichheld concludes that unconditional, hierarchical loyalty has simply been replaced, and not with a vacuum. "Free markets have replaced it with something far superior – mutual, earned loyalty; loyalty that works in two directions."

In the new order, it turns out, stakeholders, whether they are customers, employees, or triple bottom line campaigners, want to be (and to be treated as) partners. In fact, the same "zero defection" targets that Reichheld proposes for companies wanting to be "loyalty leaders" can be cross-applied to broader stakeholder relationships. Companies may not be able to keep their customers, employees or triple bottom line stakeholders forever, but the greater the mutual, earned respect and loyalty the greater is the chance that the organization will be sustainable.

Co-opetition

When Barry Nalebuff and Adam Brandenburger chose "Business is War" as the first phrase in their book *Co-opetition*, their intent was to skewer this notion.[13] They accept that the traditional language of business certainly makes it sound as though business is war: "outsmarting the competition, capturing market share, making a killing, fighting brands, beating up suppliers, locking up customers. Under business-as-war, there are the victors and the vanquished." But anyone involved in business today knows that often it just isn't like that. "You have to listen to customers, work with suppliers, create teams, establish strategic partnerships – even with competitors. That doesn't sound like war."

As they explain, the real business world often involves cooperation when creating a pie and competition when it comes to dividing it up. It's not Tolstoy, with endless cycles of war followed by peace followed by war. "It's simultaneously war and peace." Or as Novell founder Ray Noorda put it: "You have to compete and cooperate at the same time." Nalebuff and Brandenburger then use game theory to work out ways of avoiding "lose–lose" and "lose–win" outcomes, where everyone loses or you set up the pie in such a way that only other people win, and instead pursue "win–win" outcomes. There is no reason at all why the same principles cannot be pursued in relation to the "win–win–win" outcomes required by sustainability's triple bottom line.

So if business is viewed as a game, who should we include as key players? The answer is customers, suppliers, competitors, and *complementors* – those who provide complementary products, services, or other inputs. "Thinking complements is a different way of thinking about business," Nalebuff and Brandenburger contend:

> "It's about finding ways to make the pie bigger rather than fighting with competitors over a fixed pie. To benefit from this insight, think about how to expand the pie by developing new complements or making existing complements more affordable."

Co-opetition offers a number of rules for companies and stakeholders choosing to travel this path. Simply stated, they are as follows:

- Every player should be aware of the potential added value they bring to the game. How will the game be different if you are in rather than out?
- There needs to be at least a basic set of rules. Often, to build trust, these rules need to be spelled out and agreed early on.
- Perceptions need to be taken into account: different people view the world differently. The way we see the game, and the way we think others see the game, influences the moves we make.
- There need to be boundaries: a game without boundaries gets too complex to analyze or play. Players need to agree on what those boundaries are or should be.
- Attention needs to be paid to different types of rationality and irrationality. In any game, different players can be perfectly rational but, seeing the value added, rules, and boundaries in different ways, end up playing in very different ways.

In sustainability partnerships, as in all other walks of life, dismissing actual or potential players as "irrational" closes the mind. It makes much more sense to expand the mind by trying to work out how others see the world, the game, and its rules. "To us," say Nalebuff and Brandenburger:

> "the issue of whether people are rational or irrational is largely beside the point. More important is remembering to look at a game from multiple perspectives – your own and that of every other player. This simple-sounding idea is possibly the most profound insight of game theory."

It is also one of the simplest, yet most effective ingredients in the expanded stakeholder approach to capitalism.

Trust

Every now and then you come across a book that you can feel changing your thinking as you turn each and every page. Francis Fukuyama's *Trust*,[14] which I read on a flight to South Africa, had this effect on me. Best known for his 1992 best-seller *The End of History and the Last Man*, Fukuyama (formerly deputy secretary of the US State Department's policy planning staff, then a Rand Corporation analyst) subsequently turned his attention to an area likely to be central to the sustainable development agenda: trust – and what he describes as "social capital." This was before the Asian crash, remember.

With capitalism increasingly in the ascendant around the world, *The End of History* argued that different countries were coming to share increasingly similar political and economic institutions. Now that the Cold War is considered to be over, *Trust* concludes that the most important issue facing Europe, the USA, and other industrial democracies is economic competitiveness. And here Fukuyama offers a chilling conclusion: the tendency of countries like the USA and UK towards individualism will undermine their economies. By contrast, he argues, the success of the rapidly growing economies of East Asia is rooted in often overlooked forms of social capital, such as trust, sense of community, and social integration.

Fukuyama is hardly alone in making this case: *The Economist* pointed out that "hardly an issue of the *Harvard Business Review* or the *California Management Review* appears without the word 'trust' emblazoned on the cover." One key reason for this is that many current trends in management, among them downsizing, reengineering, and the culling of middle managers, are forcing companies to place more responsibility on, and faith in, their front-line employees. Now growing numbers of companies are finding that this internal need for trust is mirrored in the external world. Just as they need to work much more closely with smaller numbers of trusted suppliers, so they also feel the need to involve a growing range of external stakeholders, including sustainability campaigners, in setting their business priorities.

In conventional business terms, trust cuts the costs and delays involved in project development and other processes. It can help to secure a licence to operate. But as environmental, and other triple bottom line, factors increasingly shape markets, the growth of trust between individual companies and their stakeholders will also help hone competitive edge and provide an important source of new business ideas. But companies investing in trust will still need to cultivate a degree of paranoia (in the sense in which Intel's Andy Grove uses the word) and schizophrenia (as discussed above).

Boardroom Views

Damn It, This is Important

Most company directors are fairly comfortable with the idea of commercial partnerships and many accept the need for social and community partnerships. But environmental and sustainability partnering is still way down the curve. Environmentalists, in particular, are often seen as a form of virus which should be kept as far away as possible from the vital organs of a company or industry. That view will change.

A small but growing number of CEOs and other business leaders are waking up to the need to involve even some of their fiercest critics in the process of deciding what their companies should do next. Listen to Monsanto CEO Bob Shapiro:

> "We have to reduce – and ultimately eliminate – the negative impacts we have on the world. But even if Monsanto reached its goal of zero impact next Tuesday, that wouldn't solve the world's problems. Several years ago, I sensed that there was something more required of us than doing no harm, but I couldn't articulate what it was."[15]

So Shapiro pulled together a group of about 25 critical thinkers, including some of the company's up-and-coming leaders, and sent them off to ponder the issues with a number of non-traditional thinkers, including Paul Hawken, from the outside world. In short, this was a very focused form of partnership. "That off-site meeting in 1994 led to an emerging insight that we couldn't ignore the changing global environmental conditions," recalled Shapiro:

> "The focus around sustainable development became obvious. I should have been able to come up with that in about 15 minutes. But it took a group of very good people quite a while to think it through, to determine what was real and what was just puff, and to convince themselves that this wasn't a fluffy issue – and that we ought to be engaged in it."

The Monsanto people came away "emotionally fired up," said Shapiro. "It wasn't just a matter of 'Okay, you threw me an interesting business problem, I have done the analysis, here is the answer, and now can I go back to work.' People came away saying, 'Damn it, we've got to get going on this. This is important.' " Watch that space.

Experience suggests that such outcomes are much more likely when companies bring the outside world in. Indeed, wherever we look, business is learning to listen to and consult with new types of stakeholder. As Cor Herkströter of Shell put it in the wake of the Brent Spar and Nigerian controversies:

> "Naturally we have listened very closely to our customers. We have listened very carefully to government and to our staff. They, after all, were the institutions, the bodies, we had always dealt with. Of course, we also dealt with environmentalist groups, consumer groups and so on, but we tended to let the public affairs department deal with them. They were important – but they were not as important as government, industry organizations and so on."[16]

That, at least, was the prevailing wisdom, but these controversies signalled an important shift in triple bottom line politics. "In essence," Herkströter admits, "we were somewhat slow in understanding that these groups were tending to acquire authority. Meanwhile, those institutions we were used to dealing with were tending to lose authority. We underestimated the extent of these changes – we failed to engage in a serious dialogue with these new groups." The key message: "We learnt we had to be much more open to the world around us."[17]

Bubbling Under

Going Dutch

Sustainability partnerships can be initiated – and led – by government agencies, companies, NGOs, or other stakeholders. One government-led partnership approach which certainly ought to spread is based on "covenants," or voluntary environmental agreements between business and government. Indeed, although the idea may be difficult to export in its entirety, it has attracted interest from a number of other countries including Germany and Italy in Europe and, in the Americas, Argentina and the USA.[18] Rooted in the Dutch political and business tradition of consensus and consultation, the approach also benefits from the fact that Dutch companies tend to belong to one or more sectoral organizations – making it easier to negotiate sector-wide agreements with government.

Since the first experiments of the 1980s, more than 75 environmental covenants have been signed. These have committed a wide range of sectors to meeting targets in such areas as energy efficiency, greenhouse gas reduction, and the control of volatile organic compounds. So, for example, some 150 companies operating in the surface treatment sector signed up to an energy efficiency covenant with the economic affairs ministry which aimed for a 20% improvement between 1989 and 2000. And the approach, despite some NGO criticisms, appears to be making headway. When the chemicals covenant was reviewed, it turned out that 107 out of 125 companies committed to the agreement had already installed the management systems needed to monitor progress.

The main criticisms have been that the covenants do not go far enough and, because they tend to be based on intimate discussions between government and a particular sector, they are not as democratic as the traditional legislative processes. But there are also real advantages. As KPMG partner George Molenkamp put it:

"From the government's point of view, the covenant creates a wider base of support from within industry. If the government tried to reach the same goals through legislation, it would be time-consuming and not necessarily very effective. Through voluntary agreement it is possible to do difficult things that could not easily be laid down in law."

This approach, it hardly needs saying, is not applicable to all problems and all circumstances. To work, it not only requires sectoral bodies with the ability to negotiate agreements with governments, but also governments where the fundamental policies and targets are not changed with every new administration. Above all, voluntary agreements will always require the pre-existence of a reasonably comprehensive and sophisticated framework of legislation, to ensure that any "free-riders" are identified and dealt with.

Eco-infrastructure

One emerging recognition is that, however much a single company may be able to do on the eco-efficiency front, in the end sustainability will depend on the progress of entire concentrations of industry, complete value chains, and whole economies. As a result, we see growing interest in the provision of eco-infrastructure, as for example in the concept of the eco-industrial park (EIP). The central idea here is that by sharing resources, whether in the form of efficient energy production or of state-of-the-art waste management, companies can significantly boost the overall eco-efficiency of a local or regional economy.

"We see eco-parks as a community of companies working together to improve individual and group performance in all environmental areas," explained the US Environmental Protection Agency (EPA):

> "There is a large menu of options for doing this, including energy efficiency in building and process design, innovations in park infrastructure, created wetlands to process stormwater, and shared environmental management services. Most of these options translate into bottom line benefits to the companies."

Of course, as *Tomorrow*'s then US editor, Carl Frankel, put it:

> "There are many unknowns to contend with. Example: sooner or later a critical player in a multi-company waste recycling system will re-locate or go bankrupt. When that occurs, how do you keep the entire system from collapsing? More immediately, how do you reassure potential EIP participants that there isn't a fatal design flaw? Another problem involves the difficulty of quantifying the economic and environmental benefits of EIPs for candidate companies. The bottom line is that full-scale EIPs are still essentially untested."

For participating companies, it also potentially adds one more level of uncertainty, particularly if they come to depend on the outputs of others nearby.

In the Netherlands, meanwhile, there are plans for developing an "Environmental Technology Valley," based on the Silicon Valley model and including at least one business park catering for up-and-coming eco-companies. And a series of proposed schemes have been surfacing across the USA. The President's Council on Sustainable Development strongly backed EIPs and anyone wanting to keep a finger on the EIP pulse should keep an eye on Chattanooga, Tennessee. Since the late 1980s, according to councillor David Crockett (a descendant of the legendary pioneer), the city has aimed to be a "living laboratory" for sustainability policies, technologies, and design. Four EIPs are in the works, a couple on old "brownfield" industrial sites, one on a "greenfield" site in a pristine valley on the edge of town, and one – which is planned to have zero emission manufacturing facilities – in the south central business district. Such schemes will depend for their success on long-sighted regulators, communities, and companies, but they certainly look like an idea whose time is coming.

Industrial Ecology

Nor are these eco-industrial parks developing in a vacuum. Behind them stands a rapidly-evolving field of research and practice known as "industrial ecology." Whether the focus is on designing and operating cities, EIPs, or individual companies, the idea is "based upon a straight-forward analogy with natural ecological systems," as Robert Frosch put it, "where nothing that contains available energy or useful materials is lost."[19]

But evidence that the approach does work can be seen every day of the working week around the "industrial symbiosis" in Kalundborg, Denmark. The scale of the environmental benefits has been consider-able. By 1995, $60 million had been invested by the participating companies and organizations to launch 16 materials and energy exchange schemes, which were already producing $10 million a year in surplus.[20] Although none of the cooperative initiatives had been required by legislation, annual oil consumption had been cut by 45,000 tonnes, coal consumption by 15,000 tonnes, and water consumption by 600,000 cubic metres. In addition, carbon dioxide and sulphur dioxide emissions had been cut, respectively, by 175,000 tonnes and 10,200 tonnes a year.

It is no surprise that ecosystems thinking is now coming into man-agement consulting: as any ecologist knows, the output of one organism becomes input for others, and organisms may both compete and cooper-ate. Among the names of interesting thinkers that have popped up in the area of industrial ecology and metabolism are Brad Allenby, Bob Ayres, and Hardin Tibbs, but the field is now wide open for its own ver-sion of such entrepreneurs as Steve Jobs or Richard Branson to get it on the road commercially.

Winners, Losers

Are You In or Out?

Winners, whether they are companies or national or regional econo-mies, will learn how to earn the loyalty of their key stakeholders (see Case Study, p. 240). Success in these areas will help considerably with such challenges as building employee morale and generating new busi-ness ideas. Companies with active, extended webs of partners will be much better prepared for emerging trends, their antennae scanning ho-rizons well beyond the reach of many of their competitors.

Note that the rules of partnership will change as the partnerships evolve. The Management Institute for Environment and Business (MEB) has reviewed the evolution of environmental partnerships in the USA, and defines four different types of partnership. These are: *pre-emptive* or *resolution* partnerships, which are designed to defuse an already or potentially hostile situation; *coalescing* partnerships, in which rivals join forces to accomplish their goals; *exploration* partnerships, based on opportunistic attempts to research or investigate issues of joint concern; and *leverage* partnerships, whose aim is to find win–win (or win–win–win) opportunities that will allow each party to make modest investments in return for relatively high gains.[21] The rules of the game will clearly vary depending on the style of partnership adopted.

Most companies developing advanced eco-efficiency and sustainability management tools recognize that they need a multiplicity of inputs to the relevant processes if they are to provide robust suggestions for future product development and marketing. But they also need to recognize that adopting the right tools and developing the relevant management systems is only part of the challenge. If they need to build public credibility and stakeholder engagement, and most companies do, they need to build wider partnerships – so that their stakeholders share a sense of ownership in the approaches adopted. Given that different partners will bring different rationalities to the table, however, learning how to sustain these partnerships will be a tough challenge. One outside possibility is that the unions – increasingly marginalized during much of the 1980s and 1990s – could find a new role as far-sighted brokers in relation to triple bottom line resources and performance.

The losers, often, will be those left out of the really significant sustainability partnerships. Sometimes this will be a result of the company's perceived failures in the past, sometimes it may itself be a cause of subsequent business failure. But one thing can be guaranteed: no company, industrial sector, or national economy will succeed in defining and meeting its triple bottom line responsibilities and targets without developing much more extensive stakeholder relationships and partnerships than would have been the case even in the recent past.

Three Keys to the 21st Century

The fifth sustainability revolution focuses on partnerships, requiring that we understand and use the following keys to sustainable enterprise:

CASE STUDY

NORTEL, CANADA:
SHARED SAVINGS

Suppliers usually do best when they maximize their sales to customers. Often, however, the result is that both the customer and the environment turn out to be losers. Now the telecommunications company Nortel is testing the "shared savings" approach to chemicals use reduction in Canada and waste minimization in Britain.[22] The company, which is active in some 90 countries, employs more than 60,000 people, and had a turnover of US$10.7 billion in 1995, launched a Product Life Cycle Management program in 1992 designed to root out inefficiencies.

Partnerships with suppliers are seen to be fundamental to both commercial and environmental success. Nortel's shared savings approach focuses on the relationship between supplier and customer. This is structured so as to provide both with financial incentives to improve their environmental performance, for example by curbing resource consumption and waste generation. The new approach is badly needed: recent trends in Nortel's resource efficiency had been moving in the wrong direction.

In 1993, the company disposed of 8,851 tonnes of solid waste to landfill in the British Isles. Its target has been to cut this figure by 50% by 2000, but by 1996 landfill disposals had jumped by 80% to 15,892 tonnes. Part of the problem had been better reporting, but the pressure is now on to cut waste arisings dramatically. Interestingly, however, the company found it hard to find suppliers able to meet its new needs. The waste industry proved to have little experience of shared savings contracts, but as growing numbers of customer companies move in this direction, suppliers and contractors will have no option but to work out new ways of partnering with customers to boost efficiency – both in cost and environmental terms.

♦ The role of complementors and of partnerships will be crucially important both in the development of the global sustainability agenda and of the triple bottom line strategies of particular companies and entire industry sectors. More and more, companies and NGOs will be drawn towards government–industry–NGO symbioses.

♦ *Earned* loyalty is the wave of the future. Companies must be prepared to be challenged in depth by potential and current complementors and partners. These challenges will be a key part of the value of such relationships. And the choice of partners, as in every other area of human life, will be critical.

♦ Building trust represents one of the most vital investments we can make in social capital creation. Remember, however, that poorly constructed relationships may well turn into "monkey traps," constraining the ability of one or more partners to do the things they are in business to do – and undermining trust.

Notes

1. David Watts, "Kidnappings help to undermine gold-diggers from the West," *The Times*, 17 May 1996.
2. Marieke Favrod, "Monkey trap," *Adbusters*, Spring 1996.
3. Tom Patey, "Graduates focus on green issues and multinationals," *European*, 16 May 1996. *The European Graduate Survey 1996* is available from Universum, Box 7053, 103 86 Stockholm, Sweden, or on +46 8 679 48 00.
4. Jonathan Adler, *Environmentalism at the Crossroads: Green activism in America*, Capital Research Center, Washington, DC, 1996.
5. "10 [Germans] who make a difference," *Time*, 30 September 1996.
6. Ed Ayres and Hilary French, "The refrigerator revolution," *World Watch*, September/October 1996.
7. Martin Wright, "Task force first," *Tomorrow*.
8. John Elkington and Shelly Fennell, "Shark, sealion or dolphin?," *Tomorrow*, March–April 1997.
9. "Unilever and WWF lay path to 'sustainable fish' logo," *ENDS Report 254*, March 1996.
10. Dudley Lynch and Paul L. Kordis, *Strategy of the Dolphin: Winning elegantly by coping powerfully in a world of turbulent change*, Arrow Books, 1990.
11. Frederick F. Reichheld, *The Loyalty Effect: The hidden forces behind growth, profits and lasting value*, Harvard Business School Press, 1996.
12. Frederick Reichheld, *The Quest for Loyalty: Creating value through partnership*, Harvard Business School Press, 1996.
13. Barry J. Nalebuff and Adam M. Brandenburger, *Co-opetition*, HarperCollins Business 1996.
14. Francis Fukuyama, *Trust: The social virtues and the creation of prosperity*, Hamish Hamilton 1995.
15. Joan Magretta, "Growth through global sustainability: An interview with Monsanto's CEO, Robert B. Shapiro," *Harvard Business Review*, January–February 1997.
16. C. A. J. Herkströter, *Dealing with Contradictory Expectations: The dilemmas facing multinationals*, 11 October 1996, Amsterdam.
17. Andrew Lorenz, "Streamlined Shell powers head," *Financial Times*, 26 May 1996.

18. Ronald van de Krol, "Partners in grime," *Financial Times*, 1 May 1996.
19. Robert A. Frosch, "Industrial ecology: A philosophical introduction," *Proceedings of the National Academy of Science* **89**, February 1992, pp.800–803.
20. Panagiotis Karamanos, "Industrial ecology: New opportunities for the private sector," *Industry and Environment* **18**(4), United Nations Environment Programme, October–December 1995.
21. Matthew Arnold and Dirk Long, *The Power of Environmental Partnerships*, The Dryden Press, Fort Worth, Texas, 1994.
22. "Nortel: Shared savings for chemicals and waste reduction," *ENDS Report 267*, April 1997.

◆ 10 ◆

TIME

Nanoseconds To Go

A 300-year plan is "long time" thinking
with a vengeance.

And, probably, on the right path.

Building the infrastructure of a
sustainable economy will take unusually long-term
thinking, planning, and funding.

The re-perception of time is probably the most fundamental of all of the great shifts now facing our capitalist societies. Revolution 6 requires that our "wide" time perceptions are increasingly complemented by "long" time thinking. Most trends currently point in precisely the opposite direction.

Revolution	Focus	Old paradigm ❱	New paradigm
6	Time	Wider	❱ Longer

Have you ever had the feeling that someone has sat on the fast-forward button and that time is speeding up? If so, you are not alone. "Everyone lives in what I call the Nescafé world and expects instant results," was the way Sir Evelyn de Rothschild, chairman of merchant bankers NM Rothschild, summed up the challenge of operating in what Tom Peters dubbed the "nanosecond nineties."[1] This is a bad enough problem for merchant bankers, but far worse for the sustainability movement. *For time, it turns out, is one of the most critical dimensions of the sustainability transition.*

Increasingly, executives running the new global businesses use time as a competitive weapon. One of the most successful computer companies of recent years has been Dell, which talks in terms of "velocity." By this it means squeezing time out of every step in the process of getting a computer to a customer, from taking the order, through making the machine to collecting the cash. "Speed is everything in this business," explained company founder Michael Dell.

But recognize what is going on here. "The ultimate purpose of the time-based competitor," concluded George Stalk and Thomas Hout of the Boston Consulting Group:

"is not maximising speed and variety, but owning the customer. Speed and variety are just tools allowing one to do more for the customer, to solve his problems, to reduce his costs – in short, to help him compete and make money."[2]

True, but in the ensuing decade it has often felt as if speed was being pursued for its own sake. In the old days, we might have said that the needle on the changeometer showed every sign of being forced off the clock, but in these digital times there seems no upper limit to the speeds we want to, or can, attain, with due application of globalized operations and state-of-the-art technology.

Listen to George Everhart, the American president of Fujitsu PC in California. He recalls that his team worked non-stop for months to develop the BIOS (basic input–output system) for the firm's new series of Lifebook notebook computers. But, he insists, everybody slept:

"When the work had been done in Japan, they would ship it here in the morning, our time. We did validation testing, wrote it up and shipped the results back to them in the evening. I would say we gained probably three quarters of an extra month that way."[3]

On the threshold of the third millennium, it is hardly surprising that Stephen Hawking's book *A Brief History of Time* became a dramatic best-seller.[4] It is inevitable, of course, that the world's thoughts should have turned to the time dimension as the millennium approached. This always happens at the end of a century. In 1901, for example, a popular London magazine described the future as "one of the best advertised institutions in the world."[5] And the end of a millennium cranks up the power with a vengeance.

Time Dimensions

But how can we get a better grip on the time dimensions of sustainability? And why is it necessary to talk of a time-based revolution? Some companies have made a virtue of trying to peer into the future. Scenario planning, long identified with Shell, is discussed later in the chapter. But, first, it is worth having a look at just how long companies can expect to live; their life expectancy. Insects and other organisms that live for days, or even hours, would find it hard to think in terms of months, let alone years. Companies that live for years or decades may find it hard to think in terms of generations or of the "century time-scale" that some suggest is now essential.[6]

Born early in the 20th century, Shell should be better placed than many companies. When the oil crises of the 1970s spotlighted the finite nature of our fossil fuel resources, Shell wondered whether there would be life after oil? It also asked itself what the appropriate behavior would be when the oil did run out. Should the company accept that it had reached the end of its natural life and liquidize any remaining assets to return them to shareholders? To help decide on the best way forward, it investigated how other long-established firms had addressed this question. As Simon Caulkin recalls: "In a very large proportion the matter didn't arise. Most companies just died. They merged, were taken over, or went out of business."[7]

Of 1984's top 50 UK companies, around a fifth had passed on a decade later. Of the 1974 list, the proportion is a quarter, and of the 1965 list nearly a half. Of the original 30 constituents of the *Financial Times* Ordinary Share Index, launched in 1935, just nine survive more or less intact. And the US corporate death rates turned out to be even higher. Nearly 40% of the 1983 *Fortune* 500 had dematerialized, 60% of 1970's, and of the 12 companies making up the Dow Jones Industrial Index in 1900, GE was the only substantial survivor.

On the other hand, as Caulkin reported, some companies appear to have discovered something very like the secret of corporate immortality. Japanese companies like Mitsui, Sumitomo, and the department store Daimaru can trace their origins back hundreds of years. In the UK, Cambridge University Press received its charter in 1534. But the real industrial Methuselah is Sweden's Stora Kopparberget, which started life over 700 years ago as a copper mine and then mutated into ship-building, forestry, hydropower, iron smelting, pulp and paper, and chemicals. A couple of years ago, one of the company's environmental specialists gave me two books tracing the company's roots back to the 13th century, although precursor activities may well have started at the Falum Mine's Great Pit as early as the year 850.[8] The difference here, however, is that the copper mountain was the reason for the existence of a number of loosely related stages of exploitation, rather than for a single company surviving for over 1,000 years.

More positively, although the average corporate life expectancy might be in the region of 40–50 years, there may be several hundred companies around the world which have been operating for between

100 and 150 years. This imbalance between the broad mass of companies and the long-winded few is a reflection of many factors, but perhaps the most important is the fact that in a capitalist world companies that fail to deliver shareholder value are starved of capital and die. Alternatively, if companies are badly run, then mergers and hostile takeovers will often help to provide them with new management.

Some corporate critics would argue that long-lived corporations are not necessarily a good thing. Stephen Viederman of the US Jessie Smith Noyes Foundation warns that long-lived companies, like long-lived bureaucracies, are very likely to become increasingly arrogant over time. "I could make a case for a limited time horizon, going back to the origin of the corporation," he argues. "A corporation would be chartered for a specific period of time and for a specific social purpose."[9]

This is a useful point. But anyone interested in the subject of corporate life expectancy will find current research suggesting that, while individual managers and even management philosophies may age, there is no inevitable process of decline for companies – and therefore no reason why they should not try to think long term.

Why Worry?

Long *vs*. Wide

There are at least three reasons for business and the sustainability movement to worry about time. The first is the short-sighted over-exploitation of natural resources. Think of the way the UK treated its windfall North sea oil reserves, blowing natural wealth accumulated over millennia in the space of a few decades.[10] The second is the creation of persistent environmental degradation, some of which may not become obvious until well outside the normal corporate planning framework. Recall what ecologists say about the impact of acid rain. "Soils take hundreds of thousands of years to develop. If their chemistry is changed dramatically, it's a major impact. It will take a very long time for them to recover."[11] Third, and perhaps most interestingly, there are the profound changes taking place in the ways in which time itself is perceived, valued, and managed.

But there is a further complication, which concept artist Laurie Anderson posed in the question on her album *Bright Red*, "Is time long, or is it wide?" This question was later picked up and played with by Stewart Brand, perhaps best known as the man behind one of my favourite publications ever, *The Whole Earth Catalog*, but also a co-founder of the Global Business Network (GBN).[12] His interpretation of wide time was "everything-happening-now-and-last-week-and-next-week," while long time is a "deep, flowing process in which centuries are minor events." The wide view of time sees events as most influenced by what is happening at the moment, while the long view inclines to the idea that the causes of many of today's issues and challenges lie deep in the past.

A perfect example of the collision of wide and long time came as I drafted this chapter. The trigger was a proposal to build 77 executive homes on a field where in 1471 Edward IV routed the Lancastrians at the Battle of Tewkesbury in one of the decisive engagements of England's Wars of the Roses. English Heritage's Battlefield Register sums up the importance of such sites as follows: "If, as Winston Churchill wrote, battles are the 'punctuation marks of history,' then battlefields are the fragmentary pages on which those punctuation marks were written in blood."[13] Many wide timers would argue that interest in the past is unhealthy, and long timers that our ability to recall and learn from history is a necessary condition for intelligent decisions.

Wide timers, who would include most of those employed in the computer hardware and software industries, find the boundaries of wide time opening out yet further with the exponential growth of cyberspace in general and of the World Wide Web in particular. "It's useless to try to imagine what the Web might be like in, say, 2045," says Brand, "so we don't bother." Then he asks an interesting question. "Does this mean that technoids and their camp-followers are responsibility-impaired? Could be." It turns out that lots of them are.

Anyone who has read Douglas Coupland's *Microserfs*,[14] which focuses on the lives of coders and programmers working at Microsoft, will recognize the emerging worldview. "We live in an era of no historical precedents," says Karla, on her way south after quitting Microsoft to join a new California start-up:

"History is no longer useful as a tool in helping us understand current changes. You can't look at, say, the War of 1709 (I made this date up, although no doubt there probably *was* a War of 1709) and draw parallels between *then* and *now*. They didn't have Federal Express, SkyTel paging, 1-800 numbers, or hip replacement surgery in 1709 – or a picture of the entire planet inside their heads."

But, even if Generation X-ers do now have the planet as part of their hard-wired mental imagery, what sort of triple bottom line responsibility might this new worldview encourage? Especially in a world where "environment" means MS-DOS – and where the hero's response to a

SPOTLIGHT

HANFORD: COLD WAR BATTLEFIELD

The 20th century has thrown many shadows – and the longest-lasting will probably be the environmental ones. Take the extraordinary contamination at the US government's nuclear complex in the desert of the southeast Washington State. "If we don't get a handle on this mess now," said Senator John Glenn of Ohio, "future generations will be left with a ballooning payment constituting both an environmental and budgetary disaster."[15]

Among other things, the site was the source of the plutonium used in the A-bomb dropped on Nagasaki and has since evolved into what *Scientific American* described as "a nightmarish agglomeration of decaying, contaminated facilities that each consume tens of millions of dollars a year just to be kept safe or stable." Since 1944, it is estimated that the Department of Energy and its predecessors pumped 1.3 billion cubic metres of liquid waste and contaminated water into Hanford's soil. The site contains 177 huge underground tanks of high-level nuclear waste, at least a dozen tons of plutonium, five "gigantic and profoundly contaminated" buildings where plutonium was extracted from irradiated nuclear fuel, and over 2,000 tons of irradiated fuel held in basins which, in an earthquake, "could become lethal, radioactive dustbins."

Having spent $7.5 billion in seven years on clean-up, DOE expects to spend at least $1 billion a year at Hanford for the next 40 years. But huge though Hanford is, it only accounts for about a fifth of a DOE programme to close down a large part of its nuclear weapons enterprise over the next century, give or take a decade or two. Estimates of the clean-up costs range from $230 billion to more than half a trillion dollars – well in excess of the $375 billion, in current dollars, that it cost the US to research and build tens of thousands of weapons, and to detonate the 1,000 or so tested.

"The stuff we're dealing with can't go away until it decays," said James D. Werner, director of strategic planning in the DOE's Office of Environmental Management. Much of the waste will take thousands of years to cool down. In what was officially described as a "national sacrifice area," some of the damage is likely to be, in human terms, permanent, however much money might be thrown at it. Clean-up technologies either do not exist or, even if they did, could never make much of an impression. "It's hard to explain this history in a rational way," commented an attorney with the Natural Resources Defense Council. But another way to look at Hanford is as a devastated battle site of the Cold War which was never fought.

documentary programme about codfish being gill-netted into extinction in Newfoundland is to go out "to Burger King to get a Whaler fish-wich-type breaded deep-fried filet sandwich while there was still time."

The long-term costs of short-term thinking are nowhere more apparent than at the US government's Hanford nuclear complex, where the clean-up is likely to take at least 75 years in the first instance – and last for many thousands of years thereafter (Spotlight, p.251).

And what about the long timers? No one disputes that history counts. You need only think of the history of the Jewish diaspora over thousands of years, of the Irish conflict over hundreds, or of the suspicion of the US federal government still found among the descendants of those dumped in Montana and other wildernesses of the "Great American Desert" as late as the early years of the 20th century. Indeed, there are those who would track the roots of the bomb that destroyed the Alfred P. Murrah Federal Building in Oklahoma City back to the scams through which the US government helped to "drop people on to an expanse of land which looked suspiciously like the surface of the moon."[16] As in Northern Ireland, Bosnia, or Kosovo, a sense of grievance caused generations ago still echoes strongly in today's world.

In retrospect, much of the environmental revolution has been about the collision between long and wide time. "Environmentalists are supposed to be the long-view specialists these days," Stewart Brand notes, "but I think we do it poorly. I was trained as an ecologist, so I know how extremely limited our "longitudinal studies" are – about the length of time it takes to get a graduate degree. Since it is the long, slow fluctuations and cycles that most influence everything in ecology, we still don't have the most important information on how natural systems actually work over time." So, however clever we think our latest environmental impact tools are, the chances are that they are pretty much at the same stage that the personal computer was at when Steve Jobs and Steve Wozniak were first fiddling around with the box of chips and wiring that was to become the first generation of Apple computers.

Calamity Callers

Another problem, as Brand points out, is that environmentalists have usually tended to be "calamity callers." He adds, "We are the leading apostles of 'things are getting worse.'" The few voices which are more positive – among them René Dubos, who coined the phrase "Think globally, act locally" and wrote a book on how nature and humanity could blend, *The Wooing of the Earth*, and, more controversially, Greg Easterbrook, with his *A Moment on Earth* – tend to get drowned out. Ultimately, of course, neither the Cassandras nor the Pollyannas are completely right or wrong: it is all a question of balance, a balance that can shift and be shifted. But there is no question that short-term thinking tends to short-change many of the values implicit in the sustainability agenda.

Whatever risks we are discussing, we need to find ways to extend our thinking beyond the usual time-frames. How can we do this? One Japanese millionaire, Katsuhiko Yazaki, has set up the Future Generations Alliance Foundation to consider such questions. When he held a conference in Kyoto in 1994, one of those present was Nicholas Albery of the Council For Posterity. Among the ideas Albery came up with in short order were: a permanent Internet conference on the needs of future generations; the appointment of legal guardians for endangered species and ecosystems; and the establishment of a "court of generations" to represent and protect the future.[17]

Another, unrelated, suggestion, advanced by Danny Hillis, one of the pioneers of massively parallel computing, is to construct a Millennium Clock (Spotlight, p.254). A great, mythic idea, and hopefully a stimulant for the myth-of-sustainability-engineers of the future. But another, rather more pragmatic idea might be to continue funding for some of the long-term research projects whose ultimate payoff will flow from the very fact that they have been running for more than a century (Spotlight, p.255). This issue is one to which we shall return in Chapter 13, although with proposals that are rather more mundane.

What's New, Gurus?

Shipwrecked

Let's consider five gurus, three books. The first, *Longitude*,[18] is about as far from a management text-book as it is possible to get. But the sustainability community could learn much from Dava Sobels' extraordinary account of John Harrison's attempts to build a clock which would simultaneously keep time on ships at sea and help their captains and navigators to keep track of longitude. To plot an accurate course, you need both your latitude (which you can calculate from the stars) and your longitude. Britain, which had the world's largest merchant fleet by the late 17th and early 18th centuries, was losing too many ships for comfort and offered the then extraordinary sum of £200,000 for anyone who could come up with an answer.

THE MILLENNIUM CLOCK

Why bother making plans when everything will change? 2010 is too far off to plan for, and 2030 too far to think about. Why? One factor, says inventor Danny Hillis, is simply the way we name our years. "Those three zeroes in the millennium form a convenient barrier, a reassuring boundary by which we can hold to the present and isolate ourselves from whatever comes next."

But there is more to it than that.

> "It feels like something big is about to happen: graphs show us the yearly growth of populations, atmospheric concentrations of carbon dioxide, Net addresses, and Mbytes per dollar. They all soar up to an asymptote just beyond the turn of the century. The Singularity. The end of everything we know. The beginning of something we may never understand."

So what can be done? The long-timers of the past thought in a very different way. When the oak beams in the ceiling of College Hall at New College, Oxford, needed replacing in the last century, the carpenters used trees that had been planted in 1386 when the hall was built. Hillis notes: "The 14th century builder had planted trees in anticipation of the time, hundreds of years in the future, when the beams would need replacing."

How can we prod our brains into thinking in long time? Hillis suggests the Millennium Clock. It ticks once a year. The century hand advances once every century – and the cuckoo comes out on the millennium. "I want the cuckoo to come out every millennium for the next 10,000 years," says Hillis. "If I hurry, I should finish the clock in time to see the cuckoo come out the first time."

One friend dubbed the machine "The Clock of the Long Now." The real problem, however, is how to ensure that the thing lasts for 10,000 years. The only way to survive really long term is to be made of "materials large and worthless, like Stonehenge and the Pyramids, or to become lost." Better still, someone suggested, a very convincing TV documentary should be made about the clock being manufactured and hidden. "Don't actually build one. That would spoil the myth if it was ever found." In the end, Hillis concludes, maybe this would be the best idea. "Pure information," he says, "lives the longest. Bits last."[19] Any sustainable corporation will need to develop its own version of the "Clock of the Long Now."

KEEPER OF THE LONG-TERM CONSCIENCE

It all started over 150 years ago. John Lawes and Henry Gilbert, founding fathers of modern agricultural science, sowed the first wheat on a 12-acre plot at Rothamsted in 1843. They wanted to measure the effect of various soil treatments on crop yields, from applying nothing at all through to full dollops of artificial fertilizer. As the *Financial Times* put it, Lawes and Gilbert had little idea of what they had begun, but "these remarkable trials illuminate contemporary debate about the long-term effects of intensive food production, the limits of bio-diversity and the impact of global warming."[20]

Lawes was an entrepreneur who produced synthetic fertilizer by grinding animal bones, then treating them with sulphuric acid at his 16th century manor house. The profits he made from the resulting "superphosphate of lime" helped found the Rothamsted Experimental Station, a leading UK agricultural research institute, and start large-scale crop trials. One area collapsed after a century of nitrogen fertilizer treatment, which had allowed a fungus to build up and ravage turnip crops. "Today we may be starting farming systems which may take equally long to collapse," warned Rothamsted's leading expert on the experiments.

In 1882, another area was simply abandoned to see what happened. A century later, it became critically important when the agricultural industry began to wonder what would happen if large areas of farming land were retired – or "set aside" – for conservation purposes.

A side-benefit of the trials was that a system of drains under each plot has allowed scientists to monitor inputs of pollutants from other sources. Astonishingly, just 10 years after the first PCBs were produced in the US during the late 1930s, they were detected in Rothamsted soils – having traveled across the Atlantic in the atmosphere. Some pollutants, like sulphur from acid rain, provided a useful additional source of fertilizer – and have had to be replaced as acid rain emissions dropped sharply. The contribution of rising atmospheric carbon dioxide levels to plant growth is also being monitored, with early trials suggesting that – at least with wheat – the additional CO_2 boosts growth, but higher temperatures cancel that effect out.

The ongoing experiment, in the words of Rothamsted director Professor Ben Miflin, is "a keeper of the long-term conscience." It's worrying, then, that among the casualties of recent cut-backs in international environmental research have been a number of "time-series" research programs whose records extended back over decades.

Having done a school project on Harrison in the early sixties, I knew the bare bones of the story, but not the full details of his 40-year struggle to persuade the powers that were that the answer might lie in an accurate clock, or chronometer, and not in the stars. This is not the place to retell that story; instead, let it serve as a metaphor. As Charles Handy put it:

> "the longitude story may have another very modern counterpart. For want of a way of measurement, sailors of old lost their way, drowned or starved. Businesses today may also be in danger of losing their way for want of proper measurement."[21]

Handy had in mind the mismatch between the value of a successful company's measurable assets and market values, which can be five to 20 times higher. Something, clearly, is going unmeasured. "Presumably," he concluded, "it is the unseen intellectual property in the business, its brands, its research and patents, the know-how and talents of its people." Today, growing numbers of experts are trying to work out how to measure a company's intellectual assets, knowing that "unmeasured assets, such as talent, don't get nurtured."

A few weeks before I came across Handy's extrapolation from the *Longitude* saga, I had made my own, but – perhaps not surprisingly – in the direction of measuring sustainability. That's the glory of the story. Our current inability to measure, let alone understand, how we measure up to any sensible set of triple bottom line performance indicators is seen by many as a fundamental problem. No one has yet offered a giant sum for the answer, but maybe the likes of Bill Gates might be persuaded?

Corporate Methusalehs

One of the very best books on the subject of corporate life-spans is *Built to Last*, by James Collins and Jerry Porras.[22] What they did, in their own words, was to take:

> "a set of truly exceptional companies that have stood the test of time – the average founding date was 1897 – and studied them from their very beginnings, through all phases of their development to the present day; and we studied them *in comparison* to another set of good companies that had the same shot in life, but didn't attain quite the same stature."

They compared Boeing with McDonnell Douglas, Ford with GM, Motorola with Zenith, Procter & Gamble with Colgate, and so on. They looked at the companies in their start-up and mature phases. They looked at their responses as they negotiated dramatic changes, including world wars, depressions, revolutionary technologies, and cultural upheavals. And, throughout, they asked what it was that distinguished the truly exceptional company?

Their aim was to rise above the blizzard of fashionable management buzzwords and fads, and explore the deep patterns in corporate evolution. Interestingly, they discovered in the process that:

> "many of today's buzzwords – employee ownership, empowerment, continuous improvement, TQM, common vision, shared values, and others – are repackaged and updated versions of practices that date back, in some cases, to the 1800s."

None of the companies, they found, had been able to avoid major mistakes and setbacks at some point in their history. Some were experiencing difficulty as the book was being written. But the research showed a key point; that visionary, long-lived companies all displayed a remarkable resiliency. As a result, they also turn in extraordinary long-term financial performances. If you had made three equal $1 investments in a general market stock fund, in a fund investing in the comparison companies used by Collins and Porras, and in a visionary company stock fund in 1926, the first investment would have been worth $415 by 1990 and the second $955. "But your $1 in the visionary companies stock fund," Collins and Porras note, "would have grown to $6,356 – over six times the comparison fund and over fifteen times the general market."

Along the way, the book shatters a number of myths about long-lived companies. Visionary leaders, for example, turn out to be unnecessary, indeed often actively harmful when it comes to a company's long-term prospects. Even more striking, while profit maximization and boosting shareholder wealth are important, they have not been the dominant driving force or even the primary objective through the history of the visionary companies. *Instead, the best companies turn out to pursue a cluster of objectives and are guided by a core ideology – including core values and a sense of purpose beyond the financial bottom line.* Interestingly, however, there is no "right" set of core values. "Core values in a visionary company don't have to be 'enlightened' or 'humanistic,'" we are told, "although they often are. The crucial variable is not the content of the company's ideology, but how deeply it believes its ideology and how consistently it lives, breathes, and expresses it in all that it does."

Other myths that bit the dust include the idea that "the only constant is change" (outside, maybe, but not in a company's core values), "blue-chip companies play it safe" (visionary companies are not afraid to set themselves BHAGs, or "Big Hairy Audacious Goals"), "visionary companies are great places to work" (they can be for those who fit well, but those who don't fit are flushed out like viruses), and "highly successful companies make their best moves by brilliant and complex strategic planning" (a great deal of this turns out to be a matter of accident, but these companies are all for experimentation, trial and error, and opportunism).

So, if you are looking to help build a sustainable corporation, some basic guidelines would include the following:

♦ focus on creating the company, not on great ideas, ego gratification or the accumulation of personal wealth;
♦ don't over-simplify by imagining it always has to be either/or – work out ways of having both/and;
♦ recognize that profits reflect success in meeting other goals;
♦ preserve the core values;
♦ set clear, compelling and stretching goals;
♦ encourage devotion to the company's goals, even if some see the result as a cult-like culture;
♦ "try a lot of stuff – and keep what works;"
♦ where possible, bring on home-grown management;
♦ compete with your own best performance: "good enough never is;" and
♦ work to ensure that all the above are aligned in the culture and the minds of all key stakeholders.

Asked how they would advise a company like IBM, during the throes of its unparalleled humbling by a new generation of IT upstarts, Collins and Porras had an interesting recommendation. Any company which wants to live on into the future has to launch revolutions before its competitors do, even if the end result is the loss of the markets for products or services which previously produced the bulk of the company's revenue. Change will come; the real issue is who will drive – and own – it?

Artists of the Long View

If any one thing is certain about today's business environment, it is uncertainty. Revolutions, whether they focus on virtuality or sustainability, come thick and fast. So how is the corporate head to be kept above the water? One way companies try to impose order on the future is to develop vision statements. Indeed, many of the great companies that Collins and Porras researched had state-of-the-art vision statements. But did these statements account for their commercial success and status as "visionary" companies? Not at all.

In fact such statements turned out to be just one step along the long road of integrating the company's values, goals, and strategies into every part of its fabric. Visionary companies, we are told, create a total environment "that envelops employees, bombarding them with a set of signals so consistent and mutually reinforcing that it's virtually impossible to misunderstand the company's ideology and ambitions."

But at a time of massive change, even companies with the most consistent internal ideologies and cultures need to challenge their thinking about what might happen over time. Evolutionary biologists, waking up to the fact that evolution is rarely a straight-line progression, talk of "punctuated equilibrium" – in which dramatic environmental changes trigger huge evolutionary jumps in relatively short time-scales. As a corporate parallel, imagine a company, industry, or economy that was totally in tune with an unsustainable world order, and which was then suddenly persuaded of the need to drive Factor 4 or even Factor 10 change through its system for decade after decade.

Like the individuals of which they are made up, corporations have blind spots. Corporate planners used to, and some still do, aggravate the problem by portraying the future as a series of straight-line extrapolations of existing trends. These days, they may put in a few kinks to suggest feedback from the wider world, but the underlying trend is still assured. To tackle such blind spots, and to shrug off the assumptions that they breed, companies like Shell have made huge investments in scenario planning.

"Scenarios are a tool for helping us to take a long view in a world of great uncertainty," explained Peter Schwartz in his *The Art of the Long View*:[23]

"The name comes from the theatrical term 'scenario' – the script for a film or play. Scenarios are stories about the way the world might turn out tomorrow, stories that can help us recognize and adapt to changing aspects of our present environment. They form a method for articulating the different pathways that might exist for you tomorrow, and finding your appropriate movements down each of those possible paths. Scenario planning is about making choices *today* with an understanding of how they might turn out."

Is this the perfect tool, perhaps, for straddling the wide/long time divide? Scenario designers rarely consider possible future storylines or plots individually, as Schwartz noted. Instead, they consider the ways in which different plots or scenarios might handle the same forces. So what about the sustainability challenge? Schwartz suggested that we might see either an evolutionary plot or a challenge and response plot.

In the "evolutionary" plot, more of the same – more refinery explosions, nuclear melt-downs, biological waste mishaps, chemical leaks, or rainforests razed – progressively leads us to ecodisaster, or at least to a gradual winding down of real productivity and wealth generation. Alternatively, the "challenge and response" plot might suggest a series of interlocking trends leading towards an "ecoboom." "This late in the game," as Schwartz put it:

> "the urgency of building a 'sustainable growth' society would inspire unusual innovation and change. Somewhere out there, the Aristotle Onassis of the 2000–2010 era is growing up. Spurred by the challenge of these years, he or she will figure out a way to entrepreneur intelligently managed transportation, for example. At first, he would fill only a niche that exists because of the environmental threat, a niche that gradually expands to the full system."

Alert readers may recall a reference in Chapter 7 to Onassis, whose whaling ships used to illegally hunt whales. We must hope that the entrepreneurial class of the early 21st century will be more law-abiding. But the point is the same. Scenarios are only valuable if they provoke our thinking, changing our choices and, ultimately, behavior. Opening up our thinking to emerging solutions and opportunities, rather than simply to impending problems, clearly has a great value. Later on, we will look at three sustainability scenarios, each of which assumes success in this direction – but each of which develops in a very different way. But, first, how does the time challenge look from the boardroom?

Boardroom Views

Son's 300-year Plan

The time dimension is increasingly squeezed, but not everybody running companies these days is a wide-timer. Asked where he saw his company in 10 years, Japanese entrepreneur Masayoshi Son of Softbank replied: "What I"m really thinking about is the 300-year plan." His goal is to develop much of the long-term infrastructure needed by computers and the Internet. "Technology changes very often," he argued:

> "The paradigm shifts once every 10 years or so. But the infrastructure tends to stay around much longer. Sometimes, for a technology company, size becomes a negative factor. A large company's strength in the last technology can slow down its move into the next technology. However, as an infrastructure provider, largeness itself becomes the strongest factor in sustaining the infrastructure."[24]

A 300-year plan may or may not help, but this is long-time thinking with a vengeance, and is, probably, on the right path. Son's fortunes may collapse. The debt burden he took on to buy a large stake in Asahi National Broadcasting, alongside Rupert Murdoch, may overwhelm Softbank. But Son's basic logic seems sound. Building the infrastructure of the future economy, particularly if it is to be sustainable, is going to take very long-term thinking, planning, and funding indeed.

And, every so often, one also stumbles across an example of a business taking a wildly different, long-time view of responsibilities inherited from the past. Take the case of Englishman Ian Johnston, who inherited Thortergill Gorge in 1971. Along with the site, which his ancestors had sold for mining in the 1780s as too steep for farming, Johnston also felt he had inherited a "debt to Nature," which he was determined to repay.[25] By the time the mine established on the site closed in the 1920s, the valley, with its streams and waterfalls, had been buried under thousands of tons of rock and spoil. Over a period of a quarter century, Johnston and his family have restored the Gorge, even selling their industrial supplies distribution business in order to fund the work.

By the standards of today, such behavior is little short of madness. Johnston may have been awarded a pewter plate by *Country Life*, as the magazine's "Countryman of the Year," but any head-hunter scouting for directors to help companies build a competitive position well into the 21st century would probably have given him a wide berth. However, there are elements of both these stories which reflect a different logic, a different understanding of time and the opportunities and responsibilities that long time can bring. If we managed to get at least part of the world onto the tracks leading to a more sustainable future, Son and Johnston might find themselves being courted as business visionaries. A case of the apparent lunatics taking over the commercial asylum.

Does Sustainable Mean Privately Held?

Another entrepreneur who has tried to build his company to last is Ingvar Kamprad, founder of IKEA, the giant furniture and housewares business. Far from coincidentally, the company has a well-developed environmental conscience. "I don't want to take great personal credit for our environmental efforts," said Kamprad. But, he noted, "If your goal is to serve people in general, then you know they are very interested in a sound situation in the environment."[26]

Unfortunately, he concluded that financial markets and the media are unlikely to help in this respect. "We have worked many years to build a long-lasting enterprise in many countries," Kamprad explained. "Shareholders want short-term rewards. They demand annual profits and a rising pattern of earnings. That is against my way of thinking." As a result, IKEA has rejected any public sale of shares.

This is not the place to discuss whether or not IKEA as currently constituted is sustainable in the long term. More interesting is the question raised by Kamprad's assessment: does any sustainable business have to operate on a "skunk-works" basis, hiding its real motives from the rest of the world, and particularly from financial analysts? On this evidence, it seems likely. But there are also at least signs that some of the biggest names in finance are recognizing the dangers of short-termism.

Take Henry Kravis, seen by many as "the Napoleon of late 20th century capitalism, a ruthless megalomaniac who can terrify even the most hard-bitten and battle-scarred industrialist."[27] Even before he won the biggest-ever takeover battle in corporate history, he was renowned on Wall Street as the ultimate symbol of the "greed is good" philosophy. And the epic battle for R. J. R. Nabisco made him into a financial megastar, immortalized in the best-selling book *Barbarians at the Gate*. But as a result of the experience, Kravis decided to stay away in future from socially unacceptable industries like tobacco and gambling. He also explained that, "We are looking for opportunities that are more long-term in nature, where we can put in a larger amount of equity."

Leopards may change their spots, even erstwhile barbarians take to farming, but it is in the very nature of capitalism that others will pick up those spurned investments even if Kohlberg Kravis Roberts (KKR) do not. That said, it is remarkable how fast the director class, driven by the financial markets, can sometimes shift once it is clear which way the wind is blowing. This is a theme to which we return in Chapter 11.

Racing the Clock

The subject of time, and its management, has been discussed in many management best-sellers. "Time cannot be seen or touched," say Charles Hampden-Turner and Fons Trompenaars in their book, *The Seven Cultures of Capitalism*.[28] "It is not a thing at all, but an experience of the human mind." But it is clear that different cultures view and manage time in significantly different ways. Some cultures view time as sequential, always running out. Others view time as circular, with the present feeding back rich experience to help us improve our chances of benefiting from tomorrow's inevitable opportunities. The implications of the two different approaches are profound.

Countries like the USA, the UK, Sweden and the Netherlands seem more oriented to sequential time, focusing on speeding things up. According to Hampden-Turner and Trompenaars, Japan, Germany, and France tend to be more interested in synchronized, parallel time. The results of these differences can be seen in how companies view their own people: in a "sequential culture, a "rationalizing" company will tend to see employees as a cost and waste, whereas in a synchronous culture they are more likely to be seen as a potential resource for the future, worth training and investing in.

In the sequential culture, time is an enemy, "an implacably hastening and expensive train of events that must be used fully" and products are seen as "maturing over time, going from high novelty and profitability to routine operations, lower margins, and eventual death." By contrast, in synchronizing cultures, time is a friend "who keeps coming around, providing fresh opportunities for engagement on each occasion" and products tend to be regarded as "self-renewing over time, the 'genes' of one product giving life to the next generation and the next."

Asked to plot the past, present, and future as three circles of varying sizes and proximities on a line, thousands of executives around the world demonstrated the very different ways in which they experienced time. Probably the most dramatic difference was between France (where the past loomed largest, the present much smaller, and the future much smaller again) and Japan (where the experience of time was most unified or telescoped, with the past smallest, the present medium-sized, and the future largest). In the USA, there was the largest gap between the past and the present, with the present strongly overlapping with the future. By contrast, the past and present overlapped for UK executives, with the future larger but somewhat disconnected.

In terms of the sustainability transition, both the sequential and synchronous approaches have strengths and weaknesses. But it is significant that in terms of a poll of international managers reported by Hampden-Turner and Trompenaars, American corporations ranked eighteenth in a list covering 30 nations in terms of their "capacity to take a long term view." This challenge can be viewed in at least two ways: either as a massive potential constraint on getting corporate boards to think about such issues as intergenerational equity, or as an opportunity to reframe board-level thinking by provoking directors to think longer term than would be normal.

Bubbling Under

Time Horizons

The whole subject of time, long and wide, is bubbling under. As activist Jeremy Rifkin put it: "Balancing our budget with nature requires that we reorient the pace of our economic activity so that it is compatible with nature's timetables."[29] Nor is it simply a question of different cultures having different time perceptions: even individuals living and working in the same culture may have very different perceptions of time – as, indeed, may the same individual at different stages in his or her life. Organizations, too, can create their own time environments. Recall President Kennedy comparing Washington D.C. to a stupid, ill-coordinated dachshund, "whose head hung down with tears and sadness," while the message got stuck somewhere in the middle and "the tail wagged on in previous gladness."[30]

The "long run," in short, can mean very different things to different people. In the context of social concerns, the long run is often seen as extending out through the lifetimes of grandchildren, so to around 50 years.[31] At the other end of the spectrum, some individuals, and indeed some companies, consistently act as if "there were no tomorrow." In the middle ground, some governments have five-year plans and many companies get by planning product development and marketing over a two- or three-year time-scale. Perhaps, as John Gordon suggests, what our current political systems need, and lack, are "time guardians."[32]

The point at which the time dimension can collide most violently with the sustainability agenda is in relation to the impact of the discounting rates used by governments and by business. We will come back to accounting and taxation issues in Chapter 13, but the role of discount rates is also critical when considering the value of scenarios and other time-based management tools. Discounting is an economic method

THE FUTURE IS COMING TOO FAST

How can you spot tomorrow's triple bottom line priorities? That, in essence, was the question asked by the US Environmental Protection Agency (EPA) when it investigated ways not simply to clean up yesterday's problems or manage today's, but also to protect tomorrow's world.[33] The answer, the EPA concluded, is to look for six characteristics.

1. **Timing**   How soon is this problem likely to emerge, how important is early recognition, and how rapidly can the problem be reversed?
2. **Novelty**   To what extent is this a new problem that has not been addressed adequately?
3. **Scope**   How extensive – e.g. in terms of geography or population affected – is this problem?
4. **Severity**   How intensive are the likely health, ecological, economic, and other impacts of this problems, and are they reversible?
5. **Visibility**   How much public concern is this problem likely to arouse?
6. **Probability**   What is the likelihood of this problem emerging, and necessitating a response, in the future?

which gives greater weight to present needs than to future needs. So, for example, if you or I operate, consciously or not, an annual discount rate of 10%, the implication is that consumption this year will be 1.1 times better than consumption next year, 1.21 times better than consumption in two years, and so on.

This attempt to quantify time-horizons may make sense if you are an economist, but it leaves out a great deal, and the process amplifies our natural inclination to pay less attention than we ought to longer term issues and problems. So how can we all learn to see through the mists of time and make better decisions?

The Ungentle Art of Re-perceiving

Shell has long been renowned for its scenario planning strengths and the company's scenario planners have long recognized the growing unpredictability of the oil industry's business environment. Their use of scenarios flows from the recognition that conventional planning techniques often fail to prepare the planners, let alone their employers or clients, for the sorts of surprises that are becoming endemic in today's world.

So let's look back over the brief history of scenario planning. Pierre Wack, one of the architects of Shell's scenario planning system, published two seminal papers in the *Harvard Business Review* during 1985 outlining "one thing or two learned while developing planning scenarios for Royal Dutch/Shell."[34] Scenarios, Wack argued, deal not only with the hard facts of the "outer space" beyond the organization but with the softer, fluid perceptual "inner space" of people's minds. At the time, he had in mind the necessity to bridge these two realms in such a way that Shell managers experienced a creative insight that _generated a heartfelt "Aha!" as new strategic insights emerged. But effective scenarios must also capture what is going on in the inner space of the *public* mind.

When Shell pulled the two articles together to form the first in its "Strategic Planning in Shell" papers in 1986, the slim blue-covered document was entitled *The Gentle Art of Re-perceiving*. There were three key insights. First, during a time of rapid change, companies differ greatly in their effectiveness and speed in identifying and transforming information of strategic significance into strategic initiatives. Second, the sheer amount of "noise," caused by all the conflicting signals to which we are all exposed, infinitely complicates the task of choosing the right responses. Locked into traditional perceptions, governments and companies alike can suffer strategic failure. The third insight addressed the question of what can be done to address these two problems. The answer stems from the fact that the human brain is much better at discriminating significant trends from the noise when it is listening for something – or for one of several things. Hence the value of scenarios sketching out evolving realities.

The Brent Spar controversy suggests that failures in this "gentle art" will continue to result in ungentle, highly bruising controversies which force the business world to re-perceive the emerging environmental agenda in public.[35] Globe-straddling Shell is well placed to recognize the growing worldwide concern that current patterns of development are unsustainable. But it may have made the mistake of assuming that the environmental debate is now focused on pragmatic questions of efficiency rather than on more fundamental concerns linked to a growing aversion to environmental risk.

Not that the use of scenarios ever guarantees the "right" outcome. Shell first began to include environmental factors in its scenarios in the 1980s, but anyone who tracks the debate will know that there is as yet little agreement on what "sustainability" means, let alone on how it might be applied to particular industrial products, processes, corporations, sectors, or economies. This problem is likely to be even more complicated where the issue cuts across international borders. In the case of the Brent Spar, Shell UK might have weathered the storm, but its sister companies operating in more environmentally sensitive European countries, particularly Deutsche Shell, were much harder hit.

It is also becoming clear that environmental issues cannot be considered in isolation from an increasingly interconnected, competitive, and fast-moving global economy. The result is a business world marked by growing complexity, drawn-out time-scales for action, and a growing number of unpleasant surprises.

Managing Complexity

To survive, let alone succeed, in an increasingly complex world, companies and institutions will need to develop strategies which provide clear, integrated frameworks for action, yet which are sufficiently resilient and flexible to cope with the unexpected. Indeed, as the concept of sustainability becomes part of mainstream political discourse, so we also see a growing recognition that the challenge is compounded by its increasing complexity. "Complexity," of course, is another buzzword whose fortunes have oscillated fairly dramatically. What is clear, however, is that economic, technological, social, and environmental change is accelerating, placing new demands on decision-makers in business and government. It is also increasingly obvious that today's decision making, modelling, and analysis tools, and the theoretical frameworks on which they are based, are proving to be increasingly inadequate.

To help business people, and their various complementors, to understand and respond to the emerging trends, Alex Trisoglio, Sustain-Ability, and a range of partners developed a set of three scenarios of a sustainable Europe in 2020 for two clients: European Partners for the Environment (EPE)[36] and the Commission for the European Communities (CEC).[37] Our conclusion was that Shell's scenarios to date had been "individualist," "hierarchist," or some combination of the two. None had adopted an egalitarian or "values shift" perspective. We also argued that the "values shift" scenario – one of the seemingly more outlandish scenarios developed for European Partners for the Environment (EPE) – holds clues to necessary future shifts in business strategy.[38]

In analyzing the scenarios published up to 1995 by Shell and its key scenario planners (among them Peter Schwartz), Alex Trisoglio used the three categories developed by cultural theory.[39] These three ways of life and their associated rationalities may be summarized by three archetypal examples:

♦ **Individualist**   The "self-made" Victorian manufacturer, a prag-
matist who measures success in material terms and focuses on the
"bottom line." This person follows an individualistic personal
strategy, supports the free operation of the market as a means for
increasing wealth, and sees human skill, enterprise and risk-
taking as the keys to success.

♦ **Hierarchist**   The high-caste Hindu villager, who has considerable rights to land and water, in addition to priestly duties and the
deference of fellow villagers, and a corresponding set of duties and
allowable behaviors. Everyone in this society has a place, and
there are heavy prescriptions to ensure that social order and stability are maintained. Attention to observing the rules creates a
procedural rationality that is more concerned with the correctness
of procedure and behavior than with trying to evaluate any outcome that may arise. Soldiers of all ranks and civil servants are
other examples.

♦ **Egalitarian**   The member of a self-sufficient Western commune,
whose critical rationality rejects the inequality, coerciveness, and
harshness of the outside world in favour of voluntary cooperation.
S/he has strong group loyalties, but little respect for externally imposed rules, other than those of nature. Group decisions are
arrived at democratically, but the group tends to expend more
energy in criticizing the world outside its "wall of virtue" than in
delivering solutions. This rationality was historically the driving
force of socialism, and can be seen today in many religious sects
and environmental pressure groups.

To understand the blind spots in Shell's scenarios, Trisoglio reviewed
those published up to 1996. One conclusion was that the most professional scenario builders are not necessarily the most thorough. Shell
and former Shell employees Kahane[40] and Schwartz produce very similar sets of scenarios, containing the Utopias and dystopias as seen from
the individualist/hierarchist perspective one might associate with a
large multinational like Shell. But there was no egalitarian perspective, which would seem essential for any company trying to cope with
the sustainability agenda.

Values Shift

Our own set of three sustainability scenarios does contain an egalitarian plot, "values shift" (see Spotlight, p. 269). The odd thing was that in

SPOTLIGHT   THE EPE SCENARIOS:NO LIMITS, ORDERLY TRANSITION OR VALUES SHIFT?

Three scenarios developed for European Partners for the Environment (EPE) – a pan-European coalition of government agencies, businesses, NGOs, associations and institutes – are summarized below. Each is set a generation into the future.

Scenario 1: NO LIMITS

NO LIMITS is the individualistic scenario. It assumes that many of the environmental concerns of recent decades have been greatly exaggerated. Ecosystems, and economies, have proved very much more adaptable than had been expected. Technological progress has been rapid and economic growth based on novel information technologies, biotechnology, and new materials has generated the wealth to pay for the sustainability transition. Market mechanisms are pre-eminent, the information society is reducing human impacts on the environment, and sustainability is seen in terms of securing a rising standard of living and quality of life through technological progress.

Scenario 2: ORDERLY TRANSITION

ORDERLY TRANSITION is the hierarchist scenario. It is based on the idea that the challenge of integrating environment and economy is manageable within the existing paradigm, but assumes a need for a government-led response based on strong, integrated economic and environmental policies. The internalization of external costs is achieved by ecological tax reform. Sustainable lifestyles are driven by increasing process and regulatory pressures.

Scenario 3: VALUES SHIFT

VALUES SHIFT is the egalitarian scenario. It assumes that environmental problems become increasingly urgent and foresees that growing dissatisfaction with the responses of government and business will catalyze a strong "bottom-up" approach. Steady-state economies are seen as essential and there are major shifts in production and consumption patterns to secure a dramatic reduction in man's damaging impact on nature, to embrace a precautionary approach to forestall the catastrophes that may lie ahead, and to ensure an equitable distribution of "environmental space." The key driver is a fundamental shift in human values, based on such concepts as inter-generational equity.

Source: Towards Shared Sustainability: EPE Workbook 1.1, EPE/Environmental Strategies/SustainAbility 1995.[41]

the ensuing EPE workshops, business people found it hardest to imagine scenario 1 ("no limits"), in which the environmental challenge disappears. Those working in the public sector saw scenario 2 ("orderly transition"), based on growing public concern and increasing regulation, as perhaps the best option for them. But a surprising number of EPE participants recognized in scenario 3 ("values shift") the greatest potential threats and opportunities. We got the same response when we subsequently tested the scenarios out with the members of the European Union's General Consultative Forum on the Environment.

The Brent Spar controversy should not be read as evidence that we are moving towards a values shift on the scale outlined in scenario 3, but it does suggest – as argued in Chapter 6 – that values will be increasingly central to the environmental and sustainable development debates.

Winners, Losers

Red Dwarf

Thanks to the time dimension, sustainability is always going to be a relative concept. In the long run, our civilization, like many before it, will collapse. This may be before, during, or after the next major Ice Age. In the very long run, the human race may expand to the stars, as predicted in the writings of Isaac Asimov and Arthur C. Clarke (Spotlight, p.271) and the films of George Lukas, but ultimately our species is just as likely to become extinct. Even longer term, a few billion years out, the sun will turn into a red dwarf, consume our planet, and then settle down as a grey dwarf. But if we are more modest and adopt the century time-scale, there is every reason to believe that sustainability thinking will be critical in managing the 21st century transition from a world of five or six billion to something closer to 10 or 12 billion.

Tomorrow's long-distance winners will be those who develop a strong sense of foresight. All around, the world is being reshaped by dramatic changes in the quantities of information available, the collapse of the old barriers of distance and changing time perceptions – all trends with major strategic implications for governments, industries, and companies. Interestingly, however, there is a growing sense that organizations wanting to develop the art of foresight need to have a sounder understanding of the past. The lesson from the past is that knowledge of history helps foresight – and foresight, in turn, helps those who want to build power and influence.

3001

At a time when the world was getting excited about the impending third millennium, only one man on the planet was already at work thinking about the fourth: science fiction writer Arthur C. Clarke. In the world of 3001, sketched out in his book *The Final Odyssey*, Clarke imagines: a new form of unlimited "vacuum" power based on harnessing energy contained in the space between atoms; people being equipped with "braincaps," fitted by neuro-engineers to enhance intelligence; swarms of micro-robots (or "microts") doing the housework; non-meat diets; and elevators which carry people up to an orbiting space city.

Remember, Leonardo da Vinci designed parachutes, machine-guns, helicopters, and submarines some 500 years before they came into widespread use. But, in the end, the details of such visions matter less than the fact that Clarke has shown that it is possible to stretch our imaginations 1,000 years into the future. As a mind-stretcher, perhaps we should ask ourselves which company, or companies, might still exist in 3001, and why.

So, just as some armed services have been wondering whether sustainable development and environmental security issues might not be part of their future, so we may have something to learn from the best of current military thinking. Visit Fort Leavenworth, where the US Army trains its top brass, and you will find a strong, even growing, interest in history's lessons.[42] "Ancient history has everything," explains military historian Robert Epstein. "There is nothing that can ever happen that won't have an echo from the classical past." One major contrasted this approach with today's world, in which the electronic media are "about *now, now, now*, with all the depth of a credit card." The danger, he noted, is that the political focus increasingly narrows down to what can be done – and achieve a visible pay-off – in a very short time-scale.

Will the same apply to society's response to sustainability challenges, with the media deciding on the basis of viewability and short-term audience ratings which issues are important and which not? The answer, we all know, is that it happens already, and some of the trends highlighted in Chapter 7 can only make matters worse.

But the scale of the challenge is what makes life interesting. If the transition is planned and implemented in the right way, the winners will be maximized and the losers minimized. Winners and losers there will be, but this does need to be a zero sum game, in which for every victory there has to be a defeat. Instead, foresight and careful management can also maximize the number of win–win and win–win–win outcomes.

Three Keys to the 21st Century

The sixth sustainability revolution focuses on time, requiring that we understand and use the following keys to sustainable enterprise:

♦ First, and most obviously, the sustainability transition requires greater attention to the time dimension, particularly long time. Not only companies but also economies and societies must increasing be "built to last." This may seem to fly in the face of the current push towards ever-wider time horizons, but the evidence, at least from long-lived companies, suggests that long sight is essential for this most basic indicator of sustainability.

♦ Second, as time widens and the future becomes ever more complex, scenario-based tools will become increasingly important for governments and business alike. But, be warned, pick the wrong scenarios and you can be blinded to the new realities emerging around you.

♦ Third, to ensure a switch from extractive to restorative modes of operation (see Chapter 13), society needs to work out ways of representing the needs of future generations in today's decision making. Our political institutions, company boards, and other decision-making systems must learn to recruit and listen to "time guardians."

Notes

1. Sarah Cunningham, "A patrician in the Nescafé world," *European*, 16–22 May 1996.
2. George Stalk, Jr. and Thomas M. Hout, *Competing Against Time: How time-based competition is reshaping global markets*, The Free Press, 1990.
3. Jeffrey Batholet and Jeremy Kahn, "Meet GloboBoss!," *Newsweek*, 25 November 1996.
4. Stephen Hawking, *A Brief History of Time*, Bantam, 1988.
5. Asa Briggs, "The march of time," *History Today*, November 1996. See also Asa Briggs and Daniel Snowman, *Fins de Siècle: How centuries end, 1400–2000*, Yale University Press, 1996.

6. Jean Grove, "The century time-scale," in Thackwray S. Driver and Graham P. Chapman (eds), *Time-scales and Environmental Change*, Routledge, London, 1996.

7. Simon Caulkin, "The pursuit of immortality," *Management Today*, May 1995.

8. Sven Rydberg, *Stora Kopparberg: 1000 years of an industrial activity*, Gullers International AB, 1979; Sven Rydberg, *The Great Copper Mountain: The Stora story*, Gidlunds Publishers, 1988.

9. Stephen Viederman, personal correspondence.

10. Richard Thomas, "Plunder! A tale of oil and greed," *Guardian*, 15 June 1996.

11. "Acid rain's dirty business: stealing minerals from the soil," *Science*, **272**, 12 April 1996.

12. Stewart Brand, "Two questions," *Scenarios: Special Wired Edition*, Wired 1995.

13. Stephen Goodwin, "Tewkesbury torn between homes and its heritage," *Independent*, 25 January 1997.

14. Douglas Coupland, *Microserfs*, Flamingo, 1995.

15. Glenn Zorpette, "Hanford's nuclear wasteland," *Scientific American*, May 1996.

16. Jonathan Raban, "Terror in the flatland," *Guardian*, 5 October 1996.

17. Nicholas Albery, "How to spend millions," *Guardian*, 5 January 1995. A longer paper, "If you were a multi-millionaire wanting to help future generations ...," was submitted to *Futures* magazine.

18. Dava Sobel, *Longitude: The true story of a lone genius who solved the greatest scientific problem of his time*, Fourth Estate, 1995.

19. Danny Hillis, "The millennium clock," *Wired Scenarios*, 1995.

20. Alison Maitland, "The 153-year-old experiment," *Financial Times*, 17 February, 1996.

21. Charles Handy, "Time for inspirational measures," *Management Today*, November 1996.

22. James C. Collins and Jerry I. Porras, *Built To Last: Successful habits of visionary companies*, Century Business, 1994/1994.

23. Peter Schwartz, *The Art of the Long View: Scenario planning – protecting your company against an uncertain world*, Doubleday 1991/Century Business 1992.

24. Anon, "Softbank's Son: I have a 300-year plan for success," *Newsweek*, 9 September 1996.

25. Michael Hornsby, "How green is the valley my ancestors ruined," *The Times*, 9 October 1996.

26. Hale Richards, "IKEA founder is still part of the furniture," *European*, 22 February, 1996.

27. Rufus Olins, "A civilised barbarian," *Sunday Times*, 10 November 1996.

28. Charles Hampden-Turner and Fons Trompenaars, *The Seven Cultures of Capitalism: Values systems for creating wealth in the United States, Britain, Japan, Germany, France, Sweden, and the Netherlands*, Piatkus 1993.

29. Jeremy Rifkin, *Time Wars*, Simon and Schuster, New York, 1987.

30. John Gordon, "Conflicting time-scales: Politics, media and the environment," in Thackwray S. Driver and Graham P. Chapman (eds), *Time-scales and Environmental Change*, Routledge, London, 1996.
31. Malte Faber and John L.R. Proops, "Economic action and the environment: Problems of time and predictability," in Thackwray S. Driver and Graham P. Chapman (eds), *Time-scales and Environmental Change*, Routledge, London, 1996.
32. *Op. cit.*
33. United States Environmental Protection Agency, Science Advisory Board, *Beyond the Horizon: Using foresight to protect the environmental future*, EPA-SAB-EC-95-007, January 1995.
34. Pierre Wack, "Scenarios: Uncharted waters ahead," *Harvard Business Review*, September–October 1985; and "Scenarios: Shooting the rapids," *Harvard Business Review*, November–December 1985. Reprinted as *Scenarios: The Gentle Art of Re-perceiving*, Shell International Petroleum Company Ltd, London, March 1986.
35. John Elkington, "Sparring partners," *Guardian*, 28 June 1995.
36. John Elkington, Sascha Kranendonk and Alex Trisoglio, *The EPE WorkBook: Towards Shared Responsibility*, European Partners for the Environment with SustainAbility, London, UK, 1994.
37. Environmental Strategies, IIED and SustainAbility, *Vision 2020: Scenarios for a Sustainable Europe*, scenarios developed for the General Consultative Forum on the Environment and the Commission of the European Communities, XI/120/97, 1997.
38. John Elkington and Alex Trisoglio, "Developing realistic scenarios for the environment: Lessons from the Brent Spar," *Long Range Planning*, **29**(6), December 1996.
39. M. Schwartz and M. Thompson, *Divided We Stand: Redefining politics, technology and social choice*, Harvester Wheatsheaf, London, 1990.
40. A. Kahane, *Global Scenarios for the Energy Industry: Challenge and Response*, Shell Group Planning, London, 1991.
41. Elkington, Kranendonk, and Trisoglio, *The EPE WorkBook*, op. cit.
42. Robert D. Kaplan, "Fort Leavenworth and the Eclipse of Nationhood," *The Atlantic Monthly*, September 1996.

CORPORATE GOVERNANCE

Stakes in the Future

The centre of gravity of the debate
has shifted from PR to
competitive advantage and corporate governance –
and from factory fence to boardroom.

Revolution 7 will focus on a shift from "exclusive" to increasingly "inclusive" forms of corporate governance. The profound business implications of the sustainability agenda mean that the role of the corporate board, and of company directors, is rapidly moving to centre stage.

Revolution	Focus	Old paradigm ❱	New paradigm
7	Corporate Governance	Exclusive	❱ Inclusive

It was a strange experience. Late in the day, Monsanto CEO Bob Shapiro "arrived" at the head of the roundtable by video-link. The idea was that I would give him an overview of the proceedings to date, aided by the 15-or-so stakeholders from around the globe who were taking part in this session on sustainable business opportunities for the giant US herbicides-to-Nutrasweet corporation. Monsanto had been thinking hard about how to build sustainability concepts and priorities into its business plans and strategies – and the hope was that the stakeholders would identify a set of opportunities to which it could apply its skills, technology, and other resources. To the surprise of many of the Monsanto people taking part, however, the stakeholders had seemed to veer off at a complete tangent from the expected topics of discussion.

Instead, it turned out, they wanted to discuss such things as corporate governance issues and the social dimensions of sustainability. Startled, one Monsanto executive asked me afterwards,"What's corporate governance got to do with environmentalists?" My answer is summed up below, but, as luck would have it, Monsanto's own question would be answered just a week or two later when *The Wall Street Journal* reported that Monsanto, like ICI, Hoechst, and a number of other major chemical corporations before it, had decided to break up its business into separate chemicals and life science companies.

Indeed, it is increasingly clear that a growing proportion of corporate sustainability issues revolve not just around process and product design but also around the design of companies, of "business ecosystems" and, ultimately, of markets. *The best way to ensure that a given company fully addresses the triple bottom line is to build the relevant requirements into its corporate DNA from the very outset and into the parameters of the markets it seeks to serve.*

This challenge always intensifies as the world economy goes through one of its regular frenzies of mergers or demergers. In a globalizing economy, the pressure to merge can only grow. At the same time, however, many of the conglomerates resulting from previous outbreaks of the "urge to merge" now look ripe for break-up. The authors of *Break Up!* argue that some parts of the world now face a period of demerger as intense as the conglomeration trend was in the sixties and early seventies.[1] Whichever way the scales tip, the inevitable restructurings pose major challenges for those trying to build triple bottom line thinking into the affected companies.

Traditionally, corporate governance has focused on the ways in which organizations, particularly limited companies, are managed, and on the nature of the accountability of managers to owners. In the UK, the debate was given a big push in 1992 when the Cadbury Report introduced a code of practice which the UK Stock Exchange now requires listed companies to report against. Similar initiatives have been surfacing in other industrialized countries. Those who work in the field will probably resist the expansion of the corporate governance agenda to cover corporate accountability to a wider range of stakeholders, but that expansion now seems inevitable.

Another reason why corporate governance and the role of boards will be under the spotlight is that campaigners now recognize how shallow their hold on the corporate psyche often is. Indeed, the weakness of the corporate world's support for the sustainability agenda became abundantly clear in 1994, when the Republican Party gained control of the US Congress for the first time in forty years. The result was to set in motion "a no-holds-barred assault on business-as-usual in the federal government," in the words of *Tomorrow*'s US editor, Carl Frankel.[2] "Among the targets: substantial portions of the system of environmental protection built up over the previous 20 years." And where were all the US companies that had so fervently declared themselves "green" only a few short years ago? Nowhere to be seen. Greg Wetstone, legislative director for the Natural Resources Defense Council, put it bluntly: "We have not seen any of the Fortune 500 companies out in front in terms of seeking to restrain the Republican attacks on the environment."

Of course, not all Republicans – nor all Fortune 500 companies – believed in regulatory roll-back; some genuinely wanted to maintain or improve environmental protection standards, while making the relevant systems more effective and, crucially, more cost-efficient. But the seeds of doubt were sown – or, in the case of existing cynics, watered and fertilized – by the lack of business support during these troubled times.

Skepticism about the degree of corporate commitment to sustainable development is not the only reason why we have no choice but to be critically concerned with corporate governance. In particular, we need to focus on the ways in which boards, constrained by shareholders and financial markets, prioritize their agendas. The sustainability transition simply will not happen if the corporate brain cannot be switched on and "locked in" to the new agenda. At the same time, we also need to focus on the ways in which companies are, and need to be, structured or restructured to meet changing market requirements.

The debate, in short, has moved from the corporate security perimeter, where many of the first wave controversies raged, through the lobbies, laboratories and executive offices, right up to the boardroom (see Figure 11.1). As a result, the language of the boardroom is beginning to change (see the Appendix). This is important, because the boardroom is where much of the action will take place in the first couple of decades of the new century. At the same time, boards worldwide now find themselves under unparalleled scrutiny from activist shareholders and others on a wide range of issues. What is at issue here is whether many boards can even successfully run the financial aspects of their businesses. This is a crisis in terms of trust; of social capital. As a result, its resolution will be a necessary condition for a timely, resource-efficient sustainability transition.

Why Worry?

Green Walls – and Worse

The sustainable development community is increasingly interested in corporate governance issues because there is growing evidence that the

Triple bottom line agenda handled by:

Strategists, Investor Relations, Board

↑

Process & Product Designers, Marketers

↑

Environment Managers, Planners

↑

Public Relations, Legal Advisers

FIGURE 11.1   Corporate Citizenship → Competitive Strategy
(*Source:* SustainAbility).

boards of many major corporations are, to put it mildly, dysfunctional. Listen to consultants Arthur D. Little (ADL). When they surveyed managers of environmental, health, and safety (EHS) at 185 US corporations, they concluded that most EHS managers are blocked by a "green wall" between the top management processes addressing environmental and business issues. As a result, most company boards are both deaf and blind when it comes to monitoring the emerging agenda. Many, as a result, end up acting dumb.

The contributory weakness is a lack of integration between the economic and environmental bottom lines of the sustainability agenda, partly caused by the failure of EHS managers to convince their boards of the importance of the environment. This is a problem we also came across in our own work in the late 1990s, with growing appeals from managers to help communicate the importance, scope, and urgency of the triple bottom line agenda at board level. But it is clear that there are far deeper problems at this level in the corporate world. The old order is breaking down, and even, in some cases, rotting. "All over the world the media is fixated by the lack of competence, unreliability, untrustworthiness and sheer greed of directors," as Bob Garratt puts it in *The Fish Rots from the Head,*[3] the book's title drawn from an ancient Chinese saying. He goes on to say:

"There are plenty of examples to draw from and the mixture of fraud, corporate collapses, political or economic scandals related to companies, cronyism, graft, and nepotism to be found in the US, UK, France, Germany, Japan, Italy, Spain, Australia, Hong Kong or China, to name just a few, are sufficient to keep the media fuelled for many years to come."

German Giants Humbled

These problems are even surfacing in countries where company boards have a reputation for working like well-oiled machines. Take Germany. Long held up as a model of managerial excellence, the country has been in turmoil as a succession of scandals has scythed through the ranks of its industry captains. As the *European* put it:

> "During the years of the *wirtschaftswunder* – the post-war economic miracle years – the country's businessmen enjoyed respect afforded to few other mortals. Hermann Abs at Deutsche Bank, Heinrich Nordhoff at Volkswagen, Günter Quandt at BMW and Reinhard Mohn at Bertelsmann belonged to a seemingly untouchable generation. They were the men behind 'Made in Germany.' "[4]

Today, by contrast, their successors have suffered a devastating loss of respect and prestige.

A few years ago I was appointed to the European Commission's new General Consultative Forum on the Environment, charged with working out how to implement sustainable development across the Union. I looked forward to meeting the 30 or so other members, drawn from across the EU and from the worlds of government, business, research, and environmentalism. One member who failed to put in an appearance was Heinz Schimmelbusch, chairman of Metallgesellschaft, the blue-chip metals giant. He had been fired after amassing massive debts of nearly DM10 billion through speculation on the oil futures market. As a result, the company is now a shadow of its former self.

Nor was it just Metallgesellschaft that found itself humbled. An unbelievable roll-call of corporate names – among them Commerzbank, Daimler-Benz, Mannesmann, Opel, Siemens, and VW – were blighted by police raids, investigations, or prosecutions. The management disasters cut across the whole range of sectors: AEG in electrical goods, Balsam in sporting goods, Bremer Vulkan in shipbuilding, Dornier in aircraft manufacturing, Klöckner-Humboldt-Deutz in engineering, and so on. Even Deutsche Bank found its gleaming reputation being seriously tarnished at the hands of Jürgen Schneider, a former property developer who accumulated unsound loans of billions of Deutschmarks, and Peter Young, the rogue fund manager at Deutsche Morgan Grenfell in London.

Not that German industry was ever squeaky-clean. "For decades, laws against commercial crime were ineffective and a generation of deferential public prosecutors were happy to turn a blind eye," the *European* recalled:

"Legions of directors enjoyed free 'home improvements' when business was slack. Moreover, the world-beating German export effort did not rely just on high-quality products: to this day, bribes used to obtain overseas contracts are tax-deductible expenses."

The scandals, however, helped spur deep soul-searching. German president Roman Herzog summed up the mood of resentment when he noted that "job losses have become evidence of managerial success; social duty has been sacrificed to profits." Business ethics professor Karl Homann concurred: "Competition is the basis of a modern economy," he said. "But it makes moral behavior difficult for the individual."

And the country's belief in the new spirit of enterprise also took a hammering when teenage tycoon Lars Windhorst, hailed as Germany's answer to Bill Gates and advanced by Chancellor Helmut Kohl as a role model for German youth, turned out to have feet of clay. "This is a boy who believes in the future, who believes in himself," Kohl had said. "That's exactly what I want, that 18- and 19-year-olds should take a risk and go out into the world instead of calculating their pensions."[5] But, when the prosecutors announced that they were investigating Windhorst for possible misrepresentation, what was described as a "capitalist fairy tale" began to unravel.

Altars of the Short Term

None of this means that capitalism is intrinsically "wrong" or "bad." But the evidence that capitalism needs firm, long-sighted triple bottom line management is growing ever stronger. Meanwhile, behind the scenes, deep changes were under way in Germany's business culture. Companies like Deutsche Bank and Daimler Benz had already indicated that they saw a growing shift away from Germany's post-war consensus model of business, towards a more Anglo-Saxon approach based on "shareholder value." Whereas the old approach put a greater emphasis on a company's community and wider social responsibilities, the new approach puts profits first and tends to have a much shorter time-horizon. Watch events at DaimlerChrysler.

This could well bring some immediate commercial benefits, but there will be inevitable downsides because of the way the Anglo-Saxon model of capitalism treats the time dimension, let alone such areas as social or natural capital. Indeed, many see the scandals that have hit the City, London's great financial sector, as compelling evidence of the negative impact of short-termism on the wider business culture. When Morgan Grenfell followed Barings into the financial maelstrom, Will Hutton, editor of the *Observer*, concluded that "what lay behind Morgan Grenfell's fall from grace is the same deep-seated short-termism and hunger for higher returns that has afflicted British industry and which is now gnawing at the City. Peter Young, the fund manager concerned, was anxious to maintain the high performance of his funds, not least because his remuneration and bonuses were tailored to how well he did. Nothing could be more tempting than structuring some artificial [unquoted] companies to guarantee success."[6]

But, as Hutton argued, the fund manager:

> "did not create the pressure. His employers wanted the investment performance, because they wanted to grow Morgan Grenfell's asset management business quickly – and the best way to attract clients is to show that money grows faster under your stewardship. Not over five or 10 years, but remorselessly quarter-by-quarter. Mr. Young and his bosses were locked in a merry-go-round in which all the incentives were to turn a blind eye, to cut corners and bend rules."

Nor do such pressures just affect the financial markets. Inexorably, inevitably, the demand for high returns enters the "warp and woof" of boardrooms – and can distort the structure of their decision-making. Each time there is a scandal of this sort, the media and other analysts say things like: "Few understand why trustees, the board of directors and the compliance team failed to pick up the trail" of the problem early enough to nip it in the bud.[7] Too often, the answers include short-termism, greed, flawed systems, and incompetent directors or trustees.

Much has been written about the fixation of markets like Wall Street on quarterly earnings. "It is always possible to improve profits for a time by reducing the level of our investment in new-product design and engineering, in customer service, or in new buildings and equipment," said the late David Packard, co-founder of one of the 20th century's most respected corporations, Hewlett-Packard:[8]

> "But in the long run we will pay a severe price for overlooking any of these areas. One of our most important management tasks is maintaining the proper balance between short-term profit performance and investment for future strength and growth."

Packard's words underscore the collision between the interests of would-be sustainable corporations and the here today, gone tomorrow perspective of the financial markets.

Meanwhile, the poor calibre of many of today's directors signals a wider issue. Although individual directors may be picked out as scapegoats, precariously little attention has been focused on the ways in which boards as a whole operate. Many business people would probably argue that scandals and upsets are inevitable if the market economy is to deliver the goods, with victims like Barings and Morgan Grenfell playing the role of necessary victims on the altars of short-term returns. But this is to overlook growing evidence of systemic failures in the capitalist system. As the *Observer* put it: "Amid the weighty abstractions – about structure, principles, regulation, relationships – the body that is legally responsible for making them live, the board of directors, has almost escaped scrutiny."[9]

Invading the Boardroom

This is especially worrying because the role of a board director is, by its very nature, hugely challenging. Bob Garratt points out that boards must, among other things: balance the short and long term; be simultaneously entrepreneurial and prudent; have their finger on the pulse, yet be capable of a dispassionate view; and act responsibly towards stakeholders while driving the business forward commercially.

Given the secrecy surrounding much of what goes on in boardrooms, it is hardly surprising that the media tend to salivate when protesters invade company shareholder meetings. "Newbury protesters take battle to boardroom" ran one headline during the protracted dispute over the Newbury bypass.[10] [I confess to having taken a particular interest in the extraordinary controversy about the proposed construction of a new road through areas occupied over months by doughty treedwellers, having had one daughter and two young colleagues among the protesters.]

Disrupting the annual meeting of Costain, the construction company, Friends of the Earth displayed banners with slogans like "Costain: on the road to bankruptcy." Such campaigns obviously can have a major influence on the thinking of boards, particularly if they are well-timed and the company is at all sensitive about its reputation and image. But, longer term, it is no good simply to invade the AGM, and even the boardroom, and then to retreat. Only if boards are able to handle their core commercial activities effectively can we begin to have any confidence that they will make business sense of the triple bottom line. And only if growing numbers of sustainability activists adapt to the boardroom environment will we have any real chance of stopping the capitalist juggernaut tearing off down the road to triple bottom line bankruptcy.

What's New, Gurus?

Business on Top

If you want a deeply pessimistic vision of where all this may take us, try David Korten's book *When Corporations Rule the World*.[11] As far as he is concerned, the many pressures driving corporations in unsustainable directions mean that anyone who expects them to make a serious commitment to the triple bottom line agenda is suffering from a naïve, and even dangerous, delusion. In fact, he has a much higher opinion of the ability of corporate boards to take over the world than to run it once in control.

Jonathan Charkham, on the other hand, is much more optimistic. "The way business is run matters to us all, wherever we live," he argues in *Keeping Good Company*,[12] a fascinating and fairly upbeat study of corporate governance in five countries. Formerly an adviser to the Governor of the Bank of England and a member of the UK Cadbury Committee, Charkham had a more than academic interest in the subject.

"The subject of corporate governance has attracted increasing attention on both sides of the Atlantic in recent years," he points out:

"for good reasons. Every country wants the firms that operate within its borders to flourish and grow in such a way as to provide employment, wealth, and satisfaction, not only to improve standards of living materially but also to enhance social cohesion. These aspirations cannot be met unless those firms are competitive internationally in a sustained way, and it is this medium- and long-term perspective that makes good corporate governance so vital."

These issues are becoming ever more important as the international markets become increasingly competitive, as the "the economies of the Far East gather speed and the former Communist states enter the fray." In this new world, Charkham insists, countries "will need to take a long hard look at the way other systems work and keep their own under review; to tolerate a poor system is to impose upon oneself an unnecessary competitive handicap."

The need for appropriate systems of corporate governance is not now in dispute – nor is the role of governments in establishing the relevant rules. "Everywhere the company or corporation is a creature of statute not nature," Charkham notes:

"designed to encourage the agglomeration and continuity of power that the sophistication of modern economies requires. Such a concentration of resources, however beneficial the intention, inevitably leads to effects on those inside and outside an individual corporation. It is not government's duty to double-guess individual commercial decisions – but to ensure as best it can that the structure it creates for companies contains checks and balances that are effective in resolving the tensions between differing legitimate claims."

In a world where many corporations are richer and more powerful than many sovereign states, the challenge for governance systems is "to give power to those best able to use it – and to remove it from those who use it poorly or evilly." Charkham underscores the fact that many of those running corporations are not so much the current versions of yesterday's pirates as the heirs of those who built great cathedrals and other creations and enterprises that have lasted down the centuries. There is plenty of evidence, he says, "that the men and women in business are not dedicated just to getting the most for the least personal effort. Many are by nature and instinct builders who invest themselves in their enterprises and may well in some cases continue to do so long after their economic needs have been satisfied."

So, by implication, the better the system of governance, the greater the chance that we can build towards genuinely sustainable capitalism. The purpose of governance systems is to help companies draw on the constructive vitality of their people, while containing the effects of their inevitable weaknesses. Even the most talented business people cannot sustain the highest quality of decision-making forever.

The key tests of a system of governance, Charkham suggests, revolve around questions on such issues as dynamism and accountability. First, then, does the system "permit the management of an enterprise to drive it forward without undue fear of governmental interference, litigation, or displacement?" And, second, does the system:

"ensure that in exercising its freedom management is effectively accountable for its decisions and actions so that the necessary standards are maintained and the appropriate remedial action can be taken in a timely way if they are not?"

Charkham accepts that there is a case for a third criterion, focusing on a company's "social" performance. But he argues that in a competitive market economy, however imperfect it may be, companies find it:

"difficult to sustain success over time, and society is best served when companies concentrate on that and not other causes, however desirable in themselves, because the social consequences of failure are not costless. Fortunately, social and economic behavior often run together."

True, but the triple bottom line of the sustainability agenda will mean that successful boards will need to continuously test their priorities and performance to see whether they *do* run together. The challenge for national governments and international government agencies will be to evolve corporate governance systems that help – rather than hinder – them in this task.

Rotting from the Head

Some board-level problems flow from what seems to be a profound misconception of what it is that boards are intended to do. How, for example, does the average company board see its position within the company? The answer, typically, is as the apex of a pyramid – with the main focus on internal affairs. The result, as Bob Garratt argues in *The Fish Rots from the Head*,[13] is that directors:

> "have an understandable, but not forgivable, inclination to find any excuse to intervene in the managerial system as soon as they see a crisis occurring, or to create a crisis themselves so that they can continue to demonstrate their managerial prowess."

Instead, Garratt insists, the role of a direction-giver is to apply a "brain-on" rather than a "hands-on" attitude.

This is more than just word-play. A fundamental shift in the board-level mind-set is required. Directors need to see themselves not at the apex of a pyramid but as part of the "business brain" or "central processing unit" of the company. Their role is to develop, monitor, and cope with the results of the company's internal *and* external learning processes. Furthermore, directors "need to create the political, strategic and emotional environment" for change, giving "their highest priority to ensuring that their organization is supported in its energy niches, or can migrate to new ones so that it can continue to survive and grow." As part of this task, they need to develop and communicate clear, credible visions of where the company is bound.

In fulfilling their role, Garratt suggests that directors need to address four "directorial dilemmas," each and all of which can be cross-applied to the task of tackling the sustainability agenda. So, the board must:

♦ Simultaneously be entrepreneurial, driving the business forward, whilst keeping it under prudent control.

♦ Be sufficiently knowledgeable about the company's workings to be answerable for its actions, and yet to stand back from day-to-day management and retain an objective, longer-term view.

♦ Be sensitive to the pressures of short-term, local issues and yet be informed of the broader trends and competition, often of an international nature.

♦ Be focused on the business's commercial needs, whilst acting responsibly towards its employees, business partners, and society as a whole.

To work properly, a board's learning has to be equal to, or preferably greater than, the rate of change in the company's operating environment. To achieve this:

"there must be systems for comparing regularly what is happening outside the organization, by monitoring the external environment, benchmarking and competitor analysis, and what is happening internally, through comparing customer satisfaction, productivity and financial ratios with policies, strategies, plans, budgets and projects."

The four main types of board identified by Garratt are the non-executive, executive, two-tier, and unitary boards (see Spotlight, p.288). He predicts that there will be a strong convergence towards the unitary board model in Germany, France, and even in Japan. The ways in which each type of board will handle the sustainability agenda will be somewhat different, although the basic tasks are the same. As Table 11.1 suggests, there are four main board-level tasks: policy formulation, strategic thinking, supervision of management, and accountability. Garratt notes that a well-balanced board "allows time both for thinking strategically as well as proper stewardship of the enterprise."

To build a learning organization, Garratt stresses, it is important that the board recognizes real progress and contributions – and is able to realize that mistakes will be made. "How are mistakes handled in your organization?" he asks. "In most, the idea of publicly admitting your mistakes is seen as corporate suicide, or at best career limiting. When they make a mistake, people do what they have learned to do since the cradle – they cover up." Indeed, he says:

"one of the great lies of organizational folklore is 'I'm from head

WHAT SORT OF BOARD?

Non-executive   The CEO is the only executive on the board, with all other directors being non-executive. This board is often found in the USA, sometimes as part of a two-tier structure, and in New Zealand, and is also found around the world in public or semi-public service organizations. This model risks over-concentrating power in the hands of the CEO.

Executive   This is the most common type of board, whether for family companies or multinational corporations. This board typically involves a chairman, a CEO and executive directors, and can suffer from a lack of diversity and propensity to clone membership, style of thinking, and assumptions. The CEO usually dominates and may take the chairman's role too. Typically, this model is strong on what is going on inside, and weaker on trends in the outside world.

Two-tier   This model is commonly found in Germany, the Netherlands and France, and is proposed as a universal model for the European Union. The upper (supervisory) board is concerned with strategic issues, with the lower (operational) board representing different interests within the company, particularly the unions. This model is theoretically strong, but there have been problems. The disinterestedness of the upper, supervisory board can be compromised by interlocking interests, while both boards can become politicized, trying to exclude each other and losing sight of the common purpose.

Unitary   The classic Anglo-Saxon model, found across the UK and in many parts of the Commonwealth, assumes that all directors are equal and must accept the same responsibilities and liabilities for the performance of the enterprise. Executive directors, led by the CEO or managing director, are responsible for the supervision of operations, while the non-executive directors help form policy and ensure broader accountability. Much depends on the independence and competence of all directors, so director selection, appraisal, and removal are of key importance for all stakeholders.

Based on: Garratt 1996

office, I'm here to help you.' Everyone 'knows' that that person is really here to blame the innocent, promote the guilty, and bayonet the wounded – so we cover up."

TABLE 11.1 Board-level triple bottom line responsibilities

	Short-term	Long-term
External	**Accountability** ♦ Accountability to owners, employees, customers, regulators and legislators, and to other stakeholders ♦ Sustainability audits ♦ Tactical economic, environmental or social partnerships	**Policy formulation** ♦ Stating purpose ♦ Creating clear triple bottom line vision and values ♦ Developing supportive corporate climate and culture ♦ Policy formulation ♦ Product life-cycles ♦ Monitoring external environment ♦ Strategic sustainability partnerships
Internal	**Supervising management** ♦ Supervising management ♦ Review of key business results ♦ Compliance with regulations	**Strategic thinking** ♦ Strategic thinking ♦ Setting corporate direction, targets ♦ Review of key resources ♦ Implementation processes

Based on: Bob Garratt 1996.

Yet learning often flows from mistakes admitted. It should also flow from the knowledge and experience of all the company's stakeholders, both internal and external.

Boards in different world regions have different approaches to long-term thinking. Asian companies tend to play the "infinite game," with extended time horizons, while most western companies prefer to play the "finite game," focusing on win or lose thinking. In either approach, it turns out, environmental scanning and stakeholder dialogue will be fundamentally important tools in the new order. Yamaha, for example, set up a "listening post" in London, which the Japanese company sees as the world's music capital. And, whatever the company's business, a key challenge, as Garratt points out, is to "spot the 'weak signals' that may identify future significant change." In doing this, boards tend to do better if they include people with a diversity of backgrounds and thinking styles.

Whatever its business and whichever countries a company operates in, however, the board's simplest, and most complex, tasks focus on accountability. Increasingly, Garratt argues, boards have "got to be much clearer about their values and ethics and more aware of, and skillful in their use of, the new media technologies to be openly accountable." In short, they need to integrate the lessons of sustainability revolutions 2, 3 and 4. This task, Garratt argues:

> "demands a more holistic approach by the board to the range of accountability issues, in particular the board's quality of thinking, its ethics and values, its obedience to the law and the consistency of its behaviors to its stakeholders define its approach to accountability."

As far as environmental responsibilities are concerned, Garratt argues that "it was the Bhopal disaster that really raised the notion of including 'green issues' in the thinking processes or boards." He concludes that:

> "It is the big fear of many boards that they will wittingly, or unwittingly, so pollute the physical environment that they will not only have to pay compensation corporately but will also be held *personally* liable and so put their own assets at risk as well as risking imprisonment."

They are right to worry, he says:

> "Polluting the waterways in Britain, developing non-recyclable packaging in Germany, greedily cutting hardwoods in Canada or Borneo, importing ivory from East Africa or Asia, can all lead boards to be held legally accountable. There is no 'limited liability' here."

Indeed, one company we worked with through the 1990s woke up when the directors of its Canadian operation were almost sent to prison for what were judged to be "eco-crimes."

Nor is it simply a question of regulators and campaigners pressuring business. We are also seeing companies beginning to bring court actions against other companies on environmental grounds. Britain's largest life assurer, the Prudential, was a case in point. It sued PowerGen for alleged damage to crops on a nearby farm following the burning of the environmentally controversial fuel Orimulsion. Such suits may well help turn up the heat under the boards of a growing number of companies.

Boards for the 21st Century

Legal risks is where Ralph Ward's book, *21st Century Corporate Board,* starts.[14] In the USA, he notes, "Federal environmental laws put directors on the spot for assuring corporate compliance programs – with penalties that can wreck a multinational corporation." He recalls how outside directors at General Motors launched a coup which overthrew CEO Robert Stempel. Directors who Ross Perot had once described as Stempel's "pet rocks" became a force to be reckoned with, a trend repeated in different parts of the world. As the experience of companies like GM and Saatchi & Saatchi suggested, the days when boards simply approved what management was already doing are clearly on the wane.

Companies like GM had been exposed to shareholder activism since the 1960s, on a growing range of social issues. Indeed, GM broke new ground in 1971 by appointing the Reverend Leon Sullivan, a black civil rights leader, to its board. He was an effective director and drafted the Sullivan Principles for corporate dealings with South Africa, a code widely adopted by other companies. During the next quarter of a century, as Ward recalls, pension fund activism tended to be associated with "liberal causes, social protest, and annual meeting gadflies who droned on until the other shareholders were ready to start throwing their chairs." Getting such activists to support consistent evolution in the broad range of board policies was "like trying to herd cats."

In the wake of the *Exxon Valdez* disaster, we saw the launch of the Valdez Principles, developed by the Coalition for Environmentally Responsible Economies (CERES). Later re-named the CERES Principles, these became a key influence on the debate, spurring the International Chamber of Commerce – which found itself unable to swallow the CERES Principles whole – to develop its own Business Charter for Sustainable Development. The CERES Coalition itself is composed of an unusual mix of campaigners and ethical investors, and now has companies such as Sun Oil and General Motors reporting according to the CERES model.

The next wave of investor activism, headed by enormous investment groups such as CalPERS, saw a rather different approach. In 1987, CalPERS (California Public Employee Retirement System) began to compile, and later publicize, a top 10 listing of "underperforming" companies. These were held to be lagging behind peer firms in shareholder return and in their willingness to go along with emerging governance reforms. By the mid-1990s, some activists were beginning to complain that funds like CalPERS were, to quote Ralph Nader, "going quiescent." But Ward has a different view: "Better to say that those who once had to shout to be heard now need only whisper."

As a result of all of these changes, boards now need to devote much greater efforts to the monitoring of such areas as regulatory compliance, potential environmental liabilities, and performance against emerging corporate ethics codes. "The most common compliance dangers seem to be environmental," Ward notes of US companies:

> "so many compliance committees are outgrowths of board environmental committees. In these cases, the committee will also tie in broader green concerns, such as liaison with major environmental groups and monitoring of environment-related issues and how they will affect the business."

Ward sees some of these practices as very likely to spread to Europe, while a range of issues and approaches that have emerged in Europe (for example, take-back legislation and design for disassembly) are flowing the other way. These new green laws will be of concern to any US board doing business in Europe," he predicts. "Beyond that, expect them to pop up on the US agenda sooner rather than later."

The growing focus on board effectiveness and efficiency can only build further. In the process, boards will find themselves called upon to broaden their horizons. "Laws on the environment, equal opportunity, restraint of trade, and labor relations are among those that force boards to trade off short-term shareholder value for longer-term social good," Ward notes. "Yet without the single, overriding goals of shareholder value, the board loses its North Star to steer by." This is why we see a growing interest in concepts like environmental shareholder value (see Case Study, p.293) and the market benefits of improved stakeholder relationships.

Boardroom Views

Riders on the Storm

Despite evidence to the contrary, many chairmen and CEOs of major companies may feel that they can ride out virtually any storm, and for a number of reasons. A key reason is that many boards are made up of insiders who tend to protect each other's interests. Dwayne Andreas, for example, stayed on as chairman and CEO of Archer-Daniels-Midland Co., the scandal-dogged US grain-processing company, despite the fact that the company had agreed to plead guilty to two price-fixing charges and pay a record $100 million to settle a federal investigation.[15] One

CASE STUDY

ELECTROLUX, SWEDEN:
BUILDING A VIRTUAL ASSET

Electrolux has achieved its position of global leadership in the "white goods" sector mainly through acquisition of other companies. One problem it has faced as a result has been that CFCs and other ozone-depleting substances keep reappearing in its portfolio, because they are part of the bought-in companies. But a cornerstone of the Swedish company's continuing evolution, now represented in virtually every country, each with its own culture and legal systems, is a corporate culture built on a shared vision and shared values, so the aim is to apply the same fundamental standards across the group.

Inevitably, as senior vice president Per Grunewald explains, "Our corporate culture is an extremely complex reality consisting of old and new units and operations with very different stages of maturity – particularly in the environmental field." The challenge, as Leif Johansson put it while still Electrolux's CEO (he later moved to Volvo), is to develop a "total approach" to the company's operations. In the process, the company will need to "integrate environmental imperatives into management strategy, and into the thousands of decisions that all our employees make."[16]

To spur the process, Electrolux is one of the companies that has been trialling the life-cycle philosophy and systems approach advanced by The Natural Step Foundation. Given that between 80% and 90% of the overall impacts associated with the company's total operations are linked to the use phase of those products, growing attention is being paid to life-cycle design and management. In addition, Electrolux is testing growing numbers of products in its Environmental Change Program, a scenario-based process designed to identify short- and long-term threats and opportunities shaped by triple bottom line issues.

But there is a fly in the ointment. "The ultimate purpose of our proactive environmental strategy," says Grunewald, "is to create shareholder value based on sustainable competitive advantages, responding to growing awareness and expectations among our customers." But the evidence to date suggests that financial analysts and markets do not appreciate all of this effort. Instead of seeing such investments as a positive investment in a new form of "virtual asset," they tend to mark down the stock of any company reporting significant environmental expenditures. The result can be a real brake on progress. The next step is to begin the task of understanding and educating some of the mainstream financial analysts and institutions.

ADM director noted that Andreas had "only made one mistake in 25 years," but others commented acidly that the ADM board had been dominated for years by insiders – making it very difficult to challenge a sitting chairman.

Or think of ValuJet, the US airline whose planes were grounded by the Federal Aviation Administration following a disastrous plane crash. Subsequent investigations of ValuJet found what the *Wall Street Journal* called "a host of shortcomings in its maintenance and safety operations." Indeed, so bad were the breaches that the union representing the airline's flight attendants demanded that the company's president and chief operating officer be sacked before the airline be allowed to fly again. In the event, they stayed on. Of course, it helped that the two top executives together owned more than 21% of ValuJet's outstanding shares. And the sole outside director ran a business that supplies ground-support equipment to the airline.

But stacking the board is not going to save chairmen and CEOs who seriously misjudge the implications and pace of the sustainability transition. It is now almost certain that, as a result of triple bottom line pressures, the 21st century will see companies having to adjust to new legislation and price structures, transformed accounting approaches, and, in sum, a very different business culture. As competitive advantage is increasingly determined by a company's or industry's ability to deliver products and services in a sustainable way, so every aspect of the typical enterprise will be changed, as will the definition of what is "typical."

Macho Mistakes

"Let us be clear," as Charles Handy put it:

> "profits – and good profits – are always essential. But the myth dies hard, the myth that profit is the purpose. I attended a gathering of senior managers in one corporation where they were discussing their new mission statement, with its declaration of intent to serve customers, society, employees and the environment with as much enthusiasm as its shareholders. The chief executive, pressed to make a personal statement of personal priorities, said: 'When it comes to the crunch I'm a bottom line guy.' The room cheered. He was macho."[17]

But, even in the depths of the second great environmental downwave, some top business people found that the macho approach was backfiring. Think of Texaco. The company's record-setting $176 million settlement of a race-discrimination suit sent shock-waves through US boardrooms.[18] The message, said Chase Manhattan director J. Bruce Llewellyn, was that the racial diversity debate will be an "ongoing issue" because the lack of a diverse work force "can hurt your profits."

Despite the scale of the furore, the Brent Spar controversy seemed to have no noticeable impact on Shell's profits. Even so, few top business people have been as impressively candid in explaining what led up to their travails as Shell's Cor Herkströter, whose views on the changing business environment were summed up in Chapter 6. His views will have influenced many top executives. Indeed, a growing number of company boards are becoming uneasily aware that the challenge facing them in the 21st century is going to be at least an order of magnitude more complex.

Bubbling Under

Pinstriped Dinosaurs

This challenge may take generations, rather than years or even decades, to fully address. Already, the management response, particularly in the field of stakeholder engagement, has been evolving for well over half a century. Nor has it always gone in a straight line. In the late 1940s, for example, David Packard attended a meeting involving people from various industries and organizations. "We began talking about whether businesses had responsibilities beyond making a profit for their shareholders," he later recalled:

> "I expressed my view that we did, that we had important responsibilities to our employees, to our customers, to our suppliers, and to the welfare of society at large. I was surprised and disappointed that most of the others disagreed with me. They felt that their only responsibility was to generate profits for their shareholders."

Packard was certainly a rare bird in the early days. But, as a result, Hewlett-Packard developed an unusual culture, summed up in the phrase "the HP Way." As Packard explained, it stresses:

> "being sensitive to the needs and interests of the community; it means applying the highest standards of honesty and integrity to all our relationships with individuals and groups; it means enhancing

and protecting the physical environment and building attractive plants and offices of which the community can be proud; it means contributing talent, energy, time, and financial support to community projects."[19]

Where Hewlett and Packard led, a growing number of companies now follow. The leaders have even set up a number of organizations, including the Social Venture Network, to exchange best practice and lobby for change. A number of them, however, have had a love-hate relationship with the financial markets. The Body Shop, like Richard Branson with Virgin, went public, then regretted it. Branson bought Virgin back, but Body Shop founders Anita and Gordon Roddick, who called City folk "pinstriped dinosaurs," found the likely cost of the borrowings to buy back their company too great. "The Body Shop would probably have been much happier as a private company," commented a NatWest analyst, "but having made the mistake of going public it is probably stuck."[20]

Will a public flotation always constitute a mistake for companies dedicated to strong triple bottom line performance? The answer is that – unless they happen to be sitting on a goldmine or have developed a technology or market which enables them to do whatever they please – most companies will find the financial markets a major constraint for years to come. Indeed, many directors who deal direct with investors and analysts will continue to have every reason to believe that the capitalist system demands macho strategies. But, as we see in Chapter 13, there is now mounting evidence that some financial institutions are waking up to the fact that a fixation on shareholder value alone can blind companies to deeper trends in their business environment.

We have even heard mainstream management gurus questioning whether focusing on a single bottom line pays, long term. "Is financial orientation most likely to benefit the investor?" wondered Robert Heller.[21] His answer was surprising. Although the natural expectation might be that a company focusing exclusively on shareholders would win out over others paying more attention to customers, employees and even local communities, this reflects a false premise. Profits and esteem often flow from non-financial factors, Heller noted, "among which the respect and enthusiasm of customers for the goods and services provided are critical. This high esteem and vigorous demand rest in turn on the co-operation and motivation of the workforce." The, apparently perverse, result is that companies which do not put their shareholders first outperform those that do.

Heller was quoting Robert Waterman's book *The Frontiers of Excellence*, which in turn drew on the research of two Harvard professors, John Kotter and James Heskett. They had looked at the 11-year records of large, established companies that gave customers, employees, and shareholders equal priority. The result, in Heller's words:

> "Compared with the shareholder-first outfits, their sales grew four times faster and they created eight times as many jobs. The financial pay-off was spectacular: eight times the improvement in share price and an astronomical 756 times greater growth in net income."

The 756 may be surprising, but Heller argued that the general principle is not. "Profit is a residual," he noted, "the result of income exceeding costs. Income is provided by customers and costs are deeply affected by the employees – from top managers downwards – who also have the power to alienate or delight the customers." The obvious question is will the same, or at least similar, trends hold for companies broadening their definition of stakeholders still further?

Body Shop chairman Gordon Roddick, when pressed to appoint a non-executive director to the company's board, responded: "If all we wanted was a non-executive director, we could have gone out and chosen a large orang-utan and put him on the board."[22] Given that the presence of a different sort of primate at board meetings might encourage directors to think about new issues, or to reframe existing issues, this experiment could even be worth trying.

Indeed, I have heard Professor Tom Gladwin of New York University encouraging at least one company to install three new chairs around the boardroom table: one for a fish, to speak for the natural world; one for the poorest person on earth, to speak for the disadvantaged; and one for a representative of the year 3001. But most boards will decide instead that they prefer to bring in individuals with relevant triple bottom line experience to challenge and support their thinking.

Twenty-first century governance, according to the United Nations Development Progam (UNDP),[23] will be more likely to succeed if it is:

♦ participatory
♦ sustainable
♦ based on the rule of law
♦ legitimate and acceptable to the public
♦ transparent, accountable, and trusted
♦ efficient and effective in the use of resources
♦ enabling and facilitative
♦ supportive of equity, equality, and gender balance
♦ tolerant of diversity
♦ able to mobilize resources for social purposes
♦ service-oriented

STAKEHOLDER CAPITALISM

The basic idea underlying stakeholder capitalism has long roots and is simply stated: business and industry should be an integral part of society, rather than a separate set of institutions with purely economic objectives. Originally, the idea was that companies would simply pay strategic attention to what key parts of society were thinking and saying. Later, the idea expanded, embracing the notion that stakeholders should have more of a sense of participation in the day-to-day affairs of the corporation. So we saw consumer advisory panels, quality circles, just-in-time inventory teams, community advisory groups, and so on.[24]

During the late 1980s and early 1990s, there was a surge of interest in business ethics. Much of the discussion focused on perceived corporate excesses, including industrial disasters, "fat cat" pay rises, business–government collusion and so on. But, recalls R. Edwards Freeman, director of the University of Virginia's Olsson Center of Applied Ethics:

"a small number of thinkers began to ask questions about the very purpose of the corporation. Should the corporation serve those who own shares of stock or should it serve those who are affected by its actions? The choice was laid bare: corporations can be made to serve stockholders or they can be made to serve stakeholders."

But it was a false choice. Most business people know that businesses cannot be built and sustained simply by obsessive attention to improving shareholder value. Clearly, shareholder value is critical: without it, a company would not have access to the capital needed to create wealth. But any modern product, from toilet paper to a Boeing 777, comes to us thanks to people working with a wide range of stakeholders to bring that product successfully to market. The real issue is not whether stakeholders should be involved; they are, many whether they like it or not. Instead, the issue, and the emerging challenge, is how to balance the interests of different groups in pursuit of triple bottom line performance.

Where key stakeholders are ignored, they will use the political process to force new regulations, standards and other forms of control. This has been true of such areas as labor, health and safety, consumer and environmental protection, and even shareholder protection regulation. If, on the other hand, stakeholders feel involved in the activities of a company or industry, it is more likely that they will be committed to ensuring that it has a future. As Freeman puts it: "Try building a great company without the support of all stakeholders. It simply cannot be sustained."

The key thing about stakeholder capitalism is that it bases our expectations not on the worst that might happen if business is left to its own devices but on the best that we can do when working together. As Freeman recalls:

"Adam Smith understood that business and ethics must go together. He wrote *The Theory of Moral Sentiments* along with *The Wealth of Nations*. Stakeholder capitalism can be a way of resuscitating what we have forgotten about Adam Smith and of building a capitalism that is human."

And, we should add, sustainable.

Winners, Losers

The sustainability agenda calls upon companies to adopt longer time-scales, to take on board the views of key stakeholders, to integrate triple bottom line thinking into every aspect of the business, and to consider reconfiguring key aspects of the company's operations. These emerging challenges make it essential, and inevitable, that the agenda will increasingly come to roost with the board. Successful companies will have ensured that the relevant issues are regularly debated at board level, that the appropriate indicators are agreed and performance monitored, and that corrective action is taken whenever a significant gap opens up between the company's commitments and its performance.

Given that well-run boards generally result in well-run companies, the ranks of the winners will be significantly skewed towards well-run companies that have accepted the challenge and dedicated adequate resources to the task of responding. The new demands of stakeholder capitalism will also mean that the most successful companies will be those that work out ways of bringing the outside world in.

A key question, to which we return in Chapter 13, is whether financial markets will work out how to discriminate between the strong and weak performers in respect of the triple bottom line? Most of the evidence to date suggests they cannot – or will not. This fact suggests that the losers may not simply be confined to the ranks of the non-performers and the poor performers, but also include some companies that misjudged the pace of change and went *too far*. This is the aspect of the challenge that has taxed companies like Electrolux (Case Study, p.293). But their very interest in this area is likely to be one of the factors that helps wake up some of the leading financial institutions and encourages them to develop the necessary tools for analyzing the shareholder value associated with good, indifferent, and poor triple bottom line performance in different sectors, markets, and world regions.

Three Keys to the 21st Century

The seventh sustainability revolution focuses on corporate governance, requiring that we understand and use the following keys to sustainable enterprise:

♦ First, the sustainability agenda will often overlap the corporate governance agenda. High performance boards are critical to the sustainability transition. More attention needs to be paid to the role of boards and directors in monitoring, understanding, prioritizing and ensuring progress towards sustainability targets.

♦ Second, the evolution of new forms of stakeholder capitalism will require companies to develop much more "inclusive" ways of handling stakeholder dialog, focused on multi-way dialog not simply one-way information flows from the company. One option is to conduct a sustainability audit along the lines sketched out in Chapter 14 – and ask key stakeholders to help in the process.

♦ Third, the membership of any board will increasingly need to reflect the diversity and time-scales of the sustainability challenge. A key question, given such board-level diversity, is how can companies sustain their unity of purpose? Part of the answer must be by the development of shared visions and targets, and by the creation of organizations that genuinely learn and evolve at a competitive pace.

Notes

1. David Sadtler, Andrew Campbell and Richard Koch, *Break Up! When large companies are worth more dead than alive*, Capstone Publishing, 1997.
2. Carl Frankel, "Where have all the green corporations gone?," *Tomorrow*, No. 2, March/April 1996.
3. Bob Garratt, *The Fish Rots from the Head: The Crisis in our Boardrooms – Developing the crucial skills of the competent director*, HarperCollins Business, 1996.

4. David Brierley, "How the mighty have been humbled," *European*, 3–9 October 1996.

5. Denis Staunton, "Germany shaken by kidology of the wunderkind," *Observer*, 14 July 1996.

6. Will Hutton, "Should we ask Germany to salvage the City?," *Observer*, 8 September 1996.

7. Adam Courtenay, "Just who manages the fund managers?," *Sunday Times*, 15 September 1996.

8. David Packard, *The HP Way: How Bill Hewlett and I built our company*, HarperBusiness, 1995.

9. Simon Caulkin, "'Ignorant' directors leave companies riding for a fall," *Observer*, 30 June 1996.

10. Nigel Cope, "Newbury protesters take battle to the boardroom," *The Independent*, 7 September 1996.

11. David C. Korten, *When Corporations Rule the World*, Berrett-Koehler Publishers and Kumarian Press, 1995.

12. Jonathan Charkham, *Keeping Good Company: A study of corporate governance in five countries*, Oxford University Press, 1995.

13. Bob Garratt, *op. cit.*

14. Ralph D. Ward, *21st Century Corporate Board*, John Wiley & Sons, Inc., 1997.

15. Joann S. Lublin, "Some chief executives are bombproof, no matter what," *Wall Street Journal Europe*, 2 November 1996.

16. Electrolux, *Environmental Annual Report 1995*, 1996.

17. Charles Handy, "What is a company for?" in *Beyond Certainty*, Arrow Books, 1996.

18. Joann S. Lublin, "Texaco case causes a stir in boardrooms," *Wall Street Journal Europe*, 25 November 1996.

19. David Packard, *op. cit.*

20. Simon Kuper, "Roddicks scrap buy-back plan," *Financial Times*, 5 March 1996.

21. Robert Heller, "Put shareholders first and finish last," *Observer*, 1 September 1996.

22. Peggy Hollinger, "Body Shop to revamp stores and rationalise products," *Financial Times*, 1 November 1996.

23. *Reconceptualising Governance*, Discussion Paper 2, Management Development and Governance Division, United Nations Development Programme, New York, January 1997.

24. R. Edwards Freeman, "Understanding stakeholder capitalism," *Financial Times*, 19 July 1996.

PART III

Transition

♦ 12 ♦

SUSTAINABLE CORPORATIONS

Spirit of Zero

So how should business leaders and corporations respond to the seven sustainability revolutions?

Turn them on their head.

Every time new phrases surface, like "clean technology" (later changed to clean*er* technology") and green products (softened to green*er* products), we rediscover that everything is relative. The "sustainable corporation" will undergo similar transmutations, but soon we will see thousands of new businesses signing up for sustainability – and pushing towards zero. Zero defects, zero waste, zero pollution, and, longer term, zero ethical stumbles.

Our collective giant leap towards sustainability is starting with small corporate steps. But even small steps can be nerve-wracking. I recall when BP executives unveiled three different versions of a new health, safety, and environment policy statement and asked a group of thirty or so stakeholders which version they preferred. Most of us had no problem in making the choice. We liked the ultra-short version, whose second line ran, "Our goals are simply stated – no accidents, no harm to people, and no damage to the environment." Not surprisingly, BP wondered whether such extraordinary goals would seem credible for a giant oil company, but our answer was clear. We know companies like BP have no hope of reaching zero impact targets any time soon, but sustainable development will depend on their willingness to set tough "stretch" goals and then, year after year, to strain towards them.

Companies like this, even those with a deep understanding of the triple bottom line agenda, would be very wary of using the phrase "sustainable corporation." Apart from anything else, the concept, while it may sound desirable, is still enormously hazy. Together with colleagues around the world, I have spent years searching for answers to the following questions: What will the sustainable corporation look like? Where will it emerge first? How will it operate? What will it sell, and how will it be paid? How will it be run, and who will own it? What will be the balance between compliance pressures and business opportunities in driving its evolution? And to what extent will markets need to be restructured to drive and support the process?

The answers are still in the process of forming. But one of my most powerful learning experiences along that path happened years ago in San Diego. The images are still unusually clear in my mind. Outside, lines of pelicans skimmed the surf line, threading between the surfers. Inside the cliff-top hotel, on the southern Californian coastline, I was talking to Richard (Dick) Mahoney, CEO of one of America's largest chemical corporations. This was 1992, year of the UN Earth Summit. The occasion was a meeting on the "sustainable corporation." The starting-point of our conversation: the corporate impact of the Bhopal disaster.

In the wake of Union Carbide's horrific upset in India, Mahoney had sent health, safety, and environmental auditing teams around the world and had committed Monsanto to massively reduce its toxic emissions. Sitting high above the Pacific breakers, he now recalled the reaction of his board when, in the wake of legislation requiring companies to report their emissions and the publication of the so-called "Monsanto Pledge," it received the first discharge data. Total shock. Nor was this simply environmental concern: the numbers showed extraordinary quantities of *product* escaping into the environment.

Now, however, we may be seeing the beginning of a shift from pollution control to sustainable development. Bob Shapiro's article in the *Harvard Business Review* signalled a profound shift in the company's thinking, from pollution prevention to sustainable development. "Businesses grounded in the old model will become obsolete and die," Shapiro predicted:

> "At Monsanto we're trying to invent some new businesses around the concept of environmental sustainability. We may not know exactly what those businesses will look like, but we're willing to place some bets because the world cannot avoid needing sustainability in the long run."

The company had launched seven sustainability teams. Number 1 focused on eco-efficiency, working closely with suppliers and customers. Number 2 worked on full-cost accounting, developing a methodology for assessing the total cost of making, using, and disposing of products. Number 3 set about building an index to check progress towards sustainability. Number 4 looked at new products and new business opportunities. Number 5 focused on water and Number 6 on global hunger. And Number 7 aimed to provide training to help Monsanto's 29,000 employees understand what sustainability would mean for them, their products and their company. Note, however, the heavy focus on economic and environmental considerations, with social factors as yet in the background. Monsanto paid a price.

The Monsanto experiment was presented as much more than a one-man crusade. "Someone asked me recently whether this was a top-down exercise or a bottom-up exercise," Shapiro recalls:

> "Those don't sound very helpful concepts to me. This is about *us*. What do *we* want to do? Companies aren't machines anymore. We have thousands of independent agents trying to self-coordinate because it is in their interest to do so."

More fundamentally still, he suggests that, "working on sustainability offers huge hope for healing the rift between our economic activity and our total human activity. Instead of seeing the two in Marxist opposition, we see them as the same thing." Fine, but not long afterwards Monsanto managed to trigger huge resistance to genetically modified foods in Europe, bringing Europe and the USA to the brink of a major trade war.

But another reason why that 1992 meeting stands out in my memory is that this was the first time I came across Tom Gladwin. Tom had written the main document for the Synergy '92 conference, where Mahoney and I had also been speakers. The title of the report, commissioned by the National Wildlife Federation's Corporate Conservation Council, was *Building the Sustainable Corporation*.[1] It provided a huge stimulus to the thinking outlined in *Cannibals With Forks*.

The 1990s saw a growing range of powerful interests moving into this field. For example, among Synergy '92's other sponsors were the International Environmental Bureau (IEB), part of the International Chamber of Commerce (ICC), and the Business Council for Sustainable Development (BCSD). Later, these two organizations merged to form the World Business Council for Sustainable Development (WBCSD). And what was interesting was that these different consortia of proactive corporations were all coming to the same conclusion: business must play a central, even leading, role in shifting the world on to the sustainable development path.

Although I criticized *In Search of Excellence* in the early 1980s because of its failure to make a single mention of the environmental agenda, by 1991 Tom Peters was publishing *Lean, Green and Clean* (see Spotlight, pp. 32–3), and arguing that by the year 2000 the world's most successful corporations would be those that got to the market "firstest with the mostest," having incorporated environmental efficiency throughout their value chains.[2] But, as we have seen, there is a big difference between eco-efficiency and sustainability. And the late 1990s saw a growing number of major corporations getting horribly scrambled as a result.

Doing the Splits

Jaroslav Valousek knows what it is like to shift between radically different environmental paradigms. When he was head of the environmental department at the Czech company Synthesia, his job, in the words of the *Wall Street Journal Europe*, was, "akin to being paid to bang your head against the wall."[3] The reason was that under the Communist regime the cornerstone of state policy was to deny there were any environmental problems. "The acrid chemical stench and thick brown haze that envelop the plant and its surroundings for many kilometers bear bitter witness to the past policy of neglect," the *Journal* reported.

But Valousek's persistence was rewarded: he became a director of Synthesia as the company went through the process of privatization. The company has been developing plans for massive environmental clean-up projects and rebuilding relations with employees and local communities. Indeed, the Czech Business Leaders Forum, an affiliate of The Prince of Wales Business Leaders Forum, decided that the chemical company's achievements were worthy of recognition with an award. And at that point Synthesia's prize product became public knowledge in the West. This is Semtex, the explosive which has been terrorists' weapon of choice for years. It was used to blow Pan Am flight 103 out of the skies over Lockerbie, Scotland, and to attack a wide range of civilian and military targets.

A spokesman for the Prince of Wales Business Leaders Forum explained:

"The reason for the prize is purely environmental. The company has demonstrated it has made excellent environmental progress. They have completely cleaned up their act. What its products are used for and where they go does not form part of the Forum's remit."[4]

Well, fine, but it is not hard to see why the controversy erupted.

As the communist world imploded, the terrorism link had proved to be a major problem for Synthesia when it had to begin raising funds on international capital markets. Given that explosives are needed for a wide range of legitimate uses, the company clearly had to work out a way of dealing with the terrorist problem. It succeeded, becoming the first manufacturer in the world to "mark" its explosive. As a result, the Semtex the company has made since 1991 can be detected at airports and other vulnerable sites by trained dogs and detection equipment.

The underlying message from the Synthesia experience is that eco-efficiency is never going to be enough to ensure acceptable triple bottom line performance. Wherever in the world they are based or operate, growing numbers of corporations are finding that even world class eco-efficiency standards are no guarantee of a safe ride.

Take Asea Brown Boveri (ABB), the Swiss-based engineering group that came under attack when it got involved in plans to build massive dam projects in Malaysia and China. Although ABB executives argued that it is better that such environmentally sensitive projects be carried out by companies dedicated to sustainability, the proposed Bakun Dam scheme came under challenge across the full spectrum of triple bottom line issues.

On the economic front, even members of ABB's own environmental advisory board, including Stephan Schmidheiny, said that they would have preferred to have seen Malaysia calling upon the company's expertise in energy efficiency.[5] On the environmental front, it was estimated that some 700 square kilometres of rainforest, an area the size of Singapore, would be flooded. And on the social front, perhaps most controversially of all, some 10,000 local people would need to be relocated to make way for the new reservoir.

Widely regarded as one of the founders of corporate environmentalism, ABB's environmental policy commits it to "promoting sustainable development." Now it found itself in the excruciating position of being targeted by over 100 NGOs and accused of "dumping outdated technology." The Bakun Dam controversy was important, noted Martin Wright, then one of *Tomorrow*'s editors, "because in its choppy waters are thrown together some of the essential tangles of sustainable development: how to ensure adequate energy supplies for booming economies; how transnational companies square the pursuit of lucrative contracts with a corporate commitment to environmental responsibility; how such companies address the growing demands to extend this responsibility to social justice and human rights issues; and how to decide where, if at all, the burden of responsibility shifts irrevocably from company to government."[6]

Thirty-nine Steps to Sustainability

So how should business leaders and their corporations respond to the seven sustainability revolutions? The answer is to turn them on their head. Below, we move from corporate governance and company boards out to the marketplace and, in doing so, provide 39 steps – or perhaps more accurately, since this will be a continuing process, stepping-stones – which will be essential for any corporation determined to build sustainability thinking and targets into the very core of its policies and practices.

The panels are designed to jog the memory, drawing on the earlier discussions in Chapters 5–11. The lists of transitions under each of the seven headings are intended to be suggestive rather than definitive. Progress can be tested by asking the questions found in the proposed sustainability audit framework outlined in Chapter 14. But one thing is clear: over the next decade, the role of corporate boards will be central to the sustainability debate. As a result, there will be growing scrutiny of the structure and make-up of boards, of the processes by which accountability is achieved, and of the influence of the financial markets.

CORPORATE GOVERNANCE
Boards will increasingly focus on sustainability and the triple bottom line.

Old paradigm	**〉**	New paradigm
01 Financial bottom line	〉	Triple bottom line
02 Physical and financial capital	〉	Economic, human, social, natural
03 Tangible, owned assets	〉	Intangible, borrowed assets
04 Downsizing	〉	Innovation
05 Exclusive governance	〉	Inclusive governance
06 Shareholders	〉	Stakeholders

Leadership will be centre-stage in this top-down, bottom-up revolution. And given that public perceptions of risk are so often completely opposite from the real dangers, leaders will sometimes need to take tough, unpopular decisions. But then, as one American businessman once explained it to me: "Leaders are the guys who are willing to let the flames crawl up their pant-legs that little bit further!"

Some companies – among them BP and Monsanto – are now very clear about what they are aiming for. They know they face an incredibly tough set of challenges, but employees are left in no doubt about the direction in which they should be bending their efforts.

Unfortunately, most business leaders confronted with the sustainability challenge have chosen to shut their eyes and minds, or have even led their troops in the wrong direction. When consultants Arthur D. Little (ADL) surveyed 185 North American companies, they found that only 4% reported that they treated environmental issues as a fully-fledged part of business management.[7] And the corporate governance agenda varies enormously between different world regions. Take Japan, for example, where the country's largest stockbroker, Nomura Securities, admitted that it had been paying off the local version of the Mafia.[8] The bribes are designed to ensure that difficult questions are not asked at annual shareholders' meetings, which tend to proceed at warp speed in an attempt to ensure that top executives are not embarrassed. Hardly a conducive atmosphere for open discussions about a company's triple bottom line responsibilities and performance.

But a new business paradigm is emerging. Listen to John Baker, speaking as chairman of Britain's largest power company, National Power plc, and of the World Energy Council:

> "The last 10 years have seen a remarkable convergence between a whole range of thinkers – in business, in Government and in the green movement – that has lifted environmental issues and environmental management matters to the forefront of business thinking and business practice ... I predict that, just as good environmental practice has come to be seen as good business, so ... companies will come to terms with finding ways of working, designing, producing and marketing that are driven off concepts of sustainability."[9]

This process will involve extending conventional ideas of a company's bottom line into something much closer to the triple bottom line. Indeed, there is already early evidence that this challenge is being recognized and accepted by some business leaders. "As we pursue our strategies world-wide," said GM CEO and president John F. Smith, Jr.:

> "we accept a social and environmental responsibility as well. These responsibilities include the promotion of a sustainable economy and recognition of the accountability we have to the economies, environments, and communities where we do business around the world."[10]

One interesting concept adopted by some Japanese companies is *kyosei*, literally "living together and working together for the common good." This phrase, used by Canon chairman Ryuzaburo Kaku, has helped drive the company's dogged persistence with solar technology, in which it has invested around £100 million. As Michael Kenward explains: "if nothing else, the concept helps to justify sustaining projects long after they would have come under the accountant's axe in the west."[11]

In the process, we will need to build a much better understanding of what is meant by economic, environmental, human, and social capital. It will no longer be enough to carry out an environmental impact assessment in advance of a major project like the Bakun Dam in Malaysia: economic, environmental, and social impact studies will need to proceed in parallel. Not surprisingly, this trend has major implications for the qualities of leadership we will need in the future. As John Baker puts it:

"We need to start moving beyond simple environmental literacy towards a much more strategic capability for understanding the long-term implications of business processes and practices for the physical and social environment in which we operate. This is where the real debate on stakeholders should be, rather than where it currently is, stuck with a sterile argument on the supremacy of shareholder versus other stakeholder interests."

Happily, there is a new focus on the quality of corporate boards. As leading companies try to beef up the calibre of their executive and non-executive directors, *Business Week* recently asked: "Is good corporate governance contagious?"[12] We must hope so, although to date the focus has been on fairly narrow definitions of enhanced shareholder value. To lead business towards the distant goals of sustainability, the new generation of leaders and strategists will need to move well beyond current definitions and abandon many of the latest management fads and fashions.

In pursuing the triple bottom line, however, they will find much of value in the work of the management gurus whose work we have briefly reviewed. They would also be well advised to heed Rosabeth Moss Kanter, author of books like *World Class*.[13] Her "3Cs" are as relevant to the sustainability transition as to any other business challenge we face. They are: *concepts* (knowledge and ideas), *competence* (the ability to operate at the highest standards), and *connections* (the capacity to build the best relationships, affording access to the necessary global resources). As Kanter puts it: "managing means managing an entire context. If you strip out one element and apply one methodology, it won't work."[14]

The challenge is not to strip eco-efficiency, sustainability or anything else out of its broader context, but instead to integrate these concepts into the very mainstream of management. This is why business leaders need to shift to the broader 7-D vision required to build the sustainable corporation.

As the centre of gravity of the world economy shifts from tangible, owned assets (e.g. mineral resources, forests) to intangible assets (e.g. intellectual capital) which are borrowed, leased, or rented, the challenge will swing from automation to motivation, and from downsizing to financial, organizational, and technological innovation. A key talent will be the ability to encourage people to embrace and achieve demanding "stretch" goals.

At Xerox, for example, the goal of waste-free factories and waste-free products has led the company into such areas as "remanufacturing." This involves taking back older photocopiers and refurbishing them to the point where they can be resold or leased again. These machines are designed to be "as-good-as-new," and are covered by the company's standard three-year guarantee. In 1995, the company's worldwide recycling programs saved Xerox over $12 million. That same year, the company's Rank Xerox joint venture was recovering some 80,000 of the 120,000 photocopiers discarded each year in western Europe. Again, the benefits were remarkable: in 1995 alone, Rank Xerox saved about £50 million on purchases of virgin raw materials by reusing recovered equipment. And further costs were avoided by diverting over 7,000 tonnes of material which would otherwise have been landfilled.[15]

Or take DuPont, where the potential of the "Spirit of Zero" now pursued by the giant chemical company is illustrated by the achievement of an agricultural products team from LaPorte, Texas. They reduced their toxic emissions and off-site transfers by an astounding 99%. The turnaround was achieved through the use of closed-loop recycling, off-site reclamation, selling former wastes as products, and substituting raw materials. The potential for transportation accidents was greatly reduced with the overall savings including $2.5 million of capital and more than $3 million in annual operating costs.

Of course, one should ask just how much pollution was being discharged in the first place? The dirtier the business, the easier the earlier stages of the clean-up. But, however clean or dirty, those starting up this curve should be aware of one fundamental fact of business life. It goes under many names, including the "hockey stick effect" or, more typically, the law of diminishing returns. As you push towards perfection in any area, perhaps pushing towards 95% of the ultimate target performance, recognize that achieving the last few percentage points often comes at a much higher price. Indeed, one of the real challenges for boards in the future will be to work out ways of avoiding the hockey stick effect, where costs suddenly go off the scale, and of investing the resources saved in other priority areas. Persuading stakeholders of the legitimacy of such decisions will be a central part of the 21st century management challenge.

New environmental management standards, such as ISO 14001 and EMAS, will help provide platforms from which companies can reach for the relevant stretch goals. But they will not of themselves ensure that companies make sufficient progress in the right directions. Instead, the experience of successful companies suggests that the magic ingredient is a combination of strategic clarity, hard work, and new alliances. It seems increasingly likely that new forms of partnership will be at the very core of the emerging business order, and as a result, inclusive styles of corporate governance will become the norm. To enable this transition to get under way, we all need to change the way we view, value, and manage the dimension of time.

TIME
We need time guardians, not time bandits.

	Old paradigm	❱	New paradigm
07	Wider	❱	Longer
08	Extraction	❱	Restoration
09	Tactics	❱	Strategy
10	Plans	❱	Scenarios
11	Time bandits	❱	Time guardians

Our time horizons are simultaneously getting wider and shorter. Changes which once took tens, if not hundreds, of years now rocket by in the space of a few months, weeks, or hours. More and more happens in parallel. Lester Brown, president of the Worldwatch Institute, speaks of "the acceleration of history."[16] This acceleration, he says:

"comes not only from advancing technology, but also from unprecedented world population growth, even faster economic growth, and the increasingly frequent collisions between expanding human demands and the limits of the earth's natural systems."

Those of us born before 1950 have seen more population growth in our lifetimes than took place in the previous 4,000,000 years. And the world economy, Brown points out, is growing even faster, expanding from $4 trillion in output in 1950 to more than $20 trillion in 1995. In the single decade from 1985 to 1995, it grew by $4 trillion – more than it had achieved from the dawn of civilization to 1950. And who now expects it to stop any time soon?

In the process, however, we are practising a form of "time banditry." When we use up non-renewable resources, or compromise renewable resources, we are stealing wealth from the future. In this sense, we are time bandits, raiding the wealth of victims who are often as yet unborn. To restore the balance, we need to build a better understanding of "long time" – and to switch from extractive modes of business to modes which, over time, actively rebuild economic, environmental, human and social capital.

The problem is that commercial pressures, and most particularly the demands of financial markets, will not yet allow most business leaders to move strongly down the sustainability path. Any company announcing that it wanted to abandon time banditry and to appoint "time guardians" to its board runs the risk of seeing its stock marked down sharply. But change will come.

Some of the inherent dangers in the ever-accelerating shrinkage of commercial time were underscored while I was writing this chapter. Toyota, a pioneer of just-in-time manufacturing, found that its over-dependence on its *keiretsu*, or extended group, of suppliers could bite back. A fire at Aisin Seiki, in which Toyota had a 25%-plus stake, left the giant car company without sufficient stocks of vital brake parts.[17] It was forced to halt all its manufacturing lines in Japan, and the disaster also hit production at hundreds of other companies supplying Toyota, which had no option but to stop their production of Toyota parts.

Despite such shocks to the system, however, Toyota is unlikely to abandon its *kanban*, or just-in-time, approach. In the same way, of course, the pressure on financial markets to progressively shorten their time-scales is unlikely to reverse any time soon, despite evidence that short-term thinking can damage our wealth. But, as explained in Chapter 13, some parts of the financial world are beginning to respond to the ongoing paradigm shift. In response, they are experimenting with new ways of measuring the value that successful environmental and broader triple bottom line strategies can add over time. Indeed, new research suggests that such strategies can significantly boost profitability and help to attract investment.

When ICF Kaiser, one of the largest US engineering consulting groups, studied the financial data on over 300 of the largest US public companies over a long period, the conclusion was inescapable: the volatility of the stock reduced after the introduction of environmental programmes.[18] Among the companies which scored highly were DuPont, IBM and Polaroid. ICF Kaiser's conclusion was that:

"Adopting a more environmentally pro-active posture has, in addition to any direct environmental and cost-reduction benefits, a significant and favourable impact on the firm's perceived riskiness to investors and, accordingly, its cost of equity capital and value in the market place."

To succeed, companies must switch from tactics to strategy. And, in a complex and fast-paced world, they also need to test their plans against a range of scenarios. But, in the middle of all of this, we should beware of switching people off by overstressing the message that "time is running out." Too much gloom can be counter-productive. Indeed, the sustainable corporation will need a sense of fun and a good deal of humor to get it through the challenges ahead. Not that you have to go as far as Southwest Airlines, the Texas-based company renowned for its wacky style.[19] Ring the Southwest reservations agent and, after a while, you hear a recorded message. "If you have been on hold for more than five minutes," it says, "push 8." So you push 8 and the voice returns. "This didn't speed your call," it soothes, "but don't you feel better? You can push 8 as often as you like until an operator is free to take your call."

Anyone trying the same trick for those in search of outstanding triple bottom line performance may risk triggering new forms of outrage, yet the basic message stands. Humor can help us cope with most challenges. Indeed, if we know how to make life fun, we are more likely to attract and hold partners. But remember the words of Noël Coward: "Wit ought to be a glorious treat, like caviar; never spread it around like marmalade."

PARTNERS
Today's green business networks will catalyze tomorrow's sustainability *keiretsu*.

	Old paradigm	❯	New paradigm
12	Deregulation	❯	Reregulation
13	Enemies	❯	Complementors
14	Subversion	❯	Symbiosis
15	Unconditional loyalty	❯	Conditional loyalty
16	Rights	❯	Responsibilities
17	Green business networks	❯	Sustainability *keiretsu*

You rarely, if ever, heard laughter in the early meetings between business people and activists during the first environmental wave and downwave. These people were deadly serious about their need to protect their respective interests. These days, however, there is often laughter; indeed participants often describe the meetings as "fun." That, I suspect, is one of the most powerful indicators that partnership approaches are beginning to engage. Some business people may still try to undermine the environmental movement, a process sometimes described as "brownlash," but many understand, as one executive once said to me, that trying to nail the likes of Greenpeace is tough. "How do you kill Santa Claus?," he asked.

We are learning to see each other not as enemies, but as potential partners and complementors. In the process, the focus is switching from mutual subversion to the evolution of new forms of symbiosis. When Royal Dutch/Shell announced that it would in future invite environmental and human rights groups to participate in some of its more sensitive projects in the developing world, it sent a powerful message to other companies worldwide. "We should use the increased scrutiny of NGOs as a tool to strengthen our performance," argued John Jennings, as chairman of Shell Transport and Trading. And he noted that the challenge would be to extend the net sufficiently widely, "including those who wish you were not there."[20]

A sense of fun should not imply that there is complacency. Indeed, as *Fortune* recently put it, the challenge for all companies is to "Kill complacency before it kills you."[21] One reason why growing numbers of companies are bringing in triple bottom line partners is to help challenge their thinking and to smash complacency. John Kotter, the Konosuke Matsushita professor of leadership at Harvard business school, notes that the best way to remove complacency is to turn up the heat in your organization. He advises companies to:

"set higher standards both formally in the planning process and informally in day-to-day interaction; change internal measurement systems that focus on the wrong indexes; vastly increase the amount of external feedback everyone gets; reward both honest talk in meetings and people who are willing to confront problems; and stop baseless happy talk from the top."

In short, disrupt the (unsustainable) status quo. Often, we have brought triple bottom line campaigners into client companies. It can work a treat. Time and again, we have seen companies challenged at close quarters by activists and other stakeholders from Europe, North

America and the Asia-Pacific region. The outcome is almost always the same. If those participating rise to the challenge, all sides emerge from the sessions energized, and the company people say they have a much sharper view of what the outside world wants in the way of improved triple bottom line performance.

The sustainability challenge requires much more than public statements of support by CEOs. The real focus of attention should be on the corporate culture. Listen to Dr Vicki Lafare, an American specialist in unravelling corporate cultures and reshaping them to deal with rapid change:

> "I think the key issue for corporations that hope to become sustainable – and are committed to sustainable development – is one of alignment, starting at the top and going all the way to the bottom. Corporate policies, procedures, practices, real systems – everything must be in line to support their goals."[22]

Agreed, but in some companies we have found that you have to work with the grass roots to get the transition started, because the senior management are either distracted or asleep.

There are many ways in which companies can mobilize their human resources. They can follow Skandia's example, mapping and measuring their internal intellectual capital. They can develop processes for building and conserving that capital. They can use new technologies, such as "groupware," to enable employees to access shared knowledge resources via Intranets. And they can adopt new, softer management approaches, which encourage managers and other employees to develop their capacity for sustained creativity-on-demand, with books like John Kao's *Jamming*[23] suggesting that the improvisational styles of jazz can help manage today's increasingly virtual organizations.

Outside partners can also help enormously in this process, bringing different perspectives and experience to bear, providing new tools and benchmarks, and helping to hold management and others to account for progress. Growing numbers of companies worldwide are developing "strange alliances" with triple bottom line campaigning organizations, among them BP, S.C. Johnson, McDonald's, Monsanto, Novo Nordisk and Unilever. In doing so, such companies are having to recognize that stakeholder dialogue is not simply a way of getting your opponents close enough in to ensure they really hear what you are trying to say. Indeed, as Peter Senge put it in *The Fifth Discipline*:

> "All too often, 'proactiveness' is reactiveness in disguise. If we simply

become more aggressive fighting the 'enemy out there,' we are reacting – regardless of what we call it. True proactiveness comes from seeing how we contribute to our own problems."[24]

If companies are to be trusted by their partners, they must learn the art of principled negotiation. If they are to sustain critical triple bottom line partnerships, they must learn to understand their partner's real needs and achieve consistency over time. It makes no sense, for example, to profess support for a social agenda, and then have one's own industry – or, worse, one's own company – fight to remove regulations or standards designed to promote that agenda. On the other hand, we all know that regulations and standards can be made more efficient and effective. So if change is needed, fight for *reregulation*, not deregulation.

Companies should not expect unconditional loyalty from their triple bottom line partners, any more than they would in other areas of their business. Loyalty will depend on the degree of perceived progress. It may be acceptable for green or sustainable business networks to be talking shop today, for example, but the real future need will not be for words but for action. The networks that survive will very likely be those that successfully evolve into "sustainability *keiretsu*." Like the giant Japanese value chain groupings of companies, these organizations will combine to develop and offer a range of products, infrastructures, finance, and other services for sustainable development. And for the stakeholders wanting to stay the course, the focus will need to switch from their rights to involvement in processes to their responsibilities for outcomes.

LIFE-CYCLE TECHNOLOGY
Focus on sales alone and you risk losing out to competitors stressing lifetime value.

	Old paradigm	❱	New paradigm
18	Responsibility to factory gate	❱	Stewardship throughout life cycle
19	Sales	❱	Lifetime customer value
20	Product and waste	❱	Co-products
21	Environmental LCAs	❱	Triple bottom line LCAs
22	Product	❱	Function
23	Trial and error	❱	Biomimetics

Technology has helped create our problems and will also help to solve many of them. In the process, we will learn to design processes and products with their life-cycle performance in mind. In the wake of the first environmental wave, pesticide manufacturers were among the first to recognize the need for "product stewardship." Instead of simply handing over highly toxic substances to customers regardless of their ability to use them safely, far-sighted chemical companies woke up to the fact that this was a form of commercial suicide. To protect their own futures, they would have to take at least some responsibility for the handling of their products from "cradle to grave." In effect, they were bundling environmental services with their products. The cost of doing so may be one of the factors driving the evolution of much safer alternatives.

Practice remains imperfect even in the world of pesticides, but the product stewardship concept is also taking root in other markets. So, for example, packaging manufacturers are increasingly subject to "take back" requirements, an approach designed to encourage much higher levels of recycling. This, in turn, is reinforcing the trend for companies to shift the focus of their attention from raw sales to lifetime customer value. Clearly, if this approach is to pay off, there is a real benefit in companies being around for the long haul. Competitors that are in and out of the business will simply be unable to afford the investment in the environmental services and infrastructures needed to sustain a market presence long-term.

Not surprisingly, we are seeing the twin areas of life-cycle assessment and life-cycle design evolving in response. The pace of development may at times seem frustratingly slow for practitioners, but viewed from the perspective of "long" time we have made dramatic progress during the post-1945 period. So LCA can focus on boosting the net contributions of a material, process, product, or development in terms of financial capital (e.g. life-cycle costing), natural capital (e.g. life-cycle environmental accounting) or social capital (e.g. life-cycle social accounting). And we are also seeing life-cycle assessment and design professionals beginning to toy with the problem of integrating the economic, environmental, and social dimensions of emerging market requirements.

These new perspectives will drive companies in a number of directions. It is inevitable, for example, that successful companies will increasingly take responsibility for the triple bottom line performance of suppliers. Simultaneously, companies producing high levels of waste will either be forced to drop these inefficient technologies or, in a subtle twist, to evolve sophisticated co-product strategies. Tioxide is one company which has invested a great deal of effort in turning materials which once went to waste into a range of products, from insulating wall-board through to magnetic tape. Such companies increasingly recognize that they will need to make much greater efforts to ensure that materials which once went to waste are increasingly produced to standard specifications suited to the needs of particular downstream customers.

Consider the toxic, but highly useful and valuable, mercury that goes to waste every time a fluorescent tube light is junked. In the UK alone, up to 80 million fluorescent tubes are available for recycling every year, although few are actually recovered. The mercury in these products accounts for just 0.01% of their weight, but two companies have been working on technology designed to achieve "seven nines" purity levels in the recovered mercury – that is, 99.9999999% pure mercury.[25] This, in turn, will significantly increase the value of the reclaimed metal.

As the pressures to recycle and "close the loop" intensify, companies will form new alliances to provide the necessary infrastructure to pull back and recycle materials. Take the mobile telephones which have become such an intrinsic part of modern business life. In 1996, around 15 million were sold across the European Union alone. Although their useful life is anywhere between five and 15 years, most are disposed of after 1–5 years because of rapid advances in technology.[26] In an attempt to ward off new laws designed to force recycling, five manufacturers – Motorola, Ericsson, Nokia, Alcatel and Panasonic – which jointly account for 99% of the EU market came together to test out a range of "take back" schemes, initially in the UK and Sweden. In this case, the task is complicated by the fact that products are small and the recovered materials have little, if any, value. Worse, the distribution channels are complicated, with most products sold to individuals who have no responsibility for returning them. If the pressures continue to grow, however, the likelihood is that these distribution channels will need to be restructured and it may even be that leasing will become more popular, with ultimate recycling included in the price of the leasing package.

The drive for "zero waste" technologies and products will intensify. The focus will inevitably shift from the "product" to the "function" it is meant to serve. If you are a power utility, the long-term challenge will not be to supply kilowatts or therms, for example, but to supply heat, illumination, or other benefits. But these new services will not be immune from life-cycle pressures. As the modern economy becomes increasingly service-based, these services will themselves go through life-cycles.[27] Triple bottom line pressures will drive this evolutionary process and companies that fail to recognize that you can't offer the same service forever will go out of business as surely as did the horse-buggy-makers when Henry Ford got into his stride.

Nor will the pressures be confined to industries that are used to being in the spotlight. For example, the need to cut out waste will be one of the key factors spurring the virtuality revolution. Take the world of fashion. Design is often a hit-or-miss affair, with the overwhelming majority of ideas being binned long before they reach the stores. Now we see the Virtuosi project pooling the resources of companies such as BT, BICC and GPT, working alongside government agencies and universities, to develop a "virtual reality design studio."[28] The goal of the project is to allow people in different places to share a 3-D view of a proposed garment and to collaborate in its design. The garment can be modelled by a real or virtual mannequin and the designer, or buyer, can experiment with changes to the fabric, cut, or length. The mannequin can be made to move by using voice commands such as "face me" or "raise your arm." Meanwhile, Ford is using variants of the same technology, dubbed "C3P," to build "virtual assembly lines" which will help cut the production time for a typical car by as much as a third.[29]

Any such technological changes will require cultural changes in the companies and industries adopting them, however. There will be strong resistance to many of the necessary changes: the challenge for management will be to break through this resistance in such a way that a company's human resources are mobilized in support of the necessary transitions. Change management, as a result, will rocket up the sustainability agenda. And what is interesting about the experience of pioneering companies like the Body Shop, Ben & Jerry's, and Levi Strauss is that they have demonstrated that employees can be strongly motivated to achieve clear triple bottom line visions.

Another trend which will be driven by the acute need to dematerialize our economies is the shift from trial-and-error approaches to the development of new materials, products, and systems, to a growing use of the insights and tools of *biomimetics*. This involves using biological models when designing new technology: for example, a penguin's flippers may suggest a way of propelling future ships which is more energy-efficient than conventional propellers. Indeed, if you want an insight into inspired design, look no further than the nearest garden. Nature is full of extraordinary clues on how to build stronger, lighter and more sustainable materials. Indeed, researchers worldwide are increasingly probing this relatively unexplored treasure-chest for clues on how to make better materials for everything from bullet-proof vests to jet engines.[30]

Biological materials, however, also have their economic disadvantages: wool shrinks, wood rots. This is where the evolving science of biomimetics comes into its own: by copying, and improving on, nature's designs, it is on the threshold of making major technological and commercial contributions. Take nacre, better known as mother-of-pearl. Although nacre is 95% chalk, it is 3,000 times stronger than bulk chalk thanks to its composite structure. Following the clues provided by mother-of-pearl, scientists have now made materials which are three to four times stronger than steel and could provide new super-tough materials for use in jet engine blades. From hedgehog spines (which could help design running shoes that better absorb impact) to the lethal toxin produced by puffer fish (which may provide a cure for prostate cancer), biomimetic advances will very likely encourage us to view our wild neighbors with greater respect.

TRANSPARENCY
Closely monitored targets will replace empty, if well-meant, promises.

Old paradigm	》	New paradigm
24 Closed, except financial reports	》	Open, triple bottom line reports
25 Need to know	》	Right to know
26 Facts and science	》	Emotions and perceptions
27 One-way, passive communication	》	Multi-way, active dialogue
28 Promises	》	Targets

How do you maintain the necessary levels of commercial confidentiality when operating in a business environment which will increasingly be like a global goldfish bowl? This is one of the questions to which would-be sustainable corporations are going to have to find workable answers. The transparency revolution will be a key factor driving each of the other six sustainability revolutions, but, as we shift between the "closed" traditional paradigm and the new "open" paradigm, its capacity to spring surprises on even the best-intentioned of companies will ensure that it attracts more than its fair share of business attention.

Most companies continue to assume that increased transparency will hurt their bottom line. Foreign tobacco companies, for example, worry that stringent health regulations in countries like Thailand will force them to disclose trade secrets, damaging their businesses.[31] But this is far from a foregone outcome across the board. Take the experience of Dutch banks ABN Amro Holding NV and ING Groep NV. Both banks decided to pre-empt changes in government regulations by revealing how much money they had put aside to cover unspecified risks such as losses from derivatives trading or sudden rise in non-performing loans.[32] The result was that their share prices soared and analysts rushed to upgrade earnings estimates. Of course, the outcome might have been very different if companies were forced, or even volunteered, to reveal unduly low reserves, high environmental liabilities, or appalling social conditions deep down in their supply chains.

And recognize that the transparency revolution is already generating second and third order problems of its own. Those inundated by the extraordinary flows of information now coursing around the planet by fax, e-mail, and the Internet, are even beginning to complain of "information fatigue syndrome." David Shenk has described the problem in terms of "Data Smog."[33] His theory is that as we all become immersed in a growing tide of news, opinions, reports, and rumors, many of them contradictory, we will increasingly be information-rich but knowledge-poor. Information starvation will be followed by information obesity. Companies must learn how to cope with triple bottom line information flows, or risk being blind-sided, swept away, drowned.

Whether driven by new regulations, emerging political movements or a recognition that commercial efficiency demands greater levels of transparency, we will see a continuing shift from long-established "need to know" requirements to new "right to know" approaches. The US Freedom of Information Act provides one model of how greater transparency can be promoted by government, driving greater transparency throughout a society. Inevitably, the leakage of potentially sensitive _information through purely national freedom of information initiatives will bypass and, in a growing number of cases, undermine the attempted secrecy of less advanced countries and states.

Telecommunication technologies such as television, satellites, and the Internet will be critically important in creating the global goldfish bowl. But the very fragmentation of many such media will mean that the likelihood of any one company, or campaigning group, having full 360° vision will be very low. Instead, we will often see the "X-ray environment" switching on in an erratic, unpredictable way which keeps both governments and corporations perpetually off-balance. If even Intel can trip up, then so can any of us.

This problem is likely to be aggravated by the excruciatingly blinkered nature of much prime-time TV coverage. Only 3% of the prime-time TV output in the UK, for example, features the developing world. Worse, according to the Third World and Environment (3WE) Project, the proportion is falling steadily.[34] Given that over 70% of viewers cite TV as their primary source of information on world affairs, such findings raise a question-mark over any assertion that TV coverage on its own is going to illuminate, and, even more importantly, force the world to tackle, key triple bottom line issues. Trends in this area are being monitored by groups like the Independent Broadcasting Trust (IBT), but the chances are that we will have to devote growing efforts to ensuring that triple bottom line perspectives and information percolate forcefully through the media.

Anyone wanting to communicate effectively in this increasingly noisy and fragmented mediaverse will need to learn new rules, and new tricks. Some companies will develop "stealth" ploys for slipping in under the radar of campaigners, regulators, and competitors. Consider one recent example from the tobacco industry. New brands of weird-looking cigarettes have been hitting the streets in the USA, with names like Politix, Planet, or Icebox. They are made by The Moonlight Tobacco Company. Those seeking to steer clear of "big, nasty American" tobacco companies, and even some hardened anti-smoking campaigners, might feel inclined to treat such companies more gently. But Moonlight Tobacco turns out to be none other than R. J. Reynolds Tobacco, the second biggest cigarette manufacturer in America.[35]

The implicit message, as one marketing consultant put it, is, "We are not these big bad guys. We are really just small entrepreneurs, people like you, and you should support us because we are hip like you guys are." The headline of the *Financial Times* piece on Moonlight was "The giant who lurks behind a smokescreen." And we can be sure of one thing: even in the emerging goldfish bowl, at least some big corporate fish will find effective ways of cloaking their current activities and future plans from triple bottom line campaigners. Imagine other companies replacing the phrase "hip like you are" with "sustainable as you would want us to be."

Inevitably, many will be caught out. More positively, however, the evidence also suggests that growing numbers of far-sighted business leaders will be exerting every sinew to develop the skills needed to engage positively with the new agendas. In doing so, they will come to depend increasingly on their younger staff. In the past it might have been simply a question of learning how to speak in sound-bites and keep your hands on the table, so that viewers did not subliminally wonder what you were trying to hide. Increasingly, however, business must recognize that the challenge today is not so much to deflect external pressures by building a wall of facts and science but to effectively engage the public's emotions and perceptions. NGOs have often been spectacularly good at this and companies have much to learn from them, not just in a technical sense but in terms of the values which directly or indirectly underpin the most effective communication.

The range of interesting reporting initiatives grows by the day. So, for example, Australia's largest greenhouse gas emitter, Broken Hill

Proprietary (BHP), has published a revealing report on its emissions and efforts to control them.[36] As the corporate reporting trend continues to evolve, companies will need to ponder whether and how to integrate social accounting and auditing information into their environmental reports. More fundamentally still, they will increasingly need to reflect on how to integrate triple bottom line reporting into engaging, credible, and, above all, useful forms of communication. As part of this process, we will see an accelerating shift away from one-way, passive styles of communication to multi-way, active dialogue. None of this means that companies will abandon printed documents, but instead that they will increasingly try to involve a wider range of stakeholders in working out what and how to report. And growing numbers of companies will also be exploring the Internet and World Wide Web as a means both of communicating their triple bottom line targets and performance and of encouraging active feedback from stakeholders.

In the process, business leaders will need to switch from spur-of-the-moment promises to published targets. Increasingly, too, these targets will need to be integrated with sectoral and national sustainability targets and aspirations. This is an area where we need much better coordination between the efforts of governments, businesses, campaigners and ordinary citizens.

VALUES
Who will satisfy the demand for caring capitalism?

	Old paradigm	❯	New paradigm
29	Careless, uncaring	❯	Careful, caring
30	Control	❯	Stewardship
31	Me	❯	We
32	Monocultures	❯	Diversity
33	Growth	❯	Sustainability

In the past, it was part of the *macho* approach to management to project a tough image. If this meant coming across as uncaring, or even in some instances careless, this was part of the price business leaders were prepared to pay. Nor will this change any time soon. Faced with calls for it to stand trial in the USA for alleged human rights violations in Burma, where it has a $340 million stake in a natural gas project, Unocal took radical steps: it had no plans to leave Burma, so it started to "de-Americanize" its operations. It is slowly moving assets out of the USA to Asia, so that it is less vulnerable to US mores in the future.

The realities of globalization will ensure that business leaders are forced, or at least encouraged, to take commercial decisions which result in major social or environmental impacts. Recall the Belgian government issuing an angry protest to France over what it called the "brutal and unacceptable" decision by the French carmaker Renault to close its Belgian factory, with the loss of 3,100 jobs.[37] The Belgian prime minister expressed "indignation and stupefaction," but investors in Renault applauded the decision: the company's shares promptly jumped 13%.

Renault defended its decision by saying that it planned to transfer production to existing plants in France and Spain, where the same number of cars could be made with just 1,900 staff. Of course, there were many other factors at work, among them the crippling social contributions faced by employers in Belgium, which have hampered the Belgian government's efforts to tackle the country's high unemployment figures.

Such decisions and, probably, the political indignation they trigger, will be an inevitable part of our future, whether or not we shift towards a sustainable economy. Globalization will drive tremendous transformations and trigger huge dislocations. But, in the midst of all this, cultural changes around the world are making it harder for business leaders to simply project an image of ruthlessness. While financial analysts may mark up a company's stock when it moves to slash costs, social analysts are likely to raise real questions about the implications for local communities and society. As a result, a growing political, if not always yet financial, premium is likely to be attached to corporate boards which can demonstrate that they are fully aware of (and selectively responsive to) triple bottom line issues.

"When we talk of changing values," said Jehangir Ratanji Dadabhoy Tata, for decades chairman of India's Tata Iron and Steel Company, "we are sometimes inclined to think only of changes for the worse."[38] This, he noted, was wrong-headed, since there have been many changes for the better. He pointed to "the growing acceptance by industry and business of their social responsibilities to the underprivileged sections of society and to the environment." He was speaking in 1983, ironically the year before the horrendous Bhopal disaster. Does that mean he was wrong? Not at all. Indeed Tata has continuously provided a model of excellence for other Indian companies. But the message is that the necessary values transition is still in its embryonic phase.

Some companies will choose to tackle these issues separately from their core businesses. Whirlpool, for example, has the Whirlpool Foundation, which has a clear focus on such social issues as lifelong learning, cultural diversity, and contemporary family life. The company also funds research on the attitudes of women to work, the family, and society. No doubt, some of the relevant insights feed back directly into the company's core business strategies, but this is a less direct mechanism than companies which decide to integrate triple bottom line thinking into every relevant aspect of their core businesses.

Wherever it operates, a company is likely to find that any major business action inevitably triggers a proportionate and opposite political reaction among stakeholders. As a result, whether the focus is on financial, natural, human, or social capital, the emphasis will shift from simple control to active stewardship. In some cases, we may well see a growing focus on how we can deliver "enough" rather than "more." The claim that we are moving from a "me" society to a "we" society may seem exaggerated, but after years of market-driven change we should expect to see some profound transformations driven by emerging (or resurfacing) values in this area.

In parallel, the sustainability transition will require that we shift the emphasis from economic growth (with its focus on quantity) to sustainable development (with its focus on economic, environmental, and social qualities). This, in turn, will utterly depend on our capacity to think in longer time and to recognize that quality depends on our ability to recognize, respect, manage, and sustain diversity.

Expect a backlash against agricultural, economic, socio-cultural, and even political monocultures. Genetic, ecological, and cultural diversity will often be highly prized, as – too often – the supply shrinks. A key area in which the value of diversity is increasingly appreciated is ecology. Recent research shows that the more diverse an ecosystem, for example, the better it is in absorbing carbon dioxide, and moderating global warming. As a result, a waste management company like WMX now finds it essential to set itself the goal of ensuring that its operations result in no net loss of biodiversity.

As far as social diversity is concerned, most of us who think of a sustainable future tend to think in terms of a global future which would suit our own individual, corporate, or national interests. This seems unlikely. A sustainable world is very unlikely to be homogenous. Sustainable lifestyles won't come off production lines like early Fords. Instead, like plants evolving a variety of shapes, colours, and reproductive strategies around their common core of chlorophyll-based photosynthesis, so future lifestyles are likely to be spectacularly diverse, even though they must increasingly converge around overall resource efficiency.

Indeed, one model of 21st century business could be the famed, Montreal-based Cirque du Soleil, which I had the pleasure of seeing while writing *Cannibals With Forks*. Cirque's 1,250 performers and other staff members come from 17 countries, speak 13 languages, and are often scattered across the globe in troupes from Las Vegas to Latvia. The organization recognizes that diversity is a crucial aspect of its success, and manages accordingly. A human relations executive accompanies every group and employees, whether they walk tightropes or manage wardrobes, are peppered with a steady stream of bulletins and newsletters from headquarters. The idea, as *Fortune* put it, is "to make sure highfliers know they've got support from the ground."

Business, when faced with demands for diversity, often responds with "mock diversity." In relation to staffing, this led to the early employment of ethnic individuals to "sit by the door" and give the impression of diversity. Now, by contrast, some companies are recognizing that diverse companies do better in diverse markets. Ernst H. Drew, as head of the US chemical company Hoechst Celanese, learned the lesson by watching problem-solving groups at work. "It was obvious that the diverse teams had the broader solutions," he recalled:

"They had ideas I hadn't even thought of. For the first time, we realized that diversity is a strength as it relates to problem solving. Before we just thought of diversity as the number of minorities and women in the company, like affirmative action. Now we knew we needed diversity at every level of the company where decisions are made."

The much-heralded "triumph of capitalism" may be just one more sign of the growing homogenization (or "Coca-Colonization") of the world economy, but, even as the process of globalization proceeds, the pressure to recognize and express ecological, economic, social, cultural, and political diversity will intensify. Future sustainability will depend on the outcome.

None of this will mean that life will become easier in the business world. Indeed, as the travails of Monsanto in Europe, of Shell in Nigeria, and of BP in Colombia have shown, recognizing and addressing the full range of triple bottom line responsibilities will tax the resources, patience, and vision of even the best companies. The human rights challenge, whose growing importance was illustrated by the priority it was given by the incoming Labour Government in the UK during 1997, will severely test the resolve and values of a growing number of corporate boards.

So, as the values shift proceeds, how much leverage can companies bring to bear on regimes infringing basic human rights? "Company influence is limited, but real, and readily wielded for tax or regulatory concessions," noted Sir Geoffrey Chandler.[39] In a fascinating personal odyssey, Sir Geoffrey had been the architect of Shell's first statement of general business principles, and later moved on to chair Amnesty International's UK business group. Companies tend to argue that the business of business is business, but Sir Geoffrey pointed out that if the business world's influence were to be used for the improvement of human rights "the world could have a powerful weapon for its betterment and companies a better climate for their investment."

Nor should campaigners alone hold the high ground on these issues. "Companies also contain people with ideals," Sir Geoffrey argued, "who may come face to face with violations, and must ultimately force their companies to act of their own volition rather than be shamed into action by world opinion." Companies, he stressed:

> "have a clear choice: to use what influence they have, or to do nothing. There is no activity without risk. If they speak out they may incur the anger of government. If silent, the certain price is reputation – which is, of course, everything."

MARKETS
The shift from compliance to competition could see the role of NGOs transformed.

	Old paradigm	❭	New paradigm
34	Externalization of costs	❭	Internalization of costs
35	Compliance	❭	Competitive advantage
36	Country-by-country standards	❭	Global consistency
37	Adding volume	❭	Adding value
38	Production growth	❭	Sustainable consumption
39	Disruptive NGO campaigns	❭	Disruption as commercial strategy

Ever since the Industrial Revolution, business has been under intense pressure to externalize as many economic, social, and environmental costs as possible. This pressure has been at the root of such social ills as slavery, child labor, deforestation, and pollution. Unfortunately, left to their own devices, markets will often continue to deliver a wider range of externalized costs alongside their undoubted benefits. One key to ensuring that markets increasingly deliver the right, sustainable results is to engineer pricing and accounting systems in such a way that the prices, as Ernst Ulrich von Weizsäcker of Germany's Wuppertal Institute puts it, "tell the truth."

TROPICAL MARINE CENTRE, UK:
CLOSING IN ON ZERO

The spirit of zero can be found in all sorts of businesses. While writing *Cannibals*, for example, I was asked to visit a small company, Tropical Marine Centre (TMC), alongside one of the investment team from the National Provident Institution (NPI), which runs a series of "global care" investment funds. As a member of NPI's environmental advisory committee, I had expressed concern about the tropical fish business of Cranswick plc, one of the companies in which NPI had invested. NPI had originally invested on the strength of Cranswick's "high welfare" pig farming operation, but we were concerned that the company's TMC subsidiary might be less appetizing for ethical investors.

I confess my mind was already pretty much made up when I set off with NPI analyst Alex Gozzi to meet TMC's top management. "Ornamental" tropical fish are wonderful to watch, clearly, but most are still caught in the wild. Yet what we saw confounded many of our expectations. Yes, TMC, which employs some 50 people, is now Europe's largest supplier of marine livestock, marine fish feed, and associated aquaria products. Yes, most of the fish are still collected in the wild. And, yes, the tanks in meticulously clean holding areas contain live corals taken from reefs which are now among the world's endangered ecosystems.

Yes, but managing director Richard Sankey turned out to be every bit as much an environmentalist as most of the campaigners we work with. Having set up TMC in 1970, he has used the business to campaign for higher standards throughout the value chain. Whereas many of his competitors have accepted high mortality rates among the fish they catch, ship, and sell, Sankey decided to aim for "zero loss." Today, thanks to efforts right back down to the point of capture, TMC is tantalizingly close to zero loss across the board, and has achieved the target with some species.

Those who do the catching are trained in the dangers of overfishing and in the principles of sustainable fisheries. Shipping is handled in a way which means a minimum of stress to the fish in transit – and there is a carefully programmed acclimatization process once they arrive in the UK. Antibiotics are not used at any point in the operation, on the basis that they are generally a desperate remedy for poor fish husbandry. And the company is also captive breeding a number of species, with tank-bred clownfish the main success to date. We were also very much taken by the fact that TMC has developed breeding methods for such threatened species as the seahorse – and has been helping with seahorse conservation projects in the Philippines and Vietnam.

But the real clincher, as far as I was concerned, was the lobbying TMC had been carrying out in an attempt to stop one of the most destructive activities as far the reefs of the Philippines are concerned: cyanide fishing. Late in the Second World War, when the occupying Japanese had withdrawn and Filipinos were starving in their hundreds of thousands, some bright spark discovered that if you took the cyanide which was used to protect copra plantations against pests and dumped it in the sea, the result was that multitudes of stunned fish floated to the surface. Fine, perhaps, in the midst of a famine, but the cyanide fishing continues to this day, and the impact on reef and sea-floor habitats is staggering.

Sankey and his colleagues have helped to permanently change standards in the marine fishkeeping industry. If we tried to ban the trade, it would go underground and standards would inevitably deteriorate. So, to my surprise, I caught the London train believing that if TMC can radically boost the number of species it breeds and keep the pressure up on the cyanide front, then this small company has probably earned its place in the sustainable investment portfolio.

This is an area which still requires massive investment of intellectual resources. While this work proceeds, there also needs to be a shift from compliance-based corporate strategies, in which companies try simply to meet the standards which regulators require, to much more proactive strategies designed to build competitive advantage. The competitive challenge posed by the triple bottom line is illustrated by the experience of the Body Shop International.

"How can you ennoble the spirit," founder Anita Roddick once remarked self-deprecatingly, "when you are selling something as inconsequential as a face cream?"[40] Part of the answer, the Body Shop concluded, was to link the company's marketing strategy with the campaigns of groups such as Amnesty International and Greenpeace. Unfortunately, as *Fortune* put it, although the strategy paid off in spades, the company's top executives "began spending an increasing amount of time launching environmental projects rather than revamping the company's ageing product line. The head of finance was detailed to help set up a windmill farm in Wales," designed to ecologically replace the electricity used at the company's UK headquarters offices. Meanwhile, the market for the company's core products was not standing still. The Body Shop lost ground to competitors, among them Bath & Body Works, particularly in the US market. None of this is an argument for not addressing the social and environmental dimensions of the sustainability agenda, but the Body Shop's problems underscore the importance of performing well against all three bottom lines.

In facing up to this challenge, companies will need to recognize that the transparency revolution will increasingly mean that they will have to shift from approaches based on country-by-country standards towards greater global consistency. As they do, new financial funds will emerge dedicated to tracking and investing in companies committed to best practice. Kleinwort Benson, for example, launched its Tomorrow's Company investment fund to test the conclusion of the "Tomorrow's Company" inquiry that in a changing world a company must maintain five key relationships: with investors, employees, customers, suppliers, and the community.[41] Kleinwort Benson, in short, is betting that the "real world" of the stock market will move in favour of stakeholder capitalism and away from more basic, numbers-based investment strategies.

This investment strategy may well pick up some environmental drivers, but will it fully capture the necessary trend from adding volume to adding value? Time alone will tell. But it is clear that the sustainability transition will require continuing, intensifying pressure to shift the global economy – and the corporate strategies of individual companies – from atoms to bits, with inputs of natural capital being replaced with inputs of our only infinitely expandable renewable resource; knowledge or intellectual capital.[42]

In the process, we will be driving towards the seven goals of eco-efficiency.[43] The first of these is to reduce the material intensity of goods and services; the second to reduce their energy intensity; the third to cut toxic dispersion; the fourth to enhance material recyclability; the fifth to maximize the sustainable use of renewable resources; the sixth to extend product durability; and the seventh to increase the service intensity of goods and services. In the process, it will be essential to refocus our ambitions from production growth to sustainable consumption.

Says the World Business Council for Sustainable Development (WBCSD):

"As the world becomes increasingly crowded and acceptable sinks for wastes and pollution more difficult to find, and as valuable resources become scarcer and ever more expensive, companies which manage their resources more efficiently will gain a competitive advantage. In addition, business will be challenged on the actual value it provides. Consumers will ask whether the function is really needed: and, if it

CASE STUDY

GOLDEN HOPE PLANTATIONS, MALAYSIA: GIVING UP SMOKING

On a recent visit to Malaysia, I had the opportunity to visit an oil palm plantation owned and operated by Golden Hope Plantations Berhad, listed on both the Kuala Lumpur and London stock exchanges. Some years previously, the company had been elected to the UN Global 500 Roll of Honour – an award normally reserved for individual environmentalists or small campaigning groups. The key reason for the election was that, in 1989, it had introduced its "zero burning" policy.

Instead, of burning huge numbers of old oil palms on its plantations, Golden Hope switched to a process based on shredding and composting on site. The changes not only dramatically improved local air quality but also helps return organic matter to the soil. At the palm oil mill that I visited, the partly treated organic effluents produced during the milling of the fruit (once highly polluting) were being used as a fertilizer substitute among the oil palms.

Among other projects designed to drive the company towards the goal of zero emissions, work is under way on turning materials like palm trunks, fronds, and empty fruit bunches into useful materials – like particle, oriented strand, or gypsum boards. Rubberwood, too, is also being developed as an alternative to tropical rainforest timbers for use in such areas as furniture making. The company's research is now directed to cloning palms that produce both high quality latex and, at the end of their lives, high yields of rubberwood.

The company still has a long way to travel, but group chief executive Encik Abdul Rahman bin Ramli was clearly committed to putting the "spirit of zero" into practice at Golden Hope. As he explained in a speech to a conference organized by the UN University's Zero Emissions Research Initiative (ZERI), Golden Hope is working towards a vision of the future based around "zero defects, zero inventory, zero wastes and, of course, zero emissions."[44]

is, whether particular products and services are the right answer to that function, or whether there are alternatives."

Many business people associated with organizations like WBCSD hope that the sustainability transition will be a simple matter of eco-efficiency and total quality-style continuous improvement. Don't count on it. The sustainability agenda is much more likely to catalyze huge discontinuities in today's markets. And these discontinuities will come on top of the massive adjustments caused as economies like those of China, Indonesia, and India start to compete in world markets for food and other commodities. The key question is should companies wait for the sustainability-led discontinuities to happen or, where it makes sense, step in and help to cause them, in effect turning to market disruption as a commercial strategy? This is the theme to which we now turn.

Notes

1. Thomas N. Gladwin, *Building the Sustainable Corporation: Creating Environmental Sustainability and Corporate Advantage*, National Wildlife Federation Corporate Conservation Council, 1992.
2. Tom Peters, *Lean, Green and Clean*, The Tom Peters Group, 1991.
3. Amy Barrett, "Czech chemical firm contends with stain from its past: Semtex," *Wall Street Journal Europe*, 11 February 1993.
4. Jimmy Burns, "Prince in row over Semtex award," *Financial Times*, 16–17 March 1996.
5. Leyla Boulton, "Dialogue over a dam," *Financial Times*, 5 February 1997.
6. Martin Wright, "Energy, economics and ethics collide," *Tomorrow*.
7. Ronald McLean and Jonathan Shopley, "Green light shows for corporate gains," *Financial Times*, 3 July 1996.
8. William Dawkins, "Tradition on a knife-edge," *Financial Times*, 13 March 1997.
9. John Baker, column in *Green Futures*.
10. John F. Smith, Jr., in GM's *1995 Environmental Report*, General Motors, USA.
11. Michael Kenward, "Canon goes flat out," *Director*, March 1997.
12. Anthony Bianco, John A Byrne, Richard A. Melcher and Mark Maremont, "The rush to quality on corporate boards," *Business Week*, 1997.
13. Rosabeth Moss Kanter, *World Class: Thriving locally in the global economy*, Simon & Schuster, 1995.
14. Trevor Merriden, Rosabeth Moss Kanter, *Management Today*, February 1997.
15. *Xerox Corporation: Environment, Health and Safety Progress Report 1995*, Xerox Corporation, 1996. See also: "Rank Xerox: Towards waste-free products from waste-free factories," *ENDS Report 261*, Environmental Data Services, October 1996.
16. Lester R. Brown, "The acceleration of history," *State of the World 1996*, Worldwatch Institute, 1996.

17. Michiyo Nakamoto, "Toyota slams on the brakes," *Financial Times*, 7 February 1997.
18. Nancy Dunne, "Green policies attract investment, says study," *Financial Times*, 28 January 1997. The study reviewed was *Does Improving a Firm's Environmental Management Performance Result in a High Stock Price?* by Stanley J. Feldman, Peter A. Soyika and Paul Imeer, ICF Kaiser, Fairfax, Virginia, USA, 1997.
19. Richard Tomkins, "The seriously funny airline," *Financial Times*, 11 November 1996.
20. Robert Corzine, "Shell to Consult Pressure Groups," *Financial Times*, 17 March 1997.
21. John P. Kotter, "Kill complacency before it kills you," *Fortune*, 5 August 1996.
22. Whitman Bassow, "Get an attitude," *Tomorrow*, No. 5, September/October, 1996.
23. John Kao, *Jamming*, HarperBusiness, 1996.
24. Peter Senge, *The Fifth Discipline: The Art and Practice of the Learning Organization*, Century Business, 1993.
25. Andrew Baxter, "Light flickers on a recycling problem," *Financial Times*, 14 February 1997.
26. "Take back schemes launched for mobile telephones," *ENDS Report 264*, January 1997.
27. Tony Jackson, "When service is not included," *Financial Times*, 20 January 1997.
28. Vanessa Houlder, "Virtual couture," *Financial Times*, 10 December 1996.
29. John Griffiths, "'Virtual' assembly lines will help Ford cut costs," *Financial Times*, 14 April 1997.
30. Julian Vincent, "Tricks of nature," *New Scientist*, 17 August 1996.
31. Ted Bardacke, "Thai dilemma for tobacco companies," *Financial Times*, 2 May 1997.
32. Anya Schiffrin, "Voluntary disclosure aids ABN Amro, ING," *Wall Street Journal Europe*, 28 January 1997.
33. Edward Welsh, "'Information fatigue' saps the e-mail set," *Sunday Times*, 20 April 1997.
34. "What in the world are we watching?," *Fast Forward*, International Broadcasting Trust, no 27, Winter 1997.
35. Richard Tomkins, "The giant who lurks behind a smokescreen," *Financial Times*, 3 February 1997.
36. *BHP Greenhouse Report 1996*, Broken Hill Proprietary Company, Melbourne, Victoria, Australia, 1996.
37. Niel Buckley and David Owen, "Belgium attacks 'brutal' Renault," *Financial Times*, 1 March 1997.
38. Jehangir Ratanji Dadabhoy Tata, "Changing values," in *Keynote*, Tata Press Limited, 1986.
39. Sir Geoffrey Chandler, "People and profits," *Guardian*, 14 November, 1996.

40. Charles P. Wallace," Can the Body Shop shape up?," *Fortune*, 15 April 1996.
41. Simon Caulkin, "Reaping the profits of tomorrow's world," *Observer*, 24 November 1996.
42. Nicholas Negroponte, *Being Digital*, Hodder & Stoughton, 1995.
43. World Business Council for Sustainable Development, *Eco-efficient Leadership for Improved Economic and Environmental Performance*, 1995.
44. Abdul Rahman bin Ramli, *Towards Zero Emissions: Maximising the utilisation of the biomass of the oil palm industry in Malaysia*, paper presented to Second Annual World Congress on Zero Emissions, 30 May 1996, published by Golden Hope Plantations Berhad, September 1996.

◆ 13 ◆

MAINSTREAMING

Market Makers

It is often much more effective to get a 20% solution into millions of homes than to get an 80% solution into tens of thousands.

If markets are to work for sustainability, extraordinary efforts will be demanded from political figures, opinion formers, and business leaders. A key driver of change will be the growing fear that those who fail in the transition will see economic value migrating to those who succeed.

The central challenge for the first half of the 21st century will be to make markets work strongly and consistently in support of sustainable development. Those campaigning for triple bottom line progress need to become market makers, bringing technologies and approaches that have so far been on the periphery of the modern world directly into the mainstream. However much we may wish it otherwise, sustainable corporations and industries will not evolve spontaneously. Instead, their development will require well-directed government intervention and focused market pressures, sustained over decades.

One of the few commensurate challenges which the market economies have had to address was that of world communism. Ironically, the success of the capitalist economies in outpacing the communist economies has helped to create – or release – a growing range of triple bottom line expectations which must now be recognized and managed. Indeed, the global context to the sustainability transition is a fundamental reorientation of global thinking towards markets. As the World Bank put it in its *World Development Report 1996*, this is the "transition of countries with centrally planned economies – in particular, central and eastern Europe, the newly independent states of the former Soviet Union, China, and Vietnam – to a market orientation."[1]

The transition "from plan to market" will directly impact about one-third of the world's population. The heavy hand of bureaucratic control and central planning typical of state-run economies meant that they were ill-prepared to compete in world markets. As a result, the World Bank notes, they were "incapable of sustaining improvements in human welfare." The negative effects were increasingly obvious right across the triple bottom line balance-sheet.

"Although these systems guaranteed employment and social services, they did so at the cost of productivity, overall living standards, and – importantly – the environment, which has been severely damaged in some countries by distorted prices, inefficient use of natural resources, and antiquated plant."

Huge resources are now being devoted to thinking through the new institutional structures necessary to drive and sustain these market changes. At least three key institutional developments are seen to be critical. First, good laws and effective means for their enforcement. Second, strong financial institutions, to encourage saving and channel it to its most productive activities. And a third essential institution, still missing in many countries, is good government, at both local and national levels, coupled with effective systems of corporate governance.

As the World Bank stresses, however, "institutions do not develop in a vacuum." More practically:

"reformers' top-down efforts to develop strong legal and financial institutions and to change government behavior must be complemented by bottom-up demand for such reform. This demand will not spring up overnight, and it will often require deep changes in incentives, attitudes and experience."

Precisely the same can be said of the "sustainability transition." The very phrase, of course, is still wide open to interpretation. "What on earth is the sustainability transition?" asked Professor Tim O'Riordan when writing about the role of ecotaxation in the transition.[2] He noted that it is "a wonderfully 'flakey' phrase" covering how any society and economy can "move from a present, non-sustainable state to a future, less unsustainable state." However, as he then points out, "we are embarked upon it, so we might as well try to get to grips with what it would look like and what it will involve."

The seven revolutions outlined in Chapters 5 through 11 are just part of the answer in terms of what will be needed to get the transition going, and to keep it rolling once under way. Each of the revolutions will itself need to be guided, nurtured, resourced, and explained. For sustainable corporations, industries, and economies to evolve and thrive, we must also increasingly engineer markets – and the institutional structures that govern them – with sustainable development priorities in mind.

Markets, it should be stressed, rarely promise a smooth ride. Anyone who thinks otherwise might usefully read Bernice Cohen's *The Edge of Chaos*, which explores the underlying structure in the world's recurrent financial booms, bubbles, and crashes.[3] Crashes and bubbles, she demonstrates, "seem to be an inherent part of industrial capitalism." The legendary US investor, Benjamin Graham, compared the behavior of the stock market to that of a manic depressive. At times, the views of investors veer from "the ridiculously high to the absurdly low" as excessive optimism gives way to equally extreme gloom.

Are bubbles and crashes a thing of the past? Hardly. They appear to be closely linked to human psychology, most particularly to social psychology. While we can certainly understand them better by applying chaos and complexity theory, they seem to be as inevitable as the weather. As a result, those responsible for guiding and driving the sustainability transition must learn to minimize the risk of their occurrence, predict their arrival when conditions are heading in the wrong direction, cut the damage caused when they arrive, and manage sustainable recoveries where bubbles or crashes have happened.

Not that stability is particularly desirable in a world which we know to be unsustainable. Enormous changes are needed, which will create a dynamic business environment for decades, even generations. Nor do we have much choice in the matter of whether we buy into, and operate within, the market transition. "Revolutions, by their nature, do not operate with the consent of the governed," argues William Greider in his *One World, Ready or Not*, sub-titled "The Manic Logic of Global Capitalism:"[4]

"A revolution, whether it is driven by political ideals or economic imperatives, is always the work of a radical few who seize power and impose new values and social arrangements on the many. While the process is inescapably undemocratic, that complaint is beside the point. Human history does, on occasion, advance by such decisive breaks from the past – epic transformations that destroy the comfortable old identities and compel people, for better or worse, to adopt new understandings of themselves."

This is what the process of globalization is already doing to us, whether we live in Washington DC or Warsaw, Paris or Phnom Penh, Toronto or Tokyo. This transition cannot fail to be hugely disruptive, at all levels. But at least business people do have options: we can decide to let the disruption happen to us or we can develop ways of working with the flow of the disruption. For much of the time, as Tom Peters has put it, business is immersed in a "sea of similarities." Jean Baudrillard called it a "Xeroxed world."

But, as Jean-Marie Dru put it in his book *Disruption*, "faced with this situation, companies understand that they cannot go on doing things as they've always done them. Too often, without realizing it, they fall into another kind of conformity. To impose order on change, they plod down the same worn paths."[5] He continues:

> "After we have restructured, reengineered and rediscovered the importance of the client, what's left? What enables something to happen? What's left is what makes the real difference: creativity. Creativity as a tool for change."

And it is the creativity of business and markets that must now drive the disruptions that sustainability demands.

Being customer-driven, as Dru points out, is no guarantee of coming up with the right answers. There are real limits to being consumer-led. "After all," he argues, "the consumer can't imagine the future any better than anyone else." And that is one of the reasons why companies are beginning to form strategic alliances with triple bottom line partners, to enhance the flow of new thinking and business concepts.

In the past, campaigners, the media, policy-makers, and regulators were the main sources of the triple bottom line discontinuities which so disrupted business. And campaigners will continue to work out extraordinary new ways of grabbing public attention. Greenpeace, for example, made a last-minute bid to take part in the UK government's 17th licensing round for oil and gas exploration. It applied for 127 blocks on the continental shift, announcing that if successful in its bid (a wildly unlikely outcome), it would not undertake any oil and gas exploration, but would carry out extensive wildlife surveys. Increasingly, however, companies themselves will begin to adopt disruptive strategies designed to radically improve their financial performance by meeting emerging triple bottom line needs and expectations. They will learn from groups like Greenpeace how to use "mind-bombs" to dislodge established competitors and open up new markets. And, at least for a transitional period, they will increasingly work alongside campaigning organizations to ensure that they are credible suppliers of the new goods and services.

So what are the changes that we should be calling for to help drive the sustainability transition? Clearly, to make it happen – and to keep it on course – we need to engage the talents and energy of many people. But among the most important are those discussed below: political leaders, opinion leaders, business leaders, and financial leaders. Let's look at some of the things we should be expecting from each group in turn.

Politicians

Politicians count. The problem, though, is that short electoral timescales mean that they are often extremely short-sighted. But, in the end, many sustainability issues will resolve into questions of power: who controls, who decides. This area will be full of trade-offs. If, for example, a company improves its environmental performance, yet slashes its workforce, can we say it is sustainable in the full sense of the word? These questions go to the heart of the sustainability debate, which is about combining environmental and development considerations in ways that are not "either/or," but "both/and" – the "win–win–win" balance required by the triple bottom line.

Clearly, the political dimensions of the sustainability transition will be central, yet it remains a sad fact that genuine 7-D vision remains beyond the reach of most of today's political class. Margaret Thatcher, Mikhail Gorbachev, and George Bush switched on in the late 1980s, but only Gorbachev showed any signs of staying the environmental course. But we now see a new generation of political leaders emerging, among them the then US vice president Al Gore and members of the UK New Labour Cabinet elected in 1997, with its various environmental and human rights pledges.

Luckily, extraordinary times often call forth extraordinary leaders. So if we are right about the nature and scale of the sustainability challenge, we are very likely to see a new generation of leaders emerging. Part of the challenge will be to identify them early and to nurture and support them as they emerge.

A New Focus on the Future

Whether we do it with a strong political vision (a man on the Moon by 1970, for example, or Singapore as a "wired society"), a Ministry of the Future, the use of scenarios, or the burial of a Millennium Clock, we must work to develop a longer time-frame for our thinking on such areas as investment, science, and education.

During a period of global history when time-horizons are shrinking, this represents one of the most profound political challenges ahead. But, whether we think of the reconstruction of the old communist regions, the narrowing of the North–South divide, the development of new eco-efficient technologies, or the education of the next generation of business leaders, we must find ways of accepting responsibility for the longer term consequences of our actions, and, as a result, learn to manage extended time-scales. Businessman Masayoshi Son may be able to think 300 years ahead, and science-fiction author Arthur C. Clarke 1,000 years, but for most of us being able to imagine the future just 15–20 years ahead would be a great step forward. Some of the most profound changes will have to come in the world of finance, discussed from page 364. Without these changes, even the most far-sighted visionaries will continue to be hamstrung.

A New Focus on Governance

The sustainability transition will depend on markets, and markets, in turn, depend on sound systems of international, national, and corporate governance. Yet traditional forms of governance are increasingly failing us. Around the world, the political and business establishment is under pressure to share power and, to a lesser extent, responsibility. Stakeholder capitalism, in one form or another, will be a clarion call for the 21st century. Long-lived companies, among other things, will have worked out how to engage their stakeholders and sustain long-term, productive relationships. Governments and public sector agencies face the same challenge. Initiatives like the European Union's Consultative Forum on the Environment and Sustainable Development, the UK Advisory Committee on Business and the Environment (ACBE), and the US President's Council on Sustainable Development are useful early steps in this direction.

New sources of authority are emerging in our societies. Grass-roots activists, non-governmental organizations, and new business groupings are playing an increasingly important role in shaping national and international policy. Fine, but are governments mainly run in reaction to the latest lobbying, headlines, and focus group studies really going to be able to sustain the sort of long-term thinking that the sustainability transition requires? Hardly. Instead, we must rediscover the importance of politics and governance, helping to shape governments and policies which are anticipatory, market-oriented, enterprising, and empowering, yet also prepared and able to care for the less privileged.

Capitalism is unlikely to be sustainable unless we address the widening gap between rich and poor, whether it be within industrial societies or between the developed and developing worlds. Those who feel ignored or uncared for are hardly likely to fulfill their side of the sustainability bargain. Now, after a period in which politicians of every stripe have argued that "free is good" – as in free markets, free trade, free competition, and the free movement of technology and ideas – we see growing evidence of a powerful counter-trend. Increasingly, critics of free market capitalism argue that the invisible hand cannot do it all, and that many people need a helping hand.[6] Even George Soros, the staunch anti-communist investor who has given millions to support democracy in Eastern Europe, argues that unbridled self-interest and laissez-faire policies could destroy capitalism from within.

Inevitably, his arguments attracted a storm of criticism, yet there is truth on both sides. "Perhaps we should be saying: 'Free is good – but read the fine print,' " said Claudia D. Goldin, an economic historian with Harvard University. Markets can be efficient, but are not necessarily equitable, which makes it increasingly important that we develop a new sustainability-focused politics based on a recognition that we are all in this together. Even more importantly, just as the post-1945 Marshall Plan helped to catalyze decades of economic prosperity, so a carefully constructed new deal with the have-nots of the developing world could help to promote a period of sustained prosperity both north and south of the equator.

The role of corporations, and particularly of transnational corporations, will be central in all of this. But if they are to act in the right ways, governments will need to carry out major surgery on the markets which help to shape their behavior. In the old days of computing, for example, an IBM had the power to create the market with massive machines. In today's world, we increasingly see much smaller players like Netscape arguing that "the Net is the computer," with much of the most significant activity happening outside the company, in its markets and business environment. Most 21st-century companies will be in Netscape's situation, rather than the old IBM's, with respect to triple bottom line governance.

Recent years have also seen a massive upsurge in the debate on corporate governance, although the definitions used vary widely. Some commentators see it as concerned solely with the relationship between a company's shareholders or owners, its management, and its board of directors. Others define it more broadly, arguing that it covers all these relationships but also, in addition, the relationships between a company's management and a wider range of stakeholders.

Organizations like Britain's PIRC (Pensions and Investment Research Consultants) increasingly link corporate governance with such issues as environmental protection, employment conditions, and human rights. And the tide of history seems to be moving in their favor. Although the group failed to force Shell to adopt a shareholder resolution requiring external auditing of its environmental and human rights performance, PIRC joint managing director Anne Simpson noted that Shell, and other companies, "have had a crash course in why the environment and human rights need to be integrated into business strategy and fully reported to shareholders."[7]

Within days, the mining group Rio Tinto (previously RTZ-CRA) was announcing that it would embrace sustainable development. While campaigners outside shouted "Rio Tinto stinks," executive chairman Robert Wilson pledged the company to publishing its first environmental report and said that the company was open to suggestions on how to take on board social and environmental concerns. Clearly, another company to watch as a barometer of the pace of triple bottom line change.

A New Focus on Regulation

You would scarcely credit it when listening to some free market proponents, but markets depend on predictable, effective, and cost-efficient regulation. Developed and applied in the right way, legislation helps business. In its absence, you risk rapid degeneration into the sort of lawless anarchy we have seen in countries like Albania and parts of the old Soviet Union. Even in the developed world, there are many areas where the laws still need tightening and enforcing more effectively, but many political leaders tend to duck calls for tighter controls, or even re-regulation, preferring to leave the problems to later administrations.

In part, this flows from a fear of failure. Yet the evidence shows that even apparently drastic changes can be achieved as long as there is sufficient political commitment. The most spectacular example of industrial change in recent years has probably been the shift out of ozone-depleting substances like CFCs. The best study to date focused on the US economy's experience and was produced by the World Resources Institute (WRI).[8] As WRI president Jonathan Lash put it, "Less than a decade ago, (CFCs) were entrenched in the US economy. More than a 100 billion dollars' worth of equipment relied on CFCs." At the time, US industries used a third of all CFCs produced worldwide. Today that picture has changed out of all recognition. Industry, not surprisingly, argued that it could not possibly afford to make the transition to substitutes, yet today it has developed alternatives for virtually all previous CFC applications. In case after case, the WRI report notes, "firms have eliminated CFCs faster, at lower cost, or with greater technological improvements than ever imagined."

Among the critical factors in achieving this success were: environmental goals that were sufficiently flexible to be easily adapted to new scientific evidence; the use of economic instruments (including tradable consumption permits and a tax on ozone-depleting chemicals); and entrepreneurial government programs designed to help spread best practice, together with the necessary skills and funding.

There have been arguments that we can do without regulations, yet nothing could be further from the truth. New laws may not always be the most efficient way of reshaping markets, but experience shows that they can be effective if well designed. Again, German industry protested mightily about the proposed takeback law, which assigns extended producer responsibility to all companies that develop, manufacture, process, or market products in the country. But once the law came into force late in 1996 they set to work trying to understand how the new "circular economy" and closed-loop value chains might be created and operated.

Clearly, the early costs will be high, as companies struggle to take back and reprocess products and materials which were never designed to be recovered, remanufactured, or recycled. But longer term the closed loop logic should become second nature. As for the corporate casualties, German research suggests that small and medium-sized companies will be most vulnerable.[9] Among the problems they face are lack of time, lack of information, and unfocused apprehension about the likely costs and competitive impacts. Among the possible remedies are government support programs, green business networks, and the provision of free or cheap advice and information over the Internet.

One key is to believe that change for the better is possible. Indeed, there are a growing number of success stories to demonstrate that the reshaping of markets with triple bottom line objectives in mind can work. Consider California's recent experiments with reformulated (or oxygenated) gasoline. The new fuel may cost 10 cents a gallon extra, but most motorists accept that the benefits have been worth it: there has been a 50% cut in concentrations of airborne benzene, a known human carcinogen.[10] The beneficial impact of the new fuel has been equivalent to taking 3,500,000 cars off California's roads. Not surprisingly, countries like Finland, France, and Germany are following in California's wake.

And once in place, the laws must be enforced. This dimension is too often forgotten in the rush to get new rules on the statute book. But even countries like Spain, where such issues have long been low on the agenda, is showing signs of a new determination. The owner of a textiles company, sentenced to a four-year prison term for dumping untreated sewage into one of Catalonia's main rivers, became the first person in Spain to be imprisoned for an environmental crime. Indeed, in some parts of the world the number of "sustainability criminals" fined or imprisoned could well become an important early indicator of national progress.

A New Focus on Pricing, Subsidies, and Taxation

Markets can be guided in many ways, but economic instruments, most notably taxation, are among the most powerful tools at our disposal. According to the OECD, the number of market-based instruments in industrial countries increased by 50% between 1989 and 1994.[11] Such instruments use market forces to encourage producers and consumers to cut their triple bottom line impacts. A typical approach might be to put a price tag on emissions, so as to discourage air or water pollution, or to charge for access to national parks, so that peaks in visitor numbers are smoothed and revenues boosted.

A key part of the problem is that today's prices often mislead us. As Ernst Ulrich von Weizsäcker of Germany's Wuppertal Institute has forcefully argued over many years, we need to ensure that prices increasingly tell the truth; the economic truth, the social truth, and the ecological truth. As he puts it in *Factor Four*, written with Amory and Hunter Lovins of the Rocky Mountain Institute,"We need economic *perestroika* built on economic *glasnost*, for if our prices tell lies, they cannot guide true choices."[12]

In America, for example:

"the social costs of driving – related both to the conversion of fuel into smog and to congestion, lost time, accidents, roadway damage, land use and other side-effects of driving itself – are largely socialized. 'External' costs approaching 1 trillion dollars a year, perhaps a seventh of the American GDP, are borne by everyone, but not reflected in drivers' direct costs."

Yet there is clear evidence that proper pricing can work. Take the case of Singapore. As Weizsäcker and the Lovins point out, the city-state could easily have become "another bumper-to-bumper Bangkok," yet today it is:

"rarely congested, because it taxes cars heavily, auctions the right to buy them, imposes a $3–6 daily user fee on anyone driving in the city centre and puts the proceeds into excellent public transport. This level playing field, where cars and (public mass) transit both pay their way, yields a liveable city."

Increasingly, too, new electronic gadgetry will enable governments or operators to levy such charges automatically, without the need for toll-booths.

Factor Four should be required reading for politicians and policy-makers around the world. One area where they will increasingly take action is in relation to the extraordinary range of subsidies which currently distort markets. "Governments don't intend to waste money or destroy the environment," as David Malin Roodman puts it, "but the fact is, most are obsolete or ineffective, and are hard to defend even before the taxpayer, consumer and environmental costs are added in."[13]

There are many examples of the triple bottom line impacts of misconceived subsidies. Let's take just three of those quoted. First, government subsidies for the global fishing fleet have helped produce enough boats, nets, and other equipment to catch twice the available fish. Second, in addition to what drivers pay in gas, car, and road taxes, US taxpayers directly subsidize drivers to the tune of 70 cents for every gallon of gas or diesel fuel sold. And, third, the cost of protecting a hard coal job in Germany through subsidies had reached $72,800 a year by the late 1990s. It would be cheaper to shut down the mines and pay the miners not to work.

More positively, it is clear that there is now a growing range of market-based instruments, including deposit-refund systems used in the packaging sector, subsidies (such as grants, soft loans, or accelerated depreciation for desirable activities), and tradable permits. The purpose of the last of these is to allow polluting industries more flexibility in deciding how they spend limited financial resources across various pollution sources, while permitting governments to maintain a firm limit on the total volume of polluting emissions.[14]

Probably the most controversial economic instruments are taxes. Tax reform is rarely easy, but it is increasingly clear that a range of environmental taxes (or eco-taxes) have a central role to play in the sustainability transition. Among the benefits which they are expected to bring are greater flexibility than legislation, clear signals through markets to producers and consumers, and the prospect of revenues which can, if allowed to, be used to fund specific environmental tasks or to reduce labor costs and thereby boost employment.

"I want to increase the tax on pollution to make further cuts in the tax on jobs," was the way UK Chancellor Kenneth Clarke introduced his new landfill tax in 1994.[15] Among the other pioneers in green tax reform in the European Union are countries like Denmark, Finland, the Netherlands, and Sweden. Although early enthusiasm for energy taxes has often been blunted by fears about the impact on competitiveness, the beginnings of a significant shift of taxation from labor to resources and pollution cannot be long delayed. The challenge for political leaders is not now to debate whether we need such a shift, but to work out how, when, and where it should be implemented – and how to maximize the "soft effects" (i.e. changes in attitudes) of such measures.

In Sweden, the evidence suggests that tax reform can deliver the "goods." In one of the world's largest exercises in using taxes to protect the environment, beginning in 1984, there was a 30% reduction in acid rain between 1989 and 1995.[16] The taxes have encouraged power generation companies to invest in desulphurization equipment and buy low-sulphur fuels. Interestingly, the tax revenues have been recycled. So, for example, sulphur tax revenues have been used to pay for new desulphurization equipment. Other Swedish green taxes cover nitrogen fertilizers, pesticides, the scrapping of cars, and gravel extraction. As an indication of the impact, the fertilizers tax has led to an estimated 10% reduction in use.

Another idea which deserves more attention is that of the so-called "Tobin tax," originally proposed by Nobel laureate James Tobin. The idea is to levy a small tax (say 0.2%) on foreign exchange transactions. This would be an insignificant burden on genuine investments, but might be a useful deterrent to transactions that are mainly speculative.[17]

A Tobin tax could be applied to any sort of financial transaction, but the underlying logic applies with particular force to the global foreign exchange market, which now totals over $1 trillion a day – and adds relatively little to global wealth. Such a tax might help temper the wild swings as "hot money" sluices around the world, while even a 0.2% rate would raise billions of dollars which could be spent on sustainable development priorities.

Opinion Leaders

Public opinion counts, too. In fact most politicians these days won't move without it blowing strongly from behind. Without public understanding and support, sustained over time, there can be no sustainability transition. Happily, in the global village it is ever easier for citizens to get information, and participate in debates, on the triple bottom line issues of the day. Unhappily, however, much of the information we receive is hugely confusing. Public opinion is shaped by a plethora of influences, most notably the media, activists, and, although they would often deny it, public opinion pollsters.

Most people would conclude that scientists seem to change their minds almost at the drop of the proverbial hat. "You got a guy with four PhDs saying no fish were hurt, then you got a guy with four PhDs saying, yeah, a lot of fish were hurt," said one juror in the *Exxon Valdez* hearings. "They just kind of delete each other out."[18] It may keep the scientists paid, but it does little for coherent public opinion or political thinking on these subjects.

There are those, particularly in the USA, who argue that the environmental movement has lost its way, becoming removed from its traditional grass-roots support and overly comfortable with opponents who are playing a long game designed to undermine its agenda. Certainly, as Mark Dowie puts it in his book *Losing Ground*, if environmentalism is:

"to become 'the single most important movement of the twentieth century,' as historians and social scientists have predicted, the movement needs to be as large as the environment itself. Environmentalism needs to penetrate every institution, ideology, and religious faith in our culture. It needs to be seen as a social as well as a political movement."[19]

More positively, some leading campaigners are beginning to beam out a rather different message to the public. "Environmental groups aren't going to solve the world's problems," as Jeremy Leggett of Greenpeace put it. "Industry will."[20] But industry, along with its various complementors, has a great deal of learning and adapting to do. The problem is that the public is generally less interested in an issue like global warming than it is in something which, like ozone depletion or "mad cow" disease, is perceived to threaten our health or safety more directly and immediately. And that is where we now need to see different types of opinion former emerging, with campaigners, businesses, and government interests coming together to explain to the public why particular issues *are* important – and to spotlight and promote solutions.

A New Focus on Shared Responsibility

Markets depend on rights and on responsibilities. To date, we have tended to focus more on our rights than on our responsibilities. This must change. In the sustainability transition, our own mind-sets will be crucial, whether we are acting, for example, as consumers, voters, parents, employers, or employees. And our mind-sets are strongly influenced by our education and training, by our experience, and by the information sources we use. If we are to support the right political and business decisions, we need to understand the issues and trust those who explain them to us. This is why the concept of "social capital" is so important. Whichever issue we choose to focus on, there needs to be a judicious balance between emotion, politics, and economics. But judicious is hardly the word you would use to describe much of what passes for media coverage today.

"Ultimately," as *Scientific American* put it in relation to the huge Alaskan oil-spill:

"it is the frame of the television set and the mind-set of the media that dictate people's responses to images of oiled animals. The public wants the animals saved – at \$80,000 per otter and \$10,000 per eagle – even if the stress of their salvation kills them."

Or, as one scientist put it, "You have to balance the show and the science."

The question is do editors and journalists today have the interest, capacity, or time, to build their audience's knowledge, rather than simply providing them with horror stories or entertainment? In short, can they balance the show and the science in a way that leaves us all a bit wiser? We know that undiluted good news rarely builds readership or viewer ratings, but a key part of the challenge must be to work out ways of using both existing and new media to help make the necessary information both accessible and digestible. Meanwhile, organizations like Sweden's Natural Step, with its "four commandments" or system conditions (see Spotlight, p. 354), are helping to reduce the complexity into manageable messages.

In this context, the need for a greater sense of shared responsibility can only grow. The concept has been central to the European Commission's Fifth Environmental Action Programme, *Towards Sustainability*, and has also been a central plank in the platform constructed by the multi-stakeholder grouping European Partners for the Environment (EPE). These, in fact, are just some of the institutions which are

THE NATURAL STEP

The Natural Step Foundation, founded in Sweden by Karl-Henrik Robèrt and now also established in countries like the UK and USA, proposes four "system conditions" for a sustainable world:

1. Substances from the Earth's crust must not be extracted at a rate faster than their slow redeposit into the Earth's crust.
2. Substances must not be produced by society faster than they can be broken down in nature or deposited into the Earth's crust.
3. The physical basis for nature's productivity and diversity must not be allowed to deteriorate.
4. There must be fair and efficient use of energy and other resources to meet human needs.

springing up to meet the new needs created by the sustainable development agenda, from the UN Commission on Sustainable Development and the Earth Council, through the US President's Council on Sustainable Development to the European Union's own Consultative Forum on the Environment and Sustainable Development.

None of these bodies has yet been as effective as their originators hoped, but their existence underscores the likely direction of change. Equally, the fact that they draw on many different sectors of society and of the economy illustrates the growing sense of shared responsibility for defining and implementing the sustainability agenda. Most may be little more than talking shops, but, hopefully, some of them will begin to lever real change when their thinking and priorities start to flow through in the form of new political visions, laws, and economic instruments.

A New Focus on Choices

Markets, in the end, are all about choice. But how many of us can really say we fully understand the economic, social, and environmental choices we now face? How many of us receive direct feedback on the impacts associated with the choices we have already made? Precious few. For the sustainability transition to make real progress, we need clear choices, real choices, both commercial and political. We also need feedback from those in authority on how we are doing against agreed triple bottom line targets. Initiatives like Agenda 21 and national sustainability plans are a good start, but this is an area which is pretty much where aviation was at the time of the Wright brothers.

Opinion leaders, including politicians, play a central role in the new global economy. They influence our thinking and priorities far more profoundly than most of us are prepared to accept. We need to ensure that they do much more to inform the public on the choices that are already available – and on the sorts of choices that might be available if sufficient numbers of people were prepared to invest in the sustainability transition. These emerging needs represent major commercial opportunities for those who spot them in time, just as Ted Turner spotted the need for a global news service and hung in there with his embryonic CNN.

Too often, however, as during the CFC transition, the choices we are presented with are artificially stark. We are offered a choice between environment and jobs, between cold homes and global warming, between order and chaos. Yet these are not real choices: they are political levers, designed to force us to moderate our demands. Such false choices need to be exposed for what they are. The public needs to be shown what is possible, if the will, the money, and, most importantly, the quantum leap creativity can be found.

Business Leaders

Many of today's business leaders come from a generation which was acutely aware of markets and, to a degree, of corporate governance issues. But they have tended to be less concerned about values, corporate transparency, product life-cycles or really long-term thinking. 7-D vision, in short, is simply not one of their strong suits. Competitive pressures and the dictates of the financial markets make an already grim situation worse. Nor are these issues particularly high on the agenda for many of the business schools training up their successors. But things are beginning the change.

Not that you would guess it by looking at the business news. And there are good reasons. Too many of today's business leaders continue to lay off thousands of people while, at the same time, taking massive pay-rises. Their communication of the future they are driving towards varies between poor and disastrous. Too often, it seems, they also have little understanding of the social consequences of their actions. As Peter Drucker has put it:

"Few top executives can even imagine the hatred, contempt and fury that has been created – not primarily among blue-collar workers who never had an exalted opinion of the 'bosses' – but among their middle management and professional people. I don't know what form it will take, but the envy developing from their enormous wealth will cause trouble."[21]

These side-effects of unfettered markets and human greed have the potential to undermine any embryonic trust which society may have in business leaders – and, as a result, the capacity of the business world to make the necessary contributions to the sustainability transition. But there are signs of a dawning recognition of the challenge. "The problem is that the business community is not seen to be central to society, nor to be playing its part in creating a just society," warned Tim Melville-Ross, who heads Britain's Institute of Directors.[22] "The problem may be aggravated by an unwillingness, or even an inability, by business leaders to understand it." As we move into the 21st century, he noted, we need a movement to promote business ethics, to make the world of business more attractive to young people. "Something more like a movement is required," he argued, "applying pressure over a long period to change behaviour and attitudes."

Pressure is now coming from some unexpected directions. Among other recent initiatives, Business in the Environment (BiE), a consortium of major companies, recently published its first benchmark survey assessing the environmental commitment of the FT-SE 100 companies (see Case Study, p. 358). The initial reaction in many boardrooms was one of utter horror that their own peers should do this to them, but increasingly we see even some of the first year's hold-out companies agreeing to take part in the survey in the coming years. They recognize that this is a tide that can only build.

A New Focus on Triple-win Business Concepts

Markets depend on new business concepts for their evolution. The triple bottom line of sustainable development will also spawn huge numbers of new business concepts, many of them successful. But to get to this point, we need to stir the pot of business thinking, education, and training vigorously. Thinking and practices which for the most part still remain on the periphery of the business mainstream need to be firmly folded into the emerging heartland of 21st century business.

It is always tempting, when challenged on the question of how far we have come, to focus on "green industries" or "green exports." There are important growth sectors here, certainly. US exports of environmental technology alone grew 50% between 1993 and 1995, for example, reaching $14.5 billion. But the sustainability transition requires a great deal more than clean-up technology and environmental consulting. We also need to turn conventional markets, and conventional business thinking, on their heads.

This is a mainstream challenge which must impact all sectors of industry and commerce, and we should be responding to it with an appropriate level of imagination and energy. One of the most useful reviews of business progress to date in dealing with a range of triple bottom line issues is *Business as Partners in Development*, a report by Jane Nelson of the Prince of Wales Business Leaders Forum.[23] She argues that:

"the greatest opportunity for harnessing the power and potential of business as a partner in development lies firstly, in motivating and mobilizing the talents and energies of the millions of people who work in the business sector and secondly, in mainstreaming a greater sense of innovation, entrepreneurship, individual responsibility and social and environmental awareness into their daily working lives."

She also speaks for many when she concludes that:

"We know what the economic, environmental and social problems are. The need now is to focus on solutions. At one level the solutions are technology, finance and institutions. Ultimately, however, these are just the 'mechanics.' The core issue is about changing attitudes, values and approach. It is about thinking and acting in non-traditional ways. It is about a new way of governance – at both societal and corporate level."

The latest values revolution has only just begun to stir the corporate pot, and the effects will intensify as growing numbers of companies respond and require their corporate partners to do likewise. Ethical challenges are surfacing more than they used to. So, for example, France's Lyonnaise des Eaux faced tough ethical scrutiny during its initially hostile bid for the UK's Northumbrian Water.[24] The French group had been the subject of allegations about its links with politicians during the 1980s. Instead of ducking the challenge, however, Lyonnaise des Eaux set up three new board sub-committees, one of which took charge of ethical policies. An executive director was made solely respon-

CASE STUDY **BUSINESS IN THE ENVIRONMENT, UK: PLAYING FT-SE WITH THE BOARD**

A slim blue document has been dropping on to boardroom tables across the United Kingdom, sparking glee in some companies, and apoplexy in others. The first attempt to benchmark the "environmental engagement" of the Financial Times Stock Exchange 100 (FT-SE 100) has had precisely the effect that Sir Anthony Cleaver, as chairman of Business in the Environment (BiE), had hoped for. Top people in scores of major companies have been keeping the telephones in their corporate health, safety, and environment departments ringing off the hook.

Which is as it should be. The events of the last couple of years have shown that environmental controversies can rock companies to their foundations. "Business operates within a constantly changing and dynamic economic landscape," says Sir Anthony, also chairman of AEA Technology plc, which sponsored the BiE project, in his foreword to BiE's *Index of Corporate Environmental Engagement*. "Fine," some of his business peers have been saying, "but we can do without our own kind making things harder for us on the environmental front!" They will not have been amused to see that BiE intends to produce the Index annually and, as Sir Anthony bravely concludes, "it is also our hope that the impact of Index will reach well beyond the FT-SE 100, to the wider business community."

No problem there, it seems. Corporate boards, some of which are already besieged on a range of corporate governance issues, are waking up to a transformed landscape. Some are showing considerable interest, wondering whether they can adapt in time and in good order. Other FT-SE companies display every sign of shock and denial. Their distress, I suspect, flows not so much from what is being said in the survey report, but from who is now saying it – and the potential longer-term commercial implications.

Although I should declare an interest, given that SustainAbility worked closely with BiE in developing the methodology and final report, the Index has been very much a shared effort. Early versions were tested on BiE board members, including the chairmen, CEOs and environmental practitioners of such companies as BT, General Accident, General Utilities, National Westminster Bank, Norsk Hydro and J Sainsbury. These "beta" versions were critiqued by BiE's advisory group and then test-driven in two pilot studies by BiE corporate members and by FT-SE 100 retail companies. The twin aims were to alert board directors to the emergence of environmental benchmarking and to push environmental issues sharply up – or, in some cases, on to – the boardroom agenda.

❯

The Index does not rate environmental performance or impact. Instead, it aims to gauge progress in environmental management. The ten indicators eventually selected for the Index range from the existence of measurable targets through to supply chain challenge programs. Overall, it shows most FT-SE companies well advanced with the basic tasks of adopting policies and allocating board-level responsibilities, although the Retail, Financial and Services, and Property and Transport sectors stumble even in this area. Reasonable progress has been made in setting objectives and targets, and addressing stewardship and communications, but much less in such areas as internal audit processes and supplier challenges.

It was perhaps unfortunate that when the *Financial Times* ran the results of the survey, it used progressively darker shades of green to distinguish the five "quintile" rankings of companies. Some companies have queried whether competitors with policies and management systems coming out of their ears really have the right values in their hearts and minds? An interesting point, given that a number of environment-intensive companies, among them Shell, ICI and RTZ, appeared in the top quintile. But, more than anything else, the Index is designed to provoke the director class and to shake complacency.

sible for ethical matters, codes of conduct were drafted for both the group and its subsidiaries, and wrong-doers were fired.

The group's directors, the *Financial Times* reported:

"have attempted to embrace a wider range of values, stressing duties not only to shareholders, but to employees, customers and to the community at large – particularly in environmental matters and urban affairs."

Greater transparency, on everything from environmental performance to the stock options payable to the chairman, has been a key part of the new order.

Interestingly, at the time of the changes, 43% of the group's turnover was generated outside France, and 30% of its shareholders were foreign, mainly from Switzerland and the Anglo-Saxon countries. In those countries, according to René Coulomb, who took over as group director responsible for ethics, "people are much more serious" about corporate governance and ethics issues. In many countries, clearly, corruption is still the name of the game. Refuse to play by these rules and you are not in the game. Over time, however, the transparency revolution will help spread triple bottom line values around the world.

OK, transparency and values are of little help when the markets are structured in the wrong way, so that all the pressures force you to behave in ways which you know are unsustainable. Let's take, as a topical example, the world's fisheries; a real test-case of sustainability. The world's media regularly run stories on how over-fishing is emptying the seas and oceans of their most important commercial fish stocks.[25] Commercial fishing is an example of a massive industry with often conflicting economic, social, and ecological objectives.

Today's methods of controlling vessel numbers, mesh sizes, quotas for catches and by-catches, and so on are hugely complex, but you don't need to be a brain surgeon to know that many of our great fisheries, and the industries and communities that depend upon them, are unsustainable. It's an extraordinary fact, too, that the world's governments currently spend over $50 billion a year to subsidize a fishing industry worth $70 billion. No doubt there are concealed triple bottom line objectives here, including the sustenance of local communities and employment, but something is clearly going wrong.

No-one disputes that universal solutions to such problems are unlikely. The most effective remedies will vary from country to country. But those fisheries that have introduced market mechanisms have generally done well. These typically work in the following way. Fishermen acquire a share (quota) of the resource and harvest it in the most desirable manner, generally trying to maximize returns on their investment, subject to whatever legal constraints the government has implemented. Since the fishermen own or lease the quota, each share owner has an incentive to ensure that the stocks are harvested in such a way as to ensure future sustainability. Moreover, in cases where these stocks are transferable (i.e. they can be sold on), the system can also favor the most efficient fishermen.

So far, of course, such market approaches cannot be used on the high seas, where no individual country has exclusive jurisdiction – so access to the resource cannot be limited. But this is another challenge for the future. How do we put in place (and then effectively police) regimes which help conserve and rebuild our natural resources? Market approaches will be a key part of the answer, with the added benefit that they can, when properly designed, ensure a healthy degree of self-policing.

In other areas, a wide range of new initiatives are developing to test sustainable business concepts out in the real world. In the USA, for example, the Management Institute for Environment and Business

(MEB) is working with large corporations and business schools to develop knowledge and methods for integrating environmental and social goals into business planning and decision making. Through its Sustainable Enterprise Initiative (SEI), it aims to deepen its relationships with a select number of companies as they jointly explore ways to integrate economic, environmental, and social objectives through every aspect of their businesses. Three areas on which SEI is focusing are: design for the environment; profit and loss management; and performance indicators and measurement.

Since engineers estimate that 80–90% of the cost of a typical product, and some 80% of its environmental impact, is determined at the design stage, this is the logical place to start. Key focus areas will include designing for optimum material, energy, and water efficiency, and designing for disassembly, remanufacturing and recycling. The profit and loss (P&L) statement is a basic management tool used by general managers to guide operations, investments, and sale projections. Hence, building environmental, health, and safety considerations into the P&L is a powerful means of ensuring that a business unit seriously addresses the integration issue. And the axiom that "you manage what you measure" also holds true in the environmental, health, and safety area, and will also inevitably hold true right across the triple bottom line agenda. As a result, there will be a growing demand for sustainability indicators which have been pilot-tested and de-bugged to the point where they perform well in the real world.

A New Focus on Value Chains

Markets operate through value chains – and companies now need to work with their value chains to deliver sustained triple bottom line performance through the product life-cycle. As the centre of gravity of the economy shifts, new industrial sectors will suddenly pop into the spotlight. Take remanufacturing. In the USA, this unglamorous, little-noticed industry which returns discarded durable products to as-new condition, involves over 70,000 small to medium-sized companies employing nearly 500,000 people.[26] Similar unsuspected opportunities will pop up all over the place as the sustainability transition takes hold, offering new markets for companies large and small.

Or consider the relatively unsexy area of office carpeting. A US commercial flooring company has launched an innovative program aimed at selling "functionality" rather than any particular product. A true life-cycle business concept. Working closely with fiber producers, Interface has developed a new product line by remanufacturing products, converting "old" products into new carpeting or floor tiles. The customer then "leases" the product, or, to put it another way, leases the comfort the carpeting provides. Once the carpet reaches the end of its useful life, a new floor covering is supplied to replace the old and the "spent" product is remanufactured and reintroduced into the market after refurbishing, remanufacturing, or a fashion facelift.[27]

Value chains can also be used as powerful levers for change in industries which have not yet decided to make the necessary changes. Nor will the pressures be confined to environmental issues. The International Labour Organization (ILO), for example, is among those calling for a new system of "social labeling" to guarantee that internationally traded goods are produced under humane conditions. Among the areas that would be covered are: acceptance of the freedom of association and collective bargaining; the prohibition of forced labor, including child labor; and the ending of discrimination between workers.[28]

When corporate customers get agitated about triple bottom line issues, they can often exert enormous influence on their suppliers. Reports *Business Week*:

"Shin Won Honduras is cleaning up its washrooms. The South Korean clothing subcontractor in San Pedro Sula is buying fire extinguishers, installing emergency exits, and checking the ventilation – all in the hope of winning business from J.C. Penney Co. 'Penney wants so many things,' says manager Heung-Tae Kim. Meanwhile, other customers, among them Reebok International and Seers Roebuck, have laid down the law: No underage workers."[29]

This is the emerging business reality. "Thirteen people came to check us from Levi's," noted a lawyer for Seolim, a joint Korean–Honduran venture aiming for a contract with the US company. "You can't fool these people." Campaigning organizations know that they can use the combination of consumer power and value chains to bring intense pressure to bear on some industries. At the same time, companies are beginning to realize that they must use consumers and value chains to "pull through" life-cycle improvements in triple bottom line performance, just as brands like "Intel" and "Nutrasweet" have been pulled through in such areas as personal computers and soft drinks. In some cases, this will be one more reason for business people and campaigners to work together.

In steering the sustainable business debate into the mainstream, we will also need to recognize that it is often much more effective to get a 20% solution to a particular problem into 20 million homes than to get

an 80% solution into 100,000. Of course, these options may not be mutually exclusive, but, as Microsoft has shown, if you can get the basic platform into people's lives you can then continuously improve it. However,
only if people use the more sustainable technologies and systems
instead of the less sustainable alternatives will the promised advantages be realized.

And recognize just how fast technology is now evolving. Brian
Arthur, Citibank Professor at the Santa Fe Institute in New Mexico,
carried out some rough-and-ready calculations and estimated that the
pace of technological evolution is currently running "at roughly 10 million times the speed of natural evolution. Hurricane speed. Warp
speed."[30] Clearly, the sustainability community is going to have to
invade the world's R&D labs, and fast!

Some of the best work will be done outside the giant labs, in
"skunkworks" or in institutes which are currently outside the mainstream. Consider the Rocky Mountain Institute (RMI). The inventor
Paul MacCready once likened Amory Lovins of RMI to a grain of sand in
an oyster; the irritating catalyst that causes pearls to form. An interesting metaphor. As RMI itself notes:

> "Free and fair markets often produce the best pearls; they just need a
> little sand to get them started. By putting the right information into
> the right hands at the right time, the Institute stimulates technolo-
> gies and techniques that work better and cost less. That those pearls
> also happen to benefit the environment need not concern the
> oysters."[31]

The resulting pearls may be "hypercars" that offer dramatic improvements in fuel efficiency and emissions-per-kilometre, or they may be
garments made in safe factories employing reasonably paid people. But,
whether we work in traditional labs or in new ones, the aim will be the
same. To build sustainability thinking into the entire life-cycle, from
conception to resurrection. In the process, we will trigger a process of
value migration which will dwarf what happened to the auto industry
when the OPEC oil shocks hit or to the mainframe computer industry
when PCs came along.

A New Focus on Educating Tomorrow's Business Leaders

This is a critical need. Luckily, there are a number of interesting initiatives designed to fill the gap between today's typical business education

and the likely needs of tomorrow's business leaders. Leading companies are developing their own internal courses. Some of the better business schools now cover aspects of the triple bottom line agenda as a matter of routine, although almost never with the degree of integration proposed in the preceding pages.

In addition, one of the leading international student bodies, AIESEC, is represented in over 700 campuses in more than 80 countries and has initiated a series of projects in this area. Among other things, it has created a web-site with the World Business Council for Sustainable Development, explicitly designed to help business students around the world to come to grips with the sustainability agenda.

Financial Leaders

The question is no longer whether such discontinuities will happen, but when, who will drive them, and who will lose or gain as a result. Worryingly, many of these potential risks and opportunities are outside the boxes in which most financial market people operate. But that will change. Indeed, groups like the World Business Council for Sustainable Development (WBCSD) are beginning to explore ways of demonstrating to financial analysts and others how strategic environmental investment by companies can actively create shareholder value.

The insurers, not surprisingly, were the first to work up to the risks implicit in the environmental regulation of industry, particularly in such areas as asbestos contamination, radioactive wastes, and site and groundwater contamination. But now banks and other lenders are also becoming concerned. The financial analysts will take longer to wake up, because of the very nature of their business, but their time is coming.

A New Focus on Value Migration

Markets are all about risk, but some risks are routinely ignored. Markets, too, have their blind-spots. Indeed, financial markets tend to go through many of the standard human reaction phases when confronted with new evidence that particular companies or industries are going to come under pressure. They start with denial, move on to grudging acceptance, and then, eventually, start to look for the emerging opportunities. Naturally, these opportunities are not always in the sustainability mainstream. So, for example, analysts may wake up to the fact that, with CFCs in increasingly short supply, certain critical users are going to have real problems with substitutes, driving up CFC prices. So they identify and pile into the stocks of the few remaining major producers.

But underlying all of this are deeper trends with profound implications for the value of investments. CFCs are only part of the transition. What happens when we start to squeeze out carbon-based fuels, or road transport, or chlorine compounds? In the process, we will see extraordinary shifts in the centre of gravity of our economies. Read Adrian Slywotzky's *Value Migration*.[32] His basic premise is simple. As industries or companies develop, they go through a period of value inflow (where they begin to absorb value from others whose business designs are outmoded), then through a period of stability (where they are well matched to customer priorities and overall competitive equilibrium), followed by a period of value outflow (as better business designs emerge).

Between 1983 and 1992, for example, IBM is estimated to have lost $70 billion of market value as competitors, particularly Microsoft, scooped up new markets and customers. Environmental and other triple bottom line factors can have precisely the same effect, be it on products, companies, industries, or even entire economies. For example, when the US Vinyl Institute commissioned a study of the market prospects for vinyl, or PVC, through to the year 2020, the conclusion was that potential growth could take the industry to as much as $61 billion in value by 2020.[33] On the other hand, environmental pressures could limit the industry to less than $23 billion over the same period. The $38 billion difference between the two scenarios indicates the economic value of the "triple win" game that the vinyl industry must now learn how to play.

Financial institutions and analysts that get ahead of this curve and ride it through will likely benefit hugely. So it should come as no surprise to find some major financial organizations beginning to align themselves with the emerging reality. This is why Norway's largest insurer, Storebrand, has joined forces with US money manager Scudder, Stevens & Clark to launch the Environmental Value Fund. The Fund uses a Sustainability Index which calculates separate benchmarks for each industry according to eight environmental criteria: global warming, ozone depletion, material efficiency, toxic releases, energy intensity, water use, environmental liabilities, and the quality of the environmental management system.[34] So, for example, a company's global warming rating is calculated by dividing its revenues by tonnes of CO_2 produced.

And does the approach work? Time alone will tell whether investors consistently earn an "environmental dividend" over and above the market average. But when a "back test" was run to see how the fund would have performed over the previous years, it showed an annualized return of 22%, eight points higher than the benchmark Morgan Stanley World Capital Index.

In the end, however, the mainstream thinking of financial centres like Wall Street, London's City, and Tokyo will only change when it is clear that triple bottom line issues are having a real, significant impact on profits and dividends. And, noted David Lascelles of the Centre for the Study of Financial Innovation, analysts do not see companies as locked into the same line of business for ever.[35] "The hallmark of a successful company," he explained:

"is its ability to adapt to variations in markets. So even environmentally responsible companies may never have to face up to the sustainability issue. An unsustainable business does not necessarily die: it can diversify into something else."

Don't count on diversification, however. Those who have tried it know that it is rarely the easy path to anything. And even if you do decide that diversification is the answer, consider working through some of the sustainability audit processes outlined in the next chapter. In the process, you may well find that your core businesses are unsustainable as currently configured. But, just as likely, you may discover that key parts of your business could play a central role in the sustainability transition.

Notes

1. World Bank, *From Plan to Market: World Development Report 1996*, Oxford University Press, 1996.
2. Tim O'Riordan, "Ecotaxation and the sustainability transition," in *Ecotaxation*, edited by Tim O'Riordan, Earthscan Publications, 1997.
3. Bernice Cohen, *The Edge of Chaos: Financial booms, bubbles, crashes and chaos*, John Wiley & Sons, 1997.
4. William Greider, *One World, Ready or Not: The manic logic of global capitalism*, Simon & Schuster, 1997.
5. Jean-Marie Dru, *Disruption: Overturning conventions and shaking up the marketplace*, John Wiley & Sons Inc, 1996.
6. Karen Pennar, "A helping hand, not just an invisible hand," *Business Week*, 24 March 1997.
7. Simon Caulkin, "Amnesty and WWF take a crack at Shell," *Observer*, 11 May 1997.

8. Elizabeth Cook (editor), *Ozone Protection in the United States: Elements of success*, World Resources Institute, 1996.

9. "German firms respond to product takeback law," *Business and the Environment*, February 1997.

10. Christopher Parkes, "US breathes more easily," *Financial Times*, 17 April 1997.

11. Paul Ekins, "Taxing times for the big new idea," *Green Futures*, No. 2, December, 1996.

12. Ernst von Weizsäcker, Amory B. Lovins and L. Hunter Lovins, *Factor Four: Doubling wealth, halving resource use*, Earthscan Publications, 1997.

13. David Malin Roodman, *Paying the Piper: Subsidies, politics, and the environment*, Worldwatch Institute, 1997.

14. Jean-Philippe Barde and Stephen Smith, "Do economic instruments help the environment?," *OECD Observer* **204**, February–March 1997.

15. "A new momentum towards green tax reforms," *ENDS Report 257*, June 1996.

16. Fred Pearce, "If you want to be green recycle your taxes," *New Scientist*, 5 April 1997.

17. Robert Kuttner, "A tiny tax might curb Wall Street's high volatility," *Business Week*, 3 March 1997.

18. Marguerite Holloway, "Sounding out science," *Scientific American*, October 1996.

19. Mark Dowie, *Losing Ground: American environmentalism at the close of the twentieth century*, The MIT Press, 1995.

20. Julia Flynn, Heidi Dawley and Naomi Freundlich, "Green warrior in gray flannel," *Business Week*, 6 May 1996.

21. Robert Lenzner and Stephen S. Johnson, "Seeing things as they really are," *Forbes*, 10 March 1997.

22. Roger Cowe, "IoD calls for 'business ethics,'" *Guardian*, 18 April 1997.

23. Jane Nelson, *Business as Partners in Development: Creating wealth for countries, companies and communities*, The Prince of Wales Business Leaders Forum, in collaboration with the World Bank and the United Nations Development Programme, 1996.

24. Andrew Jack, "Water music," *Financial Times*, 2 February 1996.

25. William Emerson, "Can private property rescue fisheries?," *OECD Observer* **205**, April–May 1997.

26. Professor Robert T. Lund, *The Remanufacturing Industry: Hidden giant*, reviewed in *Business and the Environment*, March 1996.

27. Edwin G. Falkman, *Sustainable Production and Consumption: A business perspective*, World Business Council for Sustainable Development, 1996.

28. Robert Taylor, "ILO chief in appeal for 'social labelling,'" *Financial Times*, 23 April 1997.

29. Elisabeth Malkin, "Cleanup at the *maquiladora*," *Business Week*, 29 July 1996.

30. W. Brian Arthur, "How fast is technology evolving?," *Scientific American*, February 1997.
31. "Playing the Market: Using competition to get others to practice what we preach," *Rocky Mountain Institute Newsletter* **7**(1), Spring 1996.
32. Adrian J. Slywotzky, *Value Migration: How to think several moves ahead of the competition*, Harvard Business School Press, 1996.
33. Gary Gappert et al, *Vinyl 2020: Progress, challenges, prospects for the next quarter century*, The Vinyl Institute, April 1996.
34. Ann Goodman, "Green funds: fuzzy no more," *Tomorrow*, No. 5, September/October, 1996.
35. David Lascelles, "View," *Green Futures*, No. 1, October, 1996.

PART IV
Toolbox

♦ 14 ♦

SUSTAINABILITY AUDITING

How Are We Doing?

So how does your company or organization
measure up against today's
– and tomorrow's –
triple bottom line requirements?

For some, the word "audit" conjures up the image of gray men in gray suits ticking boxes. But, to be successful in preparing any organization for the changes now in prospect, sustainability auditing needs to engage internal and stakeholders in the colourful task of refocusing the company.

Fine, you may say. We understand that sustainability is going to be a priority on the 21st century business agenda. We already have, or are putting in place, policies and management systems covering many of the areas included in the triple bottom line agenda. But how well is your organization doing against the emerging indicators and expectations?

♦ Are the issues now emerging in the "shear zones" fully plotted and tracked on your radar screens?
♦ How would a selection of the more challenging stakeholders from different countries evaluate and describe your targets and achievements?
♦ And how would your achievements to date compare with best practice among your competitors, in sectors which your customers, shareholders, potential new recruits and other stakeholders watch closely?

There is only one way to find out. Carry out a sustainability audit. To do so, it will help to understand the full range of tools now available in the sustainability toolkit. For example, triple bottom line performance can be vetted by using impact assessment, auditing, and life-cycle assessment methods.[1] The real challenge, however, comes in assessing the risks and opportunities in the shear zones, where the different dimensions of sustainability overlap. Indeed, one of the key reasons that the triple bottom line is now becoming a board-level agenda item is that success depends on careful prioritization and integrated strategies.

Sustainability audit frameworks are still evolving. But it is essential that any such audit covers all three dimensions of sustainable development, and, most importantly, the interfaces between them. Any company organization wanting to assess the sustainability of its management systems, operations, value chains, and markets also needs to consider the likely impacts of the seven sustainability revolutions.

So, to briefly recap, here are some of the key conclusions that we have reached to date:

♦ **Chapter 2**   We asked whether capitalism is sustainable. The conclusion was that it all depends on what it is that you are trying to sustain. But there are now good reasons to believe that we can evolve sustainable forms of capitalism if business and, equally importantly, the world's financial markets can get to grips with the seven sustainability revolutions.

♦ **Chapter 3**   We looked at the two great waves, and ensuing downwaves, of environmentalism, and reviewed some of the likely characteristics of the next wave. One key characteristic, alongside the increasing complexity and pace of development, will be a new focus on the triple bottom line.

♦ **Chapter 4**   The triple bottom line, in turn, will require new forms of accounting, auditing, reporting, and benchmarking. At the same time, troubling new issues are already surfacing in the "shear zones" between the bottom line agendas.

♦ **Chapter 5**   The sustainability community must now recognize that Sustainability Revolution 1 will mean that triple bottom line goals and targets will increasingly need to be met by working with business and through markets.

♦ **Chapter 6**   Revolution 2 will mean that diverse human and societal values will be on the boardroom agenda as never before. This trend, coupled with the spread of high-technology communication media and the erosion of traditional centres of authority, creates the "ghost in the system" with which boards will now need to wrestle.

♦ **Chapter 7**   Revolution 3 will turn the global business environment into the electronic equivalent of a goldfish bowl. As a result, business thinking, commitments, and actions will be under scrutiny as never before. Some companies will try to develop "stealth" maneuvers, in the hope of slipping in underneath society's radar, but most will have no option but to play the game by the new rules.

♦ **Chapter 8** Revolution 4, in turn, will mean that growing numbers of companies will themselves try to switch on focused forms of the "X-ray environment," in an attempt to understand the triple bottom issues potentially lurking in their supply chains. As a result, life-cycle thinking will be a key feature of 21st-century business.

♦ **Chapter 9** Revolution 5 will accelerate the process of alliance-building and partnership development between leading companies and a growing range of actual or potential "complementors." These partnerships will also help to drive Revolutions 1–4, 6 and 7.

♦ **Chapter 10** Revolution 6 will be based on, and spotlight, new ways of perceiving, valuing, and managing time. None of this will be friction-free, however. The collision of different time-perspectives, whether wide or long, will be a key feature of the 21st-century business environment.

♦ **Chapter 11** Because of all the above, Revolution 7 will require that corporate governance systems evolve rapidly – and that corporate boards begin to understand the full range of changes likely to be required by stakeholder capitalism. Stakeholder dialog is likely to be among the most important of these new requirements.

♦ **Chapter 12** Here we ran through "39 steps to sustainability," which will be essential for any corporation determined to build sustainability thinking and targets into the very core of its policies and practices. In each case, we focused in on a number of old-to-new paradigm shifts needed to drive the sustainability transition.

♦ **Chapter 13** Recognizing that all of this represents perhaps the most profound challenge our species has yet faced, we then focused on necessary changes in such areas as governance, regulation, and taxation, together with the implications in terms of such areas as shared responsibility and value migration.

This is a huge agenda, clearly. But it is manageable, so long as a company or organization understands the direction and pace of change – and has ways of measuring progress against a range of key triple bottom line performance indicators. Below, we run through some of the basic questions that will almost certainly need to be asked when designing and conducting a sustainability audit.

Corporate Governance

♦ Does our Board have the ability not only to see things in the round, in what is often called 360° vision, but also to view the world and emerging challenges in "7-D?" If not, what would it take to acquire the necessary skills?

♦ Is the triple bottom line agenda likely to become a societal concern in the countries and markets where we operate? How might we find out?

♦ Does our Board genuinely understand that sustainability is a new form of value which society will demand and which successful businesses will deliver through transformed markets?

♦ Is sustainability something to which this company is already committed, or something to which it should now commit?

♦ Should the main focus be on corporate citizenship or on competitive advantage?

♦ How do we assess the likely upsides and downsides of adopting, or failing to adopt, a competitive triple bottom line strategy?

♦ Which aspects of our management of economic, social and natural capital are likely to be most important – and, potentially, most controversial?

♦ Which performance indicators will be most useful in our sector, value chain and markets?

♦ Which board member(s) is(are) responsible for integrating and driving our triple bottom line activities, against which benchmarks and audited by whom?

♦ Which existing voluntary codes of conduct have we already signed – and which should we sign next? What are the implications and requirements?

♦ Are we clear on what changes will be needed? Will it involve a revolution or a series of continuous improvement programs?

♦ Are there appropriate champions in each business area?

♦ Do we have the right balance between advice and challenge in our non-executive directors and elsewhere?

Time

♦ Does our Board fully understand the tension between "wide" and "long" time – and the implications for our triple bottom line performance?

♦ How will the time dimension influence the way that the triple bottom line agenda impacts our company, industry and markets?

♦ Do our plans, objectives, and goals combine long-term thinking with short-term targets and rewards?

♦ What would happen if we radically stretched (or shrank) the time-scales involved in our business?

♦ Have we developed scenarios for our different business areas – and, if so, do they cover each of the seven sustainability revolutions?

♦ How could the focus of our value chain move from environmental extraction to restoration, and to full triple bottom line engagement?

♦ Do the investment, R&D, and product stewardship time-scales involved in our markets favour sustainability programmes?

♦ If triple bottom line performance is not currently rewarded in our markets in an appropriate time-scale, what would it take to turn things around?

Partners

♦ Does our Board understand the "2 + 2 = 50" power of "strange alliances"?

♦ Do our existing partners, up and down the value chain, understand the triple bottom line challenge?

♦ As the sustainability transition builds, can we maintain or achieve competitive advantage without new forms of stakeholder partnership?

♦ Which stakeholders should we involve in developing our sustainability audit – and how? Which current critics might become future "complementors"?

♦ If asked, would our key internal stakeholders (particularly employees) say that we are "walking the talk?"

♦ Where partnerships are needed, how do we choose strategic triple bottom line partners, particularly from amongst the ranks of campaigners?

♦ How do we develop and sustain such relationships? What are the likely benefits, and how can we maximize them? Where are the downside risks, and how can we minimize them?

♦ Are we doing enough to build bridges and track organizations with which we are not formally partnering?

♦ What are our customers and competitors doing to engage their stakeholders?

♦ Is partnership-based disruption by a competitor possible?

Life-cycle Technology

♦ To what extent is our Board aware that its triple bottom line responsibilities no longer end at the factory fence but increasingly extend to stewardship through the life-cycle of the company's products?

♦ How well do we understand the trends in such areas as life-cycle assessment, design for the environment, and industrial ecology?

♦ How does the life cycle of our business look when viewed through triple bottom line lenses?

♦ Where would we be vulnerable if the "X-ray environment" were to switch on in relation to our products, markets, or value chain?

♦ Have we carried out any form of need test on our main products?

♦ What would happen if customers started to focus on "functions" rather than on the products we supply?

♦ Have we audited strategic suppliers not only against the obvious eco-efficiency requirements but also against the outside risks (e.g. environmental oestrogens, carbon risks, environmental justice, and human rights)

Transparency

♦ To what extent do our Board believe that if they can just keep their heads down, they can avoid the sorts of challenges that have buffeted companies like Shell and Texaco?

♦ Are we communicating our triple bottom line commitments, targets and performance to all appropriate stakeholders?

♦ Have we genuinely moved beyond sustainability promises to triple bottom line targets?

♦ Is our communication credible and effective? Does it engage the emotions and perceptions of target audiences? How do we know?

♦ How does our performance against key triple bottom line indicators and benchmarks compare with that of our competitors, and with emerging best practice in other sectors?

♦ What implications will the Internet have for the transparency of our operations?

Values

♦ Does our Board understand that the business of business is not simply about the creation of economic value, but also, increasingly, about honoring a growing range of social and ethical values?

MAKING IT HAPPEN

It's done. The champagne corks have popped. In a no-holds-barred AGM or press conference, the chairman or CEO has announced the company's conversion to the cause. The triple bottom line is now part of the language. Board members and employees are enjoying the warm glow as they leave the ranks of the public's enemies and, hopefully by the evening news or next morning's papers, join the list of white knights.

And then the chill hits. How are we going to make all of this *happen*? Faced with this question, many business leaders turn to management consultants, among whom McKinsey & Company are unquestioned market leaders. So what would McKinsey suggest a company does to make the necessary changes happen for strong triple bottom line performance? I asked Pieter Winsemius, once the Netherlands' Environment Minister and now head of McKinsey's environment practice.

One of the biggest barriers to change, he notes, is that a company's internal systems too often fail to support top management's message. To prove his point, he offers Figure 1, based on a recent McKinsey survey of companies. On the left, the responses show 78% of respondents in three major companies strongly agreeing that the environment should be among the top three priorities of line management. By contrast, on the right, 66% feel that their companies fail to reward line managers for excellent performance in this area.

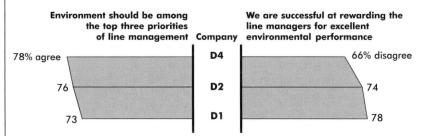

FIGURE 1   Outdated systems fail to support board's message

The result   Despite further attempts by the board to revive interest, progress slows or stalls. Recognizing that such problems can undermine even the best-laid plans, Winsemius and his colleagues turned to psychology research and mapped out the key steps that successful corporate managements have taken in moving from words to effective, sustained action. Figure 2 summarizes the results.

❭

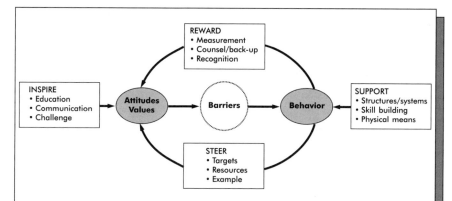

FIGURE 2   Instruments for making change happen

The first step is to INSPIRE all of those who work for, or alongside, the company. This is designed to reinforce or shift attitudes and values in the appropriate directions. It involves education, internal, and external communication, and a clear definition of the challenge. Think of Bob Shapiro at Monsanto or Cor Herkströter at Shell.

Inevitably, however, even the most committed boards often find that their new initiatives run into a range of internal and external barriers. What to do? Winsemius advises two linked steps at this point: STEER and REWARD. Targets need to be set, adequate resources allocated, and examples of successful approaches widely communicated. High-fliers also need to be steered into the new area, to signal serious intent. At the same time, progress towards the right attitudes, values, and behaviors needs to be measured and rewarded. Recognition for achievement is crucial, but as Figure 1 suggests, incentive systems at all levels should also financially reward the right actions. For those who find the transition a struggle, there needs to be counselling and other forms of back-up.

And then, as appropriate behaviors begin to emerge, they will need support. They must be reinforced, spread, and developed by new structures and systems. Initially, these may be solely internal, but life-cycle thinking dictates that eventually they will need to embrace all key stages in the company's value chain. New skills, fueled by training and information, will almost certainly be needed, particularly for those whose role it is to integrate different aspects of triple bottom line performance. Finally, but equally important, all involved must be given the means to make the new behaviors both possible and, eventually, second nature.

Source of figures: Pieter Winsemius, McKinsey & Co, Inc.

- ♦ What are this company's values? What are the values of our customers and other key stakeholders? Are they congruent? And how do they relate to the triple bottom line of sustainability?
- ♦ Do we have a values statement? If not, should we have one – and how should it be developed?
- ♦ Are our values in line with the emerging sustainability agenda? If not, what are the nature and scale of the gaps to be bridged?
- ♦ To what extent do we cascade our values through the organization, and through our value chain?
- ♦ Have we tested our values with key stakeholders such as our customers? Or with young people, including our new recruits, or young people we would like to recruit?

Markets

- ♦ Is our Board thinking of sustainability as a corporate citizenship issue, or as a key factor in competitive advantage in 21st-century markets?
- ♦ How do our markets currently value triple bottom line commitments and performance, and under what circumstances might this change in future?
- ♦ As the sustainability transition builds, are our markets likely to grow, stall, or shrink?
- ♦ Will triple bottom line pressures drive changing regulations, standards, or stakeholder expectations with the potential to transform our markets, or the markets served by our customers?
- ♦ Have we looked at the potential market implications of the sustainable production and consumption debate for our products or services?
- ♦ Are our markets sensitive to triple bottom line disruption?
- ♦ What would happen if competitors, or customers, began to apply demand side management strategies?
- ♦ To what extent are insurers, lenders, and financial analysts in our sector prepared for the sustainability transition? If the answer is that they are ill-prepared, what should we be doing to help them understand and support the necessary changes?
- ♦ Will our markets be subject to the law of diminishing returns, or of increasing returns? What difference might a successful triple bottom line strategy make?

♦ How might the Factor 4–10 agenda, and the drive towards a "restorative economy" impact our markets, and what might we do to influence customer demand and financial market pressures in the right directions?

Once the key issues are identified, the next step is to make the necessary changes happen. This, as anyone who has run a health and safety, total quality, or other similar corporate change program knows, is where the real problems often start. As many case studies dotted through *Cannibals With Forks* suggest, SustainAbility has a long track-record of helping corporate clients through the process of change. But while finalizing the book, I co-presented to an international business conference alongside Pieter Winsemius of McKinsey. He used the two figures shown in the Spotlight (p. 378) to explain some of the barriers he and his colleagues often encounter in such change programs. I found them helpful, and hope you do too.

Note

1. Peter Groenewegen, Kurt Fischer, Edith G. Jenkins and Johan Schot, *The Greening of Industry Resource Guide and Bibliography*, Island Press, 1996.

CODA

Closing the Gap

As we enter the 21st century and the
third millennium, the triple bottom line agenda
is shifting into overdrive.

Try eating soup with a fork. It's difficult. And it is at least conceivable that the 21st-century business environment will be so fluid that it defies analysis, forcing executives to fall back upon hunch, or instinct. But there are also signs of hope. Growing numbers of major companies are beginning to align themselves with the sustainability agenda and to pursue win–win–win solutions to market challenges. Their value chains will be encouraged to follow suit.

So where next? The human brain, above all, is a pattern-recognition organ. Sometimes, it succeeds in extracting real patterns from chaos and disorder. But sometimes it descends into dreams and hallucinations. Let me conclude *Cannibals With Forks* with a very personal view on some of the patterns I now see developing. You judge whether they are real, or hallucinations.

First, let's consider the bigger picture. In 1848, Karl Marx and Friedrich Engels published their *Communist Manifesto*. It took more than a generation for the thinking of this grouping of revolutionaries to take hold and transform the world. Then it seemed, for much of the 20th century, that some form of socialism or communism would be our future. But in 1947, a century after Marx and Engels published their manifesto for change, the foundations were laid for the counter-revolution.

In April of 1947, in Switzerland, the Mont Pelerin Society held its first meeting. This early think-tank, which opposed totalitarianism whether of the left, right, or centre, is now credited with having decisively shifted the political economy of the world away from collectivism in favour of free-market economics.[1] Highly secretive though it may have been, the society – which included among its early luminaries people like F. A. Hayek, Milton Friedman, and Karl Popper – helped spawn nearly 100 like-minded think-tanks, making the free-market movement truly international and helping to inspire the politics of leaders like Ronald Reagan and Margaret Thatcher.

Once again, it took more than a generation for the ideas of this group of thinkers to take root and transform our world. In the same way, the thinking of the sustainability movement will take at least a generation to transform our world and our vision of the future. If we date the process from the publication of the Brundtland Commission's report, *Our Common Future,* in 1987, then we still have 20–30 years before the process really gets into its stride. But the pace of change is accelerating. In retrospect, it is clear that 1995 marked a critical year in the development of this new, broader-based agenda for business and for society.

In controversies like those triggered by the Brent Spar, the executions of Ken Saro-Wiwa and his colleagues, and the extraordinary political and economic convulsions caused by "mad cow" disease, we saw real evidence of the values shift discussed in Chapter 6. The size of the gap between today's world and anything approaching a sustainable future was increasingly clear, although few business leaders, or politicians for that matter, seemed to have much of a clue on ways of bridging the chasm.

But the string of controversies that erupted through the mid-1990s helped bring the agenda into much sharper focus. Indeed, it was as if a number of seed crystals had been dropped into a series of supersaturated solutions. Anyone who remembers carrying out this experiment in the school laboratory knows that a solution teetering on the edge of crystallizing into a solid can be provoked into making the "phase change" by dropping in a surprisingly small object. The same is true of human politics, where particular events or figures can trigger reactions which were previously almost unimaginable. Interestingly, too, once the political phase change has happened it can be extremely difficult to reverse the reaction.

Inevitably, many of the students using the web-site developed by the World Business Council for Sustainable Development (WBCSD) – described in Chapter 13 – will find themselves wrestling with aspects of the triple bottom line agenda during their careers. Indeed, few things are as certain since the process of globalization, as described in earlier chapters, now embraces not only economic dimensions but also social and environmental dimensions. We are seeing evidence of financial superconductivity, as described in Chapter 5, but we are also seeing evidence of social and political superconductivity, often catalyzed by unexpected side-effects of economic globalization. So, for example, as western lifestyles invade the developing world, the World Health

Organization (WHO) expects an epidemic of chronic diseases, including a doubling in diseases such as diabetes and cancer over the next 25 years. According to WHO director Dr Paul Kleihaus:

> "There is a dramatic trend for globalisation of the Western lifestyle and a parallel globalisation of the associated diseases. We had expected this, but we are nevertheless surprised at the pace at which this is happening. Cancer rates are soaring in countries which hardly knew the disease a few years ago."

Changes in diet and the growth of smoking in Asia and Africa appear to be mostly to blame.[2] Ironically, the growth of developing world cigarette markets is enabling the tobacco companies to pay off their liabilities in the West!

The challenge will not only be to spot areas where such effects are about to surface but also to develop ways of measuring progress against the triple bottom line, which is where "shadow pricing" and similar techniques potentially come in. As the pace of change accelerates and the world becomes more complex, the risks associated with blind-spots, highlighted in the Executive Summary, can only grow. Hence the value of close dialog with a range of stakeholders, given that their networks and radar-screens are likely to pick up trends and issues which may slip in under your own organization's radar. But corporate boards need to recognize that the very fact that we are seeing powerful globalization trends does not mean that we will inevitably see homogenization of the world's social or environmental agendas, no more than we will see complete economic homogenization.

The environmental revolution resulted, in large part, from a values meltdown in the main capitalist nations. Indeed, as Charles Hampden-Turner and Fons Trompenaars explain in *The Seven Cultures of Capitalism*,[3] one result of the sustainability revolutions outlined in earlier chapters might simply be to create one more culture of capitalism. Given that the triple bottom line approach can involve transitional costs to business, this outcome would be problematic. The pace of change would be severely slowed by the need to compete with others – from pragmatic entrepreneurs through to outright black marketeers – with shorter term concerns and fewer (or different) principles. Clearly, a far more desirable outcome would be for all cultures of capitalism to progressively internalize sustainability thinking.

For this to happen, we will need "sustainable corporations." As I finished off this book, *The Stakeholder Corporation* by David Wheeler and Maria Sillanpää appeared:[4] it is highly recommended. And read anything on the subject by Tom Gladwin. But we also need new forms of international governance if such corporations are to appear, evolve, and flourish.

Sustainable corporations and sustainable markets will rarely evolve of their own accord. Indeed, one of the most interesting trends in the closing few years of the 20th century was the evolution of a much stronger appreciation of the central roles played by governments, governance systems, and regulation in the civilization of capitalism. As Robert Kuttner puts it in *Everything for Sale,* a book bearing the revealing sub-title "The virtues and limits of markets,"[5] much post-1945 wealth creation flowed not from raw capitalism of the variety now being commended to emergent nations around the world, but from the "mixed economy." The idea underpinning this approach was that:

"Market forces could do many things well – but not everything. Government intervened to promote development, to temper the market's distributive extremes, to counteract its unfortunate tendency to boom-and-bust, to remedy its myopic failure to invest too little in public goods, and to invest too much in processes that harmed the human and natural environment."

No one disputes that market economies tend to out-perform their command-and-control competitors, but that does not mean that we should abandon everything that smacks of a command-and-control approach. Regulation is essential to the effective and efficient working of markets, particularly in pursuit of emerging triple bottom line objectives. But, increasingly, we must learn to develop regulatory frameworks which operate, as far as possible, through market processes and are intrinsically procompetition.

In a mixed economy, as Kuttner argues:

"the state intervenes to protect citizens from a variety of assaults that laissez-faire forces would otherwise produce. These include the spewing of pollutants into the air and water, the manufacture of dangerous products, the coercive power of private business to condition employment on unsafe working conditions, and other 'contracts of desperation' that do not reflect truly voluntary transactions."

Supporters of unbridled capitalism may argue that it is up to investors, workers, and consumers to work out whether particular market offerings are safe, efficacious, and, ultimately, sustainable. But, as Kuttner concludes:

"the consumer can't be expected to know with precision if her hamburger is poisoned, if the lawnmower will cut his foot off, if the water is safe to drink. The factory worker can't know whether an industrial compound risks producing cancer ten years into the future. The individual citizen doesn't have the basis to insist that the local public utility burn cleaner fuel or develop lower-polluting technology – except via government regulation."

After two decades of celebrating markets and denigrating governments, we are probably on the threshold of a new era in which the triple bottom line agenda helps to give governments and regulation new forms of legitimacy. Both will play central roles in developing the market instruments and technologies necessary for the sustainability transition. But to make all this happen, we must increasingly learn how to mobilize the potential winners. For, as Machiavelli argued some 500 years ago:

"There is nothing more difficult to plan, more doubtful of success, nor more dangerous to manage than the creation of a new system. For the initiator has the enmity of all who would profit from the preservation of the old institutions, and merely lukewarm defenders in those who should gain by the new ones."

There is still a tremendous amount of work to be done on waking up those responsible for running the interlinking worlds of politics, economics, and business. One way to attract the attention of boards, we have found, is to develop the right scanning systems and metrics. For example, as explained in Chapter 13, we helped Business in the Environment (BiE) to develop its Index of Corporate Environmental Engagement, based on ten environmental benchmarks.[6] It was clear that boiling all of this complexity down into a single barometer-like set of readings had helped. "The Index was snappy enough to seize attention and appeal to boards' competitive instincts," said Paul Pritchard, environmental adviser at Royal Sun Alliance, one of three insurance groups ranked in the bottom quintile.[7]

Eventually, similar surveys will be done on the sustainability of major companies and key sectors of the economy. It may even be possible to link such indexes to likely value migration caused by future regulations or market shifts. There are huge advantages to be had from switching the business brain on to the need to compete in terms of triple bottom line performance, but there are dangers here, too. After years of downsizing and intensive, face-to-face competition, there is a growing recognition that we must increasingly focus on innovation – on disrupting today's markets with radically different products and services offering Factor 4 or 10 improvements, coupled with real consumer benefits. As W. Chan Kim and Renée Mauborgne put it recently in the *Harvard Business Review,* "don't focus on beating competitors."[8] Focus, instead, on breaking out of the trap of today's diminishing return markets and aim to break into the increasing return markets of the future.

The law of diminishing returns, the "hockey stick effect" discussed in Chapter 12, is well understood by economists. But we are now also seeing the so-called law of "increasing returns" being developed and promoted by economists such as W. Brian Arthur (based at Stanford and the Santa Fe Institute), Paul Krugman (Stanford), and Paul Romer (University of California at Berkeley). Described by Arthur as the tendency for something that gets ahead to get further ahead, this new law has dramatic implications for corporations considering developing new sustainability-related products and services. "The more people use your product," as Arthur puts it, "the more advantage you have – or, to put it another way, the bigger your installed base, the better off you are."[9]

Of course, this law could also help fuel the growth of an industry that, ultimately, was unsustainable in some way, at least for a while. The most extreme current examples of the operation of the law of increasing returns come from the computer software business. But, at the same time, there is absolutely no reason why it should not come into play in the sustainability transition. The key questions are when, where, for whom and for how long? Happily, there is a burgeoning literature produced by those at the cutting edge of a completely new paradigm now emerging.

One of the most stimulating books I have read on this whole area is Kevin Kelly's *Out of Control.*[10] In predicting a period of evolution when our machines, companies, and economies become much more akin to biological and ecological systems, he notes that:

> "Anything which alters its environment to increase production of itself is playing the game of increasing returns. And all large, sustaining systems play the game. The law operates in economics, biology, computer science, and human psychology. Life on Earth alters Earth to beget more life. Confidence builds confidence. Order generates more order. Them that has, gets."

The emerging sustainability movement must learn to exploit these new principles of evolution and development.

We must learn to coordinate triple bottom line change in ways that help to transform the conditions in which governments, companies, and ordinary people operate, whether acting as citizens, consumers, or investors. In the process, too, Kelly encourages us to learn to honor our errors. "Even the most brilliant act of human genius," he notes, "in the final analysis, is an act of trial and error."

The history of social and economic development has been one of risk. What distinguishes the modern era is that we are getting much better at analyzing and managing many risks, but our scientific and technological inventiveness means that new risks are continuously being generated. In his book, *Against the Gods*, Peter Bernstein shows how a small group of thinkers "put the future at the service of the present," by "showing the world how to understand risk, measure it, and weight its consequences."[11] In the process, he argues, they converted risk-taking into "one of the prime catalysts that drives modern Western society."

By contrast, many of the campaigning groups that have grown up to promote different triple bottom line issues are by their very nature risk-averse. Typically, they have been happier telling others what not to do than advising on, and taking responsibility for, possible solutions. The watchdog role will remain critically important right across the sustainability agenda, but this must also be matched with a more constructive approach to engagement with those in business who have, or who can help develop, the tools and other resources needed for the sustainability transition. To play this role well, they must develop a different view of risk and of failure.

As Kelly concludes, "Evolution can be thought of as systematic error management." The path to relative economic, social and ecological sustainability is guaranteed to be littered with failures of every nature and scale. If we recognize them and learn from them, the transition will proceed faster and in more resource-efficient ways. If, on the other hand, we prefer the short-term comfort of burying our failures, or of blaming scapegoats, the transition will be significantly slowed, or could even be derailed completely.

Meanwhile, for those who fear they may have missed the glory days of environmentalism, never fear. Through waves and downwaves alike, the process of greening our minds and industries may have been under way for nearly forty years, but the process of putting the world economy on to a more sustainable footing has only just begun. Indeed, this is an agenda which will still be current when today's business students are reaching retirement age. As the great plates represented by the three bottom lines grind up against one another, some issues and campaigns will disappear into the political equivalents of the subduction zones which drag down areas of the sea-floor into the seething magma below. But, at the very same time, we will see growing numbers of uplift zones, where new issues, and new opportunity spaces, will surface and be colonized by both existing and new forms of business activity.

And my own personal challenge in this area, at least for the next year or two, was crystallized for me a month or two before *Cannibals With Forks* hit the bookstands. I was at a small lunch on the top floor of the headquarters of one of the world's most powerful corporations. We were being asked whether we would help the company reposition itself in relation to the three dimensions of sustainable development. However, one of those present confided that the use of the phrase "triple bottom line" had been quite specifically banned within the company. The very top management preferred to talk in terms of the "three pillars" of sustainable development, or the "three legs of the sustainability stool."

My response was that "pillars" and "legs of stools" make sustainability sound static. It hasn't been, it isn't, and it won't be. Instead, we need to capture, and, increasingly, to manage, the hugely powerful underlying dynamics. "In two years," I predicted, "you will be using the phrase 'triple bottom line' without thinking about it." Yet, even as I said it, I knew that if we succeed in making this happen, everything will have changed.

Business in the 21st century, in the new millennium, will, in a very real sense, be operating in a new world. A key area to look for early evidence of change will be in the language used by business (see Appendix). We know change is needed. Let's make it happen.

Notes

1. Richard Cockett, "Secret society for world freedom," *Sunday Times,* 13 April 1997.
2. Ian Murray, "World health crisis as West exports its lifestyle diseases," *The Times,* 5 May 1997.
3. Charles Hampden-Turner and Fons Trompenaars, *The Seven Cultures of Capitalism,* Doubleday 1993; Piatkus, 1994.
4. David Wheeler and Maria Sillanpää, *The Stakeholder Corporation: A blueprint for maximising stakeholder value,* Pitman Publishing, London, 1997.
5. Robert Kuttner, *Everything for sale: The virtues and limits of markets,* a Twentieth Century Fund book, Alfred A. Knopf, 1997.
6. Business in the Environment, AEA Technology and SustainAbility, *The BiE Index of Corporate Environmental Commitment,* Business in the Environment, 1996.

7. Leyla Boulton, "Companies compete to clean up their act," *Financial Times*, 15 April 1997.

8. W. Chan Kim and Renée Mauborgne, "Value innovation: The strategic logic of high growth," *Harvard Business Review,* January–February 1997.

9. James Aley, "The theory that made Microsoft," *Fortune,* 29 April 1996.

10. Kevin Kelly, *Out of Control: The new biology of machines*, Fourth Estate, 1994.

11. Peter L. Bernstein, *Against the Gods: The remarkable story of risk,* John Wiley & Sons, 1996.

APPENDIX

Notes for a Sustainable Business Phrase-book

One of the best places to watch for early warning signals of impending market changes is the vocabulary used by successful business people. Even if sustainable development experts speak your own language, however, they still sometimes seem to be speaking a foreign language. Each of us needs to build our own phrase-book. The following are among the interesting words and phrases coming up the curve, which any self-respecting student of sustainability should now be able to define.

benchmarking   Developed in such areas as Total Quality Management (TQM), benchmarking involves the comparison, ranking or rating of different business processes, units or companies against standards. The aim: to identify ways of improving the performance of operations, systems, processes. Environmental benchmarking is a growth area.

biodiversity   The word, a contraction of "biological diversity," is sometimes used as a synonym for "Life on Earth." But its specific meanings, referring to the number, variety, and variability of living organisms, will be central to 21st-century values, thinking and action.

business ecosystems   As traditional industry boundaries erode, new types of multi-industry coalitions and networks are emerging. Think of the Microsoft-Intel (or "Wintel") business ecosystem. The real test for 21st-century businesses will be to outperform their rivals at creating the new business ecosystems needed to build and sustain competitive triple bottom line (q.v.) performance.

complementors   Those actors in an economy or society who supply complementary products, services or inputs to businesses or business ecosystems (q.v.). Increasingly, these can include actors once thought hostile, including competitors and campaigning groups.

co-opetition   A business approach which recognizes that in the new economy companies may often end up working alongside, or even through, their competitors. Key players are seen to be customers, suppliers, competitors, and/or complementors (q.v.).

demand side management (DSM)   DSM can be applied in any industry where a product can be replaced by a service. The central principle is that a company or utility learns to provide (and have customers pay for) services (e.g. heated rooms, lighted spaces) rather than kilowatt-hours or therms of gas. Often, the market needs to be provided with new price signals or other incentives.

eco-efficiency   Involves the delivery of competitively priced goods and services that satisfy human needs and bring quality of life, while progressively reducing ecological impacts and resource intensity throughout the life cycle, to a level at least in line with the Earth's estimated carrying capacity.

ecological footprints   The size and impact of the "footprints" of companies, communities, or individuals reflect a number of interlinked factors, among them human population numbers, consumption patterns, and the technologies used. A more challenging version of the concept is "environmental space," as developed by Friends of the Earth Netherlands/Milieudefensie.

eco-taxes   The use of economic, and in particular fiscal, instruments for environmental protection is gaining support. Examples include charges and taxes on polluting emissions and products, tradable emission permits, and deposit-refund schemes. The aim is to achieve environmental or broader sustainability policy objectives more effectively and at lower cost.

environmental justice   In the same way that certain social groups or communities may be economically disadvantaged, so they may suffer disproportionate health, safety, or environmental problems. Linked issues can surface around various types of industrial facility, from oilfields and chemical production complexes to major airports.

environmental management system (EMS) standards   The main international EMS standard is ISO 14001. There are also emerging regional EMS systems, notably the European Union's Eco-Management and Audit Scheme (EMAS).

Factor 4/10   Key terms in the thinking of Germany's Wuppertal Institute and the US Rocky Mountain Institute. To be sustainable during a period when human populations will likely double and average living standards increase significantly, industry needs to increase its resource conversion efficiency by a minimum Factor 4 (i.e. 75% reductions in resource consumption for any unit of production). Given that western societies typically consume 20–30 times more than their less developed counterparts, the Carnoules Declaration calls for Factor 10 improvements (i.e. 90% reductions).

full-cost accounting (FCA)   Although this is an area in need of much further work, the Holy Grail is to develop accounting methods which account for all the key costs of a project or activity, not just the financial costs.

industrial ecology   Discipline which focuses on the design, development, operation, renewal, and decommissioning of industrial facilities as ecological systems, with an emphasis on the optimization of resource efficiency.

industry covenants   Some countries, particularly the Netherlands, are encouraging selected industry sectors to agree voluntary targets – and encourage member companies towards those targets, as an alternative to new regulation. The threat of regulation, however, is always in the background.

joint implementation (JI)   Proposed as a least-cost approach to cutting greenhouse gas emissions. The idea is that Annex 1 countries under the Framework Convention on Climate Change, which have binding commitments to cut their emissions, can invest in emission-reducing projects in countries which do not have such commitments.

lean production   Based on the concept of *muda*, and pioneered by Toyota, this is the Japanese approach to waste management and resource efficiency. It aims to avoid: the production of goods that no one wants or which fail to meet expectations; the use of processing steps that are not needed; and the non-productive transport of people or materials.

life-cycle assessment   The overall process of assessing the life-cycle impacts associated with a system, function, product, or service. Sometimes considered to include four stages: initiation, inventory, impact analysis, and improvement.

MIPS   Proposed by Professor Friedrich Schmidt-Bleek of Germany's Wuppertal Institute, the MIPS approach focuses on the "material intensity per unit service." The approach aims to measure the "total material and energy throughput in mass units (like kilograms or tonnes) per unit good or per mass unit of good, from cradle to grave." As the units of service clock up for a product like a car, so the MIPS "invested" in each unit of service supplied fall. The greater the durability of the product, within limits, the fewer the MIPS needed per unit of service.

natural capital   This comes in two main forms: "critical" natural capital (essential to the maintenance of life and ecosystem integrity) and renewable, replaceable, or substitutable natural capital.

outrage   Perceived risk is usually a complex, volatile mix of hazard and outrage. Experts argue that companies minimize the risk of outrage when they engage stakeholders (q.v.) in the development and operation of major projects.

precautionary approach   Policy or other action taken before the underlying science has reached absolute clarity.

remanufacturing   Pioneered by companies like Xerox, remanufacturing involves the recovery of equipment or products for servicing, upgrading, and re-sale as working systems. Potentially offers much higher environmental returns than recycling.

reverse logistics   The use of logistical and distribution systems to recover products or materials destined for remanufacturing or recycling.

social capital   A measure of the ability of people to work together for common purposes in groups and organizations. A key element of social capital is the sense of mutual trust.

solutions campaigning   Instead of simply focusing on problems, even campaigning groups like Greenpeace are now linking up with selected companies to develop and promote problem-solving technologies or approaches.

stakeholders   The broadest definition of "stakeholder" brings in anyone who affects or is affected by a company's operations. The key new perception is that companies need to expand the range of interests considered in any new development from customers, shareholders, management, and employees to such people as suppliers, local communities, and pressure groups.

sustainability   There are over 100 definitions of sustainability and sustainable development, but the best-known is that of the World Commission on Environment and Development. This suggests that development is sustainable where it "meets the needs of the present without compromising the ability of future generations to meet their own needs."

triple bottom line   Sustainable development involves the simultaneous pursuit of economic prosperity, environmental quality, and social equity. Companies aiming for sustainability need to perform not against a single, financial bottom line but against the triple bottom line.

value:impact assessment   A technique developed by Procter & Gamble to optimize the value delivered to customers and consumers, and to reduce the environmental or other impacts associated with the production, shipment, use, or disposal of products.

value migration   Market change pulls economic value from one company (or industry) and pushes it towards another. In losing control of the personal computer market, for example, it has been estimated that IBM may have lost $70 billion to new business ecosystems (q.v.) centred on companies like Microsoft. The sustainability transition will also drive value migration between companies, sectors, and economies.

values shift   Over time, human and social values change. Concepts that once seemed extraordinary (e.g. emancipating slaves, enfranchising women) are now taken for granted. New concepts (e.g. responsible consumerism, environmental justice, intra- and inter-generational equity) are now coming up the curve.

INDEX